Multiple Paths to

Literacy K-2

Proven High-Yield Strategies to Scaffold Engaging Literacy Learning Across the Curriculum

Inquiry, Play, Art, Technology, and Self-Regulation through Intentional Teaching

Miriam P. Trehearne

This book is dedicated to all teachers who believe as I do: "Better to be effective than politically correct."

"Be who you are and say what you feel, because those who mind don't matter, and those who matter, don't mind." — Bernard M. Baruch

The bottom line is that "new" or "different" is not necessarily better. The work of such notables as John Hattie, Michael Fullan, and others promotes improving teaching by building on success, on what is working (best practice), rather than simply looking to implement yet *another* new innovation or hopping onto *another* new bandwagon. That being said, we need a combination of best practice and next practice.

"There needs to be a mix of committing to best practice (existing *proven* practices that already have a good degree of widely agreed effectiveness) and having the freedom, space and resources to create next practice (innovative approaches that often begin with teachers themselves and that will sometimes turn out to be the best practices in the future)."
(Hargreaves Fullan 2012, 50–51).

"What counts in life is not the mere fact that we have lived. It is what difference we have made to the lives of others that will determine the significance of the life we lead." — Nelson Mandela, 2002

As teachers, let's accomplish a strong literacy legacy by closing the gaps, beginning on day one of preschool/Kindergarten. Let's leave education and the world better than we found it!

For permission to use material from this text or product, submit a request to Miriam P. Trehearne Literacy Consulting at miriam.trehearne@telus.net.

ISBN 978-0-9948579-0-3

Photocopying guidelines for Canada: If you are an educator at a publicly funded school in Canada, please consult your school's license with Copibec (Quebec) or Access Copyright (rest of Canada) when doing any photocopying suggested in this book. Adhering to the terms and conditions of your license allows you to copy what you need worry-free. Please note that the license includes copying done in support of educational purposes only. If you are an educator at an independent school and your school does not have a license with Access Copyright or Copibec, it is strongly recommended that you contact these organizations and obtain a license in order to allow your school to make the photocopies required/suggested in this book easily and legally.

All trade names and trademarks recited, referenced, or reflected herein are the property of their respective owners who retain all rights thereto.

Trehearne, Miriam P.

Multiple Paths to Literacy K–2

Proven High-Yield Strategies to Scaffold Engaging Literacy Learning Across the Curriculum

Inquiry, Play, Art, Technology, and Self-Regulation through Intentional Teaching

Library and Archives Canada Cataloguing in Publication

Trehearne, Miriam, author
        Multiple paths to literacy : K-2 / Miriam P. Trehearne.

Includes bibliographical references and index.
ISBN 978-0-9948579-0-3 (paperback)

        1. Language arts (Early childhood)--Canada. 2. Language arts (Elementary)--Canada. 3. Language arts (Early childhood)-- United States. 4. Language arts (Elementary)--United States. I. Title.

LB1181.2.T74 2015   372.4   C2015-905940-2

Editorial Advice and Proofreading: Ruth Bradley-St-Cyr
Indexer: Judy Dunlop
Designer: Jim Bisakowski   BookDesign.ca
Photographers: Patrick Trehearne and Bob Hart. Photographs have also been provided by numerous educators and parents and are used with permission.

About the Author

Miriam Trehearne has been a classroom teacher, resource teacher, Program Specialist (exceptional needs students), coach, Literacy Specialist, and University Associate. As a Literacy and Early Childhood Specialist, she led a very successful research-based literacy initiative (Kindergarten to Third Grade) in a large urban school district (156 elementary schools) that focused on 56 high-needs schools. Due to her many and varied roles and experiences, Miriam has become passionate in her belief that pre-school–Grade 2 are the most important grades. She believes that effective, engaging, early literacy programs are not only important but also crucial as a matter of social justice. Like Michael Fullan, she promotes improving teaching by building on success, on what is working (best practice), rather than simply looking to implement yet *another* new innovation or hop onto *another* new bandwagon.

That being said, she believes that we need a combination of best practice and next practice. Her beliefs are supported by highly credible research.

Miriam presently devotes much of her time to researching literacy best practices and presenting them to teachers, literacy coaches, paraprofessionals, school administrators, and parents, nationally and internationally. Miriam has been a keynote speaker at the Association for Supervision and Curriculum Development (ASCD) Kindergarten conference in Chicago and co-chaired a one-day institute with renowned literacy expert Regie Routman at the International Reading Association (IRA) conference in San Antonio. She can be found speaking regularly at early childhood conferences such as the National Association for the Education of Young Children conference (NAEYC), the Early Childhood Education Council conference (ECEC), and the Annual ASCD Pre-Kindergarten/Kindergarten conference as well as the annual International Literacy Association conference (ILA), the World Reading Congress, and the European Reading Conference.

Miriam enjoys working with schools and school districts doing literacy reviews often resulting in the adoption of the whole-school approach, or response to instruction and intervention, RTI. The end result: real school and often school-district improvement frequently occurs.

The key factor: The within-school variation in teacher effectiveness is reduced.

Miriam also writes books, journal articles, and literacy materials for classroom use. Four of her books have been translated into French. Her books include *The Comprehensive Literacy Resource for Kindergarten Teachers*, the 2006 Association of Educational Publishers (AEP) award winning *The Comprehensive Literacy Resource for Grade 1–2 Teachers*, and *The Comprehensive Literacy Resource for Preschool Teachers*. *The Comprehensive Literacy Resource for Grade 3–6 Teachers* was a finalist for the 2007 AEP Award. *Learning to Write and Loving it!*, Miriam's most recent book, is also a best-seller. *Center Stage Literacy*, engaging and developmentally appropriate literacy focus centres for K–2 classrooms, won the 2008 Teachers' Choice Award for Classroom Materials.

Follow Miriam at http://miriamtrehearne.ca/

Other Professional Books for the Elementary Grades: Preschool, Kindergarten, Grades 1–2, 3–6 by Miriam P. Trehearne

The Comprehensive Literacy Resource for Preschool Teachers
ISBN 0-7406-1718-4
American and Canadian Edition

Nelson Language Arts Kindergarten Teacher's Resource Book
Canadian Edition ISBN/ISSN: 0-17-618-662-X
Canadian Edition ISBN-13: 978-0-1761-8662-3
French Edition ISBN- 2-89593-484-3

The Comprehensive Literacy Resource for Kindergarten Teachers
American Edition ISBN 0-7406-0378-7

Nelson Language Arts Grade 1–2 Teacher's Resource Book
Canadian Edition ISBN/ISSN: 0-17-620-190-4
Canadian Edition ISBN-13: 978-0-1762-0190-6
French Edition ISBN- 0-17620190-4

The Comprehensive Literacy Resource for Grades 1–2 Teachers
American Edition ISBN 0-7406-3397-X

Learning to Write and Loving It! Preschool–Kindergarten
American and Canadian Edition ISBN: 978-1-4522-0313-3
French Edition ISBN -978-2-8965-0978-2

The Comprehensive Literacy Resource for Grades 3–6 Teachers
Canadian Edition ISBN 0176270302
Canadian Edition ISBN 13: 9780176270308
French Edition ISBN 2895937559 ISBN 9782895937555
American Edition ISBN 0740643177
ISBN 9780740643170

CONTENTS

3. An Effective and Engaging Classroom Environment. 79

4. Oral Language 103

5. Making Conversations Powerful 123

6. Maximizing the Effectiveness of Read-Alouds 151

7. Play, Self-Regulation, and Literacy Learning K–2 175

8. Play at Centres or Stations 195

9. Storytelling and Retelling 207

10. Key Centres that Support Literacy, Inquiry and Play . . . 241

11. Learning to Write, Writing to Learn 267

12. Assessment, Documentation and Scaffolding of Writing . 301

13. Inquiry-Based Learning: What We Really Know... 317

ACKNOWLEDGEMENTS

This literacy resource book was truly developed by teachers for teachers. **Many educators — teachers, principals, and consultants — helped in the development of this professional book.**

A special thank you to all of the K–2 teachers, students, and parents, public, Catholic, private, and charter, with whom I continue to have the privilege of working across Canada and the United States. Thanks for letting me learn alongside you. You teach me so much. And thank you to the Literacy and Numeracy Secretariat of Ontario for providing many fine on-line publications and resources.

A word of thanks to the many early childhood and literacy consultants like Colleen MacDonald (Coordinator, Elementary Student Success, Early Years Ottawa Catholic School Board) who work tirelessly to support the work of K–2 teachers in hundreds of school districts.

I would like to recognize the York Region District School Board, the largest board that I know of that stayed true to their focus on strong early literacy programs using a whole school approach, for an extended period of time. Teachers need constant support over time. Thank you in particular to Bill Hogarth, Lyn Sharratt, Denese Belchetz, Beate Planche, Deborah Sinyard, Sandy Giles, and the many others who continue to provide strong educational support from outside a school district.

In addition, thank you to the following individuals from the Thames Valley District School Board: Valerie Nielsen, Superin–tendent of Student Achievement, Diana Goodwin (formerly Learning Supervisor, Program Services, Community and School Programs), Rose Walton (Learning Coordinator Literacy JK–Grade 6), and Kim Gains (Speech/Language Pathologist). This school district's focus on and research in the areas of oral language and early literacy is very valuable and, in my experience, quite unique.

And thank you to principals like Karen Mitchell (Sacred Heart School, Paris, Ontario) who realize that preschool–Grade 2 are the most crucial times for learning and who go above and beyond the call of duty to support their teachers and students.

In particular, my thanks go to the teachers whose stories this book celebrates, the many others I have visited, too numerous to name, and in memory of Jo Simpson of Oswego, Illinois:

- *Jane Beeksma, Kindergarten teacher, Sunalta School, Calgary Board of Education
- Clarice Bloomenthal, formerly K-2 teacher, Calgary Board of Education, Saanich School District
- Diana Bruni, Kindergarten teacher, Transfiguration of Our Lord Catholic School, Toronto Catholic District School Board
- Amber Bowden, Kindergarten Teacher, Kamloops, British Columbia
- Karen Dance, Grade 1–2 teacher, R. L. Graham Public School, York Region District School Board
- Sue Ann Goshima, Kindergarten teacher, Gustav H. Webling Elementary School, Aiea, Hawaii
- Bonnie Gremont, Preschool Coordinator, Kindergarten teacher, The Leo Baeck Day School, Toronto
- *Angie Harrison, Kindergarten teacher, W. J. Watson Public School, York Region District School Board
- Alissa Hurwitz, Kindergarten teacher, R. L. Graham Public School, York Region District School Board
- Colette Lau, Kindergarten teacher, Gustav H. Webling Elementary School, Aiea, Hawaii
- Heather McKay, Kindergarten teacher, Andrew Sibbald Elementary, Calgary Board of Education
- Christina Nicola, Kindergarten Teacher, Surrey School District , Surrey British Columbia
- Jennifer Oppenheim, Grade 1–2 teacher, Glendale School, Calgary Board of Education
- *Kas (Karin) Patsula, Kindergarten/Grade 1–2 teacher, Glendale School, Calgary Board of Education
- Jo Simpson, formerly Kindergarten teacher, Oswego Community School District, Oswego, Illinois
- Kathy Steele, formerly Surrey School District, Surrey British Columbia
- Mila Tamaoka, Kindergarten teacher, Gustav H. Webling Elementary School, Aiea, Hawaii
- Jennifer Thomson, Kindergarten teacher, Vancouver, British Columbia

*With deep appreciation to Angie Harrison, Jane Beeksma and Kas Patsula for providing numerous "Windows on the Classroom" demonstrating engaging and effective classroom practice. In addition thank you to Angie for sharing her technological insight.

Thank you to my home board, the Calgary Board of Education, and all of its teachers and administrators. I learned so much! Thank you to Laura Devitt, Principal Guy Weadick School, Joan Green, Principal Mountain Park School, and Judy Hehr, Calgary Board of Education Trustee. Thank you to Steacy Collyer, Executive Director of Calgary Reads. Thank you to Christine Gordon, Professor Emeritus, University of Calgary, for taking on the Early Literacy Research Project. It is through such research that educators continue to learn and grow.

And a special thank you to Donna Michaels, former Chief Superintendent of Schools, Calgary Board of Education, who supported the Calgary Early Literacy Research Project. She believes in the centrality of strong early literacy programs at the core of everything teachers do and understands that equity and equality are not necessarily the same things.

I would also like to acknowledge the following wonderful educators, authors, and researchers, and the many others, who have taught us so much about early childhood and specifically how to support young literacy learners effectively: Richard Allington, Elena Bodrova, Barbara Bowman, Sue Bredekamp, Jerome Bruner, Lucy Calkins, Marie Clay, Carol Copple, David Dickinson, Nell Duke, Elliot Eisner, Deborah Leong, Anne McGill-Franzen, Donald Graves, John Hattie, Shelley Harwayne, Georgia Heard, Peter Hill, Don Holdaway, Lillian Katz, Lesley Mandel Morrow, Susan Neuman, David Pearson, Kathleen Roskos, Regie Routman, Tim Shanahan, Catherine Snow, Sharon Taberski, William Teale, and Canadians Andy Biemiller, David Booth, Jim Cummins, Adele Diamond, Stuart Shanker, and Keith Stanovich. Many thanks to world-renowned Canadian cartoonist Lynn Johnston, for permission to include one of her cartoons. It truly depicts what learning environments should be like. Thank you also to cartoonist Oleg Kuznetsov for creating the cartoon of the teacher attempting to deal with all the educational pucks teachers often feel are being fired at them. We never know what is coming at us next.

Finally, thank you to my husband for all of your support.

"Let us pick up our books and our pens. They are our most powerful weapons. One child, one teacher and one book and one pen can change the world. Education is the only solution. Education first." —Malala Yousafzai, 2013, 310

"A good head and good heart are always a formidable combination. But when you add to that a literate tongue or pen, then you have something very special. Education is the most powerful weapon we can use to change the world." —Nelson Mandela, 2003

Yes, Education First, Literacy First! Let's Make This World a Better Place

We have an obligation to develop children's literacy skills and understandings along with other aspects of their developing selves. Literacy development is a fundamental area of (human) development — one that is essential to developing the whole child (Bennett-Armistead, Duke, and Moses 2005, 15).

"How wonderful it is that nobody need wait a single moment before starting to improve the world." —Anne Frank, 1929–1945

"Destiny is not a matter of chance, it is a matter of choice; it is not a thing to be waited for, it is a thing to be achieved." —William Jennings Bryan

Jo Simpson improved the world by developing motivated and skilled Kindergarten writers. By focusing on informational text, the students developed academic (tier 3) vocabulary and background knowledge. Don't you love the voice: "Why are baby birds pink? I don't know. Because they were just born. Oh, now I know!"

A Message from Miriam: The Story Behind this Book

This book comes from my life experiences as a classroom teacher for 18 years (K–6), a Resource Teacher, a Special Needs Program Specialist, a University Associate working with student teachers, and as a parent. As Literacy Specialist K–2 for a large school district, I was given the opportunity to lead an early literacy research initiative that was very successful in improving literacy results (K–3) in 56 high needs/high poverty schools. This work involved thousands of students, including a large number of English Language Learners, hundreds of teachers, and thousands of families. Although there were challenges, the research done by the local university shows that it is possible to close the gaps! What could be more satisfying than enabling thousands of young children to improve their chances of high school graduation dramatically and to influence their life paths due to effective literacy teaching and learning in Kindergarten and the primary grades?

The research indicates that what happened in Kindergarten was the single most significant factor: "Overall the results indicated that **a strong Kindergarten program and good first teaching (Grades 1–2)** resulted in progressively 'closing the gaps' by third grade" (Gordon 2004). We do know a lot about what makes for effective schools, effective teachers, and literate students (who are the real winners).

Why Another Literacy Book?
To Celebrate, To Caution, To Inform

This particular book was written for a number of reasons: some celebratory, some cautionary, and some simply informational.

To Celebrate: K–2 Classrooms that Work!

Having worked across North America, in fact around the world, I have had the opportunity to meet some extraordinary Kindergarten–Second Grade teachers. This book allows you to hear some of their voices. And each voice is different. What is clear is that there is no magic bullet, no one way to support early literacy effectively. There are multiple paths. That being said, we do know that some high-yield strategies have proven to make a huge difference no matter the path taken. The teachers celebrated in this book share many of these high-yield strategies and instructional approaches, especially intentional explicit teaching and a high degree of student engagement and self-regulation. All the teachers demonstrate constructive relationships with their students. Visitors know when they open their doors that these classroom cultures resonate with warmth, caring, and student success. They can feel it! This book shares the gist of what we know about excellent early literacy teaching and learning. And, we know a lot!

The challenge is to provide engaging and effective Kindergarten programs that contribute to lasting positive change in literacy, cross-curricular learning, and self-regulation. And to do this the learning in Grades 1 and 2 must build on strong and engaging Kindergarten programs. Program continuity is crucial.

But after writing four professional books in English (and three in French) about preschool–2nd Grade, why write another book on the topic of early literacy? Why a K–2 professional resource?

Thank you to Laura Woods, Kindergarten teacher, Peel District School Board, for your note:
"Thank you for both putting the pressure on and lighting the path". Laura, this is all I have ever wanted to do!

To Caution: Surviving the Pendulum

We are all aware of recent pendulum swings in education, and I am worried. Many primary teachers are feeling the pressure to adopt certain approaches to teaching and learning. I begin by sharing a heartfelt caution to Kindergarten–Grade 2 teachers: avoid the latest flavour of the month. Always ask, Where is the research to support this practice? Whose research is it? How credible is it? Does it appear in a refereed journal? How would or could this work in my setting? Does this seem plausible to me? What I am already doing is working. Why implement change?

> "Millions saw the apple fall, Newton was the only one who asked why?" — Bernard M. Baruch

Teachers encourage children to question, to inquire. Teachers themselves need to do the same. Remember the tale *The Emperor's New Clothes* by Hans Christian Andersen? And be aware of the fact that one of the major problems in education is precisely the lack of specification around defining teaching practice, so that the same or similar terms can mean widely different practices. For example, is play-based learning the same as learning through play? What does play-based learning really mean anyway? What is inquiry-based learning? Is inquiry-based teaching the same as inquiry-based learning? And do any of these equate or connect to problem-based, project-based, or design-based learning? Are play-based learning, inquiry-based learning, intentional teaching, and early literacy learning mutually exclusive? The answer to the last question is a resounding no; they must not be treated as mutually exclusive. We need them all and strategic integration is the key.

My personal findings from classroom visits indicate that many teachers struggle to integrate the inquiry approach, self-regulation, play, and strong

This book is written alongside many teachers and consultants, parents and students across North America and around the world. It provides proven and practical research-based strategies and instructional approaches to use at school and at home to support literacy learning. In the book *Making Thinking Visible* (Ritchhart, Church, and Morrison 2011), important classroom examples are described as pictures of practice. Throughout this book, such pictures of practice are highlighted as "Window on the Classroom" features. These real-life examples come to life in the many photos, student writing samples, and student, teacher, and parent reflections and stories. Enjoy the varied voices!

This book also provides a focus on the *how to* of integrating effective literacy learning, inquiry-based learning, self-regulation, art, and play through intentional teaching: what does this look like, how do effective teachers strategically get it all in? Technology tips are also provided as useful tools.

> Learning through play, inquiry-based learning, intentional teaching, and early literacy learning work well when strategically integrated across the varied curricula, across the day.

> The bottom line is that "new" or "different" is not necessarily better. The work of such notables as John Hattie, Michael Fullan, and others promote improved teaching by building on best practice, on what is working, rather than looking to implement *yet another* innovation.

---

early literacy teaching and learning effectively. How does one follow the child and differentiate as needed while still providing important adult scaffolding? This book provides numerous and varied examples that demonstrate how effective teachers are making it work.

It also has become clear to me from visiting hundreds of classrooms across North America that inquiry-based learning in any two classrooms, even in the same school, is often defined in very different ways. How can we say that inquiry-based learning works or does not work when frequently educators use different definitions and very different frames of reference for *inquiry*? What do we know about self-regulation in K–2? And what do we know about play? This book attempts to provide some clarity in defining terms. Credible research and practical examples of effective "next practice," taken from K–2 classrooms, are also shared.

To Inform: What Teachers Want to Know

This book provides a user-friendly synopsis of some of the proven early literacy best practices crucial for students in Kindergarten–Grade 2 and the how-to of effective and engaging classroom practice. The major literacy focus areas for this resource are oral language (the foundation of all literacy learning), comprehension (word and world knowledge being key components), and writing. These are also curriculum gap areas (Teale, Paciga, and Hoffman 2007) that need more classroom focus. With more classroom focus in K–2, specifically in the "gap areas," we may be able to prevent the Fourth Grade slump (Chall, Jacobs, and Baldwin 1990) and the Eighth Grade cliff (Allington 2009) experienced by many students. In the process of providing the synopsis, this resource will respond to many frequently asked questions.

> **FAQ: What Teachers Want to Know**
>
> ■ What are developmentally appropriate literacy expectations or goals for students in K–2?
>
> ■ How can teachers most effectively help their students reach these goals?
>
> ■ What does the term "developmentally appropriate" really mean?

- How does research describe the practice of the most effective/accomplished K–2 teachers? What do they do?

- What does play-based learning really mean? Is it the same as learning through play?

- How does mature play differ from immature play?

- How can play and literacy learning effectively support one another?

- What do engaging and effective learning centres look like?

- What is self-regulation and how does one scaffold it?

- What does inquiry-based learning really mean?

- What does the research say about how effective inquiry-based learning really is in K–2 classrooms?

- What does effective inquiry-based learning look like?

- What is self-regulation and how does one develop this in K–2 classrooms?

- How does one develop strong literacy practice hand-in-hand with inquiry-based learning?

- What are the high-yield strategies or non-negotiables for effective literacy teaching and learning in K–2? How does it look in the classroom?

- What does a strong Kindergarten–Grade 2 literacy program look like?

- What is phonological awareness (and phonemic awareness) and how important is it in K–2?

- How much time should be allocated specifically for language arts each day and how does one fit it all in?

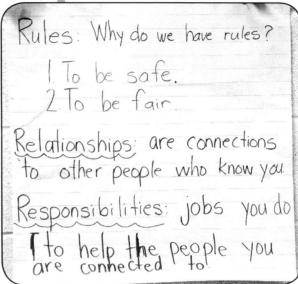

It is important that the students understand the purpose and importance of rules and work together to come up with a very few.

It is important to self-regulation that the students understand the components of writer's workshop: where they are going and how they plan to get there.

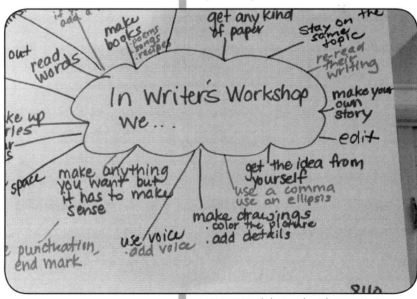

Writer's Workshop web with appreciation to Sue Ann Goshima, Gustav H. Webling Elementary School, Hawaii

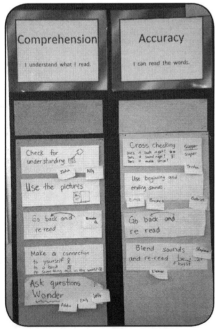

Shared reading and singing of songs is crucial to the development of phonological awareness, reading, and writing.

Students use metacognition to reflect on the comprehension strategies they are using. Adding their names indicates a level of ownership or commitment to using the strategies when needed.

■ How can one effectively organize the classroom? What does a strong classroom environment look like? What classroom materials are needed and how might they be organized? What effect do classroom colors have on student learning?

■ How can one keep students meaningfully engaged during the language arts block, enabling the teacher to work with small flexible groups? What are "the other kids doing" during guided reading?

■ How should phonics be taught?

■ How many high-frequency words (sight words) are crucial for students to know by the end of Kindergarten, Grade 1, and Grade 2? Which words are they?

■ What is fluency and how does one support its development?

■ What are the researched-based strategies that support reading comprehension?

■ How can one effectively assess and support oral language and vocabulary development?

■ How can we most effectively differentiate for ELL and second dialect learners?

■ Which literacy assessments and documentations should teachers use and how can they help to drive instruction?

■ How can one combine the writing process, writing genres, and writing traits or characteristics during writing workshop?

■ How can one motivate reluctant writers and readers?

■ What are effective mini-lessons to use when teaching writing in K–2?

■ How does one effectively assess and teach word work and spelling? Which spelling rules work in K-2?

- How do we help struggling students? What does effective early intervention look like?

- How can technology be used as a vehicle to support literacy learning in the classroom? What does the research say about the effectiveness of technology use on student achievement in K–2?

- How does literacy support the arts and vice versa?

- What role can parents realistically play in support of literacy learning and how might teachers enhance this home–school connection?

- What does worthwhile literacy homework look like?

Note: For the purposes of this publication, the word "parents" is meant to represent a single parent, two parents, guardians, and any other essential caregivers in a parental role.

Art supports cross-curricular academic vocabulary learning. Scientific drawings like this one of the ear, work well.

The Importance of a K–2 Focus: Vertical Connections

Although Kindergarten is unique in some respects, research clearly indicates that literacy learning is constantly emerging from birth and that early literacy learning should connect smoothly and seamlessly from K–2. Good teaching is good teaching. Strong Kindergarten programs, even full-day early learning, in and of themselves are not good enough. Blaming Kindergarten teachers alone for weak Third Grade literacy achievement is not just. A strong and coordinated literacy program for K–2 is required in all schools.

But what about Grade 3? There is actually very little evidence that programs designed to correct reading problems beyond Grade 2 are successful. Remediating learning deficits after they are already well established is extremely difficult. Thus, prevention using strong literacy programs is more effective over time than intervention. Clearly, the time to provide additional help to children who are at-risk of school failure is early on, when

Home-school connections
Easy-to-implement and effective strategies for involving parents/caregivers in their child's learning

Check It Out!
Recommended read-alouds and other great resources to support literacy development

Technology
User friendly tips for incorporating technology to enhance literacy learning

Apps
Apps that have proven useful in support of literacy learning

Learning Centres or Stations

Window on the Classroom
Vignettes from actual classrooms that bring the early childhood experiences and classroom practices to life

they are still motivated and confident or when learning deficits are relatively small and remediable. Thus, research around the world indicates that the "gap" in reading (and writing) widens dramatically after Grade 1 and is hard to close. An Australian study found that even by Grade 3, the learning gap was so large that for low-achieving students, catching up with their peers (in reading) was virtually impossible (Hill and Crevola 1999). That is why the focus of this professional resource, and the focus of schools and school districts, must be on K–2.

Teachers Want Practical and Like My Other Books, Practical It Is

How to Use This Resource Effectively

As with my other professional books (See p. 6), this resource enables you to access specific content or topics quickly using the table of contents in conjunction with the index. However, you may prefer to read through the entire resource in order to gain a more complete picture of early literacy development in Kindergarten–Grade 2. Reputable research, developmentally appropriate and easily implemented assessment tools, instructional strategies, samples of children's work, and descriptions of what some of the samples reveal are key components of this resource. The diagnostic assessments featured are both formative (*assessment for learning*) and summative (*assessment of learning*). Students are also encouraged to be involved in *assessment as learning*, which involves student self-reflection and metacognition.

Also included are proven teaching and organizational strategies, as well as mini-lessons and activities that effectively support strong literacy learning. The "Window on the Classroom" feature brings the early childhood experiences to life. Some of the vignettes exemplify strong classroom practice while others simply describe specific situations that teachers may connect with personally. All of the accounts come from actual classrooms.

Throughout the chapters the "Check It Out!" feature offers suggestions for teacher and student resources specifically related to that subject matter. Rounding out the contents is a list of recommended professional books, reports, and a comprehensive bibliography.

The solid research base of this professional book is detailed in the following chart.

Research Base, Beliefs, and Understandings for this Professional Book

Research Base, Beliefs and Understandings	This Professional Book
"Excellent teachers know it's both what you teach and how you teach" (Copple and Bredekamp 2009, 48).	Shares both the **what** and the **how** of effective literacy teaching and learning
Play and literacy learning naturally support each other (Copple and Bredekamp 2009; Bodrova and Leong 2004).	Provides excellent examples of teachers scaffolding effective **play-based** literacy activities and inquiries, both spontaneous and planned
The latest research on early childhood literacy learning stresses the importance of writing for its own sake but also to support early reading (both decoding and meaning), phonological awareness, and concepts of print, the reading–writing connection, and the development of the whole child (Harrison, Ogle, McIntyre, and Hellsten 2008; Shanahan 1984, 2006; Snow 1998; Graves 1994).	Provides motivating and engaging **writing activities** as well as mini-lessons to scaffold learning
Young children naturally construct knowledge, but they also need **intentional teaching**: scaffolding through modelling, demonstrating, explaining, and guided practice (McGee and Richgels 2003; Schickedanz 2004; Routman 2005; Neuman and Roskos 2007).	Supports the **gradual release of responsibility model** as one example of intentional teaching
Oral language is the foundation of early literacy learning (Dickinson and Neuman 2006; Neuman and Roskos 2007; Strickland 2006; Roskos, Tabors, and Lenhart 2004; Bredekamp and Copple 1997; Snow 1998; Beck 2002; Biemiller 2007).	Suggests practical and research-based ways to implement a **rich oral language** classroom program
Children must be provided with opportunities to apply the strategies they are taught by doing interesting activities that make sense to them; they learn best when they see a specific purpose for what they are learning (Routman 2005; Copple and Bredekamp 2009; Helm and Katz 2010).	Provides engaging, interesting, and **purposeful activities** that support literacy across the curriculum
Differentiation or "embracing" the individual child (Tomlinson 2014) is key to both academic success and happiness in early childhood.	Provides a variety of assessment tools/documentation to help drive instruction; supports **many instructional approaches and materials;** provides engaging activities and projects that provide **managed choice** for the children (Allington 2002)

Literacy learning occurs across the curriculum. Integration is natural for teachers. Through cross-curricular integration including inquiry in areas such as social studies and science, young children are able to develop literacy skills while acquiring important "big ideas" involving hands-on activities (Copple and Bredekamp 2009). Children need to be exposed to language-rich and content-rich settings that can help them acquire the broad array of knowledge, skills, and dispositions that build a foundation for literacy and content learning. (*How Does Learning Happen? Ontario's Pedagogy for the Early Years, 2014*).	Provides examples of **integrated cross-curricular inquiries and activities** that celebrate **inquiry-based learning** along with effective literacy teaching and learning
Children's oral language and their artwork together help them deepen their understanding. Art becomes a tool for thinking and makes thinking visible (Bell 2012). Art helps students synthesize all of their learning throughout the day. "Because works of art are almost always 'about' something, they can be the glue that binds the curriculum together and helps kids synthesize all of their learning throughout the day" (Christine Marmé Thompson 2015).	Provides many examples of how children's **art** and oral language develop and support one another and reveal student thinking
The home plays a key role in emergent/early literacy development (National Early Literacy Panel Report 2009; Bennett-Armistead, Duke, and Moses 2005; Gullo 2006).	Includes examples of practical and easy-to-implement **home literacy activities**
Inquiry-Based learning gives students the opportunity to observe, read, write, and work together to research as they capitalize on their interests (Katz and Chard 2000). "As children pose questions, conduct research, engage in discussions and present their findings they learn to think critically and make connections between what they are learning and their own lives" (NAEYC 2006).	Includes many examples of different types of **inquiry-based literacy experiences** that support strong student engagement and co-operation
When used appropriately, technology can support and extend traditional materials in valuable ways. It is a tool that can provide an added option for young children to learn. Research points to the potential positive effects of technology in children's learning and development, both cognitive and social (Clements 1994; Haugland and Shade 1994; NAEYC 2012).	Includes examples of developmentally appropriate, practical and easy-to-implement literacy activities effectively supported through **technology**

CHAPTER

Effective Teachers, Effective Schools

When it Comes to Teaching, One Size Does Not Fit All

One way to consider how to scaffold school/teacher effectiveness and, of course, student learning is to start with the success stories. These stories focus on how teachers, schools, and school districts, including many in high-needs communities, have proven to be effective in supporting early learning. The first three chapters do just that by first considering the commonalities among very successful schools and school districts or, as Richard Allington says, *Schools That Work Where All Children Read and Write* (2006). Success stories are provided throughout the book, celebrating teachers from very different schools, who describe what they do daily to foster student literacy success. What emerges from these success stories is that there is no single quick fix or magic bullet for teaching early literacy. No two teachers featured in this book use identical approaches, nor do they need to. What is key is to look for the commonalities, the high-yield strategies. Teachers don't need to reinvent the wheel.

>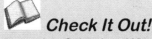
> **Check It Out!**
> Improving Schools… What Works? *Educational Leadership*, Vol. 72 No. 5, February 2015.

What Do We Really Know About Excellent Early Literacy Instruction? We Know a Lot!

Defining Literacy

It is important to start with a definition of literacy. Literacy used to be considered simply reading and writing. Not anymore. There is much talk about "multiple literacies," including arts literacy and technological literacy. For this book, I take my definition of literacy from the Ministry of Education in Ontario, Canada, 2013, 3. I love this definition because it encompasses what it means to be literate at any age:

> "The early years are just too precious to get it wrong" (Neuman 2010, 39).

Literacy is... the ability to use language and images in rich and varied forms to read, write, listen, speak, view, represent, discuss and think critically about ideas. Literacy enables us to share information and to interact with others. Literacy is an essential tool for personal growth and active participation in a democratic society.

———•+•———

Literacy involves the capacity to
- *Access, manage, create, and evaluate information*
- *Think imaginatively and analytically*
- *Communicate thoughts and ideas effectively*
- *Apply metacognitive knowledge and skills*
- *Develop a sense of self-efficacy and an interest in life-long learning*

———•+•———

The development of literacy is a complex process that involves building on prior knowledge, culture and experiences in order to instill new knowledge and deepen understanding (Ontario Ministry of Education 2013, 3).

Learning for the 21st century

Presently, there is much focus on "learning for the 21st century." The learning skills found in *Partnership for 21st Century Skills* (2005) are all scaffolded by K–2 teachers. In fact, the heart of such learning occurs in K–2:

- Information and communications skills
- Thinking and problem-solving skills
- Interpersonal and self-directional skills

"Beyond reading, writing and mathematics, we know that to achieve excellence in the future, our learners will also need to develop characteristics such as perseverance, resilience and imaginative thinking to overcome challenges. Combined with a deep sense of compassion and empathy for others, our learners will develop the skills and knowledge they need to become actively engaged citizens" (*Achieving Excellence: A renewed Vision for Education in Ontario* 2014, 5).

Closing the Within-School Gap: Effective Teachers Do Matter!

We now know a lot about both excellent early literacy instruction and the conditions associated with successful early literacy learning. We definitely know what the proven high-yield strategies are, yet many of these strategies are not common practice from school to school nor from classroom to classroom. We also know that typically there is a huge within-school gap between the effectiveness of the various teachers in any one school (Hattie 2012; Hill 1999). That is, if you take any two teachers who teach the same grade in the same school, use the same curriculum, have the same resources, the same principal, the same community, and the same heterogeneous mix of students, there is often a huge difference in effectiveness between teacher A and teacher B, year after year. One parent informed me that it is like playing Russian roulette or the luck of the draw, depending upon her child's class placement. And she is right. Doctors and lawyers are not all equally effective; the same holds true for teachers and all other professionals.

It is what teachers know, do, and care about that is very powerful in this learning equation (Hattie 2003, 3). The only variable that has even more influence on student learning than teacher variance is what students bring to the table with regard to ability. However, regardless of ability, "we have evidence that 98 percent of all children entering Kindergarten can be at grade level by the end of first and second grade" (Allington 2010, 1).

The Most Effective/Accomplished Teachers

Since there is no single right way to teach literacy, *there is no magic bullet to develop literacy*. That said, research indicates that there are some high-yield strategies, some non-negotiables that should be in effect in all early literacy classrooms. Early literacy learning is too important to be dealt with haphazardly. Moreover, effective literacy instruction does not follow the "latest flavour of the month." A key finding in all of the research is that effective teachers/schools use research-based, proven high-yield strategies, and do not abandon what works to follow the latest pendulum swing. Focusing on and supporting a few key high-yield strategies can bring quick results and create momentum for ongoing learning.

Pendulum swings often disenfranchise teachers, students, and parents. Many experienced teachers suffer as they continue to live through pendulum swings (e.g., whole language versus phonics,

As teachers, we provide a range of experiences and the instruction necessary to help children become good readers, writers, and speakers early in their school careers. All children possess the fundamental attributes they need to become literate.... The key is good first teaching
(Adapted from Fountas and Pinnell 1996).

The within-school variance in teacher effectiveness is typically larger than the between-school variance! "A student in a high-impact teacher's classroom has almost a year's advantage over his or her peers in a lower-effect teacher's classroom" (Hattie 2012, 23).

"Excellence in teaching is the single most powerful influence on achievement" (Hattie 2003, 4). Instead of always looking for the next innovation, schools and school districts need to build on success — what we already know works. Innovation does not always equal improvement.

> "Effective educators employ a variety of pedagogical approaches that can accom—modate a combination of educator- guided instruction and child-directed activity."
> (Pascal 2009, 18)
>
> Teacher-Guided Instruction + Child-Directed Activities = Optimal Learning

 Check It Out!

Great websites:
• Encyclopedia of Language and Literacy Development
http://www.literacyencyclopedia.ca
This site presents the first comprehensive, authoritative, archival, science-based, bilingual online resource focused on children's language and literacy development for the Canadian education sector. The Encyclopedia helps to provide answers to questions about children's language and literacy, answers based on relevant and up-to-date research, presented in an easily accessible format.
  ■ The National Institute for Early Education Research (NIEER)   http://nieer.org

"It is a good idea to use programs that have worked elsewhere ("research based"). But that doesn't mean the program will work for you. Teach that program like crazy with a lot of focus and intensity, just like in the schools/studies where it worked before—in fact, that's likely why it worked elsewhere. Research-based doesn't mean that it will work automatically; you have to make such programs work".
http://www.shanahanonliteracy.com/

as if the two are, or ever were mutually exclusive). I chose to be a whole language teacher. As a whole language teacher, I believed and I continue to believe that skills, strategies, and understandings are *generally* (but *not always*) taught most effectively in meaningful contexts, not in isolation. Typically, literacy skills and strategies are not limited to one subject area, but span the curriculum. Research and teacher common sense tell us this.

Other very similar debates continue: play-based classrooms versus focused intentional teaching; inquiry-based learning versus focused intentional teaching. Why would it be either/or? Why is there any debate? Different definitions of terminology make it more confusing. For example, is play-based learning the same as learning through play? What does play-based learning really mean anyway? What is inquiry-based learning? Is inquiry-based teaching the same as inquiry-based learning? And do any of these equate with or connect to problem-based, project-based, or design-based learning?

What we do know from the work of Jeanne Chall (2002), John Hattie (2013), Richard Allington (2011; 2006), Susan Neuman (2011; 2007; 2013), Tim Shanahan (2013), Catherine Snow, *Preventing Reading Difficulties in Young Children 1998, National Research Council,* and many others is that there are some high-yield strategies that have been proven to make a real difference in varied classrooms around the world, whether the classrooms are inquiry-based, play-based, both, or neither. The effective strategies are still effective and necessary with all approaches to learning, no matter the path taken. Rather than constantly reinventing the wheel, effective teachers consistently build on what has been proven to work (Allington 2006; Chall 2002; *"Improving Schools: What Works," Educational Leadership,* February 2015).

A Caution to Preschool, Kindergarten, and Primary Teachers

Teachers need to know what reputable research truly says, and question methodologies that don't make sense. Teachers teach children to think critically and question. Teachers must do the same. Ask yourself the following questions: Is there solid research to support a particular methodology? If so, whose research is it? Does the research appear in an accredited journal? Would it or could it work in my particular context? Does it make sense? Much of what we know about effective literacy teaching and learning is common sense, albeit supported by strong research.

Teachers must trust themselves and follow the children. Stand up for what is working for the children. Avoid the latest pendulum swings. Admittedly, this is often easier said than done.

Schools and school districts often introduce too many innovations, not necessarily backed up by a strong research base or coordinated with each other and with what already exists. Yet, teachers are made to feel that the latest innovation is the magic bullet. Teachers often feel like this instead:

Teachers often don't know what is coming at them next.

Essential Elements and High-Yield Strategies of Effective K–2 Literacy Programs:
Use A Whole-School Approach

Research points to a number of essential elements and high-yield strategies of effective Comprehensive Grade K–2 literacy programs. They are often included under the banner RTI — Response to Instruction/Intervention — or the Whole-School Approach. What is key is that the most effective classroom literacy programs include both effective daily classroom instruction and effective classroom intervention. The essential elements and the high-yield strategies are included in the box below.

- Teacher and student beliefs and understandings
- Time spent on literacy teaching and learning across the day
- A high level of student engagement and self-regulation
- Clear and appropriate literacy goals, benchmarks and targets

My motto: "Better to be effective than politically correct." New or different is not necessarily better. The work of such notables as John Hattie, Michael Fullan and others promotes improving teaching by building on success, on what is working, rather than looking to implement yet ANOTHER innovation.

"Again it is my constant question in education. Why do we walk away from strategies that work?"
—Karen Mitchell, Principal, Sacred Heart School, Paris, Ontario

"Baby, I've seen it all before.... I ain't gonna be your fool anymore."
—Amos Lee

Like David Pearson, I think we are all better off in *the radical middle* going somewhere, rather than stuck in the far left or far right in the ditch, going nowhere. It isn't easy, but excellent teachers avoid extremes. Exemplary teachers should not have to teach against the organizational grain!

Effective schools are not simply about the work of individual teachers. The biggest gap is the gap in teacher effectiveness between teacher A and teacher B in any one school. They are about the work of a whole school of effective teachers. This is a call-out to principals as instructional leaders.

Without strong classroom literacy programs, all the intervention in the world will simply be playing catch-up. Rarely will there be enough effective intervention available. According to John Hattie (2012, 251) the Effect Size (ES) of **Response to Instruction/Intervention = 1.07,** which strongly validates the need for both effective classroom instruction and effective intervention.

Defining Effect Size (ES): Effect size is a standardized, scale-free measure of the relative size of the effect of an intervention on student learning. It is particularly useful for comparing the relative sizes of effects from different studies. In education, effect sizes tend to be lower than 1.00 and they can even be negative, indicating that the students in the control group gained more than those in the experimental group. Effect sizes are considered large if higher than 0.80, moderate if between 0.50 and 0.79, and small if lower than 0.30 (Shanahan and Lonigan 2013). A hinge point of 0.40 is considered close to the average effect that would be expected in student learning in order to make a visible difference. That is, a year's growth from a year of schooling.

In our view, the greatest problem faced by school districts is not resistance to innovation, but the fragmentation, overload, and incoherence resulting from the uncritical acceptance of too many different innovations which are not coordinated" (Fullan, Bennett, and Rolheiser-Bennett, 1990, p. 19).

- Ongoing assessments, documentation, and effective feedback
- Intentional and focused teaching
- An effective and engaging classroom environment: materials and organization that work
- Balanced literacy, inquiry, and play as an instructional framework
- Extensive student talk within an effective classroom culture and climate with strong teacher–student relationships
- Effective early intervention
- Enhanced home, school, and community partnerships

A Whole-School Approach
RTI- Response to Instruction/Intervention E.S. = 1.07

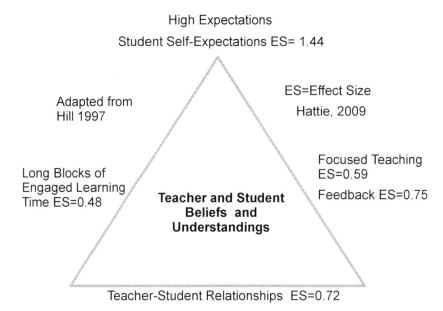

High Expectations
Student Self-Expectations ES= 1.44

Adapted from Hill 1997

ES=Effect Size
Hattie, 2009

Long Blocks of Engaged Learning Time ES=0.48

Teacher and Student Beliefs and Understandings

Focused Teaching ES=0.59

Feedback ES=0.75

Teacher-Student Relationships ES=0.72

Teacher and Student Beliefs and Understandings

Teacher and student beliefs and understandings drive teaching and are crucial to student success.

Kindergarten and Primary Students' Beliefs and Expectations: Establish a Growth Mindset and See the Engagement!

Kindergarten and primary students must see themselves as effective literacy learners. **The ES of student self-expectations is 1.44.** This is one of the most powerful influences on enhancing student achievement. According to Carol Dweck (2008), what is key is ensuring that students have the power of believing that they can and will improve or having a "growth mindset." This provides a path into the future. Students with a fixed mindset believe that they can't be successful and never will be. Students with a growth mindset believe in the power of "not yet."

In other words, I may not be able to read this book or ride this bike yet but I will! Dr. Dweck's research has shown how thousands and thousands of kids, especially struggling students, have moved from having fixed mindsets such as "I can't do this and never will be able to," to growth mindsets such as "I will get this." The classroom culture, teacher–student relationships, and teacher feedback are all key. Students benefit greatly when teachers and parents praise wisely: praise the process, the effort, the strategies, the progress, the engagement, and the perseverance.

Dr. Dweck also found that just the words "yet" or "not yet," give students greater confidence, give them a path into the future that creates greater persistence.

(See **also Making Feedback Effective,** p. 68 and **Window on the Classroom: Jane's Story,** p. 109).

Students must also see the value of literacy learning and remain engaged and motivated in literacy learning across the day (See also **Building the Brain Smarter and Stronger**, p. 118).

Kindergarten and Primary Teachers' Beliefs and Expectations

Effective Kindergarten and primary teachers are passionate about their work. Some would say they have grit. They believe that

- Teaching is not just about teaching a subject or content, but is about developing the whole child: heart, mind, body, and soul
- Early literacy learning is foundational knowledge and should be a priority focus in Grades K–2 and across the curriculum
- Virtually all students will become successful readers, writers, speakers, listeners, and viewers. Teachers keep

Student and teacher attitudes and expectations are key (Hattie 2012).

A bird sitting on a tree is never afraid of the branch breaking, because her trust is not on the branch but on her own wings. Always believe in yourself... (author unknown).

The POWER OF NOT YET!

Watch your praise!!

"When educators create growth mindset classrooms steeped in not yet, equality happens." Carol Dweck from http://www.ted.com/talks/carol_dweck_the_power_of_believing_that_you_can_improve?language=en

"Focusing on literacy involves engaging all partners in the belief that all learners can develop the literacy skills essential for life-long learning" (Ontario Ministry of Education 2013, 4).

Keep high expectations for all students (failure is not an option).

Grit can be defined as persistence, resilience, and stamina.

"Genius is one percent inspiration, ninety nine percent perspiration". Thomas Edison

high expectations for all students. They do not under-estimate what students can do.

- The child or the family should not be blamed for a student's lack of success (See chart below)
- We all learn by taking risks and making mistakes
- They are effective literacy teachers

The chart below speaks to teacher beliefs about what determines student success. There is no doubt that some schools, some contexts, and some children have more challenges than others. However, most young students who struggle with literacy are "curriculum casualties" (Clay 1987). For whatever reason(s), they do not receive the scaffolding they need at school. However, at least 98 percent of individuals can become functionally literate. Strong classroom support is key in the early years.

Myths rarely die nor fade away.

Percentage of Children Who Are Successful with Varying Levels of Home and Classroom Support		
	High Home Support	Low Home Support
Consistent High Classroom Support	100%	100%
Consistent Mixed Classroom Support	100%	25%
Consistent Low Classroom Support	60%	0%

Source: Snow cited in Allington, 1996, 66.

Kindergarten Reading: Debunking a Myth

Teacher and student beliefs and understandings are key to the degree of student success. For a long time, there has been a myth that learning to read in Kindergarten can be very damaging to students and may have long-term negative effects. Let's look at what we really know as summarized by Tim Shanahan, Chair of the Early Literacy Panel, and Member of the Reading Hall of Fame.

> "We do have a lot of data showing that literacy instruction improves the literacy skills of the kids who receive that instruction in preschool and Kindergarten, and another body of research showing that early literacy skills predict later reading and academic achievement (and, of course, there is another body of literature showing the connections between academic success and later economic success). There are studies showing

that the most literate kids are the ones who are emotionally strongest and; there is even research on Head Start programs showing that as we have improved the early literacy skills in those programs, emotional abilities have improved as well. **There are not now, and there never have been data showing any damage to kids from early language or literacy learning**, despite the overheated claims of the G. Stanley Halls, Arnold Gessells, Hans Furths, David Elkinds, and many others. We also know that early reading performance is predictive of later school success (Cunningham and Stanovich 1997; Duncan, Dowsett, Claessens, Magnuson et al. 2007; Juel 1988; Snow, Tabors, and Dickinson 2001; Smart, Prior, Sansor, and Oberkind 2005). This means that young children's reading performance tends to be pretty stable: Kindergarten literacy development is predictive of First Grade performance, First Grade performance predicts achievement in various upper grades, and the performance at each of these levels is predictive of later levels.

> Many, perhaps most, students entering Kindergarten believe that they will learn to read (and write) by the end of Kindergarten. They have the drive and believe that they will do it!

If a youngster is behind in reading in grade 3, then he/she would likely still be behind in high school, which can have a serious and deleterious impact on content learning (science, history, literature, math), high school graduation rates, and economic viability (the students' college and career readiness).

The research seems clear to me: teach kids reading early and then build on those early reading skills as they progress through school. Don't expect early skills alone to transfer to higher later skills; you have to teach students more literacy as they move up the grades (something that has not always happened)" (Shanahan 2015, http://www.shanahanonliteracy.com/2015/01/twogroups-that-are-strong-advocates-in.html).

The long-term effects on high school seniors of learning to read in Kindergarten

The Long-Term Effects on High School Seniors of Learning to Read in Kindergarten (Hanson and Farrell, 1984) is a very well researched large-scale longitudinal study of 3,959 high school seniors from 24 school districts in 10 U.S. states, published in *Reading Research Quarterly* (1995). The International Reading Association (IRA) — now the International Literacy Association (ILA) — publishes this very reputable journal of reading research. Some of these high school seniors were enrolled in Kindergarten and attended elementary schools that provided formal reading

> The essential research question is this: "Do differences in the age at which children begin receiving formal reading instruction have any measurable impact on their subsequent schooling experiences, reading achievement, attitudes, and literacy levels as young adults?"

instruction in Kindergarten. The study compares the subsequent reading and school-related experiences of these students — from Kindergarten through their senior year in high school — with those of students from the same districts who did not receive the Kindergarten reading instruction. Although the study included Kindergarten students from all backgrounds, those from at-risk backgrounds were overrepresented. This study is extraordinary, since there are very few longitudinal studies involving preschool or Kindergarten students, and even rarer are those focused on the long-term effects of learning to read at an early age.

Results showed that clear, consistent, and positive differences were associated with receiving reading instruction in Kindergarten:

> *The major finding of this study, briefly stated, is: Students who learned to read in Kindergarten were found to be superior in reading skills and all other educational indicators measured as seniors in high school. Further, this finding held up across districts and schools, as well as ethnic, gender, and social class groups. Also, there was absolutely no evidence of any negative effects from learning to read in Kindergarten. Collectively, the results provide full support for the policy of teaching reading in Kindergarten. Thus, any district with a policy that does not support Kindergarten reading should be ready to present new and compelling reasons to explain why not — beyond the old and now refuted myth that it has long-term, adverse effects on students' reading skills, attitudes, and behaviours* (Hanson and Farrell 1995, 929).

What did the Kindergarten reading instruction look like in this longitudinal study?

First, reading was defined as both decoding and comprehending text. The children were introduced to basic sight words and decoding skills, beginning with critical sounds (See more about phonics and decoding in this chapter and in Chapters 10 and 11) and reading from a set of 52 special story booklets. The story booklets, which were the central focus of instruction, consisted of illustrated stories about a series of animal characters. The children read them aloud and, to allow for additional practice and to increase parental involvement, each child was provided with a full set of these consumable booklets to take home. At the back of the booklets were discussion questions about the story characters and plot, used by the teacher or parent to verify the child's understanding and encourage discussion. In the context of an

---

Something to Celebrate

Not only did the students who received formal reading instruction in Kindergarten exhibit a clear pattern of (a) showing superior high school reading skills, (b) having higher grades and better attendance in school, and (c) needing and receiving significantly less remedial instruction in both elementary and secondary school, but many were also from much more high-needs communities with lower levels of parent education as compared with those in the control group.

---

otherwise standard Kindergarten environment, which included play, only 20 to 30 minutes of daily instructional time were devoted to the teaching of reading — a balanced Kindergarten curriculum focused on developing the whole child.

What does this research really tell us?

A number of common elements were found in this longitudinal study. The six key findings are included below.

- Students who learned to read in Kindergarten were superior in reading skills and all other educational indicators measured as seniors in high school, regardless of their social class, ethnicity, and gender.
- There were no ill effects from learning to read in Kindergarten.
- Both play and focused (intentional) literacy teaching using a balanced literacy approach are important in Kindergarten.
- Spending at least 20 to 30 minutes a day focused on reading in Kindergarten is crucial.
- Parental involvement is beneficial.
- Reading instruction should focus on more than decoding.

> Students who learned to read in Kindergarten were found to be superior in reading skills and all other educational indicators when measured as seniors in high school, regardless of their social class, ethnicity, and gender. There were no ill effects from learning to read in Kindergarten (Hanson and Farrell 1995, 929).

What does this research not tell us?
The research does not tell us that there is just one way to teach early reading.

I didn't know it was time to move on!

The Kindergarten students in Jane's class are totally smitten with reading. They absolutely love it. In June, when asked by the upcoming group of Kindergarteners what they liked best about being in Kindergarten, the majority did not hesitate: "We learned to read!" And they did! Most, in fact, could read very fluently with comprehension. Jane frequently begins her day with students "reading" independently on the carpet. No time

is wasted when they first come in. Research indicates that this is a very good routine to use at the start of the K–3 day. The little girl in this photo is so hooked on reading that she doesn't make a move when it is time to join the others who have moved on to other activities. Every one of the children in Jane's Kindergarten class joins the Reading Club by the end of Kindergarten, and often well before. Throughout the primary grades, most children go on to read (and write) a great deal on their own, and further develop their oral language and background (world) knowledge. As in the study reported above, there is no downside to early reading in Jane's class. For more about Jane and her very successful approach to early literacy, see p. 109, **Window on the Classroom: Jane's Story.**

Early Literacy: What's the Rush?

The research is clear. School systems, working with families, have a small window of opportunity in which to get children off to a strong start. Research indicates that children who begin Grade 3 struggling in reading and writing rarely catch up with their age-appropriate peers and tend to struggle all the way through high school (Snow 1998). "When children perform poorly, it is often attributed to their delayed development or disability, rather than the paucity of experiences and opportunities to explore written language and literacy understandings. Teachers need to revise their instruction, not their expectations for learning, when children are not progressing" (McGill-Franzen 1992, 57–58). All children deserve a strong start. Early childhood education is crucial to later success in school and in life:

- According to a study by Connie Juel (cited in Kameeunui 1998), the probability that a child who is a poor reader at the end of Grade 1 will remain a poor reader at the end of Grade 4 is 0.88. In addition, there is a 90 percent chance of remaining a poor reader after three years of schooling.

- An estimated 80 percent of children identified as learning disabled have, as their predominant characteristic, a serious problem in learning to read. However, there is an impressive and growing body of evidence showing that many of these reading problems, which all too frequently become permanent, are preventable if children are provided with effective intervention early (Pikulski 1998).

- There is very little evidence that programs designed to correct reading problems beyond Second Grade are successful (Allington 1998; Snow et al. 1998).

- Reading failure is preventable for all but a very small percentage of students (Pikulski 1998; Allington 2011).

- The best time to provide additional help to students who are at risk is early on, when they are still motivated and confident, and when the "learning gap" is still relatively small (Pikulski 1998).

- The International Reading Association and the National Association for the Education of Young Children (NAEYC) Joint Position Statement reports, "Failing to give children literacy experiences until they are school age can severely limit the reading and writing levels they ultimately attain" (1998, 6).

- "The receptive vocabulary scores of Kindergarten students near the end of Kindergarten were strongly related to the end of seventh grade vocabulary and reading comprehension" (Dickinson and Sprague 2001, 273).

- "Research indicates that the experiences during the first five years of a child's life have a major bearing on his or her future success in school, in the workplace, and many other aspects of a healthy, fulfilling life" (The Canadian Council on Learning 2007, 2).

- "Children in Grades 2 and 3 who lack decoding skills and a reasonable base of sight words may be condemned to school careers marred by increasing distance between them and other children unless successful remediation occurs" (Kameeunui 1993, 13).

- "A child who is eight years old and not a reader is a student in deep trouble at school" (McGill-Franzen 1992, 57).

- A very recent study, *Double Jeopardy Overview: How Third-Grade Reading Skills and Poverty Influence High School Graduation* (Hernandez 2012), confirms that students who are unable to read in Grade 3 are four times less likely to graduate when compared to students who can read proficiently. Early identification of struggling students in Kindergarten and Grade 1 is crucial to ensuring that teachers are able to provide the necessary interventions and supports to ensure that students succeed (Nova Scotia Department of Education 2009).

"We could know on the second day of Kindergarten who is at risk of becoming a struggling reader, but we typically do nothing with this information" (Allington 2011).

"The major prevention strategy is excellent instruction" (Snow et al. 1998, 172).

"By the end of second grade, students should be reading at least simple chapter books and other texts of their choice with comfort and understanding. Second grade is broadly viewed as children's last chance. Those who are not on track by third grade have little chance of ever catching up" (Snow et al. 1998, 211–212).

"Too many pre-school and Kindergarten teachers, perceiving themselves as advocates of developmentally appropriate practice, fear pushing children too much academically and fail to teach them the knowledge and skills that they need" (Bredekamp 1997, 38).

"Vulnerable children are not limited to low-income families since many 'vulnerabilities' are not income sensitive. Analyses show that the majority of vulnerable children — more than 60 percent — live in moderate, middle class and affluent families" (Pascal 2009, 10).

- Neither retention nor social promotion is the answer for struggling literacy learners. "The evidence gathered in study after study over sixty years clearly indicates that the best policy keeps children with the peers they enter school with" (Allington and Cunningham 1996, 12). Yet, social promotion — moving them on year after year — rarely sees the students "catching up." The only solution is to get the students off to a strong start in preschool through Grade 2.

Finland - a Literacy Success Story

Finland consistently has one of the highest adult literacy rates in the world. Finnish children generally start Grade 1 in the year in which they turn seven. Most attend strong preschools. There is some speculation in North America that the reason for the higher literacy rate is due to their learning to read at an older age than many North American students. However, this is a simplistic explanation which does not stand up under scrutiny. Consider the following facts:

- Almost half of Finnish children (40-50 %) are able to read when they begin school.

- The schools, the teachers and parents have high expectations for literacy education; so if the other half of the children (50-60%) is not able to read by Christmas, the teachers often consider themselves to have failed in their reading instruction.

- Six-year-old Finnish children (Kindergarten), like children in English-speaking countries, segment and blend syllables and identify rhymes. They also focus on phonics and listening to and responding to stories. They write. The work is intended to provide the foundation for further work in literacy.

- There is a greater incidence of oral work in Finland than in English-speaking countries studied. This focus on oral language is probably a significant difference.

- There is a "national culture of the book" which some analysts believe lies behind Finland's high standings in international comparative studies of attainment in literacy. Finnish society places a high value on literacy and teachers. It is reinforced in schools and home where, in both cases, the daily reading of a story to children is firmly embedded. There is a strong national culture of reading. It is a country of readers.

For more on the differences between the Finns' situation and that of the U.S. and Canada see more from Tim Shanahan@ http://www.shanahanonliteracy.com/2015/10/response-to-joyful-illiterate.html

- Teachers are well paid and highly valued in the community.

- Finland has excellent public libraries and highly-educated librarians. The number of books borrowed annually from public libraries and the number of new books for children and young people is very high.

- There is a strong regularity of the Finnish Sound/Spelling system—unlike in English where fewer than 50% of the words are phonically regular.

- The impact of parents' socio-economic background on pupil's performance is reported to be low. The differences among schools, between urban and rural areas and between regions, are small. 'Equal opportunities' is the leading principle in education policy. Differences in socio-economic status of families have little impact on students' reading achievements. In Finland, education is totally free, including lunches, travel and books. Education is comprehensive and non-selective; there are no elite or private schools.

- Elementary school classes have low pupil-teacher ratios.

- The Finnish learning environment consists of a commitment to good design. The furniture matches the users' needs. Considerable effort goes into achieving the best intrinsic design through wall coverings, lighting, furniture, equipment, fabrics and plants.

- Schools provide free warm lunches which are of a high nutritional quality.

- Finnish teachers are not preoccupied with discipline and control due to the freely co-operative behaviour of most of their pupils.

- Finland's population is approximately five and one-half million. It is a largely homogeneous society. 94% speak Finnish and 6% speak Swedish; Ethnic breakdown: 93% Finns and 6% Swedes; 1% other.

- Religious breakdown: 89% Evangelical Lutheran, 1% Russian orthodox, 9% no religion and 1% other.

- Pupils with learning difficulties get remedial teaching in addition to their regular classes. Early intervention is in place. Thirty-seven percent of First-Graders get additional support. All regular class teachers and special needs teachers have knowledge and expertise in support of learning difficulties

So, there you have it. Too many have for too long tried to find simplistic explanations or excuses for why some students struggle with reading while others don't. And often, they have blamed the "victim". The gift of time, waiting until students are older, is generally no gift at all. Comparing Finland's education system and culture to Canada's or that of the U.S. is like comparing apples to elephants. In the end the most important factors no matter the country are teacher and student beliefs, understandings, skills and teacher-student relationships. Good results in literacy call for strong co-operation between homes, schools and the whole society. **In the end, Finnish society supports literacy—schools and teachers are not alone.**

A Matter of Social Justice

Providing strong preschool, Kindergarten, and Grade 1–2 literacy programs is a matter of social justice. Adult literacy rates tell the story:

> *A devastatingly large number of people in America cannot read as well as they need to for success in life. Large numbers of school-age children, including children from all social classes, face significant difficulties in learning to read. … However, the majority of reading problems faced by today's adolescents and adults could have been avoided or resolved in children's early years* (Burns and Snow 1999, 5, 11).

Based on the results from Statistics Canada and the International Adult Literacy and Skills Survey (IALSS) 2005, 48 percent of Canadian adults age 16 and over — about 12 million Canadians — have low literacy (20 percent scoring Level 1, the lowest proficiency, in prose literacy, and 28 percent at Level 2). This means that fully 48 percent of all Canadian adults do not have the literacy skills considered necessary to live and work in today's society (Statistics Canada and OECD 2005).

The Programme for International Student Assessment (PISA) is an international study that measures the performance of 15-year-olds in reading literacy, mathematics literacy, and science literacy. Approximately 470,000 students in 65 countries participated in the 2009 PISA study, representing close to 26 million students. The overall national scores for both Canada and the U.S. decreased on the 2009 reading literacy assessment when

RELATIONSHIPS:

"**Belonging** refers to a sense of connectedness to others, an individual's experiences of being valued, of forming relationships with others and making contributions as part of a group, a community, the natural world" (How Does Learning Happen? Ontario's Pedagogy for the Early Years, 2014 p.7).

compared to the original scores in 2000. This should not be the case, considering the ongoing focus on literacy during the past 20 years. These results are especially troubling since the demands for high levels of literacy in our society are rapidly accelerating (Knighton, Brochu, and Gluszynski 2010).

The number of prison cells gauged to be built in some U.S. states is reportedly based on literacy rates in Grade 2 (Blankstein 2010, 4). There is, in fact, a strong link between low literacy levels and incarceration. "A child who can read by third grade is unlikely ever to be involved with the criminal justice system, while four of five incarcerated juvenile offenders read two or more years below grade level. Indeed a majority of them are functionally illiterate" (Lawrence cited in Blankstein 2010, 4).

> "One in three Ontario Kindergarten students entered Grade 1 'vulnerable' or 'at-risk' in language and cognitive development. Most of these students did not meet the reading, writing and mathematics standards at the end of Grade 3" (EQAO 2013).

Time Spent on Literacy Teaching and Learning Across the Day

Teachers who allocate more time to reading and language arts are the teachers whose children show the greatest gains in literacy development (Allington and Cunningham 1996). However, it is not just the number of minutes allocated to literacy learning that matters. How are these minutes used? Student motivation, self-regulation, and engagement are key.

Time in Kindergarten

Literacy learning occurs across the Kindergarten day — in whole-class, small-group, and one-to-one activities, both at centres and during cross-curricular activities. Children in Kindergarten also need large blocks of time to play, explore, investigate, reflect, and share often through inquiry and play. Inquiries often tend to be ongoing for at least several days, as does mature play (See **Mature Play**, p. 180; **Inquiries**, Chapters 13 and 14). Lots of student-talk, both student–adult and student–student, is crucial. (See **Extending Conversations**, p. 127–132; **Conversations**, Chapter 4 and 5; **Documentation** (See **Documentation and Effective Feedback,** p. 61) both reciprocal student and teacher feedback, are all crucial in Kindergarten. The possibilities for student improvement are now endless, with full-day early learning/Kindergarten being implemented in three Canadian provinces (Nova Scotia being the first) and many U.S. states. However, simply adding more time is not enough. What is done during this time is crucial.

> Lots of student-talk, adult-student, student–adult and student–student, is crucial.
> (See **Extending Conversations**, p. 131; **Conversations**, Chapter 4, 5 and 9; **Documentation** (See **Documentation and Effective Feedback**, p.61)

The role of the administrator is crucial. There must be a priority by administration when scheduling timetables that the **language arts** block is the **first priority**. "Creating the two-and-a-half hour uninterrupted blocks begins by setting that as a firm organizational guideline. Classroom teachers need time to teach. They need uninterrupted time to teach. Kids need time to learn. To read. To write. Uninterrupted learning time" (Allington 2001, 39).

How does one "get it all in" using long blocks of time for literacy learning? Integration is the answer! A natural framework for making this happen is inquiry-based learning. (See **Scaffolding an Inquiry**, p. 322; **Inquiries**, Chapter 13 and 14.)

Time in Grades 1–2

Students in Grades 1–2 need to spend at least two hours daily focused on language arts (Allington and Cunningham 1996). "Research indicates that using longer instructional blocks often results in productive and complicated work being achieved" (Allington and Johnston 2001, 161). Long blocks of uninterrupted time are most beneficial. This time must be sacred. The more interruptions and transitions, the more time lost. Frequent intercom announcements must also be eliminated. However, simply adding more time is not enough. What is done with this time is crucial. At least half the time in Grades 1–2 should see students reading and writing. Strategic cross-curricular literacy integration across the day and from day to day is also crucial. In their research on effective Fourth Grade classrooms, Allington and Johnston indicate, "Integration across subjects, time, and topics was common, rather than a compartmentalized curriculum" (2000, 17). Much of the work was longer-term in nature — lasting for a week or more — rather than a series of small tasks to be completed each day. It is likely that this research can be extrapolated to Grades K–2, including time spent doing inquiry and play because deep understanding comes from being immersed in extended inquiries and play.

Students learn to read and write by doing lots of reading and writing. Stanovitch (1986) describes the "Matthew Effect," where "the rich get richer and the poor get poorer." That is, strong readers typically read a great deal and the more they read, the better they get. Struggling readers typically read less and less as they move up through the grades, and the gap between them and their more capable peers widens more and more, year by year, even day by day!

Equally important to lots of reading and writing in Grades 1–2 is lots of student talk, both student–adult, adult to student and student–student. (See **Extending the Conversations**, and **Conversations**, Chapters 4 and 5). Intentional and focused teaching, documentation (See **Documentation**, p. 61), and student and teacher feedback are also crucial.

A High Level of Student Engagement and Self-Regulation

According to research done by Richard Allington (2002; 2006), among others, the amount of time students are truly engaged in learning is the most potent predictor of literacy learning.

Task difficulty and task interest (including choice) largely determine engagement. If a task is too difficult, students tend to give up. If the task is too easy, students are bored and often give up as well. "Managed choice" (a term coined by Allington), where students do not have an unlimited range of task or topic choices, but are often seen working on similar but different tasks or projects, has proven successful for students and teachers alike. Student voice is important, as are meaningful and purposeful tasks. The tasks, generally last several days, often span several subject areas (such as during inquiry-based learning and play), and require significant student self-regulation. They also increase student engagement. These tasks involve lots of time for extended reading and writing (Allington 2002, 2006) and inquiry (See **Inquiry**, Chapters 13 and 14; **Play**, Chapters 7–10). The most effective teachers expect students to be self-regulated (at least most of the time), and they teach them how to self-regulate (Taylor, Pressley, and Pearson 2002). (See **Self-Regulation**, Chapter 7). Classroom management (ES=0.52) and classroom routines, including having the needed materials readily available, are two other key factors affecting engagement (and self-regulation) (Allington and Cunningham 2002).

> There is a difference between engagement and simply on-task behaviour. A student who is engaged not only does the work but does it with enthusiasm (Schlechty 2001).

Clear and Appropriate Literacy Goals, Benchmarks and Targets

Begin with the End in Mind and Keep it in Mind

The work of John Hattie (2012), amongst others, shows the importance of teachers and students sharing clear learning intentions. Having high expectations, not underestimating, is also important.

The landmark work of Catherine Snow, Susan Burns, and Peg Griffin (1998), and the work of the National Early Literacy Panel (2008), indicate that young children (preschool to Kindergarten) develop into strong readers and writers when their teachers effectively focus on the following foundational areas of literacy development:

- Letter knowledge/fluent letter recognition
- Phonological, including phonemic awareness
- Letter–sound correspondence (phonics)
- Concepts about print and books
- Oral language, including vocabulary (listening and speaking, receptive and expressive language)
- Writing

What About Worksheets?
The only children who can fill in a blank or do a worksheet successfully are those who already know an acceptable answer. Some of them may find a worksheet easy and satisfying because it can be completed quickly. However, these students are not learning anything from the exercise, and those who are struggling with literacy are simply frustrated by the experience. Activities that are more open-ended allow everyone to succeed and remain engaged.

When students are motivated to learn they (more) naturally acquire the skills they need to get the work done (Robinson 2015).

Letter Knowledge (Fluent Letter Recognition and Letter-Sound Correspondence or Phonics), Phonological Awareness, and Oral Language

According to Marilyn Jager Adams (1990, 36), pre-readers' ability to recognize and name letters (letter knowledge) at the end of Kindergarten is "the single best predictor of first-year [Grade 1] reading achievement, with their ability to discriminate phonemes auditorily ranking a close second. Furthermore, these two factors were the winners regardless of the instructional approach used." However, "it is not simply the accuracy with which children can name letters that gives them an advantage in learning to read [and write], it is the ease or fluency [speed] with which they can do so. Recognizing the letters on a stop sign, without hesitation, is an example of fluent letter recognition. A child who can recognize most letters with thorough confidence will have an easier time learning about letter sounds and word spellings than a child who still has to work at remembering what is what" (43).

According to research, knowing letter names is important because they typically contain a sound represented by the letter. For example, recognizing the letter *d* helps the reader to remember that its sound is /d/. The more time children need to spend on figuring out letters, the less time and energy they will have available to use other strategies to decode print, to write, and to comprehend. Thus, letter recognition must become automatic.

Learning Letters

Teach letter shapes to learn letter names

Children often confuse similar letters such as b, d, and p; u and n; w and m; E, F, T, and L; and H and A. To reduce this confusion, children must be taught to recognize the shapes of letters and their orientation. One way to achieve this is to teach the different strokes for printing each letter. Learning to print letters is important. Kindergarten teachers should generally not worry about some letter reversals, inversions, and unconventional letter formations in student writing.

Children learn to distinguish confusing letters by doing activities involving several letters, not just one. Sorting games help children to pay attention to different letter orientations and features (McGee 2005, 98). Letter sorts are done after the mini-lessons that differentiate the confusing letters. Be sure that the children have a good grounding in one confusing or tricky letter first. They really do need to know that letter, for example *b*, before introducing a second commonly confused letter, e.g., *d*.

Develop Strong Readers and Writers: Strongest Predictors of K–1 Literacy Success

- Best Predictor: Fluent letter recognition (See Learning Letters p. 46)

- Second Best Predictor: Phonological including phonemic awareness (See Chapter 4)

- Third Best Predictor: Oral language (See Chapters 4 to 6)

"Just measuring how many letters a Kindergartener is able to name when shown letters in a random order appears to be nearly as successful at predicting future reading, as an entire readiness test" (Snow, Burns, and Griffin 1998, 113) .

Children are given letter tiles, plastic letters, and/or wooden letters providing several examples of four to six letters (limit the number of letters) that are often confused (e.g. E, F, T, L). Not only should the students sort the letters, but they should also write each letter to reinforce the letter shape and orientation. Letter sorts may also include sorting by matching upper and lower case letters and sorting pictures by matching those that begin with the same letter.

Also learning to write letters in a letter guessing game, called "let's predict" helps students to learn tricky letters. In this game the teacher begins with one stroke of the letter and gets the students to predict the next stroke and eventually the letter name. This is a great activity to do frequently after teaching children the strokes for printing each letter.

"We recommend demonstrating how to write three or four letters that can be confused, over several days" (McGee 2005, 99).

Lots of student writing (See Chapters 11 and 12) and linking letters with phonological and phonemic awareness activities supports both the learning of letters and their sounds. Writing and reading are reciprocal. They support one another. Not enough emphasis has been placed on supporting writing in primary classrooms with reading being the main focus.

Using names to teach the letters

Children are especially motivated to read and write their names and the names of others in their class. Research shows that personal name learning does promote letter learning among preschoolers (Ehri and Roberts 2006, 122).

1. Learn letters in their names (making and breaking their names)

2. Learn to recognize the letters in their friends' names

3. Learn to sort like letters, machining upper and lower cases letters

4. Learn to sort letters using different fonts

Use environmental print to learn letters and sounds

Children can learn letters and phonics from environmental print if the teacher engages them actively in using such print. Although most students recognize that there is print on the wall or on a label at a Centre, many do not recognize individual letters and words. Students often ignore environmental print, regarding it simply as wallpaper. In addition, combining letters with natural items, such as rocks and wood at a Centre, can be very engaging. Tactile learning is important.

Children's ability to read words is tied to their ability to write words (IRA and NAEYC 1998, 35).

Children learn a lot about reading from labels, signs and other kinds of print they see around them (IRA and NAEYC 1998, 33).

Learning Letter Names and the Comprehension Strategy: Predicting

1. Students print their names on sentence strips.
2. Students pair-up and share their name cards: letter names and numbers of letters.
3. Each pair joins with another and follows the procedure listed above.
4. Students 'predict' which letter will be the most popular letter in all of their class names. Say "Let's predict…What will be the most popular letter in all our names? Popular means the most of… e.g. the most popular ice-cream; election results". Explain that a prediction is an informed guess.
5. Students cut out each of the letters in their names and place each one in a separate cup labeled with the corresponding letter name.
6. Students make further predictions.
7. Students count and tally the results.
8. How close were their predictions?

Check it out!

The following alphabet knowledge sites:

www.songsforteaching.com
www.rocknlearn.com , and
www.jazzles.com;

AK sites with a variety of children's AK learning games:
www.internet4classrooms.com/ kplus_alpha.htm ,
www.abcya.com/Kindergarten_ computers.htm, and
www.playkidsgames.com/ alphabetGames.htm.

There is evidence that the beginning (a, b, c) and ending (x, y, z) of the alphabet are more easily remembered than the middle (Stahl 2014, 264). Thus, they would require less focus in general.

Is There a Best Protocol for Teaching Letters?

Jones and Reutzel (2012) developed the Enhanced Alphabet Knowledge (EAK) protocol for teaching letters that has proven very successful. In this protocol, brief explicit lessons are taught using multiple instructional cycles. A new letter is taught each day. All letters are taught explicitly at least once. The letters that are harder for children to learn receive more practice. There are at least four instructional cycles:

- Cycle 1 teaches the initial letters of the students' names
- Cycle 2 teaches all of the letters in alphabetic order
- Cycle 3 is based on the letter-name pronunciation advantage, such as b, d, j, k, p, t, v, f, l, m, n, r, s. These are letters that have the letter sound pronounced in the letter name.
- Cycle 4 teaches ambiguous letters such as h, y, and w that cause children the most difficulty.

Ongoing assessment determines student grouping and regrouping and ongoing teaching as needed.

The Enhanced Alphabet Knowledge Lesson Components (adaptation of Jones and Reutzel 2012, 463, in Stahl 2014, 264).

COMPONENT	TIME	DESCRIPTION
Letter-name identification	1–2 minutes	Children name targeted upper and lower case letters.
Letter-sound identification	1–2 minutes	Teacher models letter sounds and how they are formed in the mouth. Children make the sounds. Short vowels are taught.
Recognizing letters in text	3 minutes	Find the letters in a text and make the sounds.
Producing the letter form	4–5 minutes	Teacher demonstrates letter formation and the children form the letters on paper, dry-erase boards or with clay, pipe cleaners, or Wikki Stix.

There is no definitive evidence to recommend only one particular sequence for teaching letters or letter sound correspondences. That being said, we do know that the most commonly used initial consonant sounds are f, m, s, t, and h. Teachers often choose to begin with these letters. The next initial and final constant sounds usually taught are l, d, c, n, g, w, p, r, and k. These letters are followed by j, q, v, and x. Vowel sounds are taught beginning with short vowels, then moving to long vowel sounds, and then vowel pairs (Morrow and Morgan 2006, 35).

Should upper and lower case letters be taught at the same time?

Again, there is no simple answer for this. However, the 52 letters (upper and lower case) represent 40 letter shapes. It is obviously easier for a child to learn upper case S with lower case s or a C and a c than learn a B and a b or an R and an r. According to Adams in her landmark book *Beginning to Read: Thinking and Learning About Print*, it is unwise to try to teach both upper and lower case forms of all 26 letters at once to children who have little letter knowledge. That is, upper and lower case should be taught at different times. Special care should be taken to avoid confusion of letter names and sounds (Adams 1989, 129). We know that many children beginning Kindergarten do not understand the concept of a letter or a sound.

Young children generally learn capital (upper case) letters earlier and more easily, perhaps because the shapes are less confusable. Additionally, environmental print consists predominantly of upper case letters which parents and caregivers often point out to preschoolers (e.g., look at the *S* in the stop sign or the *M* in McDonalds, Ehri and Roberts 2006, 113).

The second best predictor of reading success in Grade 1 is a child's ability to discriminate between phonemes (individual letter sounds) at the end of Kindergarten. Phonemic awareness is one aspect of phonological awareness. It involves

1. *An understanding that oral language is composed of a series of individual sounds*

2. *The ability to play with these sounds*

(See Phonology and Phonological Awareness p. 104; The Sound (Phonemic Awareness) Segmenting Centre: A Three-step Intervention Framework that Works p. 105)

"Enhancing children's letter knowledge and phonological awareness skills should be a priority goal in the Kindergarten classroom" (Snow 1998, 188). However, no matter how skilled the child is in alphabet letter knowledge and phonological awareness, he or she still needs a strong understanding of both the concepts about books and about print, and a strong foundation in oral language and background knowledge. Oral language proficiency (See Chapters 4–6) — both receptive (listening) and expressive (speaking) — includes vocabulary knowledge and is a third strong predictor of future literacy success that lasts well into high school.

Generally a good rule according to current learning theory is to start with the more easily visualized uppercase letters. In each case, introducing just a few letters at a time, rather than many, enhances mastery (IRA and NAEYC 1998, 35).

Learning word families (also called rimes or phonograms) is also important to early decoding in reading and encoding in writing. (See **Common Phonograms or rimes**, p. 298).

Phonological awareness involves the understanding or awareness of the structure of oral language — that oral language is comprised of words, and that words consist of syllables, rhymes, and individual sounds or phonemes. ES=0.86, this is very high.

How Important is Phonics and How is it Best Taught?

It is important to start by defining the term *phonics*. As defined by Strickland (1998, 5), phonics refers to instruction intended to develop an understanding of the alphabetic principle (i.e., that letters represent sounds), as well as knowledge of the sounds represented by those letters or letter combinations. Teachers and researchers generally agree that phonics is important. The debate arises regarding the best way(s) to teach phonics: in isolation, in context, or both? No one phonics program or approach provides THE answer! What works best is following the children, not following a program. Chall's findings (1967) still hold up. Early and systematic instruction in phonics leads to better achievement in reading than later, less systematic instruction. And writing activities are very important in establishing letter-sound relationships.

Phonics instruction is very important. It is more important in Kindergarten and Grade 1 than in any of the other grades. But it is not letter knowledge and phonics instruction in isolation alone that is important. Children should have many opportunities for meaningful reading and writing experiences. Research undertaken by Manning and Kamii (2000) revealed that children who were taught phonics in an isolated manner advanced less and became more confused during the Kindergarten year than those who learned phonics in context.

Canadian longitudinal research, undertaken by Linda Phillips, Director of the Canadian Centre for Research on Literacy used a specific explicit phonics program called "MAP," *Meaningful Applied Phonics: Explicit Phonics Through Direct Instruction* with half of the students, beginning in First Grade. The control group was taught using a more balanced literacy approach. Third Grade results indicated that it is better to support a strong comprehensive balanced literacy program rather than spending huge amounts of time on phonics drills. "The lesson was clear: phonics is important, but deal with it first and fast and get on with reading" (and writing) (Phillips, Norris, and Steffler 2007, 16).

A helpful phonics guide
The phonics guide that follows was introduced by Steven Stahl and the Centre for the Improvement of Early Reading Achievement.

> In systematic phonics programs, a planned set of phonics elements is taught sequentially. "The use of a planned and sequential approach to teaching phonics is recommended, as is integrating instruction in phonemic awareness skills with phonics" (The Council of Ministers of Education, *Canadian Education Statistics Council: Key Factors to Support Literacy Success in School-Aged Populations* 2009, 29).

> Effective phonics instruction should not dominate instruction and should not be boring. Students need to spend most of their time doing authentic Language Arts activities such as writing for a purpose, reading, and being given many opportunities for oral language activities such as discussion, songs, rhymes, and play.

Kindergarten

Consonants
Introduce Consonant Digraphs (e.g., ck, ph, ch)
Introduce Consonant Blends (e.g., st, str, bl, br)
Introduce Short Vowels
Introduce Simple Rimes or Word families (e.g., at, in it, am)

Source: Steven A. Stahl, *How Can I Help Children Crack the Code?* CIERA, 2001.

Writing: The Reading–Writing Connection

In her landmark research, Dolores Durkin (1966) discovered that the parents and caregivers of children who had learned to read before coming to Kindergarten had read with their children. However, they did more than this. They did "literacy on the run" on a regular basis — they sang with their children, rhymed, pointed out letters on signs, and wrote to and with their children. They also gave their children many writing opportunities. It became clear that early readers generally are very interested in writing and many write long before they read.

Canadian researchers, Harrison, Ogle, McIntyre, and Hellsten (2008) reviewed K–3 studies on early writing conducted in Canada, the United Kingdom, and the United States. The findings, published in a paper titled "The Influence of Early Writing Instruction on Developing Literacy," indicated that early writing

- Supports the development of phonological awareness, the alphabetic principle, and phonics
- Enhances early reading (word identification, decoding, passage comprehension, and word reading) and often precedes early reading (See **Window on the Classroom: Wags in Diana's Class,** p. 273).

Writing and reading develop reciprocally, but more emphasis has been put on the teaching of reading than the teaching of writing in many classrooms. Early writing is one of the three curriculum gap areas described below.

Curriculum Gaps: What Areas Need More Attention?

The research described by Bill Teale in his article "The Curriculum Gap Ensures a Continuing Achievement Gap" (2007) is important. This research indicates that the following key areas are often neglected in early literacy classrooms:

Consonant blends are two or three consonants that together create a distinct sound (e.g., st, bl, br, str).

Consonant digraphs are two consonants together that represent one sound (e.g., ck, ch, sh).

> I would argue for a steady dose of teaching in the areas that we cannot test easily (comprehension and oral language), and a variable amount of teaching of those skills that we can monitor such as phonics and fluency. http://www.shanahanonliteracy.com/search/label/RtI

- Oral language, including vocabulary (word knowledge), world knowledge (background knowledge and comprehension), listening and speaking, and receptive and expressive language (See Chapters 4–6)
- Reading comprehension (See Chapters 3–4)
- Writing (See Chapters 11–12)

Closing Thoughts

The areas that need much attention are clear. Close the curriculum gaps by also attending to the remainder of the high-yields strategies clarified in the following two chapters. The literacy goals described in Chapter 2, Chapter 11 and the Oral Language Checklist p. 114 will help to guide this work.

Literacy Goals for Grades K–2

A Goal Is a Dream with a Deadline

It is important to begin with the end in mind, clear and appropriate literacy goals, benchmarks and targets. Grade 2 is the defining time. By the end of Grade 2, students will

- Develop the knowledge, skills, and understandings of effective literacy learners

- See themselves as successful literacy learners

- Be motivated and enjoy reading, listening to text read aloud, writing, problem solving, learning about the world, and sharing their thoughts

The IRA and the NAEYC published a joint position statement titled *Learning to Read and Write: Developmentally Appropriate Practices for Young Children* (1998). The document clearly lays out the following continuum for children's development in early reading and writing.

Continuum of Children's Development in Early Reading and Writing

Children at any grade level will function in a variety of phases along the reading and writing continua. The lists presented below are intended to be illustrative, not exhaustive. For more detailed benchmarks and targets, mini-lessons, engaging activities, and proven instructional approaches, see the following chapters.

"If you don't know where you're going, any road will get you there."
—Lewis Carroll, *Alice's Adventures in Wonderland*

Phase 1: Awareness and exploration (goals for Preschool)

Children explore their environment and build the foundations for learning to read and write.

Preschoolers...	So preschool teachers...	And family members should be encouraged to...
■ enjoy listening to and discussing storybooks ■ understand that print carries a message ■ engage in reading and writing attempts ■ identify labels and signs in their environment ■ participate in rhyming games ■ identify some letters and make some letter–sound matches ■ use known letters or approximations of letters to represent written language (especially meaningful words like their name and phrases such as *I love you*) ■ wonder about many things	■ share books with children (including Big Books, fiction, non-fiction, and poetry) and model reading behaviours ■ talk about letters by name and sounds ■ establish a literacy-rich environment ■ reread favorite stories ■ engage children in language games ■ promote literacy-related play activities ■ encourage children to experiment with writing ■ extend conversations ■ scaffold play and inquiry	■ engage their child in conversation, provide the names for things, and show interest in what their child says ■ read and reread stories and non-fiction texts daily ■ encourage their child to recount experiences and describe ideas and events that are important ■ visit the library regularly ■ provide opportunities to draw and print ■ join in during play

Phase 2: Experimental reading and writing (goals for Kindergarten)

Children develop basic concepts of print and begin to engage in and experiment with reading and writing.

Kindergarteners...	So Kindergarten teachers...	And family members should be encouraged to...
▪ enjoy being read to and can retell simple narrative stories and non-fiction text	▪ encourage children to talk about reading and writing experiences	▪ read and reread narrative stories and non-fiction texts to their child daily
▪ use descriptive language to explain and explore	▪ promote inquiry	▪ encourage their child's attempts at reading and writing
▪ recognize letters and letter–sound matches	▪ scaffold literacy-related play activities	▪ allow their child to participate in activities that involve reading and writing (e.g., cooking, making grocery lists)
▪ show familiarity with rhyming and beginning sounds	▪ provide many opportunities for children to explore and identify sound–symbol relationships in meaningful contexts	
▪ understand left-to-right and top-to-bottom orientation and familiar concepts of print	▪ help children to segment spoken words into individual sounds and blend the sounds into whole words (for example, by slowly writing a word and stretching the sounds)	▪ play games with their child that involve specific directions (such as Simon Says)
▪ match spoken words with written words		▪ become a participant in their child's imaginary play
▪ write letters of the alphabet and some high-frequency words	▪ frequently read aloud interesting and conceptually rich stories, non-fiction texts, and poetry	▪ have conversations with their child during mealtimes and throughout the day
▪ wonder about many things	▪ provide daily opportunities for children to write	▪ support their child's specific hobby, interest, or inquiry
▪ begin to see themselves as writers and illustrators	▪ help children to build a sight vocabulary	
	▪ create a literacy-rich environment for children to engage independently in reading, writing, and frequent talk	

Phase 3: Early reading and writing (goals for Grade 1)

Children begin to read simple stories and can write about a topic that is meaningful to them.

Grade 1 children...	So Grade 1 teachers...	And family members should be encouraged to...
■ read and retell familiar stories ■ use strategies (rereading, predicting, questioning, contextualizing) when comprehension breaks down ■ use reading and writing for various purposes on their own initiative ■ orally read with reasonable fluency ■ use letter–sound correspondence, word parts, and context to identify new words ■ identify an increasing number of words by sight ■ sound out and represent all substantial sounds in spelling a word ■ write about topics that are personally meaningful ■ attempt to use some punctuation and capitalization ■ see themselves as readers, writers, and illustrators	■ support the development of vocabulary by reading aloud daily, using fiction, non-fiction, and poetry; teaching and encouraging students to use new vocabulary; selecting materials that expand children's world knowledge and language development ■ scaffold inquiries ■ encourage and extend conversations ■ model strategies and provide practice for identifying unknown words ■ give children opportunities for independent reading, writing, and frequent talk ■ read, write, and discuss a range of different text types (poems, informational books) ■ introduce new words and teach strategies for learning to spell new words ■ demonstrate and model strategies to use when comprehension breaks down ■ help children build lists of commonly used words from their writing	■ talk about favorite storybooks and non-fiction texts ■ read to their child and encourage the child to read to them ■ suggest that their child write to friends and relatives ■ bring to a parent–teacher conference evidence of what their child can do in writing and reading ■ encourage their child to share what he or she has learned about writing, reading, and cross curricular content (e.g., science) ■ encourage and extend conversations ■ support their child's specific hobby, interest, or inquiry

Phase 4: Transitional reading and writing (goals for Grade 2)

Children begin to read more fluently and write various text forms using simple and more complex sentences.

Grade 2 children...	So Grade 2 teachers...	And family members should be encouraged to...
■ read with greater fluency ■ use strategies more efficiently (rereading, questioning, and so on) when comprehension breaks down ■ use word identification strategies with greater facility to unlock unknown words ■ identify an increasing number of words by sight ■ write about a range of topics to suit different audiences ■ use common letter patterns and critical features to spell words ■ write an increasing number of "no excuses" words correctly in context ■ punctuate simple sentences correctly and proofread their own work ■ spend time reading daily and use reading to research topics, inquire ■ see themselves as readers, writers and illustrators	■ create a climate that fosters analytic, evaluative, and reflective thinking ■ teach students to write in multiple forms (stories, information, poems) ■ ensure that students read a range of texts for a variety of purposes ■ teach revising, editing, and proofreading skills ■ teach strategies for spelling new and difficult words ■ model enjoyment of reading and writing ■ encourage and extend conversations ■ scaffold literacy learning and inquiries across the day	■ continue to read to their child and encourage the child to read to them, fiction, non-fiction and poetry ■ engage their child in activities that require reading writing and talk ■ become involved in school activities ■ show interest in their child's learning by displaying their written work ■ encourage their child to share what he or she has learned about writing and reading and cross curricular content (e.g., science) ■ visit the library regularly ■ support their child's specific hobby, interest, or inquiry ■ encourage and extend conversations

Phase 5: Independent and productive reading and writing (goals for Grade 3)		
Children continue to extend and refine their reading and writing to suit varying purposes and audiences.		
Grade 3 children...	*So Grade 3 teachers...*	*And family members should be encouraged to...*
■ read fluently and enjoy reading ■ use a range of strategies when drawing meaning from text ■ use word identification strategies appropriately and automatically when encountering unknown words ■ recognize and discuss elements of different text structures ■ make critical connections between texts ■ write expressively in many different forms (stories, poems, reports) ■ use a rich variety of vocabulary and sentences appropriate to text forms ■ revise and edit their own writing during and after composing ■ spell words correctly in final writing drafts ■ see themselves as writers and illustrators	■ provide opportunities daily for students to read, examine, and critically evaluate narrative and expository texts ■ continue to create a climate that fosters critical reading, personal response, and inquiry ■ teach students to examine ideas in texts ■ encourage and extend conversations ■ encourage students to use writing as a tool for thinking and learning ■ extend students' knowledge of the correct use of writing conventions ■ emphasize the importance of correct spelling in "published" written products ■ create a climate that engages all students as a community of literacy learners	■ continue to support their child's learning and interests by encouraging and supporting their inquiries ■ find ways to highlight their child's progress in reading, writing, and oral language ■ stay in regular contact with their child's teachers about activities and progress in reading, writing, and talk ■ encourage their child to use and enjoy print for many purposes (such as recipes, directions, games, and sports) ■ build a love of language in all its forms and engage their child in conversation

Source: Adapted from "Learning to Read and Write: Developmentally Appropriate Practices for Young Children," *The Reading Teacher* 52: 193–216. Copyright 1998 International Reading Association. This is a joint position statement of the International Reading Association and the National Association for the Education of Young Children.

Although the lists above provide mainly a good sampling of developmentally appropriate reading and writing practices for young children (K–3), *an area that we now know needs more focus is the area of oral language (including background knowledge), which is the foundation of all literacy learning.* That is why this book provides **the Oral Language Observation Checklist (p. 114)** as well as extensive examples of effective techniques and practical and proven activities for use in supporting oral language development across the school day.

Ongoing Assessments, Documentation and Effective Feedback

There are two main types of educational assessments — formative and summative. The main purpose of educational assessment is to support ongoing leaning often through effective feedback.

Formative Assessment

The goal of formative assessment is to *monitor student learning* to provide ongoing effective feedback that can be used to improve teaching and student learning. Ongoing observations determine what each child knows (or thinks he or she knows) and cares about. Such observations help teachers to identify patterns in behaviour and make judgments about a student's educational needs. Documentation of student learning and providing effective and immediate student feedback is crucial (See **Documentation and Effective Feedback** p. 61 and examples captured throughout the book.)

According to the International Reading Association (2013), formative assessment consists of the varied daily interactions between students and teachers that provide feedback for the teacher to differentiate instruction, and by students to enhance their learning experiences.

Student–teacher (adult) conversations provide some of the best assessment data and oral language scaffolding for students (See Chapter 5).

Formative assessment is

- **Purposeful:** It provides information (feedback) that can be used in setting learning goals and understanding how well those goals are being met.
- **Collaborative:** Both teachers and students play active roles in formative assessment.
- **Dynamic in nature:** It occurs during teaching and learning ("on the run").
- **Continuous:** It provides **specific** descriptive feedback to teachers and students. Teachers use descriptive feedback to adjust their planning and teaching. Students use feedback from teachers to improve their learning.

There are typically two very important approaches to formative assessment:

According to Hattie (2009), the Effect Size of Formative Assessment is very high @ 0.90.

According to the research of John Hattie (2012), assessing student feedback is really the only way teachers can know the impact of their teaching. In other words, teachers should really listen to and watch the students. Teachers should also carefully examine the products students create. Follow the children.

- *Assessment for learning*, which can provide important student feedback and drive instruction
- *Assessment as learning* occurs when students develop important self- and peer-assessment skills

Window on the Classroom: Karen Scaffolds Student Self-Assessment

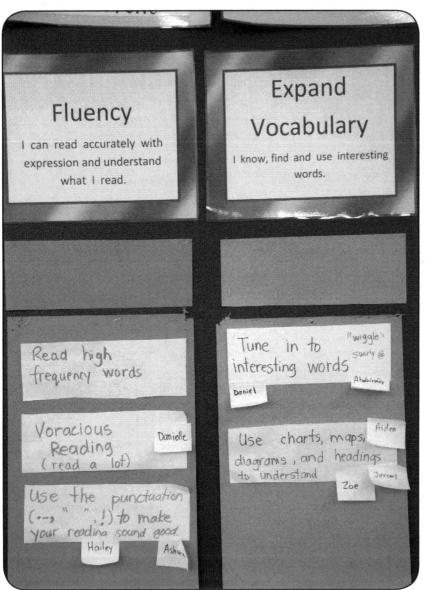

Students in Karen Dance's class are encouraged to assess their own learning and set their own goals. Karen explains: "I attached their names to their contributions on the charts where I could, because I have a strong belief in recording students' thoughts as they are said orally, as well as a belief in the ownership of what goes on the walls. Students need to feel that they are a part of the development of how their class operates throughout the day whether it is in math, science, literacy, writing etc. Attaching their names to the expected behaviour charts for our literacy block helps them be accountable for what they know how to do".

Summative Assessment

The goal of summative assessment — assessment of learning — is to *evaluate student learning over time* (such as at the end of an instructional unit) by comparing it against some standard or benchmark.

Documentation and Effective Feedback

Documentation captures learning in action. "Teaching is about human relationships. The more we as educators learn about our students, the more they are likely to learn from us" (Cummins 2007 cited in Glaze et al. 2011, 45).

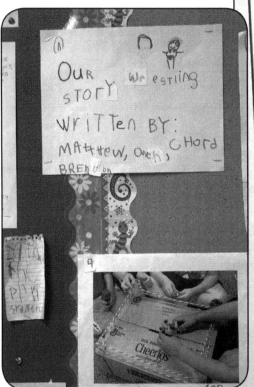

This documentation was created by the students. Consider all the ways it can be used.

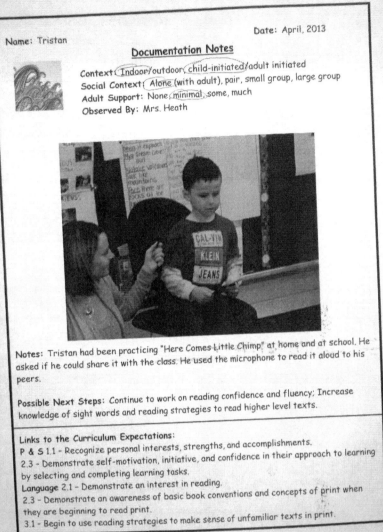

Who did the work in this documentation? Consider all the ways it can be used.

Visible thinking and learning occurs when teachers see learning through the eyes of students. Observing and documenting what children are saying, creating, and doing makes student thinking and learning visible. Documentation provides teachers, students, and parents with new insights that help to scaffold future learning. Teaching, too, becomes visible through all the choices made by the teachers and becomes evident through classroom documentation.

Documentation is not new. However, it is a hot topic now in the educational world. What may be new are additional ways teachers are now able to document, as well as new understandings of how to make the best use of documentation. "Documentation is the practice of observing, recording, interpreting and sharing through a variety of media the processes and products of learning in order to deepen and extend learning" (Krechevsky, Mardell, Rivard, and Wilson 2013, 74). It is more than a display:

> Documentation often includes samples of a child's work at several different stages of completion: photographs showing work in progress; comments written by the teacher or other adults working with the children; transcriptions of children's discussions, comments, and explanations of intentions about the activity; and comments made by parents (Katz and Chard 1996, 2).

The Documentation Process

Observing/Listening/Discussing
↓
Recording (documenting)
↓
Interpreting
↓
Responding (taking action)

Frequently these steps are nearly simultaneous, occurring "on the run," in the midst of teaching and learning.

"My prediction of 10 cubes was right!"

Observations

"I wonder if it will be to 100 cubes." Skye
"I wonder when it will be 10 blocks tall." Kaylee
"I wonder if it will be 1000 blocks tall." Alyssa

Documenting predictions tells students that the teacher was really listening and what they thought and said was worthwhile. This is an example of visible listening.

Documentation can also take the form of a simple checklist. Technological documentation, such as photos, audio recordings, and scanned work samples, also help teachers, students, and their parents to see what the students are thinking and learning, what they know, what they think they know, and what they wonder about. It also shows students that their work is valued. The analysis of the documentation by all stakeholders helps students, teachers, and parents determine the next steps. Documentation that is not analyzed and used in some way is little more than wallpaper.

Additional benefits of using documentation in the early years

Along with capturing student learning and scaffolding future learning, documentation offers the following benefits:

- Visual documentation (such as photos) strongly supports oral language (speaking and listening) assessment and development, both at home and at school.

- Through a shared discussion of documentation, students are able to understand that there may be many different perspectives or viewpoints on a single documentation item, such as a photo.

- Sharing documentation can become a social experience — a shared memory.

- "Children become even more curious, interested, and confident as they contemplate the meaning of what they have achieved" (Malaguzzi 1993, 63). Revisiting an experience often deepens understandings.

- Sharing documentation can help students think about their own thinking, helping to develop student metacognition.

- Documentation can provide a strong source for **specific** feedback and discussion.

- Sharing documentation can support students in developing retelling skills.

- Sharing documentation can be a great form of professional learning for staff members.

- Documentation is also an important kind of teacher research , See p. 218, **The Story of Success at the Thames Valley District School Board**.

- Families can become more engaged with and knowledgeable about their children's learning.

Planning for Documentation:
Make sure the documentation scaffolds learning. Teacher and student time is very precious. Consider the following questions as you plan documentation:

Purpose: Start with the end in mind. How will the documentation be used? How useful will it be?

Audience: Who will use the documentation and how? If parents are the audience, how often will a parent use the documentation?

Time: How much time will be required to create the documentation? Who will do the work?

Space: How much space will be devoted to adult-generated documentation, and how much space will be used to honor mainly student-created work?

Placement: Will the documentation be accessible to the children? Is it sometimes better situated outside the classroom for parent use?

Websites such as http://www. remind.com support the home-school connection.

Our trip to Legoland was exciting. We built towers, race cars and buildings. We saw a 4D movie and got wet! We played in the climbers and some of us went on a ride or two. We had a fun day!

Summary Learning

As the year comes to an end, it is important to think about how you will continue your child's learning throughout the summer. It is important that they are involved in some authentic reading, writing and math opportunities during the summer months.

Here are some examples;

Reading Leveled texts – http://www.oxfordowl.co.uk/reading-owl/find-a-book

Listening to stories read aloud.

Writing-craft books, procedures, diaries, I wonder books, recounts of holidays, emails, letter or cards to family and friends.

Math-sorting items, counting items, measuring items, and talking about math problems throughout the summer.

I wonder...

The students are now in a habit of talking in I wonder statements. They state I wonder statements during read alouds, during shared reading and during play situations. Over the summer, continue to engage in conversations about wonderings. Stop and observe, talk about their thinking and discuss their questions and wonderings during the summer. Together with your child seek out answers to their questions. Find books from the local library, look up information on line and do some investigations. We have observed our school pond through the fall, winter and spring. We encourage you and your family to take regular walks to our pond during the summer. Discuss the changes they notice. What animals, birds or insects do they see? Thanks for taking an active part in your child's learning.

Reminders

Thursday June 27th early release day

A reminder that Thursday June 27th is the last day of classes. Students will be dismissed at 11:10 a.m.

Report Cards

Report cards go home on Wednesday June 26th. Please sign and return the parent page on Thursday

Return Outstanding Leveled Books

All nightly reading bags were collected today. Please do a check around your home to see if there are any outstanding little leveled books.

Play Day-Tuesday June 25th in the morning 10:30-12:00 Rain Date Wednesday

Students will be involved in free flowing activities. Volunteers **must** sign in at the office and get a wrist band.

Great ideas to encourage summer literacy at home. The photo from LEGOLAND will likely promote much conversation, inquiry, and wondering.

Window on the Classroom: Angie and Documentation

Here are the guiding questions that focus my use of documentation:

- Is it documentation for students to refer back to in order to reflect and enhance their next learning task?
- If so, is the documentation done in a student-friendly manner?
- Can the child reread or picture-read the documentation and compare the information to their current learning task?
- Is the purpose of the documentation panels for parent communication?
- If so, are they hung in a location where parents can see them?
- Are they written in a fashion for quick reading?
- Are they available in different languages for parents?
- If the purpose is for parent communication, is there another way to share the information?
- Would a class blog be a better place to display the learning?
- Could parents comment on and ask questions on a class blog to become part of the learning?
- Is the documentation for the purpose of assessment of student learning? Does the documentation reflect the student's learning?
- Is the documentation saved in a manner for easy reference?
- Does the documentation belong in a student portfolio?
- How is the documentation improving student learning?

Teachers need to ask, "What is the purpose of this?" each time they engage in a task. It is important to reflect upon why we are documenting the learning; consider the specific purpose, how the process of documenting connects to this purpose and if the time investment is worth it. We have to ask ourselves if spending hours and hours transcribing audio of student conversations is necessary. Would it be more effective to transcribe and analyze a few targeted students each time?

Much is provided by documentation panels and I often wonder what the specific purpose is and if the documentation method is meeting its intended goal. I also feel pressure to replicate the proposed methodology. I am not known to conform. I am creative and I love using technology to make tasks quicker and easier.

In his novel *Fathers and Sons* (1862), Ivan Turgenev wrote, "A picture shows me at a glance what it takes dozens of pages of a book to expound". I use my digital/video camera to capture images and document learning. It can be used in many ways to document the learning process. I can use the digital photos or video in a student's individual portfolio; I can upload the photo or movies to a class blog; I can instantly email to a family; I can print the photos and display them in the classroom as a reference for learning.

I can also import the photo into Pic Collage, an app that quickly displays photos in an easy manner. I can add in children's quotes, wonderings, or new learning. I can use these digital collages online, through emails, or through print. I do not think teachers need to be bound to one method of documentation. Be creative, but more importantly, think of the purpose of the documentation. Ask if the documentation matches the purpose.

Marie Clay, John Hattie, and others recommend ongoing teacher observations and documentation of student learning, along with the very important step of providing effective student feedback. Observations, such as creating running records of student reading, help to make student thinking visible. This explains why the term *visible* has become popular when referring to educational assessment. It is no coincidence that numerous professional texts have *visible* in the title; examples include *Visible Learners: Promoting Reggio-Inspired Approaches in All Schools* (Mardell, Krechevsky, Rivard, and Wilson 2013); *Visible Learning: A Synthesis of Over 800 Meta-Analyses Relating to Achievement* (Hattie 2008); *Visible Learning for Teachers: Maximizing Impact on Learning* (Hattie 2012); and *Making Thinking Visible: How to Promote Engagement, Understanding, and Independence for All Learners* (Morrison, Church, and Ritchhart 2011).

Challenges of Documentation

Documentation generally requires teacher time to create and often space for sharing it. In addition, documentation requires teachers to slow down and follow the children, while still effectively supporting the demands of various curricula. It requires teachers to listen carefully and observe, and to know how to use the knowledge gained from documentation to scaffold student learning effectively. This is the heart of differentiation, of effective teaching and learning. Examining the documentation should also encourage teacher self-reflection and the providing of student feedback. This is all easy to say, but finding the time for effective documentation, reflection, and student feedback can be a challenge.

"If we attend to individual children as they work, and if we focus on the progressions in learning that occur over time, our detailed observations can provide feedback to our instruction" (Clay 2005, 4). Student feedback to the teacher is also very important. It allows the teacher to see learning through the eyes of the student, making student thinking visible. According to Hattie (2009), the effect size of feedback is significant at 0.74.

Three Levels of Feedback

Hattie (2012) identifies three levels of feedback:

- **Task feedback** describes how well the student has performed a given task.

- **Process feedback** describes the processes underlying or related to tasks.

- **Self-regulation feedback** describes how learners can monitor, direct, and regulate their own actions.

Specific immediate feedback given by adults and students as students work — for example, while writing or playing at centres — is generally more effective than feedback given after the fact. However, there are exceptions. Providing feedback as generic praise that contains no real learning information, such as "I like that" or "Good job" is not effective but considered empty praise. The quantity of feedback is also important. Follow the Goldilocks strategy: not too much, not too little — just the right amount. It is also important not to make feedback personal; e.g., You are a great student! (See p. 68 **Making Feedback Effective**).

Document student feedback such as student goals.

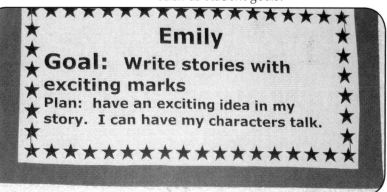

"Self-esteem comes from competence, not from false pats on the back, from constant reward, from ever-smiling teachers who pretend that children know something, when the children themselves know they do not" (Schickedanz 1994, 43).

Making Feedback Effective

Teacher–Student Feedback: "Know Thy Impact!"

What teachers say, how they say it, and what they don't say really matters. Not all feedback is good. According to John Hattie (2009), the ES is 0.75. Teachers' words can impact student achievement, both positively and negatively. "How we give children feedback is probably the most difficult for us to change, but it is probably the point of most leverage" (Johnston 2012, 34). In addition, according to Johnston, "We are not just giving students feedback; we are also teaching them to provide it. In a way, we are teaching them to teach" (36). Teaching students to give effective feedback to each other is extremely important since much of the feedback that students provide to each other is incorrect (See **Student–Student Feedback** below). How often have you heard your style of feedback repeated from one student to another? For example, a Kindergartener was sharing her art when she was interrupted with a question. She responded with "Please wait, I will take questions at the end!"

Johnston (2012) strongly suggests that teachers focus on process — the strategies used — rather than person-oriented feedback. That is, when something works or not it is due to the strategies used, not due to the person using them.

Examples of Process-Oriented Feedback	Examples of Person-Oriented Feedback
Maybe you could find another way to do this.	You know a lot about this.
You found a great way to make this.	You are so smart!*
You haven't figured out the solution yet!	I am very disappointed in you.*

* Both of these examples of person-oriented feedback may be devastating to a student. For example, praising a student for being smart can become a negative experience later when the student messes up and then thinks: "Oh no, I am not smart anymore." A fixed mindset is then established. The student frequently becomes less of a risk taker. Instead, try process feedback such as, "You found a great way to do this!"

According to Hattie (2012), Wiggins (2012), Tomlinson (2013), and others, effective teacher–student feedback has the following attributes:

- Clarity
- Builds trust (provided in a caring way)
- User-friendly

- Specific
- Focused and Manageable
- Differentiated
- Timely
- Invites Student Follow-up

What specific learning can come from "Good job!" or "Well done!"

Feedback that reflects high teacher expectations

According to Robert Marzano (2010) the following teacher actions reflect high expectations:

- Calls on the students more often
- Provides more wait time to students and self
- Uses more praise
- Asks more challenging questions
- Provides more eye contact
- Smiles more often

Student–Student Feedback

Student to student feedback in the primary grades can be effective but often is not according to the latest research of John Hattie (2009, 174). Nuthall found that most feedback that students obtained in any day in classrooms was from other students, and most of the feedback was incorrect. Teachers can improve this reality by guiding students in the process of providing effective feedback while teaching students how to "listen closely" and read with fluency by providing effective task feedback, (See mini-lesson: http://vimeo.com/38247060). Hattie believes that it is important for teachers to believe that most students can be taught to be powerful teachers in the learning equation (ES for Peer Tutoring = 0.55). Jane provides examples of how she does this daily in her Kindergarten class.

Window on the Classroom: Jane, Effectively Guiding Student Feedback

To learn how to provide effective peer oral reading feedback, students need to understand and use key reading vocabulary. The key vocabulary includes terms such as expression, smoothly, fluently, think, punctuation, and quotation marks. The vocabulary and feedback methodologies are taught using a number of instructional techniques including daily teacher read-alouds, teacher–student reading conferences, student—student paired readings, and student read-alouds to the whole class.

Teacher Think-Alouds during Read-Alouds

From day 1 of Kindergarten, I model effective read-aloud techniques to my class. I think-aloud, am using statements and prompts such as, "Listen to my reading expression. My voice goes up in the story when a question is asked." (Also see **Chapter 6 Maximizing the Effectiveness of Read-Alouds.**)

Reading Conferences: Teacher–Student, Student-Teacher

When the students begin to read home-reading books, I make time to read VERY briefly with each child in the class on a daily basis. This year this took an average of about one minute per child in the beginning. Over time, I listen less often (one in two or even three days) to those I am confident are on the right path, and with others who need more guidance, I increase our sessions to 2 to 3 minutes. I typically listen to each child read a page from the now familiar book they already read at home, which they typically are quite confident and proud to do. This allows me most often to provide a very specific compliment as feedback, usually related to the child's expression or fluency. I often preface my feedback with "You're doing what good readers do. I noticed that you were…" I often also say something like, "Your Mom/Dad must have been surprised that you are such a good reader already!" to prepare them to take a new risk with a new book. When they choose the new book to bring home, I ask them to read me one or two pages to be sure it's "just right"(after I introduce them to the title and perhaps a pattern on the first page). This is when I provide them with feedback about the strategies I see them using or not using. More of these conferences become student-initiated as the days pass.

Children at this beginning stage may vary from needing support with developing accurate tracking of words, checking the picture before they start reading, reading with expression, or looking at initial sounds to help with a word prediction. I always start with a specific compliment or two, and then add a suggestion for making their reading stronger if one is obvious. I am intentional about teaching feedback vocabulary in the whole group context and describing it in ways that make it comprehensible to young students. I use a lot of modelling to teach what fluency (or any other skill) is not, for example (by reading in a very choppy way, or a monotone way, very slowly, or even too quickly). Children can readily identify the kind of reading that sounds good or does not,

Teach the children to "read" the punctuation. A fun way to do this is through attaching actions and sounds to punctuation marks. See example from Victor Borge: https://www.youtube.com/watch?v=6bpIbdZhrzA

but through this kind of regular modelling, they become able to describe it as well. They also find these models highly entertaining! They will eventually provide their own compliments to peer readers from "I like 'your expression'/'the way your voice went up and down like real talking'/'the way you made the voice sound mad or disappointed," etc. Gradually, as I see the children's confidence grow, I invite other children (up to 3 or 4) to observe while they wait their turn for the one-to-one reading session so they learn also from the mistakes and feedback I give to their peers. Only a few children do not initially feel comfortable having others witness their efforts in this context, and those I continue to read alone with as long as I feel they need it. While in the past I have experimented with the more standard "guided reading group" concept, I feel strongly that guiding them one-on-one in this way has been much more effective and time efficient, allowing me to analyze and address each child's specific need(s) very precisely on a daily basis.

One might wonder what the rest of the class is doing while the teacher is reading one-to-one with children. During the first few months of school, I count on a minimum of half an hour daily for this task, but divide it amongst three intervals of time. By the time (mid-October) that I begin, I have six weeks of intentional teaching, modelling, role-playing and routines established. I begin by reading with children at the beginning of the day when everyone knows exactly what their routine and related expectations are and how they can save their questions, requests, outside of genuine emergencies for later. (Teaching the difference between genuine emergency and non-emergency is also essential!) Though this does take considerable rehearsal during the first several weeks to achieve, it pays off tremendously. The second 10-minute period is at the beginning of our snack time when the children wash their hands, retrieve their snacks, and chat together while they eat. Again, teaching independence and responsibility is achievable given a sufficiently dedicated effort in the first several weeks of school. Children with particular challenges who are not able to demonstrate this kind of responsibility are simply asked to join me with their snack at our reading table. This is sufficient deterrent for any others who can muster the ability to self-regulate if they wish to remain with their friends. Our third session is during Centres, when again the children have learned sufficient independence and social problem solving skills to allow me the ten minutes or more that I still need.

Paired Readings: Student–Student

As the year progresses and reading success grows, I gradually read less often with a number of children and maintain daily one-to-one sessions with others who need it the most. I still try to check in with everyone at least once a week. Instead, I do much of my observing during a daily-paired reading time, during which partners move to various places around the classroom. Their chairs are placed beside each other so that both reader and partner are able to track the print clearly. In the beginning, we practice quick book choosing and seating in the designated spots and how to choose who should read first. The children know what I will look for as I sweep past all the partners — four eyes on the page being read; once the first is finished, the second child should be starting. If they are finished both books before the teacher has cued to finish, they begin on a third book. Before each of these sessions, I ask a volunteer to demonstrate to everyone what "good reading teachers" do, and the children identify the kinds of things I say as I give feedback. I ask them to notice how I help when my student is stuck on a word and what kind of compliments I give, and then challenge them to try to do the same. As they become more specific in their word hints and compliments, I challenge them also to ask questions to ensure that their partner is "thinking about the words he is reading." I have explained that sometimes even children much older who may be reading at a very high level might *sound* like good readers but might not actually *be* good readers because they are forgetting to think. I often ask them how they think I can tell if they are good readers. It takes many of them a while to resist suggesting that the higher the level of book, the better the reader, but eventually many of them are able to suggest thinking, understanding, expression, word solving, and fluency are much better ways I can detect a good reader. When I place my students in partnerships and discover one that works especially well, I may keep that same partnership for a week or two. But I've discovered that all kinds of combinations are effective and believe that the children learn from each other's "teaching style" in different ways. Also, it doesn't seem to matter all that much if their skill levels vary. When the student at a lower reading level is observing rather than reading himself, he feels less pressure and is often able to make more accurate predictions of a word than the reader himself. I have been amazed at the growing effectiveness of the hints children give each other to solve words. They provide opposite words ("It's not 'short' but 'l...'"), act out words, suggest restarting the sentence so that the word might "pop into your head," or say things like "Why don't you say that first sound?" I make my own observation of effective teachers while the children read. Then following the session, we gather as a whole group for a few minutes to debrief. I always ask first "Did any of you have a good teacher today? And how did your teacher help you?" Then I allow those who weren't highlighted but felt they had been a good teacher to share as well.

Student Read-Alouds to the Whole Class

Once the children have begun to bring books home to practice daily, I'll often ask if anyone would like a chance to read his or her practiced book to the class. Eventually everyone asks for a turn and even when one child lags significantly behind most of her peers, she will still be keen to have the opportunity. As their reading skills improve, I'll often ask them to read only a small portion so as not to consume too much time. Following the student read-aloud, the "audience" has an opportunity to provide feedback specific to what they noticed the reader doing well. Typically, they will comment on the child's use of "expression," "volume," how well they remembered to show the pictures, or their "fluency," all vocabulary they learn well through the feedback I regularly provide when the students read briefly with me individually on an almost daily basis, especially in the first months of school. Sometimes they will highlight a particular passage and say something like, "I like how you sounded really worried when you said the part 'Oh no!'"

A number of my Kindergarten students go to a before-and-after school private daycare housed in our school just down the hallway from my class. I happily provide a basket of leveled reading books to the daycare for those children's practice and enjoyment there. I was delighted when their caregiver recently shared with me not only that she was so taken with the confident readers they were becoming, but also with her observation of how they were helping each other solve unfamiliar words. "They hardly even ask me to tell them words anymore," she said. "They just ask each other!" What especially struck her, she told me, was how often, instead of directly telling a friend the unknown word, a child would offer some kind of hint instead. The daycare provider hadn't known of the intentionality with which I had been teaching them to do this, but when I realized that it had become so natural to them that they would do it outside of the classroom without being specifically prompted, it certainly confirmed for me the value of the time and commitment I had invested in teaching them the skills to coach each other.

As a classroom observer, I was amazed at how effective Jane's students became as they enthusiastically provided each other with feedback! Jane's classroom has many effective teachers. The students benefit greatly from her intentionality!

Teaching students to provide peer feedback also improves student independence and social skills.

Student–Teacher Feedback

Again, according to Hattie (2009) the most powerful feedback is student to teacher. What is most important is listening to and watching students as they make their learning visible. It is only then that teacher–student feedback will be most worthwhile. Teachers should do less talking and instead do more listening, watching, and reflecting on student thoughts and actions.

Intentional teaching does not happen by chance; it is planned, thoughtful, and purposeful. Intentional teachers use their knowledge, judgment, and expertise to organize learning experiences for children; when an unexpected situation arises (as it always does), they can recognize a teaching opportunity and are able to take advantage of it, too (Epstein 2007, 1).

Pianta (2006) defines intentionality as "directed, designed interactions between children and teachers in which teachers purposefully challenge, scaffold and extend children's skills" (Epstein 2007, 4).

Research provides clear evidence that literacy skills improve when young children are exposed to adult– child interactions that are characterized by warmth, emotional support, and sensitivity in combination with modelling, sensitivity, direct instruction and feedback — in other words, intentionality.

Intentional and Focused Teaching

Intentional literacy learning needs to be embedded throughout the day, both at home and at school. Intentionality begins with the emotional climate created. High expectations, *clearly defined learning objectives, instructional strategies likely to help children achieve the objectives* and engaged students are key. *An "intentional" teacher aims at clearly defined learning objectives for children, employs instructional strategies likely to help children achieve the objectives, continually assesses, progress, and adjusts the strategies based on that assessment* (Epstein 2007, 4).

> "The hallmark of developmentally appropriate teaching is intentionality. Good teachers are intentional in everything they do — setting up the classroom, planning curriculum, making use of various teaching strategies, assessing children, interacting with them, and working with their families. Intentional teachers are purposeful and thoughtful about the actions they take, and they direct their teaching toward the goals the program is trying to help children reach" (NAEYC Position Paper 2009, 10).

Teachers and parents must intentionally provide developmentally appropriate and effective opportunities for children to develop literacy and other skills. Many opportunities and "teachable moments" occur spontaneously as part of everyday life, such as reading a stop sign. I call these activities "literacy on the run" (See p. 268). However, literacy experiences must not be left just to chance.

Focused teaching is an important form of intentionality. It is teaching that has a focus and that is matched to the learning needs of each student. Focused teaching typically works best when students are learning in their zone of proximal development. That is, the students are challenged just beyond what they can do independently, such as in guided reading, writing, and scaffolded play. Challenging students promotes motivation and stick-to-itiveness

(See **Self-Regulation**, Chapter 7; **Play**, Chapters 7–10; **Grit**, p. 33). Students are given many opportunities to construct knowledge and supported with the scaffolding provided by teachers, volunteers, paraprofessionals, parents, and peers.

Students often learn best using the "gradual release of responsibility" model of teaching and learning. In this approach, teachers, peers, and others model, demonstrate, and explain, with opportunities for guided practice provided. Teachers often think-aloud to bring alive the strategies they are using. What is often covert, becomes overt.

Constructivism, as in inquiry-based learning, and direct teaching are not mutually exclusive. Students often learn best when reading and writing are taught in the context of activities carried out for authentic purposes. That is, literacy is taught as part of life.

> Students need more focused teaching involving modelling, demonstrating, and coaching, and less assigning (Allington 1996).
>
> Focused teaching is one powerful strategy for scaffolding self-regulation and engagement (Boekaerts and Carno 2005). ES for direct instruction = 0.59.

Angie does a wonderful job of teaching vocabulary as she thinks aloud, "I wonder what determined means?" Notice the "let me demonstrate" stance.

> **Gradual Release of Responsibility**
> 1. **I do it.** (Adult or student models.)
> 2. **We do it.** (Students and the teacher or another mentor all work together, as in shared reading or writing.)
> 3. **We do it.** (Students and the teacher work together in a small group, as in guided reading or writing, or with a partner.)
> 4. **You do it.** (Students work independently.)

Developmentally appropriate goals, as defined by the International Reading Association and the National Association for the Education of Young Children, are "expectations for young students' achievement that are challenging but achievable, with sufficient adult support" (1998, 38).

Use of mainly whole-class instruction results in some students continually learning what they already know; for others, the lesson will be too difficult and proceed too quickly (Durkin 1990, 24). The result in both instances is developmentally inappropriate classroom instruction.

A message board provides a real reason to write.

Students spend most of their language arts block actively engaged in authentic and developmentally appropriate reading, writing and oral language activities. After a trip to a farm, a Kindergarten student is conducting a survey. When completed, she will share her results with the class.

What Effective Teachers Do

Research by Taylor, Pressley, and Pearson (2002) found that effective teachers had excellent classroom management skills. They provided scaffolded, balanced literacy instruction, often in small groups, characterized by explicit instruction in skills and strategies. As well, they gave frequent opportunities for students to read, write, and talk about text.

Student achievement was also higher the more

- Reading and writing were integrated
- Students discussed what they were reading (and writing)
- The teacher emphasized deep understanding rather than literal comprehension of text
- Discrete skills were taught in the context of actual reading (and writing) rather than out of context

Documenting Effective Teacher Practice: Follow the Students

It became apparent to me, working with schools and school districts doing literacy reviews that what is most crucial is to follow the students more than the teacher. And following the most at-risk students should be revealing. Key areas of focus include:

- Student **engagement and self-regulation** (See Chapter 7)
- Quality and quantity of student **oral language** including student-initiated, conversations and wonderings (See **Oral Language: The Foundation of Thinking and Learning**, Chapter 4)
- Level of student **play**, such as mature play vs. immature play (See **Play, Self-Regulation and Literacy Learning in the K–2 Classroom: How Teachers Make It Work**, Chapter 7)
- Student **beliefs** (See Chapter 1)
- Student **Choice** and **Voice**

"Teachers in the most effective schools provided more small group instruction, communicated more with parents, had children engage in more independent reading, provided more coaching during reading as a way to help children apply phonics knowledge, and asked more higher-level questions" (Taylor, Pressley, and Pearson 2002, 7).

See the Ontario initiative **The Student Work Study Teacher initiative (SWST).** The initiative involves three important steps: 1) a non-school-based researcher documenting raw student experiences; 2) co-interpreting the documentation with the classroom teacher; and 3) collaboratively co-planning and acting on the results. (See http://www.curriculum.org/k-12/en/projects/students-of-mystery-the-student-work-study-teacher-initiative)

A School District Documents its Success in Oral Language Development and Educator Professional Learning Using Photo Documentation such as Wall Stories, p. 218.

Closing Thoughts

Chapter 3 focusses on the additional high-yield strategies which include the how-to of establishing an effective and engaging classroom environment, proven early intervention frameworks and ways to enhance the home-school connection.

Integrating reading, writing and oral language.

An Effective and Engaging Classroom Environment

3

An effective and engaging classroom environment depends upon the choice of classroom materials, organization, the classroom culture and the instructional framework chosen.

Materials and Organization That Work

There is much discussion as to what an effective classroom environment or "learning spaces" should look like, but little published research evident and little agreement amongst educators. In addition, there is the reality that many classrooms have very little space to work with. Most classrooms are set up the way they are for many reasons, some of which are beyond the teacher's control. For example, the "open-area classroom" that I taught in and my students tried to learn in was not my choice. Often the children and teachers in the open areas could not hear themselves think!

Planning the Classroom Set-Up

When teachers have choice as to the classroom set-up, they should begin by asking themselves several questions. These include:

- What do I believe about how young children learn? (Where possible, the learning environment should be set up to support teacher beliefs about effective teaching and learning.)
- How can I provoke curiosity and wonder?
- What set-up will help to scaffold self-regulation?
- What set-up will help children learn best through play?
- What set-up will support classroom conversations?

With learning environments, as with most other aspects of education, one solution does not work for all. However, clearly some approaches place obstacles in the path of teaching and learning.

 Check It Out!
- *Spaces and Places: Designing Classrooms for Literacy* by Debbie Diller
- "Consider the Walls" by Pat Tarr

The main source of noise in a primary school classroom is the noise generated by the students themselves — the buzz in the classroom. Effective primary classrooms are full of student talk. However, noise can negatively impact self-regulation and engagement. Try to set up your classroom so that the activities that result in the most noise are in one area of the classroom. There must also be small places where children can escape the din of the classroom.

What environmental accommodations can we put into place to help students to remain engaged, calm, and learning?

Pre-Primary Classrooms in Reggio Emilia, Italy: The Environment Is the Third Educator

Reggio Emilia is a city in northern Italy known for its approach to preschool education. The school environment is the "third educator," since each classroom already has two teachers, creating a very small pupil–teacher ratio. The Reggio educator's belief is that children are resourceful, curious, competent, imaginative, and have a desire to interact with and communicate with others (Rinaldi 1998). Thus, inquiry, talk, shared problem solving, and creativity are all important, and the environment is set up to promote these effective approaches to learning. Photos, artifacts, and texts created by students and by teachers, document the learning, making it visible. Effective use of space supports inquiry and students learning together, often with a partner or in a small group. The size of the spaces created is important. Some children prefer having very small spaces, big enough for just one or two children. Such spaces often scaffold student conversations.

What We Know About Color in Education

Color — along with space, light, texture, and noise — affects the learning environment. When considering color for classroom walls, aesthetics is not the only factor. There is a direct connection between the brain and the body's reaction to color. Warm colors typically stimulate energy, resulting in an active response, while cool colors such as blue and green are more calming, resulting in a more passive response. Neutral colors such as beige, white, and gray can be calming and less distracting, but can also be monotonous and under-stimulating. Bright colors — mainly warm colors such as red, yellow, and orange — attract and stimulate young children. It is important to avoid overstimulation and under-stimulation.

Most professional books and position statements recommend that primary classrooms be colorful. "The environment should be attractive, colorful and have children's work and other pictures displayed at children's eye level" (NAEYC 1998, 49). However, when visiting many Reggio-inspired preschool, Kindergarten, and primary classrooms across North America, I have seen many walls painted neutral colors. According to Pat Tarr (2004, 400), "Walls painted in neutral colors create a sense of calmness and allow the other features in the room to stand out." In the book *Children, Spaces, Relations: Meta-project for an Environment for Young Children* (Ceppi and Zini, eds. 1998), based on the work in Reggio, there is a section titled "The Harmony of Color." It explains that we all have different color preferences and, for this reason, a living space should not be monochromatic. It is better for the space to be polychromatic so that the user can tune in to their own personal color preferences. There should be a balance between warm hues and cool hues. The book also states, "It is better to have a single color that acts as the base for holding the images that are hung on the wall and which gives the space a unifying element" (66). In other words, choose a neutral color to support and honor, but not compete with, all of the print and images on display, especially children's work. These recommendations are based on research conducted in Reggio Emilia preschools; however, no original peer-reviewed research appears to be available.

There is limited published research on how physical environmental factors such as color actually impact learning. Some researchers found that noise levels were lowest in light-colored classrooms. Cool colors produced relaxation; bright and warm colors produced alertness. However, no difference in student achievement was evident. "After examining 200 studies of school environments, Higgens, Hall, Wall, Woolner, and McCaughey (2005, 22), came to the conclusion that there "is conflicting evidence, but forceful opinions on the effects of color" with studies producing inconsistent results. Teachers need to make their own decisions regarding the walls, the colors, and the environment. Resist pressure to follow a bandwagon.

What colors and textures support the intended learning? For example, what reading centre colors are warm and inviting to you as an adult? Is it necessarily the same for children and for all children?

This reading centre is full of bright color. Do the children not appear engaged?

Encourage children to read wherever they are comfortable. They will read all around the room. Let them choose.

Multiple Paths to Literacy

Environmental Print

A print-rich environment is crucial. Books, posters, charts, documentation panels, wall stories (See **The Power of a Wall Story Centre** p. 208), inquiry posters (p. 324), celebrations of student work, word walls, and centres (Chapters 8–10) are important. However, it is the actual use of the print by students, teachers, and sometimes parents that counts. Students should be engaged in daily activities creating and using the environmental print or it will simply remain decorative. Consider who and what the displays are for. Get down and look at the classroom environment from the perspective of the children. Look at the walls. Is there a balance between filled and empty spaces? Or, is there "visual chaos and clutter?" (Tarr 2004, 4).

Remember: "More does not mean better. In a room cluttered with labels, signs and such — print for print's sake — letters and words become just so much wallpaper" (Neuman, Copple, and Bredekamp 2000, 38). The walls do tell the story.

(For more examples from Alissa's classroom, see **Window on the Classroom: Alissa's Class Where the Walls Tell the Story**, p. 237).

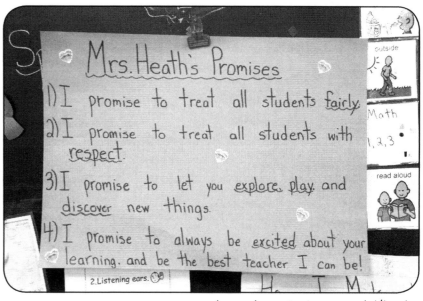

A very important message! Alissa's walls told me a great story.

Books, Magazines, Newspapers, Centre Materials

Students in classrooms with library centres read about 50 percent more books than children in classrooms without (Allington and Cunningham 2002). Students need to read a variety of kinds of print, representing many different difficulty levels and genres. Each classroom needs many hundreds of books (Big Books and Little Books) for guided, shared, independent, read-aloud, and home reading. A large percentage of non-fiction is crucial.

> "We need to get enticing, just-right books into each student's hands" (Allington and Cunningham 2002, 4). Books provoke students to wander, wonder, and discover.

Book boxes or book bags encourage the reading and rereading of just-right books. There are books that students can read fluently with good comprehension. In Kindergarten, the children are encouraged to pick any books to look at and to share with a partner. Grades 1–2 students pick their own just-right books (6–10 little books or fewer chapter books) to go in their book boxes. Typically, book exchanges occur once or twice a week. Reading and rereading is encouraged. The result is more students really reading and fewer students faking it. When a day of the week is selected as the book exchange day, students spend much less time constantly exchanging books. The books are always readily at hand for down time. Students learn that there is no point in using the refrain, "Teacher, I am finished." They know that reading is an excellent choice and is, in fact, an expectation. There is something very special about having your own book bag or book box housing your very own book choices.

It is important for students to think about what good readers do when reading independently and to self-assess.

"As with all criteria, no specific quantity (of books) can serve all classrooms equally well. For instance, beginning readers can, and should, read multiple books every day. In the exemplary first grade classrooms we studied, it was common for children to read 10 or more titles every day (counting rereading of books). Thus, 500 titles do not go as far in first grade as they do in a fifth-grade classroom where children might be expected to read a title a week. But by fifth grade, there is often both a wider range of achievement and a wider array of books that might be included than in a first grade collection. I should also note that many of the exemplary teachers we studied had classroom collections in the 1500 book titles range" (Allington 2001, 55).

Student Self-Assessment of Independent Reading

I picked a just right book to read:

- a book I enjoyed ☐ **YES**   ☐ **NO**

- a book I could read and understand ☐ **YES**   ☐ **NO**

I got started reading right away. ☐ **YES**   ☐ **NO**

I spent all of my time reading the book and thinking about what I was reading. ☐ **YES**   ☐ **NO**

When I got stuck I used a fix-up strategy. ☐ **YES**   ☐ **NO**

When I think about my reading I know I can improve by_
_____.

Centres need to be full of engaging hands-on materials, some provided by the students and others by the teacher, all promoting choice. Promoting sensory explorations (using the senses to investigate) is important. Non-specific or open-ended props, such as a paper plate, spur the imagination, creativity, and mature play. A Wonder Table leads to great discussion and inquiry. (See Chapters 7, 8, 9 and 10 for many examples of great centres and definitions of mature and immature play).

Technology as a Tool for Literacy Learning

There is no clear agreement as to what exactly technology looks like, or should look like, in Kindergarten and the primary grades. Typically, one may see any of the following being used: computers and software programs, applications (apps), tablets, smartphones, overhead projectors, digital cameras, document cameras, digital microscopes, CDs and recorders (such as at the Music/Listening Centre), DVDs, talking word processors, and the Internet, along with e-books (with adult support), and interactive whiteboards (e.g., Smart Boards).

Interactive whiteboards are gaining in popularity in elementary schools; they are typically used to support word work, modelled and shared reading, and modelled, shared, and interactive writing. They allow children to interact with the text as they write (for example, to find, circle, and manipulate words, letters, punctuation, and graphics). Interactive whiteboards also promote thinking skills, as children can use them to solve problems and answer questions.

Talking word processors are great to use. They allow children to hear a voice reading what they have created, whether it is text scribed for them, text they have written themselves, or a combination of the two. How exciting for them when they realize that the letters have turned into spoken words!

Window on the Classroom: Technology

In one classroom I visited, the Kindergarten teacher used the interactive whiteboard to help children write answers to questions related to a science unit. Using the SMART Notebook program, she dragged down the shade screen to reveal just the question "What is in the egg?" at the top of the page. Next, she pulled the shade screen down further to uncover the picture clue (a frog). The children wrote their answer(s) using invented spelling (e.g., *A fg is in the ag*). The teacher then pulled down the shade screen to uncover the answer.

The interactive whiteboard can also be used to make words available to build the same answer. The interactive whiteboard provides the option of dragging words into place (*A frog is in the egg.*) before the shade screen is pulled down to reveal the answer. The children can then check to see if their answer(s) match the one provided.

Technology may very well engage children, and there are many teacher testimonials to this effect. However, teachers are not always sure what the children are really engaged in doing, and simply being engaged in using a software program does not necessarily result in learning.

Deciding on technology use

Children use technology to play, learn, and create. Technology has great potential to enhance literacy learning in primary classrooms. That being said, it is important that teachers ask themselves several important questions before using technology in the classroom:

- Is the activity developmentally appropriate? (i.e., is it consistent with how the child develops and learns, and with the child's current developmental stage?)

- Will the activity benefit the child, or will it replace other, more meaningful learning activities?

- Is the choice of technology based on how well the tool supports both learning and teaching needs?

- Can technology deliver the same or better results in terms of literacy learning than more traditional approaches?

- Are there enough manipulatives, Little Books, Big Books, puppets, art materials, and other learning materials in the classroom? Teachers and administrators should weigh the costs of technology against the costs of other learning materials and program resources to arrive at an appropriate balance for early childhood classrooms.

(Adapted from Van Scoter and Boss 2002)

How effective is technology use in supporting early literacy?

In the end, there is very little empirical research or hard data to show that current technologies have any effect, good or bad, on young children's literacy outcomes, or that they are any more effective than traditional approaches. Most of what we know about technology as a tool for literacy learning, especially in Kindergarten through Grade 2, comes from the trenches — from teachers trying new technologies themselves and sharing their experiences with one another. What is known is that "it is the educational content that matters, not the format in which it is presented" (Joint Position Paper of the NAEYC and the Fred Rogers Center for Early Learning and Children's Media 2012, 63).

Teachers have shown that technology can be a powerful tool to support an inquiry-based curriculum where children investigate big questions. For example, see **Mini-lesson: Writing a Question-and-Answer Report**, p. 122.

Even though technology can be engaging, watch the children go for the manipulatives such as blocks or LEGO® during choice time. Which tools stir their imaginations more?

Building together with LEGO® promotes imagination, co-operation, and self-regulation.

Check It Out!

"Using Technology with Kindergarten Students" by Kindergarten teacher Chris Gathers for some best-practice examples of exciting activities using technology to enhance learning in the Kindergarten classroom: http://www.4teachers.org/testimony/gathers/.

"iPads in Kindergarten: Investigating the Effect of Tablet Computers on Student Achievement" (Blackwell, 2015). Students in classrooms with a shared iPad system scored significantly higher on achievement tests taken in the spring compared to student with no iPad or their own iPad.

"Early Connections: Technology in Early Childhood Education", a great site to support teachers and parents/caregivers interested in effective technology use. Under Publications, see "Learners, Language, and Technology: Making Connections That Support Literacy" and "5 Effective Ways for Young Children to Use Technology": www.netc.org/earlyconnections/

Technology and Digital Media the Early Years: Tools for Teaching and Learning edited by Chip Donohue (2015) is full of practical examples of how to connect the dots between digital media and early learning.

"A Framework for Using iPads to Build Early Literacy Skills" by Laura Northrop and Erin Killeen, *The Reading Teacher* Vol. 66, No. 7, 531–537, April 2013.

Computers and Young Children

An excellent article titled "Reading and Language: Experts Speak Out" (PBS Parents) addresses the following questions: What do experts recommend? When should children begin to use computers? What should parents look for when buying computer games and software for young children? Find the article online at http://nunu.pbs.org/parents/readinglanguage/articles/clicking/experts.html

 Check It Out!

The International Children's Digital Library — http://en.childrenslibrary.org/ — is a great resource for all teachers, but especially for ELL children and their families. Beautiful picture books for children aged three to five are available in a variety of languages, including English, Arabic, Chinese, Croatian, Filipino/Tagalog, Danish, French, German, Hebrew, Italian, Persian/Farsi, Portuguese, Russian, Spanish, and Thai. There are also chapter books, make-believe books, true books (informational text), fairy and folk tales, real animal characters, kid characters, and books about imaginary creatures. These books can be accessed on the website at no cost.

Computers

For many children, computers are an important part of life both at home and at school, and teachers frequently look for ways to use computers to enhance early literacy learning. However, there are differences of opinion about computer use with young children. Here are some of the anecdotal findings:

- Many early childhood educators question having children spend much solitary time in front of a computer screen, especially when the activity replaces more active play involving interaction, oral language, drawing, writing, and building. Others find computers a good tool to support early literacy.

- Including a computer (or other technologies) at existing centres, such as at the Restaurant, Pizza Parlor Centre, Ice Cream Shop, or Doctor's Office Centre, demonstrates to children that technology is a useful tool in real life.

- Interactive talking books, which allow children to participate in choral and echo reading, support comprehension, vocabulary, and fluency, and may stimulate writing.

- Many very young children struggle with fine motor skills. Research indicates that children do not effectively develop keyboarding skills until at least Grade 4. This is simply a reality.

Encourage children to work together to problem solve and develop vocabulary when using technology. Children typically engage in more conversation when they are seated together at computers than when assembling puzzles or interacting at the Block/Building Centre (Van Scoter et al. 2001). The more conversation the better!

Selecting Software for Young Children

For young children to use computers successfully, it is critical to select software that is developmentally appropriate (consistent with how children develop and learn):

Northwest Educational Technology Consortium recommends that software for young children should

- Encourage exploration, imagination, and problem solving
- Reflect and build on what children already know
- Involve many senses and include sound, music, and voice
- Be open-ended, with the child in control of the pace and the path

(from "Selecting Software for Young Children," available at http://www.netc.org/earlyconnections/Kindergarten/software.html)

Open-ended software allows users to explore, discover, and make choices. It does not limit children with a set of predetermined options; rather, it encourages children to extend their imagination. For example, they can decide what to create in a picture, what ending to give a story, or in what direction to take an inquiry. Children learn by experiencing and benefit from discovering rather than being told. Appropriate open-ended software helps children reflect on what they already know, encourages creativity and engagement in learning, and is linked to improvements in measures of intelligence and non-verbal skills.

Programmed learning software, which offers drill-and-practice activities such as electronic worksheets or flashcards, often discourages creativity, imagination, and working together. These programs should not be the primary focus of computer use in the primary classroom. Limiting the amount of time they are used is recommended (Northwest Educational Technology Consortium, from "Selecting Software for Young Children," available at http://www.netc.org/earlyconnections/Kindergarten/software.html).

There are computer programs that support multi-sensory learning, which have proven helpful in supporting some struggling readers and writers. However, according to William Teale and Junko Yokota:

> *Many of the reading and writing computer applications aimed at young children are little more than electronic worksheets. They may be effective for keeping records*

A touch-sensitive tablet or an adaptive device that takes the place of a mouse is useful for those children who have limited technology at home and/or those who have fine motor delays. For more information, visit Early Childhood Technology Integrated Instructional System (http://www.wiu.edu/ectiis/). See also "Meaningful Technology Integration in Early Learning Environments" in NAEYC's *Beyond the Journal: Young Children on the Web*, September 2008.

"Young children learn through exploration and play, through open-ended activities. This is true with software and technology as well as with blocks and dress-up clothes" (Van Scoter and Boss 2002, 33).

 Check It Out!

Here are some helpful websites to support the selection of appropriate software for use with young children:

- Learning Village (http://www.learningvillage.com/html/guide.html) offers independent reviews by Canadian educators of software recommended for home and school use.

- Northwest Educational Technology Consortium (http://www.netc.org/software/index.html) provides information about software selection as well as links to online software review sites.

of the answers children get right and wrong, and they may amuse and engage children, but they teach little of what children need to become capable readers and writers. What is needed instead are computer-related activities that (1) provide authentic and meaningful literacy experiences and (2) are woven into the fabric of the integrated curriculum (adapted from Teale and Yokota, in Strickland and Morrow 2000, 18).

In the end, there are two major points taken from the research about the value of computers in supporting early literacy teaching and learning:

First, computer uses for reading and writing are only as strong as the off-computer reading and writing environment in the classroom. In other words, computer technology cannot substitute for a good early literacy program, it can only complement it. Second, computers contribute most to children's literacy development when children are able to create with them, rather than just "use" or "consume" ready-made programs … In addition, we should always remember that the issue is not computer use but literacy. The computer is a tool that can help children achieve literacy, but it is not the end in itself. (Teale and Yokota, cited in Strickland and Morrow 2000, 18–19)

Balanced Literacy, Inquiry, and Play as an Instructional Framework

Balanced literacy involves a wide variety of activities provided consistently. These activities include reading and writing to/for children, reading and writing with children, reading and writing by children as well as word work, visual literacy, oral language, and numerous forms of representing knowledge/understandings, such as through art. Balanced literacy also involves a balance of direct and indirect instruction; whole-class, small-group, and individual activities; and a balance of work with various genres. In Kindergarten and beyond, play and inquiry provide much of the authentic learning, and many feel that they are the key to student engagement in a strong, balanced literacy program. (See **Play**, Chapter 7; **Inquiry**, Chapters 13–14.)

The Daily 5™ (Bouchey and Moser 2006), like the Four Blocks™ Literacy Model developed by Patricia Cunningham and Dorothy Hall in the 1980s, is but one structure that may be used to help

Technology is only as strong as the comprehensive literacy program in the classroom. Teachers know that technology is a tool and nothing more. The focus is the literacy learning, not the technology. Whatever materials, technology, and approaches are used, they simply have to work for the teacher and the children.

"We don't stop playing because we grow old; we grow old because we stop playing."
—George Bernard Shaw

support a balanced literacy approach. (For more on the Daily 5™ and the Four Blocks™ Literacy Model, see the links in the sidebar on p. 92). We know that engagement is supported by routines and that young children thrive on routines. Whatever structure you pick, make sure it works for your students. What is important is to base your choice of activities on learning goals and individual student needs. Expect initial engagement and skill improvement when a new structure involving more reading, writing and mini-lessons is implemented. Also, be aware that often the apparent strength of the structure dissipates over time as an implementation dip occurs.

For example, there are many proven effective and engaging ways to develop fluency in addition to those listed in the Daily 5™. Individual teachers and students should make these choices. Additionally not all students need more fluency development or even the same degree of support. Some fluency activities will work better for some than others. Some students read fluently and with expression with little understanding. What about students with very weak receptive and expressive language skills? (See Chapters 4–6). What about the approximately 20 percent of students who have not achieved phonemic awareness by the middle of Grade 1?

Research reported by Richard Allington (2009b, 11) indicates that the less effective teachers thought that fair meant distributing instruction equally to all students regardless of their needs. However, the exemplary teachers knew that fair meant working in ways that even out differences between students.

Teaching Reading Fluency to Struggling Readers – Method, Materials, and Evidence, 2008 Timothy Rasinski @ http://www.coedu.usf.edu/main/departments/ce/homan/docs/Rasinski,%20Homan%20Biggs.515.106%5B1%5D.pdf

Window on the Classroom: Karen and the Daily 5™

Karen Dance intentionally differentiated for her Grade 1-2 students by adjusting the Daily 5™ to better meet their needs. "Because I had periods dedicated to writing and modeling lessons, some mornings were only Daily 3 (Read to Self, Read to Someone, and Word work) as students would use the time after the modeled or shared lesson to work on personal writing. The authors of the Daily 5™ list "Listening to Reading" as one of the components that is taught through modeling and used as a choice during the literacy block. It did not become mandatory as a component for our block, but it was modeled and offered as an opportunity during Literacy Station time (listening Centre time)". Karen knows her students and works effectively to scaffold their learning.

"Read to someone" (peer reading) is important for many reasons.

Help students to make strong connections by effectively teaching literacy integrated across the curriculum, beyond the literacy block. Reading, writing, and speaking develop best in authentic and meaningful situations as students learn about the world. Implementing an effective literacy block framework requires teacher and student understanding of effective implementation using the proven high-yield strategies. For example, two teachers will have very different levels of student success using the Daily 5™ or the Four Blocks™ depending on the manner of implementation, teacher–student relationships, student–student relationships, and the classroom culture established.

For more information on the Four Blocks™, see: http://wik.ed.uiuc.edu/articles/f/o/u/Four-Blocks_Literacy_Model_67e6.html

For more information on The Daily 5™, see: http://www.the2sisters.com/the_daily_5.html

To reflect on how to organize daily literacy instruction, see the blog by Dr. Tim Shanahan: http://www.shanahanonliteracy.com

Do not give in to pressure to embrace a literacy block framework that you feel will not meet the varied needs of your students. If it is not broken, why fix it!

Extensive Student Talk within an Effective Classroom Culture and Climate

Extensive Student Talk

Research by Allington and Johnston (2002), amongst others, shows that the most effective teachers studied (Grades 1 and 4) encouraged, modelled, and supported lots of talk across the school day. The talk was purposeful and generally problem posing (such as inquires or wonderings) and problem solving, usually related to a curricular topic such as social studies or science. Allington describes effective classroom talk as *conversational,* not *interrogational.* Very often, the students, not the teachers, initiated the questions. If teachers did initiate the questions, they were often open-ended and allowed for multiple responses rather than a single right answer. John Hattie's research (2013) on classroom discussion shows an effect size of 0.82, which is very large! For more on the "how-to" of rich conversations and thoughtful classroom talk, see **Chapter 5** and **Extending Conversations: Strive for Five**, p. 127.

An Effective Classroom Culture and Climate

Expert teachers are proficient at creating an optimal classroom climate/culture for learning, particularly to increase the probability of feedback occurring (which often involves allowing for, and certainly tolerating, student errors). They build climates where error is welcomed, where student questioning is high, where engagement is the norm, and where students can gain reputations as expert learners (Hattie 2003). In fact, feedback thrives in conditions of error or not knowing (Hattie 2012) (See **Window on the Classroom: Jane's Story**, p. 109).

Primary Building Block for Effective Classroom Cultures:
Teacher–Student Relationships ES=0.72 (Hattie 2009)

It is evident that teachers who build healthy learning communities where students want to be at school, where there is classroom cohesion, have the greatest success. "The key factor in positive classroom climate is classroom cohesion — the sense that all (teachers and students) are working together towards positive learning gains" (Hattie 2009, 103). The way the teacher treats the students is key. Hattie (2003) points out that two attributes of expert teachers are that they respect their students both as learners and as people, and demonstrate caring and commitment to them. The students feel valued. Teacher warmth and empathy is evident. Teachers really care about their students and really listen to them. There is also some evidence that self-regulation is related to positive teacher–child relationships. More positive teacher–child relationships are also related to higher academic achievement, classroom participation and engagement, and positive attitudes about school (See **Self-Regulation**, Chapter 7). These findings likely will not surprise experienced teachers. The relationships built between teacher and student, and those scaffolded among students, really make a huge difference. "A significant body of research indicates that positive, caring, and respectful relationships are the foundation for optimal learning, development, health, and well-being (*How Does Learning Happen? Ontario's Pedagogy for the Early Years, 2014, p.24*).

> "There is evidence that more 'thoughtful' classroom talk leads to improved reading comprehension" (Johnston et al. 2001, cited in Allington 2002).

> In one notable study, teacher–child conflict was related to relatively high levels of disruptive peer play and disruptive school adjustment (Shanahan and Lonigan 2013, 78).

> "The key factor in positive classroom climate is classroom cohesion — the sense that all (teachers and students) are working together towards positive learning gains" (Hattie 2009, 103). An experienced teacher would likely call this a real sense of belonging, being part of the team.

> *Students don't care how much you know until they know how much you care.* Adapted from Theodore Roosevelt

Window on the Classroom: Colette's Kindergarten Class

I knew the class was special the minute I walked into Colette Lau's Kindergarten class in Hawaii. The students and the teacher were happy, engaged, and confident. They were more than willing to share. The classroom culture was inviting. There is much to tell. But the most powerful single example concerns a young student named Kiare who wrote a letter to her teacher. Kiare shared the letter with me (See p. 95). The letter is amazing, both from the perspective of content (ideas, voice, organization, word choice) and conventions. It is really worth reading! Kiare's mother and teacher provide the context for this true story (See letters below) . It is evident that Colette is a perfect example of John Hattie's expert teacher: She respects her students both as learners and as people, and demonstrates caring and commitment to them. A very positive teacher–student relationship is evident.

Kiare 2012

Date 3-8-12

Dear Mrs lau,

you biti my heart in all difint ways you help me make me fel beter dont chang your an exleint teacher you make me cry teas of joy you say good things ubot me I thik your agehut tehcer to the next jenerash of chillgen tech them just like me you tech me so much I thik I can move on.

Your friend,
Love Kiare.

"Dear Mrs. Lau.
You brighten my heart in all different ways. You help me make me feel better. Don't change. You're an excellent teacher. You make me cry tears of joy. You say good things about me. I think you are a great teacher. To the next generation of children teach them just like me. You teach me so much. I think I can move on.
Love Kiare

A wonderful teacher–student relationship is evident in this powerful student writing.

A Letter from Kiare's Mom

Thank you very much for your interest in making Kiare's letter to Mrs. Lau a part of your professional book for teachers.

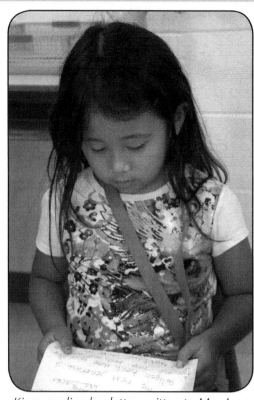

Kiare reading her letter written to Mrs. Lau

I'd like to tell you a little bit about my daughter and the impact Mrs. Lau has had on her. Kiare is an extremely, extremely sensitive child. Kiare would cry whenever she had a problem wrong. She would even cry when the class was simply being reminded to bring their forms back to school the next day, if they didn't already. Kiare is the perfect example of how positive words have such a profound impact on a child. Mrs. Lau is unlike any teacher that I ever had when I was a student, and unlike any teacher that my 19-year-old daughter has ever had. Mrs. Lau has a special gift ... she encourages them with suggestions and excitement, rather than critiquing them. For example: Instead of saying, "You need more details in your writing," she would say, "Do you think you could add more details or other interesting facts?" She has a way of saying everything in a positive way. I remember once when I was in class, she got so excited about the accomplishment of one student spelling his name that she excitedly announced it to the whole class and everyone cheered him on. Through her encouragement, excitement, and celebration of their accomplishments, they become successful and confident children. Kiare received so much encouragement from Mrs. Lau that she came home one day and announced that she was entering the school talent show. Imagine me ... the worried mother. Well, she auditioned for the talent show as a Kindergartener and made it. She was the youngest student to enter and perform in front of the entire school! She never would have done that if it weren't for the encouragement Mrs. Lau gave her. Kiare's letter really does say it all.

I wish there was a way for you to truly convey in your book for teachers the way that Mrs. Lau communicates with her students. She never points out a negative, but instead asks a question or makes a suggestion in such a cheerful and positive way that her students respond positively. I've learned so much from watching, listening, and talking to Mrs. Lau. I am a Family Resource major with emphasis on Early Childhood, with a BS degree. However, none of my courses taught me or modelled for me the way to talk to children like Mrs. Lau does. Every teacher and certainly every parent would benefit if they could talk and encourage like Mrs. Lau!!

I could go on and on about how amazing Mrs. Lau is and how I wish I could communicate just like her, for Kiare's sake, but I think you probably got the message by now. Thank you for taking the time to read my email.

A Letter from Kiare's Teacher, Colette Lau

"You brighten my heart in all different ways" … a quote from a child who has a heart of gold, and so much wisdom beyond her years. Kiare is her name, and this was an excerpt from a letter that she wrote to me in 2012. After writer's workshop one day, Kiare approached me and asked if she could read a letter that she wrote to me in private. As she read her letter, we both cried. Her words were so powerful. I couldn't believe that I was actually listening to a Kindergartner. Each word she read tugged at my heart, but her last words made me crumble … "I think I can move on." That said it all. We didn't even have to say a word to each other, as the bond we had built helped us to understand what we were both thinking. We hugged, and wiped away our tears. Kiare was so afraid to move on to first grade, and to leave me. She was ready now. Kiare has since left our school, but the bond we have built will last forever. Her inspirations have validated my teaching, my values, my beliefs. I keep Kiare's letter next to my desk to remind me daily of why I am in this profession… "To the next generation of children, teach them just like me."

Loving school does not necessarily mean finding it easy, but it does mean being and feeling successful. Expert teachers help to provide appropriately challenging tasks for the students. The teacher needs to really "know" each student and be able to differentiate as needed for each student to be successful. A joy of learning is evident. Or as cartoonist Lynn Johnston so beautifully explains in the comic strip below, students who are engaged and successful feel that learning comes naturally.

Lynn's message is an important one!

For Better or For Worse®   **by Lynn Johnston**

Reprinted with permission; © Lynn Johnston Productions Inc., 1994-02-06

    Multiple Paths to Literacy

Effective Early Intervention: Vulnerable or At-Risk Early Literacy Learners

Emerging literacy results at the end of Kindergarten are very predictive of reading and writing achievement levels at the end of Grade 1. This finding is extremely important because research indicates that there is close to a 90 percent probability that children struggling with reading (and often writing) at the end of Grade 1 will remain poor readers (and often poor writers) by the end of Grade 4 (Allington 1998). Kindergarten teachers can predict at the end of the Kindergarten year where most of the children will be in literacy learning by the end of Grade 1.

Research indicates that the children most likely to have difficulty with literacy learning are those who begin school with less prior knowledge and skill in areas such as oral language and background knowledge, phonological awareness, alphabet letter knowledge, print awareness, and writing. Background knowledge is the key to comprehension. "If we want students to learn how to think when they read (and write), they must have something to think about" (Neuman 2010, 9). How is background knowledge developed? Neuman explains: "Activities that pose problems; get children immersed in interesting topics, allow them the time to develop expertise, all contribute to knowledge gains." Additionally, solid research by Sally Shaywitz (2003) indicates that close to 90 percent of struggling readers have phonological delays.

The good news is that teachers, beginning in Kindergarten, can prevent this negative spiral from occurring for at least 98 percent of young learners. We do know what makes a big difference for struggling literacy learners. A research-based, proven form of small-group or one-on-one intervention, provided at least three to five times a week for twenty to forty minutes a session, is crucial (Gersten et al. 2009). If the students' primary need is in the area of oral language and/or comprehension, then small group intervention will often work better than one-on-one. The intervention should be in addition to, and coordinated with, effective classroom practice across the day. In fact, the best instruction for at-risk literacy learners is long-term excellent classroom instruction that monitors and meets their needs. The number of students in an intervention group makes a difference. There exists little evidence supporting interventions where the instructional group is larger than three students (Allington 2005). "Early intervention does not guarantee continuing achievement; but, not providing

> "The mediocre teacher tells. The good teacher explains. The superior teacher demonstrates. The great teacher inspires."
> —William Arthur Ward, English novelist
> (From a book entitled: *Teachers are Special* compiled by Nancy Burke)

Well-developed skills in letter knowledge, phonological awareness, and phonics are meaningless without vocabulary knowledge (word knowledge) and background or content knowledge (world knowledge). A great deal of this background knowledge can be developed in a very engaging way through inquiry-based learning.

Check It Out!
Evaluating reading interventions using research-based features analysis by Richard Allington
https://www.okhighered. org/otc/resources/allington- intervention-rubric.pdf

early intervention guarantees failure for many children through-out schooling" (Fountas and Pinnell 1996, 193).

Which Students Need intervention?

According to many publications about the three-tier model of RTI, a school's goal is for no more than 20% of students to require additional support beyond good Tier I curriculum and instruction (Burns et al., 2005). Schools implementing effective Tier 1 and Tier 2 (small group) instruction should find no more than 5% of students requiring more intensive interventions than those provided in Tier 2 (Burns et al., 2005).

Many struggling readers have had few pre-school literacy experiences. Others struggle despite strong home support. The major characteristic of struggling readers is lack of fluency. Fluency means

- Reading smoothly
- Reading without hesitation

Some students can read fluently and with expression but with little comprehension.

Characteristics of Successful Intervention Programs

- One-on-one and small-group intervention (pupil teacher ratio of 1-3) .

- Individual attention and extra instructional time.

- Small-group supplemental instruction should target the students' needs; build skills gradually with high student-teacher interaction and frequent opportunities to practice the specific skills mainly in context, and receive feedback.

- Coordination with regular classroom instruction.

- Explicit instruction in letter-sound relationships, word identification strategies, phonological awareness, letters, words, and word patterns .

- Repeated exposure to words to encourage mastery and the presentation of words in small practice sets to provide scaffolding for struggling readers.

- Explicit instruction in techniques that will improve reading comprehension. Some strategies to teach include self-questioning (readers ask themselves questions about the text as they are reading), visual imagery (readers visualize what they are reading), and retelling (readers tell the gist of the text to someone else). Encourage student use of metacognition.

- Multiple opportunities for repeated reading of connected texts to develop fluency. The intervention should at least triple the daily reading volume. The texts should be interesting and allow for student choice.

Grade retention is not the answer — early intervention is. The research evidence is that grade retention may do more harm than good (Pagani et al. 2001; Morgan and McKerrow 2006).

Intervention Lesson Frameworks that Work

There are two well researched lesson frameworks that work. One is for students with general delays in literacy and one for those with specific delays in Phonemic Awareness.

Lesson design for students with general delays in print awareness (including phonics), phonological awareness and oral language

Students should be provided with *daily opportunities to:*

- Increase fluency through oral rereading of familiar texts

- Read new texts with teacher support

- Develop comprehension

- Develop skill in writing

- Learn a core of high frequency words

- Develop phonological awareness

- Systematically develop phonics

Lesson design for students with specific delays in phonemic awareness: segmentation, blending and manipulating individual sounds (See The Sound (Phonemic Awareness) Segmenting Centre: A Three-Step Intervention Lesson Framework that Works p. 105).

"We could know on the second day of Kindergarten who is at-risk of becoming a struggling reader, but we typically do nothing with this information" (Allington 2011, 42). "We have good evidence that even modest Kindergarten interventions can reap big rewards" (Allington 2010, 1). We also know that some students will need additional intervention in Grade 1 and perhaps beyond. However, the longer one waits to intervene, the longer it takes the student to catch up. Although First-Grade interventions are necessary for some children, the best intervention is well-designed Kindergarten instruction (CIERA 1998). Allington says it best in the title of his article, "What Schools Should Do: Start in Kindergarten on Day One!" (2011).

Enhanced Home, School, and Community Partnerships

Never too young to enjoy a good story.

According to John Hattie (2013), the **effect size of parent involvement is 0.49**, while the effect size of teacher instructional quality is 1.0+. (For a definition of *effect size*, see the margin on p. 32, 177). What this meta-analysis research tends to show is that teacher effect is generally much stronger than home effect. However, Hattie's research (2003) also shows that prior student cognitive ability (ability before coming to school) has an effect size of 1.04, which supports the research on the importance of early learning and thus the importance of the home.

We also know from this research that

- Effective teachers can close or at least dramatically lessen the achievement gaps, no matter the home environments
- Parent/home involvement is important, and the sooner the parents can be engaged, the better

It may or may not surprise readers to know that Hattie's research (2013) shows that watching television at home has a -0.18 effect size. In other words, the effect on student learning is typically negative. That is not to say that young children never learn anything from watching television, but generally it is not a good use of their time.

Closing Thoughts

No matter what background people come from, no matter their economic status, more education and higher levels of literacy are associated with better outcomes, including improved life opportunities. The best practices clearly proven to develop strong and motivated early literacy learners are revealed in research. *"A balanced developmentally appropriate language and literacy curriculum is not only beneficial but perhaps crucial in these early years"* (Neuman 1998).

> *Primary-level literacy educators who want to be truly evidence-based offer strongly balanced teaching of reading and writing skills, which includes reading excellent children's literature, writing every day, and teaching literacy skills and literacy experiences in an environment that is bubbling over with teacher attempts to motivate students' academic engagement* (Pressley 2010, 10).

While agreeing with Pressley, I would also reiterate the importance of all of the other key elements and high-yield strategies such as play and those listed below:

- Teacher and student beliefs and understandings
- Time spent on literacy teaching and learning across the day
- A high-level of student engagement and self-regulation
- Clear and appropriate literacy goals, benchmarks and targets
- Ongoing assessments, documentation, and effective feedback
- Intentional and focused teaching
- An effective and engaging classroom environment: materials and organization that work
- Balanced literacy, inquiry, and play as an instructional framework
- Extensive student talk within an effective classroom culture and climate with strong teacher–student relationships
- Effective early intervention
- Enhanced home, school, and community partnerships

There are many visible and invisible aspects of teaching and learning. There are many pieces of a challenging puzzle that expert teachers somehow, seemingly magically, put together. These teachers are typically in *the radical middle* going somewhere, rather than stuck in the far left or far right in the ditch, going nowhere. It may seem like magic to an outsider, but there is a great deal of intentionality. Many, if not all, of the proven high-yield strategies are in place. Watching an expert teacher is like watching a superbly orchestrated dance. It really takes your breath away.

"In the end it will become clearer that there are no 'proven programs,' just schools in which we find more expert teachers — teachers who need no script to tell them what to do … Are we creating schools in which every year every teacher becomes more expert?" (Allington 2006, 185).

So little time, so much to do! The next three chapters will demonstrate the dance through many practical examples of effective mini-lessons and engaging activities used by expert teachers as they focus on oral language, the foundation of all literacy learning.

CHAPTER 4

Oral Language

The Foundation of Thinking, Comprehension, and Learning

Research shows that the development of oral language is *the key* component of a successful literacy program. Oral language is the foundation of all literacy learning and all cross-curricular learning. It facilitates thinking, comprehending, making connections, communicating, and solving problems. It is the basis of reading, writing, inquiry, and play. It provides the foundation for developing social skills, self-regulation, and strong relationships. Oral language is instrumental in developing the whole child, heart, mind, and soul. That is why oral language is central to this book.

Defining Oral Language

Oral language involves speaking and listening and both of these involve thinking. Receptive language is the language that children understand or comprehend when listening and reading. Typically most children understand many more words and concepts than they are able to use. This is especially true of English language learners (ELL, or any second language learners). Expressive language is the language children use to express themselves, to communicate, through speaking, writing, and drawing. Oral language is often associated with vocabulary as the main component. However, oral language is more than vocabulary. It consists of function or pragmatics, content or semantics (which includes vocabulary), form or syntax, and sound structure or phonology (phonological awareness).

Function or pragmatics involves the speaker's and/or listener's understanding of how to communicate successfully during social situations. This aspect of oral language includes social norms related to such things as conversational turn-taking, personal space, body language, tone of voice, and appropriate behaviour with peers and others in a variety of common social situations. Since pragmatics is culturally determined, students in culturally diverse classrooms might not always share the same social norms.

Oral language provides the foundation for a child's cognitive, social, and emotional development. "As teachers of literacy, we must have as an instructional goal regardless of age, grade, or achievement level, the development of students as purposeful, engaged, and ultimately independent comprehenders. No matter what grade level you teach, no matter what content you teach, no matter what texts you teach with, your goal is to improve student's comprehension and understanding" (Rasinski et al. 2001, 1).

Content or semantics involves both the meanings of words and the connections among words. Examples of semantics include the language of classroom instruction (e.g., giving directions); classification of words (e.g., living things); multiple meaning words (e.g., *hand* as in "give me a hand" or "hand me that"); idiomatic expressions (e.g., I have a frog in my throat), and words with opposite meanings (e.g., happy, sad).

Vocabulary is one of the strongest predictors of reading comprehension. In fact, research indicates that 70–80 percent of comprehension relies on understanding of vocabulary (Pressley 2002; Nagy and Scott 2000). Vocabulary is not the sole determinant of comprehension. But it is an important one!

Form or syntax involves a set of structural rules (grammar) that govern how words and phrases are combined into sentences, and how sentences are combined into paragraphs. With very young children, teachers need to focus on modelling how to put words together in the correct sequence when creating a sentence. Using the correct forms of words, especially appropriate word endings (e.g., go, goes, going) also needs to be modelled and monitored.

Phonology and Phonological Awareness can be defined as the organization or system of sounds within a language, and how the sounds can be combined to make words. Phonological awareness is a crucial aspect of oral language. "A student's level of phonological awareness at the end of Kindergarten is one of the strongest predictors of future reading success, in grade one and beyond" (Adams, Foorman, Lundberg, and Beeler 1998). Phonological awareness involves both receptive and expressive language and the ability to attend to and manipulate units of sound in speech words, syllables, rimes, and finally phonemes, which are individual sounds. A Kindergarten child who attends to sounds will likely be able to clap out three words in the sentence *I am happy*. Kindergarten students will likely understand that the word computer has three syllables or beats. A Grade 1 student will likely be able to differentiate four syllables in a word such as California. Recognizing that the word *hat* rhymes with *cat* also involves phonological awareness. The most complex level of phonological awareness is phonemic awareness. Phonemic awareness is blending, segmenting, and manipulating words at the individual sound, or phoneme, level. A relatively easy task involves recognizing that the word *mother* begins with an /m/ sound. A sometimes-challenging task requires the child to create a rhyming word by removing the /c/ sound from cat and substituting a /b/ sound to create the word *bat*. All these skills are crucial to learning to read and write. Other fun ways to develop phonological awareness include solving riddles, or playing at a syllable centre or at a sound segmenting centre.

Play at a Syllable Centre

Having fun at the Syllable Centre by naming the item in the photo, counting the number of syllables in the name, and finding the corresponding syllable number card.

Try Riddles

- Provide the students with a word made up of a rime, e.g., h ead.

- Ask them to solve the riddles:

In a cheese sandwich, we put cheese between the slices of _____.

Someone who is not living any more is _____.

The Sound (Phonemic Awareness) Segmenting Centre: A Three-Step Intervention Lesson Framework that Works!

Use a three-step intervention lesson framework for delays specifically in phonemic segmentation, blending, and manipulating individual sounds. This lesson is based on research done by Ball and Blachman (1991) who found that this training did make a difference in early word recognition and developmental spelling

Step 1: "Say It and Move It" using Elkonin Boxes: The teacher provides manipulatives (bingo chips, tiles, or blocks) and demonstrates that one sound is represented by one manipulative. The teacher says, "This is the sound 'b.' As I say the sound, I move the block into this box." Teacher then moves the block back to where it started repeating the sound. Once the student(s) demonstrate success with single sounds repeated twice, the teacher introduces two phoneme real words (e.g., "at," "me," "it," "go," "he") and repeats the steps listed above. Then the teacher introduces three phoneme words (e.g., "sun," "fat," "zip," "lip") and repeats the steps listed above. (See photo below of Step 1-using Elkonin Boxes)

Step 2: Sound Segmentation Activities: These oral activities teach students to categorize words based on their common sounds. Use one or two activities during each lesson. The activities include:

Activity 1: Beginning Sounds, Ending Sounds, Rhymes

Activity 2: Pictures and Sound or Elkonin Boxes

Activity 3: Counting Sounds in Words

Activity 4: Sound Blending

Step 3: Letters and Sound Activities: These activities are selected to focus on one or two letter names and corresponding sounds per lesson. The difference is that now the actual letters and their sounds (phonics) are being used. For example, the sounds in the words were used in Step One, and now the actual physical letters a-t, m-e, and i-t are moved in and out of the Elkkonin boxes, not just markers.

A great partner activity using Elkonin boxes at a centre.

Check It Out!

B. A. Blachman, E. W. Ball, R. Black, and D. M. Tangel (2000). *Road to the Code: A Phonological Awareness Program for Young Children*

How Important is Oral Language in Preschool, Kindergarten, and the Primary Grades?

Oral language is crucial. The National Early Literacy Panel (NELP 2008) reports that children's skill level in oral language beginning in preschool is a great predictor of their future academic success. Note the solid and perhaps somewhat surprising research noted below:

- Long-term research reported by Dickinson and Sprague (2001, 273) shows that the receptive vocabulary scores of students near the end of Kindergarten were strongly related to their scores for vocabulary and reading comprehension at the end of Grade 7.

- More current research (NELP 2008) indicates that to get the most reliable prediction of how well preschool

Multiple Paths to Literacy

and Kindergarten students will do in reading comprehension, as they advance through the grades, one should look at all of their oral language skills including both phonological awareness and receptive and expressive language (vocabulary, grammar and listening comprehension).

- Biemiller (2005) reports that students' Grade 1 vocabulary predicts much of the variation in reading comprehension as late as Grade 11.

- Many Kindergarten children are already behind when they first open the classroom door. Students from low socio-economic backgrounds know approximately 6,000 fewer words than their middle-class peers do when they start school. Children from advantaged homes learn two to three times as many word meanings as children from disadvantaged homes where many fewer words are used (Hart and Risley 1995, 1999; White, Graves, and Slater 1990). This gap seems to increase over time.

- According to the International Reading Association (IRA), approximately 20 percent of students have not achieved phonemic awareness by the middle of Grade 1. "The research on this statistic is as clear as it is alarming. The likelihood of these students becoming successful readers is slim under current instructional plans. We feel that we can reduce this figure through the early identification of students who are outside the norms of progress in phonemic awareness development and through the offering of intensive programs of instruction" (IRA 1998).

> Children who have strong oral-language skills often have strong reading and writing skills. In contrast, children with oral-language problems are at higher risk of reading and writing difficulties (Scarborough 2001) "Children who arrive at school (Kindergarten) with weaker verbal abilities and literacy knowledge are much more likely than their classmates to experience difficulties in learning to read (and write) during the primary grades" (Scarborough 2001, 100).

> Research indicates that Canadian 4- and 5-year-olds who enter Kindergarten with the least well-developed oral vocabulary struggle with reading at ages 8 and 9 (Hoddinott, Lethbridge, and Phipps 2002). However, although this is often a reality we know that this does not need to be the case. Strong oral language support in K–2 classrooms can turn this situation around (CESC 2009).

Closing the Oral Language Gap by the End of Grade 2

"We might hope that once children enter school at age 4 or 5, there would be more opportunities for less advantaged children to build vocabulary — even to 'catch up' with more advantaged children. Unfortunately, at present there is little evidence that the school experience helps build vocabulary — especially in the Kindergarten to grade two years" (Biemiller 2009).

> A study by Dr. Sally Shaywitz (2003) found that 88 percent of the children with reading problems had phonological delays.
> "Enhancing children's letter knowledge and phonological awareness skills should be a priority goal in the Kindergarten classroom" (Snow 1998, 188).

Most children (90 percent plus) can acquire new vocabulary at rates necessary to reach "grade level" or near grade level in middle elementary school, if given adequate opportunity to use new words (repetition is important) and adequate instruction in word meanings. However, when they are "behind before they start" the pace of vocabulary growth needs to be accelerated from the minute they walk through the Kindergarten or preschool door! Without a significant focus on vocabulary and oral language in Kindergarten, these students rarely catch up (Biemiller 2001). Vocabulary knowledge will not guarantee success but lack of vocabulary knowledge will likely result in failure.

Oral language is often a curriculum casualty. From Kindergarten to Grade 2, the difference between children with small and large vocabularies continues to get larger! Research indicates that schools have very little impact on young children's vocabulary development (Biemiller 2006, in Dickinson and Neuman 2007, 43). Researchers indicate that teachers and schools do very little to promote oral language and vocabulary development in the early grades, including Kindergarten. Most vocabulary learning it appears is left to the home. This is problematic since research indicates that the size of the child's vocabulary is related to the size of their parents' vocabulary. This often results in a huge oral language gap among children. The gap between economically disadvantaged and economically advantaged children becomes evident in Kindergarten and typically persists throughout school. But, it doesn't have to. The good news is that strong oral language programs in preschool, Kindergarten and the primary grades can have long lasting and significant effects on the children, well into middle school (Dickinson and Sprague 2001, 276). The National Early Literacy Panel report (NELP 2008) indicates that programs designed to improve young children's oral language skills can be effective. However, intervening earlier rather than later is advantageous.

Scaffolding Oral Language, Listening, and Reading Comprehension: The High-Yield Strategies

Children benefit strongly when they are provided with a classroom culture that promotes strong and trusting student–teacher, student–student, and home–school relationships. Strong relationships within the classroom require creating an environment in which it is okay "not to know," where errors are an accepted and important part of learning. "We need classes that develop the courage to err" (Hattie 2009, 178). This safe environment encourages self-expression and dialogue.

As a teacher, what you say to students and how you say it really matters.

Window on the Classroom: Jane's Story

From the beginning of the year, I try to establish the concept that our classroom is a safe mistake-making environment. I have a tiny sign on the wall that has been there since my former teaching partner originally posted it. It says, "Making mistakes is a way that we learn." I tell the children that it is a reminder to me that I don't need to feel badly if I've made a mistake but instead can try to practice a better way and learn from the mistake so I do better next time. I often deliberately make a mistake myself (sometimes, with so many watchful eyes, I don't have to fake it of course!) and when I do, I ask the children, "Is it okay that I made a mistake?" It doesn't take long for them to chime in an enthusiastic "YES" and then proceed to remind me of the little quote. I just love it when I hear a child assuring another that "making mistakes is a way that we learn" or when a parent shares that a child has given the same kind of encouragement at home! Instilling this notion, of course, has terrific transfer to the process of developing cognitive skills, which often necessitates the making of many errors followed by retrials.

Sometimes mistakes result in richer learning than if everything went just fine! In fact, according to Carol Dweck (2014), students need to be encouraged to take risks, to push out of their comfort zone, to get smarter.

Children develop grit, their ability to persevere, by learning first-hand that making a mistake is just a first try. It is the way they learn. It is the way teachers learn too. It is important that the school culture encourages teachers to believe that it is okay to take risks, to say "I don't know," or to say "I need help" (Hattie 2015, 39). Some of the greatest scientific discoveries (e.g., Alexander Fleming discovering penicillin) were made by accident after a mistake was made.

Children also benefit when they are

- Intentionally exposed to and effectively taught varied vocabulary in meaningful and often related contexts (such as an inquiry and play) across the day

"Freedom is not worth having if it does not include the freedom to make mistakes".
Mahatma Gandhi

Make your classroom vocabulary rich! Teachable moments are important but so is planned intentional instruction in vocabulary development (See Research-Based Key Approaches for Intentionally Teaching Vocabulary, p. 155)

When making your classroom vocabulary-rich, it is important to use the Goldilocks principle to get it "just right" — not too much and not too little new vocabulary and words that are just right! (See **Choosing Vocabulary Words to Teach** p. 162)

There is great potential for developing academic vocabulary during inquiries.

Literacy Growth in High-Poverty Schools

In a study of high-poverty schools, Taylor, Pearson, Peterson, and Rodriguez (2003) found that more effective teachers asked five times as many higher-order questions and offered twice as many opportunities for discussion as less effective teachers did.

Mini-lesson: To show children the strength of effective, specific student–student feedback, show them the video Austin's Butterfly: Building Excellence in Student Work - Models, Critique, and Descriptive Feedback, available at this link: *http://vimeo. com/38247060*.

- Provided with at least a good balance of student speaking, listening, and reading opportunities

- Given numerous opportunities to use and reuse the vocabulary taught

- Provided with many opportunities to be part of extended conversations (such as explanations, narratives, and pretend play) that require the use of at least several sentences.

- Encouraged to use strong conversational skills when teachers ask open-ended questions that require more than a one word answer, such as yes or no; use prompts such as "Tell me more..." rather than questions; and provide a teacher wait-time of at least 3 seconds to allow the students time to think before responding. The Researching **Effective Pedagogy in the Early Years** study (REPEY 2002) in the UK found that of a total of 5,808 questions analyzed, only 5.5 percent were open-ended and encouraged children to problem solve, hypothesize, or speculate on a problem or situation.

- Given meaningful specific feedback on their remarks: Demonstrate that you have really listened to what they have to say, rather than interrogating them (See **Making Feedback Effective** p. 68).

- Effectively supported, including English language learners

Effectively Supporting English Language Learners

As of the 2006 Canadian Census, one in five Canadians (20 percent) have a first language other than English or French. More than 200 non-official mother tongues were also reported. It is important to note that Canadian research indicates that English language learners who have been learning English since Kindergarten are at no further risk of reading difficulties in Grade 3, after four years of instruction in English. A small percentage of ESL students do experience reading difficulties. But the percentage is very similar to native language learners (Lipka and Siegel 2007). In fact research done in North Vancouver by Dr. Linda Siegel (University of British Columbia) and Dr. Nonie Lesaux (Harvard University) studied 790 children who were native English speakers and 178 who were English second language learners. They found that at the end of Grade 2 with strong classroom programs and effective intervention beginning in Kindergarten, the ESL students as a group did as well and in some cases better than non-ESL students on a number of literacy measures.

Check It Out!

Much has been written on how best to support English language learners. Some of the best sources are listed below:

■ *Integrating Literacy and Inquiry for English Learners*

https://lled5040.wikispaces.com/file/view/ Integrating+Literacy+and+Inquiry+for+English+Learners. pdf/303363384/Integrating%20Literacy%20and%20Inquiry%20 for%20English%20Learners.pdf

■ *Effective Literacy and English Language Instruction for English Learners in the Elementary Grades*

http://ies.ed.gov/ncee/wwc/pdf/practice_guides/20074011.pdf

■ *Teaching English Language Learners What the Research Does — and Does Not — Say*

https://www.aft.org/pdfs/americaneducator/summer2008/gold-enberg.pdf

■ *Full Report English Language Learners: Developing Literacy in Second-Language Learners — Report of the National Literacy Panel on Language-Minority Children and Youth*

http://jlr.sagepub.com/content/41/4/432.full.pdf

■ *Executive Summary Developing Literacy in Second-Language Learner: Report of the National Literacy Panel on Language-Minority Children and Youth*

http://www.bilingualeducation.org/pdfs/PROP2272.pdf

■ *Capacity Building Series: A World of Words: Enhancing Vocabulary Development for English Language Learners*

http://www.edu.gov.on.ca/eng/literacynumeracy/inspire/ research/world_of_words.pdf

Teacher Talk Matters

According to John Hattie (2013), teachers talk between 70 and 80 percent of the classroom time. "Teachers' talking increases, as grade levels rise and as class size decreases. When teachers aren't talking, students are typically doing work on their own, so classrooms can be very isolating places for many students." (2013,9).

Ken Rowe, former research director of the Australian Council for Educational Research, found that teachers talk too fast and bombard students with excess words, leaving them struggling in a "sea of blah" and possibly contributing to unnecessary referrals for behaviour disorders. He also found that teacher's sentences are often too long for primary grade students. When there is too much information being provided by teacher talk, either nothing is processed by some students, or the message gets through but is not always understood. Boys in particular are treading water in this "sea of blah." Boredom, confusion, lack of engagement and/or behavioural issues and often identification of Attention Deficit Disorder (ADD) or Attention Deficit Hyperactivity Disorder (ADHD) often follow. In fact, evidence shows that the ears of boys as young as four process sounds more slowly and send less information to the brain than the ears of young girls. For more information on this research see the article "Children drowning in a sea of blah" by Linda Doherty, available at *http://www.theage.com.au/articles/2004/10/29/1099028201302.html*.

Research indicates that a number of techniques can be used to make teacher talk more positive for student literacy learning:

- Using rare (new and interesting) words: Students are always interested in learning new words especially those that teachers use to describe them. This will hook them.

- Limiting how much they say allows teachers to spend more time listening to what the children have to say (Dickinson and Sprague 2001, 271). However, simply increasing student talk does not necessarily increase comprehension. (For effective comprehension-scaffolding techniques, see **Scaffolding Oral Language and Comprehension** p. 108, **Teacher Questions and Prompts** p. 166, **Proven Methods to Scaffold Conversations Effectively** p. 123 and **Dialogic Reading: A Research-Based Proven Repeated Read-Aloud Technique,** p. 169.

Improve Self-Regulation through Effective Teacher Talk
A finding of a four-year Australian study of children (reported by Doherty 2004) aged four years to ten years revealed that slower speech and steady eye contact by teachers improved literacy results and reduced behavioural problems.

"Teachers who use interesting and varied words may help to create a vocabulary-rich environment — a classroom in which children are exposed to and encouraged to use varied words" (Dickinson and Tabors 2003, 7). Such classrooms develop word consciousness: "a keen awareness of words and a keen interest in them" (Graves 2005, 32).

Listen for learning happening.

How can teachers free up time for more student talk? What has to go?

An important factor that affects children's literacy development is the amount of child participation in conversations. Findings indicate that teachers do the most talking by far. Recent research reported that teachers in early childhood classrooms produced at least 80 percent of the talk, with less than 2 percent of the talk time devoted to children expressing their own ideas (Dickinson et al. 2011).

- It is also important to limit the length of large group conversations in order to support engagement. It is better to continue the conversation at another time such as on a subsequent day (Dickinson, Freiberg, and Barnes 2011).

Scaffolding Oral Language and Comprehension: The Key Focus Areas

When scaffolding oral language and any other literacy focus area, it is important to select and effectively implement the high-yield strategies intentionally on a daily basis. This intentionality goes beyond implementing random activities. The high-yield strategies for oral language development and assessment and comprehension are embedded in these key instructional focus areas:

- Assessment: Use visible learning to monitor progress and help scaffold learning

- Conversations: Make them spontaneous and strategic (See Chapter 5)

- Read-alouds, repeated read-alouds, and shared readings (See Chapter 6)

- Storytelling and retelling using photo documentation, wall stories, and story innovations (See Chapter 9)

- Classrooms that use a varied and stimulating curriculum, including inquiry, play, and Centre Activities (See Chapters 7-14)

- Explicitly Teaching Listening and Reading Comprehension Strategies (See Chapter 6).

- Writing across the curriculum (See Chapters 11–12).

When considering reading, writing, speaking and listening, listening is perhaps the most essential for academic learning (Chand, 2007). And yet it is the least taught (Tindall and Nisbet, 2008).While some students need explicit instruction in listening, all students benefit (Ontario Ministry of Education, 2008a). In general students listen much more than they read, write or speak.

Assessment:
Use Visible Learning to Monitor Progress and Scaffold Learning

Use the Oral Language Checklist below to help guide assessment and instruction.

1: Kindergarten–Grade 2

Oral Language Observation Checklist

Name:_____Date:_____
____

Teacher:_____ School:_____
____

Many of the skills will be observed daily.	Most of the Time	Some of the Time	Not Yet
Speaking and listening behaviours			
1 Begins conversations with adults			
2 Begins conversations with peers			
3 Participates in conversations			
4 Takes turns as a speaker and a listener during conversations			
5 Uses language that is sensitive to others' feelings			
6 Comments on how what he or she has "read" or heard relates to his or her own experiences			
7 Shares personal experiences and feelings			
8 Speaks clearly and fluently			
9 Understands and uses appropriate body language (e.g., gestures, tone of voice, volume)			
10 Stays on topic in a short conversation			
11 Extends conversations			
12 Interrupts appropriately			
13 Uses language appropriately to gain the attention of adults and peers			
14 Uses language to talk about their thinking (metacognition) and to reflect and solve problems			
15 Uses language rather than physical means in conflict situations			
16 Ignores distractions and stays focused on the listening task			
17 Knows the difference between a question and a statement			
18 Asks appropriate questions in response to what was heard and/or read			
19 Makes logical predictions			
20 Expresses curiosity/wonder and makes inquiries			
21 Asks for clarification for understanding			
22 Asks for help appropriately			
23 Participates in shared reading activities			

24	Demonstrates understanding of a variety of materials read aloud			
25	Uses varied vocabulary and tries new words			
26	Shows flexibility in communication, matching language and style to the audience, topic, situation, and purpose			
	Knowledge of the Meaning of Language			

27	When listening to or reading story books:
	
	   ■ Understands character traits
	
	   ■ Understands character feelings
	
	   ■ Understands character motives (what they want)
	
	   ■ Understands character relationships
	
	   ■ Understands character change
	
	   ■ Makes logical predictions
	
	   ■ Infers — makes appropriate inferences			

28	Understands how to categorize (sort) items (e.g., animals, books) and is able to articulate the reasons for the sorts			
29	Uses language to compare and contrast (same, different)			
30	Understands figurative language (e.g., idioms)			
31	Describes items according to attributes: size, shape, color, texture, and function			
32	Understands and uses spatial concepts for following and giving directions (e.g., over, under, in front, beside, between, behind, first, last)			
33	Gives one- and two-step directions			
34	Follows one- and two-step directions			
35	Follows routines (e.g., morning sign-in, centre routines)			
36	Uses the language of "who," "when," "where," and "what" in telling stories			
37	Demonstrates simple narrative structure (beginning, middle, end) in retelling			
38	Remembers story lines and characters in stories read or heard			
39	Is able to share main ideas and supporting details in fiction/non-fiction			
40	Is able to explain and justify points of view			
	Knowledge of the structure of language			
41	Uses complete sentences in speaking			
42	Uses more complex sentences with connectors (e.g., because, if, when, after, before)			
	Knowledge of the sound structure of language (phonology)			
43	Uses phonological awareness skills effectively for word solving in reading and writing			
44	Demonstrates phonological awareness skills (See http://www.isbe.net/earlychi/pdf/trehearne_chapter_2.pdf)			

"If you don't know where you are going, any road will get you there."
Lewis Carroll

Teacher Rating of Oral Language and Literacy (TROLL): A Research-Based Tool

See *http://www.ciera.org/library/reports/inquiry-3/3-016/3-016.pdf*

In the area of oral language (speaking, listening, and comprehension), the following key research-based questions taken from TROLL (Dickinson 2001), can be used to provide a general overview and to set a direction or guide instruction:

1. *How would you describe this child's willingness to start a conversation with adults and peers and continue trying to communicate when he/she is not understood on the first attempt?*

2. *How well does the child communicate personal experiences in a clear and logical way?*

3. *How would you describe this child's pattern of asking questions about topics that interest him/her (e.g., why things happen, why people act the way they do)?*

4. *How would you describe this child's use of talk while pretending in the house area, when playing with blocks, etc.? Consider the child's use of talk with peers to start pretending and to carry it out.*

5. *How would you describe the child's ability to recognize and produce rhymes?*

6. *How often does the child use a varied vocabulary or try out new words (e.g., heard in stories or from the teacher?)*

7. *When the child speaks to adults other than you or the teaching assistant is he/she understandable?*

8. *How often does the child express curiosity (wonder) about how and why things happen?*

9. *How often does the child like to hear books read aloud in the full group?*

10. *How often does the child attend to stories read aloud in full or small groups and react in a way that indicates comprehension?*

11. *How often does the child remember the story line or characters in books that he/she has heard before, either at home or in class?*

Students Use Metacognition to Self-Monitor Progress: Scaffolding Their Own Learning

Use the Oral Language bookmarks below to help guide student self-assessment. Adjust the wording as appropriate.

I was a Good Speaker

- I thought about what I wanted to say, before I began speaking.
- I thought about the audience before deciding what to say.
- I looked at the audience.
- I spoke clearly.
- I spoke loudly enough but not too loud.
- I spoke at a good pace.
- I took at least one turn.
- I stayed on topic.

I was a Good Listener

- I looked at the speaker(s).
- I used my head to nod yes or no to the speaker(s).
- I listened respectfully.
- I waited for my turn to speak.
- I paid attention.
- I was thinking about what the others were saying.
- I asked for more information when I didn't understand.

Strive to Create a Culture of Classroom Conversation: Spontaneous and Strategic

Understanding What a Conversation is Starts with Understanding What a Question is

Starting and continuing conversations often relies on asking questions. Don't assume that all young children understand the concept of a conversation, the purpose of a conversation, or how to have a conversation. Some children do not understand what a question is! Students have to learn how to both ASK and ANSWER questions.

Jane's Kindergarten Class
Teacher: "What are you doing"?
Kindergartner: "I am stretching my reading muscle!"

What is a question?

Children who clearly have no idea what a question is need lots of modelling. Start with something simple such as, "My favorite color is blue. What is your favorite color Jana…?" Think aloud to let the children know that you just asked a question. "I just asked Jana a question. Tell a partner what the question is that I just asked Jana." Then, of course, the children all become teachers; they turn and question a partner using the same sentence frame. Make sure lots of questioning occurs in real contexts such as during the rereading of a story or during the reading of a non-fiction text. Doing a shared writing of interview questions to use in a Skype interview or a face-to-face in-class interview provides a real reason to create questions (See **Window on the Classroom: Angie's Class and Skype Conversations** see p. 138 **and Visitors to the Classroom: Developing Social and Emotional Literacy through Conversations**, p. 133).

First, it is crucial that teachers develop confident children who understand that asking and answering questions, wonderings, and inquiries help them to learn. It is important for students to understand how we learn and to do this they need to be introduced to the concept of the brain and how it changes and grows bigger every time one learns something new. The more challenging the task, the more the brain develops.

Building the Brain Smarter and Stronger

Carol Dweck and her colleagues (2008) have found that children's attitudes and behaviours regarding achievement, failure, and learning in general are already in place by preschool, but can be changed. Some students believe that their abilities — their intelligence — is generally fixed from birth. They don't feel that they can improve. This is known as having a fixed mind-set. For example, some children might say, "I am not good at puzzles" or "I am not as smart as you are!" Other children have a dynamic, or growth, mind-set. These children will say, "Putting together puzzles is hard, but I will get better at it if I keep trying." Such students do not feel that their intelligence, their capacity to learn, is fixed. What students believe about themselves strongly influences their degree of learning success. It is crucial that parents and educators help children from a very early age to understand and believe in the importance of the brain, and the brain's capacity to grow and change due to general long-term experiences. Students should develop the understanding that what they couldn't do yesterday, they will likely be able to do today or tomorrow if they keep trying. Feedback can scaffold a growth mind-set (See Feedback,p. 68).

The following mini-lessons focus on scaffolding a growth mind-set by helping students to develop an understanding of the brain:

- What the brain is and what it does
- How to take care of the brain and help it to grow
- The importance of conversations to brain development

Mini-lesson: What the brain is and what it does

Your brain is in your head. It weighs a little more than a kilogram (1.3 kilo or 2.9 lbs) which is about the same weight as a small kitten. The brain does many things for you. It helps you breathe, see, smell, hear, and touch. It also helps you to think, to learn, to make things, and to feel happy, sad, hungry, and angry. Show students an illustration of the brain inside the head (See references in "Check It Out!).

Mini-lesson: How to take care of the brain and help it grow

It is important to take care of your brain by eating well, having good night sleeps, and exercising your body. You also exercise your brain and learn many new things when you play, read, write, listen to books that are read to you, and when you have conversations with other people. All of these activities help your brain to grow stronger and smarter. The more challenging the activity, the harder it is, the more the brain grows. The more you stick with something, the more grit you show, the more your brain grows. If the children are intrigued with the concept of the brain, this might then lead into an inquiry.

A beautifully illustrated read-aloud book that demonstrates success involving a challenging task requiring grit is *Rocket Writes a Story* (2012) by Tad Hills. The book deals with what it takes to be a writer. Rocket is a dog who learns that writing is challenging work, and is told to remember that stories take time. Rocket also learns how to find something worthwhile to write about by incubating ideas and by finding something that inspires him. In addition, he learns how important word choice is. Rocket is inspired to be an author and sticks with it. Owl is "captivated" by Rocket's story. Rocket's brain grows stronger and smarter from writing. A second Rocket book, *How Rocket Learned to Read* (2010), promotes making text-to-text connections.

Dweck argues that adults can help foster a "growth mindset" — the belief that the brain is like a muscle that can grow stronger through hard work.

 Check It Out!

For more child-friendly information on the brain, see the National Geographic Kids Web site — *http://kids.nationalgeographic. com/explore/science/your-amazing-brain.html* — and the following children's books:

Your Brain by Terri DeGezelle (2002): The material presented here will be highly useful for the youngest students and browsers. An easy-to-follow hands-on activity is provided at the back of the book.

Your Brain by Anita Ganeri (2003): This book introduces the structure and function of the human brain and nervous system.

The Brain by Seymour Simon (2006): This book reveals wonderful illustrations, including MRI images, and is complete with a glossary at the end.

How Bright Is Your Brain by Michael A. DiSpezio (2006): See if you really are doing what you think you are doing or is your brain tricking you? What does your mind look like, what task does it perform, and how does it accomplish it?

Mini-lesson: The importance of conversations to brain development

Conversations help your brain grow. Conversations involve questions, asking and answering. A conversation is talking to someone and sharing your ideas. Model a conversation and use think-alouds to point out the questions posed by both participants. Conversations often lead to mini-lessons with a focus on writing question-and-answer reports.

Check It Out!

Some wonderful question-and-answer books to read aloud are listed below. The first three books listed below share authentic questions asked by children aged 4 to 12. The answers are provided by world famous scientists, specialists, explorers, paleontologists, historians, philosophers, and writers, who ensure their language is accessible to elementary school children. The questions include *Can a bee sting a bee? Who had the first pet? Do animals have feelings? Why can't I tickle myself? How is electricity made? Is the human brain the most powerful thing on earth? Will the North Pole and South Pole ever melt completely? Why do wars happen? What is global warming? Where does good come from?* The experts provide personal responses and the books do not claim to offer the only answers; often there is no definitive response.

Here is a list.
A magnet likes to pull...

DYLAN

IRON

PIPR KLIP

METL

NEIL

SKOO

CIR

MEANIT.

Feb, 3/09

A Science Inquiry, A Question and Answer Report: What can a magnet pull?

Big Questions from Little People and Simple Answers from Great Minds by Gemma Elwin Harris (ed.) (New York: HarperCollins, 2012).

Does My Goldfish Know Who I Am? Big Questions and Instant Answers by Gemma Elwin Harris (ed.) (London: Faber & Faber, 2013).

Why Can't I Tickle Myself? Big Questions from Little People ... Answered by Some Very Big People by Gemma Elwin Harris (ed.) (London: Faber & Faber, 2013).

Do Bees Sneeze? And Other Questions Kids Ask About Insects by J. K. Wangberg (Golden, CO: Fulcrum Publishing, 1998).

How Do Flies Walk Upside Down? Questions and Answers about Insects by Melvin and Gilda Berger (New York: Scholastic Reference, 1999).

How? The Most Awesome Question and Answer Book about Nature, Animals, People, Places — and You! by Catherine Ripley (Toronto: Owlkids, 2012).

I Wonder Why Snakes Shed Their Skin and Other Questions About Reptiles by Amanda O'Neill (Boston: Kingfisher, 1996).

I Wonder Why Triceratops had Horns and Other Questions about Dinosaurs by Rod Theodorou (Boston: Kingfisher, 1994).

Lift the Flap Questions and Answers by Katie Daynes and Marie-Eve Tremblay (London: Usborne Publishing, 2012).

Questions Children Ask and How to Answer Them by Miriam Stoppard (London: DK Publishing, 1997).

Questions, Questions by Marcus Pfister (New York: North-South Books, 2011).

The Kids Book of Questions by Gregory Stock (New York: Workman Publishing, 2004).

Top 50 Questions Kids Ask (Pre-K through 2nd Grade): The Best Answers to the Toughest, Smartest, and Most Awkward Questions Kids Always Ask by Susan Bartell (Naperville, IL: Sourcebooks Inc., 2010). This is a great book for parents about how best to respond to children's questions and, in the process, effectively promote conversations.

What Makes a Shadow? by Clyde Robert Bulla (New York: HarperCollins, 1994).

Why Do Dogs Have Wet Noses? by Stanley Coren (Toronto: Kids Can Press, 2006).

Why Do Volcanoes Blow Their Tops? Questions & Answers about Volcanoes & Earthquakes (New York: Scholastic Reference, 2000).

Why Don't Haircuts Hurt? Questions and Answers about Your Body by Melvin and Gilda Berger (New York: Scholastic Reference, 1999).

You Asked for It! Strange but True Answers to 99 Wacky Questions by Marg Meikle and Tina Holdcroft (Toronto: Scholastic, 2000).

 For even more question-and-answer books, see the Early Literacy Telecollaborative Project (*www.earlyliterature.ecsd.net*) and click on Predictable Books.

Check It Out!

How do you use a bathroom in space?
http://www.youtube.com/watch?v=fa3nuXxM8yk

―――――

Mainly drawings with labels or captions can make a great preschool, Kindergarten, or Grade 1 report.

―――――

Mini-lesson: Writing a question-and-answer report

Reports are often a response to a question a child or adult has. What more authentic reason to write can there be than to pick a topic of interest to investigate?

1. Introduce the activity by sharing a question-and-answer book with the children as a read-aloud.

2. Brainstorm topics about which the children have questions. Create the list of questions and wonderings as a shared writing.

3. Pick one wondering from the list each week.

4. As a shared writing activity, create a question-and-answer report or a lift the flap book. (See Lift the Flap Questions and Answers by Katie Daynes and Marie-Eve Tremblay in the bibliography above.)

5. Some children will be ready to create their own question-and-answer book or report or perhaps create it with a partner.:

Provide the children with a framework for writing a report that will include

Question or wondering

- Facts

- Possible answer to question or wondering

- Drawings and labels

Closing Thoughts

This chapter provides an understanding regarding the research-base and the high-yield strategies that effectively scaffold oral language development. Conversations are key. The next chapter expands on the how-to of making conversations powerful.

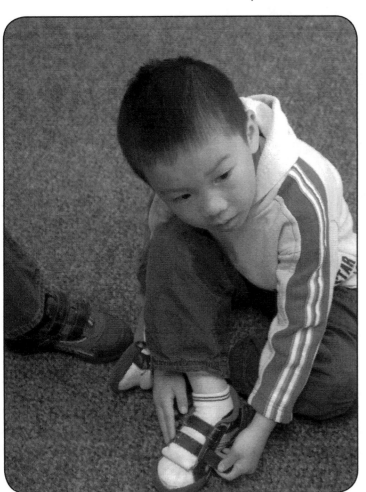

How does Velcro work?

Making Conversations Powerful

5

Proven Methods to Scaffold Conversations Effectively

Not all conversations are equal. Always use those teachable moments to embrace spontaneous conversations! In order to scaffold partner conversations effectively (Turn and Talk) plan some strategic conversations ahead. To prepare students for having conversations, consider the following ideas:

- To model for students how to have a conversation, have a brief conversation with another adult once a week, starting with the first week of school. Model a conversation on the same day every week, perhaps talking with your partner on Monday mornings and using the prompt "Tell me about your weekend" to start the conversation. Encourage the students to turn and talk to a classmate, perhaps using the same prompt to get the conversation started. Remember that some students have never heard an extended conversation at home, so modelling how to have a conversation is important.

- After the conversation, you and your partner think aloud for the students. Provide them with examples of what you tried to do to be a good listener (e.g., listening behaviours such as really paying attention to what the speaker was saying, responding in ways such as nodding, asking a question to extend the conversation, or looking directly at the speaker). Also, model what you did to be a good speaker (e.g., using appropriate volume of voice, looking right at the listener, taking turns listening and speaking and finding ways to extend the conversation). It takes many demonstrations for some students to understand the concept of how to have a conversation.

> Bond and Wasik (2009) noted that conversations in the early grades are a primary tool for oral language development within the classroom. John Hattie's research (2013) on classroom discussion shows an effect size of 0.82, which is very large!

- Model what "turn and talk" looks like. Use the Gradual Release of Responsibilityy model:

1. *"I do it": You model a turn and talk.*

2. *"We do it": Have two students who understand the process model for the class. Use a fishbowl technique, where the pair sits knee to knee and the rest of the class sits in a circle around them.*

3. *"We do it": Repeat the previous step with two different students.*

4. *"You do it": Have all students give it a go. Prompt with open-ended questions and "why" questions to stimulate higher-order thinking.*

"Yes, knee to knee, eye to eye…"

These students don't quite have the eye contact mastered, but they appear to love the sharing experience.

- Help students understand the purpose of having a conversation.

- Be sure that students understand the importance of speaker–listener proximity (e.g., eye to eye, knee to knee) and speaker and listener behaviours (e.g., making eye contact, nodding while listening, asking questions).

- From time to time determine partners so that one partner is not overly dominant, doing all of the talking, while the other is doing all of the listening. The best-case scenario is for students to take ownership in self-selecting partners, but this does not always work. When partnering, consider personalities, vocabulary, oral language skills, and compatibility.

- In order to have a meaningful conversation, students require the necessary vocabulary and concepts. Thus, plan ahead for each Turn and Talk. Turn and Talks work well during the repeated reading of a read-aloud. Identify engaging spots in the text and draw students' attention back to at least one of these after the read-aloud. Then have students turn and talk to discuss the text. Consider any vocabulary words that students could practice using during their conversations or throughout the day.

- It is also important to help students learn appropriate ways to disagree… e.g., "I disagree because…"

Window on the Classroom: Demonstrating a Conversation

While I was modelling a read-aloud in a Kindergarten classroom in Vancouver, B.C., I decided to use "turn and talk." I was near the end of reading the wonderful read-aloud titled *Hey, Little Ant* by Phillip and Hannah Hoose (a father and daughter writing team). The story consists of a dialogue between a little boy and an ant. The boy wants to squish the ant, but the ant continually tries to convince the boy that he should just let him be. It ends with a running shoe hovering over the little ant and the lines: "Should the ant get squished? Should the ant go free? It's up to the kid, not up to me. We'll leave the kid with the raised up shoe. What do you think that kid should do?" I thought, "What a motivating place for a turn and talk." So I said, "Okay, what you think that kid should do? Have a conversation — turn and talk." What I had neglected to find out before the read-aloud is whether the children had ever used this technique, which it turned out they had not. They just sat there, not knowing what to do. However, when we got by this (they were fast learners and knew what a conversation was), they did have some great conversations. One little boy said to another, "I don't think he should kill the ant because ants are God's creatures, you know." A little girl said to her partner, "I think that he should kill the ant because he might be a green ant and green ants can bite, so I think it is better to hurt him instead of letting him hurt me." Turn and talk experiences provide wonderful opportunities for documentation. Teachers learn so much about student listening comprehension and their expressive language skills, and their beliefs. This book scaffolds critical literacy by focusing on perspective and social justice.

Visit www.heylittleant.com for some great classroom activities to go along with this read-aloud. A free MP3 download of the authors singing the complete text of the book is available at this link: *http://heylittleant.wordpress. com/2011/12/02/free-hey-little-ant-song/*

Spontaneous and strategic conversations are the heart of an effective oral language classroom. Teacher–student relationships are the heart of an effective primary program. The relationships that the teacher develops with each of the students, and the connections they make with each other, are crucial to students' academic and social development.

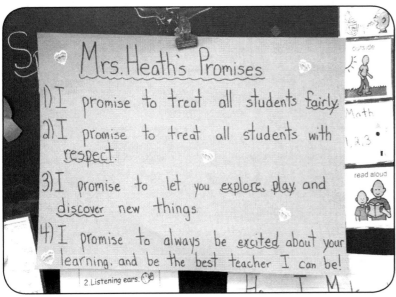

What a wonderful promise!

Language is the basis for establishing these strong relationships, and conversations provide an opportunity for developing relationships. Students and teachers initiate conversations throughout the school day, but not all are equally effective (See **Spontaneous Conversations: Grab Those Teachable Moments**, below). Purposeful strategic conversations are preplanned but not scripted. They often occur during or after read-alouds, shared reading, and play. The purpose of these conversations is to develop both vocabulary (word) knowledge and background (world) knowledge, often taken from curricular content areas such as social studies and science. Much of this vocabulary is described as academic vocabulary. Students hear the specific words in conversation and are prompted to use them. The conversation is extended with prompts such as **"Tell me more," "Explain why," or "How do you know?"** Conversations really do matter in the context of both scaffolding and assessing oral language.

Adult–child relationships in early childhood programs are important to children's security, self-confidence, and learning (Soundy and Stout 2003, 13). Language is the basis for establishing strong relationships.

A valuable form of documentation: Make a list of all of the students in your class, starting with the names of those whom you perceive to be the most verbal, and ending with the least verbal. Now circle the names of the students with whom you converse the most. Is the list a wake-up call?

Spontaneous Conversations: Grab Those Teachable Moments

Think of your class: Who is the strongest oral language user; alternatively, who is the weakest?

Most teachers can readily come up with the names of these two students. Now consider with which of these two students you spend more time conversing. Research indicates that you likely spend the most time conversing with your strongest oral language user. There are a number of reasons to explain this phenomenon. The main reason is that typically the least articulate students rarely initiate spontaneous conversations with adults. Teachers generally spend most of their day conversing with the very articulate students who often demand much of their time. Alternatively, the weakest language users need those conversations the most.

Window on the Classroom: First Thing in the Morning

I have had the wonderful opportunity to work in many classrooms across North America. Recently, in a Grade 1 classroom on a cold Monday morning in December, a young student entered and initiated a conversation with her teacher at the classroom door. "Teacher, I got new shoes on the weekend." Can you predict what the teacher said? Many experienced teachers might correctly predict that the teacher said, "That's nice. I like the color. Now, please go sit on the carpet and put them on" (or something like this). End of conversation!

Any classroom teacher who has been faced with a similar situation, with 20 or more students all arriving at much the same time, and a "stretched curriculum," with limited time, might very well have responded in the same manner. However, reputable research from David Dickinson, amongst others indicates that extending student conversations is crucial.

As much as conversations are about developing oral language and vocabulary, they are primarily about building caring and trusting relationships between the teacher and individual students. By extending the conversation with a child, the teacher is showing the child that the child's thoughts matter and that he or she is interested in what the child has to say.

Extending Conversations: Strive for Five

David Dickinson helps teachers and parents to understand what really constitutes a conversation, and how to make one happen effectively during everyday activities. He suggests that teachers and parents stay on and deepen topics over multiple turns. (See **Home–School Connections Letter to Parents — Strive for Five: Have Effective Conversations with Your Children**, p. 172). Doing this activity involves relaxed back-and-forth exchanges with *limited amounts of teacher and parent talk*. The goal is to have five back-and-forth exchanges with the child.

See **Home–School Connections Letters to Parents: Parents Who Make a Big Difference**, p. 173; and **Strive for Five: Have Effective Conversations with Your Children**, p. 172.

Using the classroom example above (Window on the Classroom), a successful "strive for five" conversation might have sounded like this:

Lexi: Teacher, I got new shoes on the weekend!
Teacher: I love the mauve color! What was the special occasion?
Lexi: It was my birthday.
Teacher: Tell me more.
Lexi: I got them at a shoe store in the mall.

Notice the varied vocabulary and the strength of the teacher word choice: *occasion, mauve*. Notice the specific detail that the teacher provides — she does not just say, "I like your shoes" or "They are nice," but instead says, "I love the mauve color!"

Effective conversational and "strive for five" strategies to extend the conversation

- Make sure that your facial expression really indicates that you are interested in what the child is saying. Attempt to maintain eye contact, even though that is often easier said than done when you have a whole class full of children wanting/needing your attention.

- Ask questions and make comments or prompts to encourage more talk. Invite the child to elaborate using open-ended statements and prompts. However, don't ask yes/no questions, which often result in the end of the talk, as the children will just nod or shake their heads in response.

- Encourage children to listen to each other.

- Don't interrupt or change the topic. Just like adults, children will be turned off by this.

- Prompt the child to talk about more than "the here and now." Encourage talk about what happened in the past and what might happen in the future.

- Provide information and encourage questioning and speculation, such as in an inquiry. These conversations can profitably go on for days.

- Share information about the meanings of words, especially academic vocabulary from content areas such as social studies and science.

- Use effective prompts such as "Say a little more about that," "Tell me more," "Explain more," "I wonder why" (thinking aloud), and "Tell me why you think (or feel) that way."

- Echo the child's thoughts ("So you think that…"), to help the child clarify his or her own thinking, and to show that you have really listened.

- Think aloud (e.g., "I remember…").

- Encourage the child to explore ideas and understand that uncertainty is a normal stage in the thinking process.

- Provide at least three seconds of wait-time for the child to come up with a response, and take the same amount of time to reflect on the student's response.

There is solid and extensive research to show the benefits of teachers using the wait-time technique. Only a teacher who is already dealing with a "stretched curriculum" would understand why such a simple technique is often forgotten in the typical classroom setting.

In terms of teacher behaviour at the elementary, middle, high school, and college levels, the following changes resulted from the regular use of wait-time:

- The use of higher level, evaluative questions increased.

- The percentage of teacher talk decreased.

- The number of kinds of questions changed (more open-ended questions).

- Teachers demonstrated more flexibility in their responses.

- Teachers' expectations for the performance of students rated as "slow learners" improved (Rowe 1986; McTighe and Wiggins 2013).

Extending the conversation on the way home. So much to share!

Effective Prompts and Questions to Extend Conversations

- Say a little more about that.

- Tell me more.

- Explain more about...

- I wonder why... (teacher thinking aloud).

- Tell me why you think or feel that way.

- So you think that...

- I remember... (teacher thinking aloud).

- Let's see, what do I know or think I know about that? (teacher thinking aloud).

- I wonder what makes e.g., a good friend (teacher thinking aloud).

- How many different points of view do we have? Let's share.

- Tell me why you think or feel that way.

- Convince me that...

- Let's think of another perspective on this — another view point.

Benefits of Wait-time

Benefits of using wait-time (teacher silence after asking question, and teacher silence after the initial student response) of at least three to eight seconds include the following:

- The length of student responses increases significantly.

- Students provide more inferences, higher-level responses, and logical arguments.

- The quality of student responses improves, especially when dealing with complex subject matter.

- Students are more willing to take a chance and speculate.

- Students ask more questions and propose more inquiries.

- There are more student–student exchanges and less teacher control of conversations.

- More students respond, resulting in fewer students declining to respond.

- Students appear to be more motivated, engaged, confident and co-operative.

- Students provide more unsolicited responses.

- More students volunteer to participate in discussions (Rowe 1986; McTighe and Wiggins 2013).

- Students generally appear to enjoy having the time to make connections.

Window on the Classroom: Extending the Conversation Works in Christina's Class!

I received the following note from a Kindergarten teacher:

Hi Miriam,

I just attended your workshop "Kindergarten Literacy: Strong Programs Make the Difference!" and I want to thank you again for another incredibly inspiring day! I am the one who had attended one of your sessions back in November and was so appreciative of the part when you talked about "extending conversation" with the little ones. I went back to school the next day and no longer "shushed and rushed" the kids into my class in the morning, as I had done in the past. Instead, I took the extra time to listen to what the kids were dying to tell me, and I encouraged them to tell me more. Eventually, I had almost every child in the class lining up before the bell rang, anxious to chat with me as soon as I opened the door. Even though entering into my classroom took a little longer each day, the children were very patient with this because they knew that they, too, would get a turn to share and to be listened to. We now bring these conversations into our circle time and just sit and talk for at least 20 minutes at the start of each day. The conversations are always varied and passionate, and the children are very respectful of listening to each other and waiting their turn. I find now that the children are even extending their ideas without as much prompting from me, and that other children are usually joining in on all the conversations. We usually finish off our circle time with a few sing-alongs/chants/dances and only then, once we have all unloaded, are we ready to start our day! I know a lot of people say that they have never seen a more bubbly, chatty, and energetic group of children — but, then again, this is what I encourage and inspire, so why shouldn't it be this way? Isn't this what a room full of five-year-olds should be like?

Sincerely,
Christina Nicola
Kindergarten Teacher, Surrey, B.C.

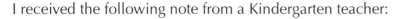

"Our data strongly indicate that it is the nature of the teacher–child relationships and the kinds of conversations that they have that make the biggest difference in early language and literacy development" (Dickinson and Tabors 2003, 11). Although young children learn much from their peers, they typically develop stronger vocabulary when they have opportunities to converse with an adult.

Get Everyone Talking Using Strategic Conversations

Think-pair-share (TPS) and "teacher wonderings" effectively scaffold strategic conversations.

Think-Pair-Share

This practical technique requires teachers to implement a longer wait-time. After listening to a read-aloud, having a discussion, or watching a video, students

- Think — experience quiet time to reflect
- Pair — form pairs and share ideas (turn and talk)
- Share — return to a larger group to share as in a class discussion

Advantages: Along with the benefits of providing a longer wait-time, this technique encourages co-operative learning and offers students the opportunity to rehearse responses with a partner or in a small group before sharing them with the whole class.

Teachers who Wonder and Think Aloud Spark Strategic Conversations

Thinking aloud is just what it sounds like — making thinking public by saying it aloud. This is an important instructional strategy or technique for the teacher to use because by thinking aloud the child experiences the teacher's thinking process and wonderings. Think-alouds also enable the teacher to demonstrate how to solve problems by thinking through possible options. Sometimes think-alouds are intentionally planned before the lessons and are used to extend the learning and possibly provoke an inquiry, but often they occur spontaneously in response to a classroom happening.

Window on the Classroom: Miriam's Classroom

One day we were celebrating a birthday with cookies from the local bakery, provided by the PTA. The children were eagerly sharing how good the cookies were. I wondered aloud, "I wonder what makes these cookies so good? It tastes like there is butter in these cookies, and cinnamon, but I am not sure. I would love to be able to make these cookies. I wonder how I could find out what makes them so tasty. I would have to know what they are made of (ingredients) and how they are made (process or procedure)." Then the children and I made a list of possible ways to find out:

- We could write a letter to the baker and ask him.
- We could phone the baker.
- We could visit the bakery.

This thinking aloud led to a class trip to the bakery. What better way to develop oral language than field trips? Incidentally, this think-aloud and the field trip had not been planned beforehand, but resulted from recognizing a teachable moment (See **Vocabulary Visits**, p. 324).

Think-alouds involve not just telling the children how you think, but showing them.

Visitors to the Classroom: Developing Social and Emotional Literacy through Conversations

Bringing the community into the classroom is one of the best ways to promote conversations and in the process develop emotional literacy and self-regulation. Emotional Literacy is made up of "the ability to understand your emotions, the ability to listen to others and empathise with their emotions, and the ability to express emotions productively. To be emotionally literate is to be able to handle emotions in a way that improves your personal power and improves the quality of life around you. Emotional literacy improves relationships, creates loving possibilities between people, makes co-operative work possible, and facilitates the feeling of community" (Steiner and Perry 1997, 11).

Roots of Empathy

Roots of Empathy, an evidence-based classroom program founded in 1996, provides an example of how bringing visitors into the classroom can develop social and emotional literacy through conversations. This program has been shown to have a dramatic effect in reducing levels of aggression among schoolchildren by raising social/emotional competence — including reducing the levels of bullying, aggression, and violence, while increasing empathy, self-regulation, and positive social behaviours. Roots of Empathy reaches elementary schoolchildren from Kindergarten to Grade 8 across three continents. At the heart of the program

Get Everyone Talking
Strategic conversations typically occur during

- Visitors to the classroom (See **Roots of Empathy** p. 133; **Ask an Expert** p. 355)
- Skype Time (See p. 138)
- Read-alouds and repeated read-alouds (See Chapter 6)
- Play and centre activities (See Chapters 7–10)
- Inquiries (See Chapters 13–14)
- Storytelling and retelling using story documentation, wall stories, story innovations, mystery boxes, and book clubs (See Chapter 9)
- Shared reading (e.g., morning message, news)

Learn much about the characteristics that make Roots of Empathy so effective: http://www. rootsofempathy.org/

is a neighbourhood infant and typically a parent, grandparent, or caregiver who visits an early childhood classroom approximately once every three weeks during the school year. The infant teaches the children so much, including empathy, as she or he grows and changes over the course of the many classroom visits. There is much more to Roots of Empathy, but this powerful activity alone, when effectively orchestrated, can result in the social, emotional, and cognitive development of the whole child for each of the children in the class.

Window on the Classroom: Miriam Observes a Visit from Baby Oren

The Kindergarten class consisted of 25 children, many of them recent immigrants, most from war-torn countries. Much preplanning and discussion occurred before each visit from Baby Oren and his mother, with further debriefing after each visit. The children began with a discussion about babies. The teacher scribed using a KWLM chart:

K: What do we know or think we know about babies?

W: What do we want to know about babies? (after the visit and/or research).

L: What did we learn about babies?

M: What more do we want to learn?

Similar to an anchor chart, a KWLM chart is a great system for documenting student understandings, and for monitoring and documenting ongoing student learning. (Also, see **Inquiry Posters and KWHLAQ Charts**, Chapter 13).

The children noted the baby's emotions: "He is smiling. He looks happy," "I think he likes the song we sang to him." The facilitator included vocabulary words such as *mood, angry, feelings, happy, sad,* and *satisfied*. The children each made up questions to ask Baby Oren's mother; some examples are provided below. What do they tell you?

What does he eat? Does he have teeth?

How does he eat with no teeth?

Does he have a bottle?

Does baby Oren ever cry?

What makes him cry?

How do you make him stop crying?

Does he ever get sad?

When does he get sad?

Does he get sad when he is hit?

I saw a policeman outside the school today.

Clearly, the last question came from a child who did not understand the concept of what a question is!

On the day that Baby Oren visited, the Kindergarten teacher had a Grade 6 student acting as a Kindergarten helper. The young man listened intently to the dialogue between the mother and the Kindergartners. When the session was over, he asked the mother if he could hold the baby. After holding Baby Oren and talking to him for a few minutes, the young man passed the baby back to the mother and asked the teacher, "Do you think someone like me who comes from a home with no love could ever be a good father?" After the conversation that ensued, it was clear that Roots of Empathy was not only working for the Kindergartners, but for a Sixth Grader as well. The conversations, key to Roots of Empathy, scaffold both social imagination and self-regulation.

Developing Social Imagination and Self-regulation

Social imagination, according to Johnston 2012, is what makes relationships work or not. It is the ability to make sense of social cues and to think through their implications. According to Johnston, there are two main dimensions of social imagination: mind reading (the ability to read facial expression and figure out what's going on in a person's mind) and social reasoning (the ability to imagine and reason about the actions, intentions, feelings, and beliefs of others from multiple perspectives). Conversations and carefully chosen read-alouds are key to developing social imagination. Social imagination in turn supports self-regulation. Self-regulation is the capacity to control one's impulses both to stop doing something (even if one wants to continue) and to start doing something (even if one doesn't want to) (Bodrova and Leong 2008). For more on self-regulation and social imagination, see Chapter 7.

Reading and rereading story (fiction) is extremely important to scaffold social imagination and self-regulation. Ministries of Education are well aware of this and stress the importance of fiction, along with non-fiction, across the curricula. "Engaging with story and text shapes and reflects our identity and develops our understanding of self and others." (From British Columbia English Language Arts Overview: **https://curriculum.gov.bc.ca/curriculum/English%20Language%20Arts/1**)

In a great read-aloud titled *Julius, the Baby of the World* by Kevin Henkes, Lilly (the same Lilly as in *Lilly's Purple Plastic Purse*) has a new baby brother. The story explores (often through inference) how and why siblings feel jealousy and other emotions at the arrival of a new baby. Social imagination and self-regulation are key to the story line. The book offers the opportunity for a powerful follow-up activity in which many students will be able to contribute to a conversation about younger siblings, based on their first-hand experiences.

Rosie and Buttercup, by author Chieri Uegaki and illustrator Stephane Jorisch, is a delightful Canadian read-aloud that also deals with sibling rivalry, experienced by so many young children. Activities such as conversations and taking on the roles of different characters "being the character" to act out the book will help the students to imagine and reason about Rosie's actions, intentions, feelings, and perspectives when she attempts to give her baby sister away. These kinds of activities can help students to develop social imagination (Johnston 2012) and empathy. Developing social imagination is key to developing positive social skills and empathy, along with problem-solving skills, self-regulation, and comprehension. According to Johnston, social imagination is what makes relationships work and relationships are the foundation of our society!

 Check It Out!

- Find several read-aloud lesson plans for *Julius, Baby of the World* at *http://www.readwritethink.org/lessons/lesson_view.asp?id=25*

- Additional lessons on building an understanding of feelings and creating emotion masks can be found at *http://www.readwritethink.org/lessons/lesson_view.asp?id=366*

- To teach children how to draw happy, sad, and angry faces, see Expressing Emotions Teaching Plan at *http://www.parentingpress.com/activity/wayifeelplan.pdf*

- To make your own vocabulary and concept board games (e.g., for feelings), go to *http://www.toolsforeducators.com http://www.toolsforeducators.com/boardgames/feelings2.php*

Other great read-alouds that support understanding emotions:

Today I Feel Silly and Other Moods that Make My Day by Jamie Lee Curtis. *This colorfully illustrated book uses comedy to help children understand the definitions for different feelings, emotions and moods, including grumpy, sad, glad, confused, frustrated, discouraged and lonely. It also provides an understanding that we feel different ways because of our moods, and that mood swings are normal.* A mood wheel on the last page allows the reader to change the little girl's expression--both her eyes and mouth to reflect different moods and feelings. *The book begins with:* "Today I feel silly. Mom says it's the heat.
I put rouge on the cat and gloves on my feet".

My Many Colored Days by Dr. Seuss This book provides a journey through different feelings and emotions, each linked to a different color. The bright and vivid illustrations really help to express the different feelings the colors are linked to. The book may help children to understand different emotions and feelings and may even help them to express their emotions.

When Sophie Gets Angry… Really, Really Angry by Molly Bang This book can be used as a tool to open up dialogue around the concepts of anger, temper tantrums and sibling rivalry. The double-page illustrations, resonating with saturated colors, reveal the drama of the child's emotions.

The Way I Feel by Janan Cain This book filled with vivid, expressive illustrations helps children to understand the many emotions, describe their emotions and understand that feelings are a normal part of life.

On Monday When It Rained by Cherryl Kachenmeister and Tom Berthiaume Using expressive pictures, the author and photographer have captured the thoughts and feelings of one small boy.

How are you Peeling? by Saxton Freymann and Joost Elffers. This book opens up opportunities for discussions about real-life situations where the students felt happy, sad, or angry. It promotes discussion of how they show feelings and how they can tell what someone is feeling.

- Singing and acting out songs about emotions like *If you're Happy and You Know It* also develops emotion vocabulary: *http://www. songsforteaching.com/charactereducationsongs. htm*

- Playing games to teach children emotion vocabulary: *https://www.naeyc.org/files/yc/file/200611/ BTJFoxSupplementalActivities.pdf*

SINGING AND ACTING

GAMES

Why not create class books of feelings!

 # Skype Time

Skype is a wonderful vehicle. It enables long distance conversations using live video. It links students, teachers and parents around the world. In the process it often develops social imagination, self-regulation and critical literacy.

Window on the Classroom: Angie's Class and Skype Conversations

I use Skype in our Kindergarten classroom as a way to broaden the students' world. Many educators have experienced a time when a student speaking on Skype says, "I live in…" and names the city. "What? I live there too!" is the reply by many in the classroom. As teachers, we giggle to ourselves as we watch the children construct their understanding of the world and how it includes others. Skype provides the opportunity to connect with other educators, classes, and experts around the world.

I understand that our youngest learners do not have an understanding of our wide world. They are much centred on their own family, their own town, and their own classroom. I believe it is my responsibility to widen their experiences so they begin to understand that there are other children in Kindergarten classrooms around the world. They may not conceptually understand the physical distances or the time zone issues, but they can understand that there are other children in classrooms around the world, building with blocks, and reading, just like us.

I use Skype in a very purposeful way. I set up times with educators through Twitter or emails. Skype has a website and a way of connecting with educators titled **Skype in the Classroom** (for details go to https://education.skype.com). I have set up Skype calls to share with classrooms around the world. We have made books during different seasons and posted the books on our class blog and on Twitter. Teachers shared the books with their students, and some created their own class books. We viewed the books and compared the information: _What does their school have that ours does? What is different? What do you notice about their schoolyard?_ Students were delighted to make connections and talk about what they saw in the books. We posted comments on blogs and developed questions before our Skype time with the classes.

My students learned that other students live in different time zones. They asked questions such as "Why can't we Skype with the class in British Columbia yet?" They learned that some classes are having lunch while we are getting ready to go home. They also learned that Kindergarten can look the same around the world, but it can also look different. Another result of our Skype time was that students learned to respect different languages. We Skyped with a primary class who wrote us a book in English and French. We listened to them read it in French. We Skyped with a Grade 6 class in Hawaii, and the students taught us how to count in Japanese. This developed a respect for differences and provided an introduction into other languages. The students also learned how seasons are different around the world.

But most importantly, my students learned about digital citizenship. Yes, this was the outcome I was most surprised about during our year on Skype. Through regular interactions with classes on Skype, my students learned some important lessons, such as listening while others are talking. They learned to respect different languages, to listen to the questions that others have, and how to have a focus for their online interaction. We did not go online without a purpose. The students prepared questions ahead of time, did some research on Google Earth, and used their online time effectively. They took turns, asked respectful questions, and valued others' work.

Linking full day early learning Ontario and British Columbia.

In our classroom, the children are used to providing feedback to others. This was apparent in the Skype calls, too. During each call, students complimented and thanked the group for participating with us. They identified what the class did well, thanked them for their time, and showed appreciation for the work that was presented or discussed. This was not the intended focus, but it was definitely one that developed throughout the year. Students may not conceptually understand how far away a class was situated, but they did understand that they could collaborate and be respectful using the Internet and apps such as Skype. The regular Skype interactions helped develop respectful digital citizens. Skyping in the classroom is about risk-taking — it's about things not always working — but most importantly, it's about being respectful and collaborating with others.

Learn how to extend a conversation on Skype and join in at *http://techieang. edublogs.org/*

Visual Literacy and Skype

Visual literacy involves "reading" pictures, graphics, signs, diagrams, graphs, and maps. For young children, visual literacy generally involves reading pictures, graphics, and signs. Environmental print is often "read" by children long before they arrive in Kindergarten. The "What Can You See?" project encourages conversations and visual literacy through Skype.

Window on the Classroom: Visual Literacy in Angie's Class

This past year, I taught Kindergarten and, in order to broaden the students' world and show them what other teachers and children see in their schoolyards, I began the "What Can You See?" project.

What Can You See?

Social media is filled with weather updates and photos portraying people's current view. In our last cold spell, the focus of tweets, Facebook posts, and blog entries were about the weather. Screen shots of the temperature on The Weather Network, photos of the road conditions, photos of sun streaming off snow banks, and photos of people bundled up to brave the weather conditions filled the screens.

Adults are eager to "see" what others see around the world. What is the weather like in another part of the world right now? What landscapes, food, or flowers do you see? The interest is high and often the topic is shared via social media. For example, one day in my Grade 3 class we were Skyping with a class in Alaska. One student asked, "What do you see in your yard?" The class held up their webcam and showed us the volcano that they view from their schoolyard. Imagine the surprise on my students' faces.

I started pondering this "What do you see in your yard?" question. Throughout the year when my students engaged in Skype calls, they often asked what the participants could see out their windows. They also always asked what the weather was like in their town. I discovered students wanted to see what others see and wanted to learn about the weather in other parts of the world. As I entered Kindergarten I took the essence of these questions and spoke with people in my Personal Learning Network and "What Can You See?" was born.

Our Kindergarten learners created iPhoto books that were printed for rereading. The files described what they could see in our playground throughout the seasons. They were also converted into QuickTime files and shared as video books. The books entitled *We Can See...*, followed a simple pattern, "We can see a..." The patterns of the books stayed the same throughout the year but the photos and observations changed. Printed photos were displayed in the classroom and on our bulletin board in the hallway. We gathered photos and grouped them together and then asked questions. What changes occurred in the milkweed plant? What do we notice about the pond in January versus the photos in September?

We walked the schoolyard with cameras in hand and took photos of the same spots in the different seasons. As a teacher, one of my key learnings was that students did not naturally link the changes in their environment to the changes in seasons. They could talk about seasons. They saw changes in their schoolyard but it took the year for them to consolidate their understanding about the effects of seasons on our pond, plants, and trees. It was an incredible opportunity for our students to look closely and examine their own immediate environment.

I extended this learning opportunity and provided a chance for the students to compare and contrast their schoolyard with others. We posted our video books and asked other schools to send us a book about their schoolyard. I also blogged about the project and tweeted invitations to join us in the "We Can See" project. Doug Peterson (@Dougpete) said on his blog, https://dougpete. wordpress.com/ "The project is simple in its premise but is only limited by the number of participants and the enthusiasm." Many teachers volunteered to participate because they felt it was a simple project that they could jump into.

Some of the colleagues who joined in did so because they felt that they had the confidence and knowledge of how to make a class book. Some educators joined in because they had a connection with me via Twitter. I discovered that once teachers began the project they had many questions that focused on the creating, formatting, and the sharing of the project. The "What Can You See?" project turned into a learning process for teachers too.

I tweeted and discussed options for creating digital books, compressing movies, and sharing links. This is how learning occurs. The educators involved conducted their own teacher professional learning inquiries. They had a focus of creating a book and sharing it with others and they investigated, played, and asked for guidance. This is how we want our students to learn and it is incredible watching teachers engage in the same process.

Jocelyn Schmidt (@MsSchmidt_YR) was the first teacher to engage in this project with our class. She sent a link to her class book/video. Our class was able to read it because it had a simple pattern. We also made many connections because it is a school in our region. Our play yard looked similar; we have a similar format with a parking lot on the side of the yard, soccer fields in the back and basketball nets on our pavement area. The students were fascinated that they had a "box" in their Kindergarten play area. The box was actually a concrete shed that houses outdoor play items. They were fascinated with the box because we did not have a bunker in our yard. I wish I had recorded the excited screams when a truck came to deliver our concrete bunker. The students immediately made connections to Ms. Schmidt's schoolyard.

Skype helps students connect with other students around the world.

After comparing our books, our class engaged in a Skype call. It went as well as can be expected. The questions were very simple, yet they came from the children. We did not lead them; the simple format came from their inquiring minds. We laughed too as we remembered that these are young learners who are very focused on their own thoughts. One of my Junior Kindergarten students stood up to respond to a question and she stated, "I have a new tiara." She was wearing it during the call and I think she wanted the class to be aware of it. What a thrill for her to share her new item with another class of Kindergarten students.

As we improved in our Skype interactions, we developed five or six questions prior to each call. We reviewed the class books several times and ensured our questions matched the information in the books. We used Google Earth to locate the Skype locations. Our students learned about different cultures. In one Skype call we learned that one of the teachers was celebrating Hanukah and she shared her celebrations with us. We connected to the pictures books we had read in class. Later, we Skyped with a class in our school district that had a large number of students who were celebrating Chinese New Year. We were able to see their special outfits and talk about their school parade.

> This project is a great support for Critical Literacy.
>
> ————◆————
>
> The "What Can You See?" project (http://wecanseeprojectsharingspace.blogspot.ca/) is another great activity to develop social imagination. (See **Developing Social Imagination and Self-Regulation**, p. 135.)

Multiple Paths to Literacy

The What Can You See? project also helped my class understand that schools can be the same but sometimes languages are different. We Skyped with a local French Immersion school. Our students listened as the class read the book in both English and in French. We also met a Grade 6 class from Hawaii. The class taught us how to count to five in Japanese. The class asked us questions about snow. They shared their photos of their school and beautiful gardens. The project opened the windows of the world to our young learners.

The project continued to grow and connections were made with classes and educators in British Columbia, Hawaii, Mexico, Switzerland, and Costa Rica, as well as other schools within our own school district. The students learned much more than what was in others' schoolyards. They learned about time zones, climates, cultures, languages, geography, and digital citizenship. The project helped our students to develop the understanding that they are one part of huge world with lots in common but also some differences and we need to respect and cherish each other.

Documenting "What she can see".

Mini-lessons to support visual literacy, critical literacy, and the "What Can You See?" project

The following visual literacy mini-lessons will help children to understand that photographs are taken from different perspectives (critical literacy), depending on what the photographer wants to show.

Critical literacy is a perspective that helps readers, listeners, and viewers to understand that everything is created from a particular perspective or point of view and with a specific purpose, author bias, and audience in mind. Students have to be helped to understand that texts are not neutral.

Visual Literacy Mini-Lesson 1: Look Book

Share with students the *Look Book* by Tana Hoban. This wordless "peek through a hole" picture book is filled with bright, colorful photos of everyday things. Readers first look through a small, die-cut circle on a black page to view a small section of a photo. Based on the colors, textures, and other details, readers then speculate or predict what the full-sized object will be as shown in the photo (e.g., a flower). Readers then turn the page to reveal the complete photo (e.g., a stand full of flowers). Children have a lot of fun predicting what the object is, and the beautiful photographs provide topics for discussion. Children also learn that what you see in pictures depends on what the photographer was trying to show. And in order to be a successful photographer one must consider what exactly you want to show, the details, and therefore how close you need to be and the angle you need to shoot from. (See **Visual Literacy Mini-Lesson 6: Practicing Photography Skills**, p. 148).

The thinking routine that supports Mini-Lesson 1 is called "Zoom In," and is described in the book *Making Thinking Visible* (Ritchhart, Church, and Morrison 2011). The thinking routines "See-Think-Wonder" and "Think-Puzzle-Explore" (See Chapter 10) are both great to use to support inquiry and looking closely. Other thinking routines described in "Making Thinking Visible" include the following:

- What Makes You Say That? A routine that requires interpretation with justification
- Think-Pair-Share: A routine for active reasoning and explanation
- Circle of Viewpoints: A routine for exploring diverse perspectives
- I Used to Think... Now I Think: A routine for reflecting on how and why our thinking has changed
- 3-2-1-Bridge: A routine for activating prior knowledge and making connections

Window on the Classroom: Kas's "Look Closely" Photography/ Art Project

Visual Literacy Mini-Lesson 2: Take Time to Smell the Roses!

By carefully examining the world around us, taking the time to smell the roses, we can see things in a different light. Imagine catching a snowflake as it falls and closely examining its shape, or searching for tiny creatures in the grass to appreciate that there is life everywhere in nature. What happens in the garden while we are busy in our classes? What if we could take some time-lapse photography and see what nature is doing while we are at work? What if we could take photos from a Kindergartener's perspective and invite our families to slow down and appreciate nature as it exists on its own clock — meaning no clock at all! In the manner of Tana Hoban's books (See **Visual Literacy Mini-Lesson 1: Look Book**), children can create frames that reveal only a small section of their own nature photographs to give a tiny "taste" of the photo to invite speculation from viewers before the frame is removed, revealing the entire photograph. Art connections occur in watercolor, sketching, etc. as children are taught how to look closely to draw and paint.

Window on the Classroom: Angie's "Look Closely" Art Project

Visual Literacy Mini-Lesson 3: Observational Paintings

Throughout the year, different provocations are put out at the art and painting centres. Students can choose an object to observe and paint what they see. I encourage them to color-blend and work on their brush strokes after I have modelled strokes and blending, while thinking aloud. The students' observational skills improve greatly with guidance and continued opportunities to create observational paintings throughout the year.

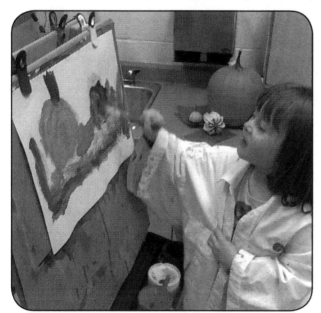

With scaffolding from Angie, great pumpkin observational paintings are created.

Introduce students to making scientific drawings. Items from home, such as onions, celery, and a turnip fresh from the garden, work well. Making scientific drawings requires close examination of objects, looking closely to create detailed and realistic art. Magnifying glasses and real microscopes are often helpful. This makes for a great Art Centre activity. Students should not use color in a scientific drawing.

Check It Out!

Use other great *Looking Closely* books by Frank Serafini (Kids Can Press) to provide opportunities for students to make text-to-text connections:
Looking Closely Along the Shore (2008)
Looking Closely Across the Desert (2008)
Looking Closely Inside the Garden (2008)
Looking Closely Around the Pond (2010)
Looking Closely Inside the Rain Forest (2010)

Modelling how to look closely and encouraging children to do the same often sparks play, discoveries, wonderings, and inquiries — and may even lead to critical literacy. (See Heather's Love Story p. 343). For many examples of "looking closely" experiences, visit *http://kidblog.org/LookingClosely/*

Visual Literacy Mini-Lesson 4: Looking Closely Through the Forest

Share Frank Serafini's beautiful picture book *Looking Closely through the Forest* (Kids Can Press, 2008). As in Tana Hoban's peek through a hole *Look Book*, young readers are instructed to look closely at the detailed photos. As in Hoban's book, readers develop their visual literacy as they are challenged to predict the identity of each close-up photograph. This causes much conversation as the children state their predictions and explain their reasons for making them. The next page reveals the entire photograph of the object that solves the mystery, accompanied by a simple but detailed description of the habitat. Unlike Hoban's book, this is not a wordless picture book. The amazing photos are complimented by rich text and this informational text needs to be revisited numerous times. However, the first time going through the book, just do a picture walk and have the children predict each time what the full photograph is from the small bit initially provided.

The following books can also be used to encourage children to look closely:

- *A Closer Look* by Mary McCarthy (Greenwillow, 2007): McCarthy begins with a close-up image and then pulls back to present a broader view. Readers are asked, "Look! What do you … see?" For example, the first page shows a large black circle against a deep red background, and the illustrations gradually zoom out to reveal a ladybug perched on a leaf. The rest of the book takes the same approach, depicting a colorful flower and then a hummingbird. The artwork is fascinating for children to examine closely, since it consists of handmade papers and collage. Each of the living things is shown from five different perspectives. The children are instructed to "open your eye, open your mind, open your imagination, and LOOK!"

- *Step Gently Out* by Helen Frost and Rick Lieder (Candlewick, 2012): Using stunning close-up photography and short stanzas of poetry, this book invites children to look more closely at the world and "prepare to be amazed." What might you see if you walked very, very quietly and looked ever so carefully at the natural world outside?

Be still, and watch a single blade of grass.

An ant climbs up to look around.

A honeybee flies past.

Fascinating facts about all the creatures shown in the book are also included.

Visual Literacy Mini-Lesson 5: Looking Closely: Focusing to Take a Picture

Window on the Classroom: Kas Focusing on Focusing

Many very young photographers need help in order to understand how to focus a camera, how to decide exactly what they want to appear in the picture, from what perspective or angle they should take the shot, and how close to the subject they should be. Many children (and adults) initially think that taking a good photo requires nothing more than pointing and shooting. In this mini-lesson and the one that follows, teachers should focus on the terms: *pose, subject, focus, zoom in, zoom out,* and *viewfinder.*

■ Begin by providing each student with a paper viewfinder — a small rectangular card with a small square hole to look through, similar to what children experience in *Look Book* (See Visual Literacy Mini-Lesson 1: Look Book, p. 144).

■ Demonstrate how to use the viewfinder by thinking aloud: "I am going to take a picture of Maya. Maya is the *subject* of my picture. I have asked her to *pose.* When I stand here and look through the *viewfinder,* I see all of Maya. But Maya is very far away. Come and take a look. I want to take a picture of her face; I will *focus* on her smile. I will *zoom in* a bit from here. Now I see Maya from her head to her waist. Come and take a look. I will move closer and *zoom in* this way. Great, now I see only her smile. Take one more look. What do you think?"

Visual Literacy Mini-Lesson 6: Practicing Photography Skills

In this mini-lesson, children will apply what they learned about taking photos in the previous lesson.

- Review with students the terms *pose, subject, focus, zoom in, zoom out, tripod* and *viewfinder.* Have the children explain each term.

- Have each child decide on a subject to photograph. Then ask the children to turn and share their idea with a partner.

- Each child decides what part of the subject he or she wants to focus on. Students turn and talk to share their idea with a partner.

- If a person is the subject, the photographer decides how the person will pose.

- Each photographer then decides exactly where to stand to take the photo. They look through their viewfinders to determine if they are in the correct place.

- The children take turns taking photos.

- They then share their photos with each other and talk about the experience.

In the process of taking this photo, the children used the terms pose, subject, focus, zoom in, zoom out and viewfinder.

Spontaneous Picture Taking

Once children understand how to use the camera, encourage them to document subjects of personal importance spontaneously and independently. Be sure to establish with children the responsibilities associated with using the classroom camera:

- The camera must be returned to its proper place right after a student takes a picture (ensure that students know where the camera is kept).

- If there is a camera case, they need to be shown how to open and close it, and should understand that the camera must always be returned to the case before putting it away.

- Some teachers like to use a sign-up sheet. Students have to sign their name when they take the camera, and check off their name when they return it. The sign-up sheet also helps to avoid disagreements about whose turn it is next.

Provide a time for children to share why they took the photo, describing what it shows and the context in which it was taken. Encourage them to use the photographs to make books, create wall stories, and create notes or letters to send to others.

Check It Out!

- *Literacy through Photography Blog* http://literacy throughphotography.wordpress.com/wendy-ewald/

- *I Wanna Take Me a Picture: Teaching Photography and Writing to Children* by Wendy Ewald and Alexander Lightfoot (Beacon Press, 2002)

Documentations of Kas' Kindergarten students' reflections on taking pictures

Tony: "We took pictures and we did some hard work. The first time was very hard, then I got used to it. We learned different ways of taking pictures, like sideways. I like best doing the poses and stuff. To take a picture we have to hold on it for two seconds and then take the picture."

Sari: "We took pictures and Ms. Patsula downloaded them on the SMART board. I learned that I have to put the string around my hand so that the camera would not fall and break. I liked to do the poses. I think the tripod needs to go higher."

Amy: "I took pictures of my friends using the tripod camera, by zooming in and zooming out. I learned how to zoom in and out."

Sam: "I did a pose like this [shows pose]. The tripod is to make the pictures go up or down."

Nikki: "I used the camera to take pictures, and we have to use a timer sometimes, but we have to run back to the spot fast so we can be in the picture. We work in groups — one person sits in the chair, and the other person starts up the camera and then runs to the chair to be in the picture. We learned that we could do different poses. The thing that I like best was starting up the camera and running into the chair. I like using the tripod because of the little rod that you could turn on it that goes up and down."

Documentation is only the first step. Most importantly, what does it tell you about student learning?

Oral Games that Support Visual Literacy

Some fun and worthwhile oral language games that support visual literacy include

- **I Spy.** One player picks an object that is visible and provides clues, such as the object's color, shape, and how it feels (e.g., "I spy something that is blue" or "round" or "soggy"). Other players take turns guessing. The one who correctly identifies the object gets to choose the next object and provide clues.

- **Can You Read My Mind?** One player thinks of an object and gives hints until one of the other players "reads their mind" For example, a player who thinks of cheese might say, "I am thinking of something that is good to eat. It may be orange or white. I keep it in the fridge."

- **Where, Oh Where.** Children have to find an example of a specified color, number, shape, or letter somewhere in the room. For example, the game might start with the question, "Where, oh where, is there something red?" (or "something round" or "the letter A"). The game goes on until all of the examples in the room are found.

Closing Thoughts

This chapter focussed on the "how-to" of making conversations powerful, a very important goal for students. The next chapter highlights the "how-to" of maximizing the effectiveness of home and school read alouds. Most teachers report that they do-read-alouds daily. But how effective is this use of time? Teachers must make the most of this time by using effective read-aloud strategies.

Maximizing the Effectiveness of Read-Alouds

Read-Alouds and Repeated Read-Alouds: What Difference Can They Make?

The vast majority of preschool and elementary teachers read aloud to their students at least once a day. Research indicates that reading aloud *effectively* is important. Therefore, teachers must make the most of this time by using effective read-aloud strategies. Generally, teachers and students tend to find read-aloud time pleasurable. Reading aloud provides the ideal context for conversations and comprehension. Reading aloud to young children *can* (though not necessarily *will*) positively affect the following aspects of children's learning:

- Language and vocabulary development (receptive and expressive): Read-alouds expose children to much richer vocabulary and language than is typically used in everyday speech at home and at school. Children gain word and world knowledge. (See **Inquiry**, Chapters 13–14).

- Understandings of concepts related to print and books

- Understandings of, and appreciation for, quality fiction, non-fiction, and poetry: Children come to understand that narrative writing includes a plot, characters, and a setting. Although there is a sequence — beginning, middle, and some form of resolution or ending — narrative writing involves more than describing a sequence of events. By the time children enter Kindergarten, most have already developed the concept of story (Tompkins 2000). They also are learning that non-fiction includes any text that is factual, and that informational text is a very important type of non-fiction. Informational text has a specific

"Reading makes my brain smarter!" said our son Colin Trehearne, age 5, who remains a passionate reader. Peter Johnston refers to books as "tools for growing minds" (2012, 56).

Books contain many words that children are unlikely to encounter frequently in spoken language. According to the website Reach Out and Read (http://reachoutandread.org/), children's books contain 50 percent more rare words than prime-time television or even college students' conversations.

It is *how* teachers and parents read aloud to young children that makes the big difference. Not all read-aloud sessions are equal!

purpose: to convey information about the natural or social world. Therefore, procedural text, such as how to make a gingerbread house, is non-fiction writing, but it is not informational text.

- Awareness of sounds and enjoyment of language, rhyme, rhythm, and sound (phonological awareness)
- Development of self-regulation and social imagination (See **Developing Comprehension of Story, Social Imagination, and Self-Regulation Using Character-Rich Read-Alouds** p. 184)
- Desire to become strong readers and writers
- Ability to see themselves as readers as they join in on refrains

A picture of engagement... But what are the proven techniques and strategies for effective read-alouds?

One-on-one, small group, whole class read-alouds

According to Tim Shanahan, chair of the National Early Literacy Panel (NELP 2008), read-alouds and shared readings can really enhance a young child's print knowledge and skill in oral language. However, all the research reviewed by the panel focused only on one-on-one or small group situations for shared reading or read-alouds, which took place either at home or at school. "The typical study of reading to kids (whether with teachers or parents) is one-on-one and small group reading, not whole class reading. The results from reading to a whole class of kids might be exactly the same, but it is also possible that attention would be so different that it might not be as potent" (Shanahan 2009). Whole class read-alouds may not consistently have as positive an effect as read-alouds conducted one-on-one or in a small group. Small group read-alouds are ideal for supporting student engagement and conversation.

Proven Techniques and Strategies: The "How-To" of Effective Read-Alouds

Since whole class read-alouds may be at times the only realistic choice, the following *proven* small-group strategies should also be used:

- Carefully selecting read-alouds including fiction, non-fiction, and poetry that span a variety of curriculum content areas. "Developing connections across books (text–text) makes learning more connected and meaningful. … Teachers can extend the read-aloud experience beyond the book itself through activities, discussions, and as a provocation for projects or inquiries" (Lane and Wright 2007, 670). For many examples of this, see Chapters 13 and 14.

- Carefully selecting of vocabulary to teach (See **Text Talk**, p. 156)

- Explicitly teaching the vocabulary and ensuring that students use the vocabulary (See **Text Talk**, p. 156; **Words in Context**, p. 159; and **Other Ways to Encourage Children to Interact with Words Taught**, p. 160)

- Using dialogic or interactive reading aloud, which supports vocabulary and comprehension (See **Dialogic Reading**, p. 169)

- Explicitly teaching concepts about print and books

- Using think-alouds and wondering-alouds (before, during, and after reading) to support comprehension

- Reading a text aloud more than once (repeated read-aloud)

- Focusing on phonological awareness, rhyme, rhythm, and song (See *http://www.isbe.net/earlychi/pdf/trehearne_chapter_2.pdf*).

- Explicitly teaching listening and reading comprehension strategies

> For a superb article on read-alouds, which lists research-based, proven strategies, see "Maximizing the effectiveness of reading aloud" by Holly B. Lane and Tyran L. Wright in *The Reading Teacher*, Vol. 60, No. 7 (April 2007), 668–675.

Explicitly Teaching Listening and Reading Comprehension Strategies

"Students benefit from teacher-directed instruction in comprehension strategies. Most struggling readers (and many not so struggling readers) benefit enormously when we can construct strategy lessons that help to make the comprehension process visible" (Allington 2001, 98). The steps include the following:

- Explaining what the strategy is
- Modelling how to use it
- Describing when to use it

The students then need many opportunities to implement the strategy using both guided and independent practice (I do it, we do it, you do it). Using the strategies will enable the students to make text–self, text–text, and text–world connections.

Which comprehension strategies to teach

Students should be taught the strategies used by good comprehenders by making connections when listening and reading. These include the following:

- * Monitoring comprehension, clarifying: Most importantly, students must learn to be aware when they do not understand when listening or reading. They must then learn to stop and use a fix-up strategy to enable comprehension. A few are listed below:

> **Fix-up Strategies to Support Monitoring or Clarifying Comprehension**
>
> - look back—reread
> - look forward—skip ahead
> - slow down (occasionally, speed up)
> - re-read out loud
> - explain what is understood, so far, to a friend
> - discuss the confusing part with someone
> - visualize
> - ask for help

- Using narrative and expository text structures
- Visually representing text using graphic and semantic organizers

- * Retelling, summarizing, synthesizing, inferring (See **Retelling**, Chapter 9)
- * Generating questions (See **Understanding What a Conversation is Starts with Understanding What a Question is**, p. 117)
- * Answering questions (See **Play On the Page and Off the Page**, p. 165)
- * Using prior knowledge/predicting
- Using mental imagery (visualizing)

*These strategies support the reciprocal teaching technique.

How Often Should K–2 Teachers Read Aloud to Their Students?

More important than the number of read-alouds is how engaging they are, how effectively they are presented, and their value versus other literacy activities. Research indicates that certain read-aloud techniques and strategies, such as Text Talk and dialogic reading, can be effective in developing both vocabulary and comprehension.

Research-Based Key Approaches for Intentionally Teaching Vocabulary

- The words have to be taught directly.
- Students have to be provided with student-friendly definitions (ones that are accurate and understandable).
- Students must use the words and be supported in using the words many times.
- The words are taught in meaningful contexts, most frequently in read-alouds and shared readings that support cross-curricular studies in content areas such as social studies and science.
- Teaching words in categories helps to develop knowledge networks. For example, teaching the words strawberries, bananas, and papayas together helps students develop the generic noun: fruit.
- Students benefit from acting out the words to help them internalize the meanings.

Teaching Vocabulary from Read-Alouds: Text Talk is Proven to Work

Most, but not all vocabulary learned before and during elementary school results from direct explanations of words, not simply by inference (Biemiller 2001).

In their book *Bringing Words to Life* (2002, 2013), Beck, McKeown, and Kucan present a strong, research-based, read-aloud strategy called Text Talk that supports vocabulary development. With this strategy, direct instruction in vocabulary occurs *after* the text has been read and discussed, so there is a strong context in which word-meaning introduction and instruction takes place. The basic steps in Text Talk have been adapted and are listed below.

REVUPS, an adapted Text Talk

REVUPS is an acronym formed from the six steps below. The teacher generally selects three or more vocabulary words to teach from a text. Direct instruction occurs *after* the text has been read aloud and discussed. Students are encouraged to use the words frequently.

R **Step 1: REREAD and REPEAT the word in context:** Find the vocabulary word in the text and reread the sentence aloud. Children repeat the word aloud.

E **Step 2: EXPLAIN the word:** Use a child-friendly definition to explain the word's meaning. For example, "In the story, Leon was embarrassed because he always stood out in a crowd. To be embarrassed means 'to feel uncomfortable, to feel shame, or to be ashamed.'"

V **Step 3: VOCABULARY examples**: Provide further examples of the word used in a sentence. For example, "I would feel embarrassed if I were eating in a restaurant with my family and I knocked my glass of milk all over the floor. I would also feel embarrassed if I hit a baseball and it broke our neighbour's window."

U **Step 4: USE the word.** All children use the word by completing a sentence stem. For example, for the word "embarrassed," the sentence stem might be "I would feel embarrassed if…"

P **Step 5: PARTNERS share examples.** Students share their examples with a partner. Use a turn and talk approach so all students share an example. For example, the teacher might say, "Tell a partner about something that would make you embarrassed. Try to use the word *embarrassed* as you talk to your partner." It is advisable to provide students with a sentence stem (See Step 4). Encourage the children to listen carefully to their partner, as some students will [later] be asked to play "I Remember" (See below).

S **Step 6: SHARE examples with the class.** A few students share their own examples with the class.

Adapted from Beck, McKeown, and Kucan (2002, 50–54).

Other Lesson Suggestions for Teaching Vocabulary

- **Playing "I Remember":** This effective strategy was developed by Jerome Harste. Encourage the children to listen carefully to a read-aloud or conversation, and then ask them to share something they remember from it.

- **Repeating the word at the end of the lesson:** Ask, "What is the word we have been talking about?" Children say the word aloud.

- **"Reading" a picture:** Use a picture from a read-aloud to reinforce the meaning of a word. For example, "Take a look at the picture on page 12. Let's find Leon in the picture. Leon looks embarrassed in the picture. How did the author draw him to look embarrassed?"

- **Acting out the word:** Students use their bodies (facial expression or actions) to demonstrate their understanding of the word. For example, "Think of a time when you were embarrassed. Tell your partner why you were embarrassed. Now show your partner how you looked when you were embarrassed."

- **Using all the words:** "The lesson concludes with a short activity or game in which all the target words from the story are brought together. Each of these activities is initiated with a statement like, 'We've talked about three words (words are specified). Let's think about them some more'" (Beck 2003, 5–6, *http://www.aft.org/pubsreports/ american_educator/spring2003/words.html*). The purpose of this activity is twofold: to help children look for relationships among the words, and to broaden the scope of each word, beyond the read-aloud context.

- **Revisiting all of the words:** Provide opportunities for children to interact on an ongoing basis with the words taught. Frequent encounters with the words are important.

- **Posting the vocabulary words on the wall:** Place the words taught on word cards under the title of the book or a copy of the book's cover. Encourage students to use the words in conversation, and explain that they can put a check mark beside a word each time they use it. (See the examples from Jennifer's and Amber's classrooms in the two Window on the Classroom features below.)

Window on the Classroom: Jennifer's Classroom and Text Talk

I wanted to say how much I enjoyed the professional development day with Miriam Trehearne last Friday. She was so inspiring, and I learned a lot. On Monday, I started the vocabulary activity she explained, and all I can say is WOW!!! On Tuesday morning at 9:03 a.m., I had a lineup of about ten students wanting to tell me a sentence they had used at home when they were interacting with their parents or siblings, and in which they had incorporated one of the vocab words we had worked on the day before. The students were so excited to share their sentences with me and to put a check mark beside the word! One of the vocabulary words already has 15 check marks, and it is only Wednesday! One student even brought in a picture he had drawn of two people having a conversation. In the speech bubbles, he included a sentence that used that vocab word. I am reading Miriam's book now [*Learning to Write and Loving It*], which I bought at the professional development day, and I look forward to incorporating more of her ideas into my teaching. Thank you for such a wonderful professional development day!!!

Jennifer Thomson
Kindergarten Teacher
Vancouver, B.C.

Window on the Classroom: Amber's Classroom and Text Talk

Hi Miriam,

I started the vocabulary words under the copied book covers, and the kids are excited to use the words in their writing. It is wonderful to listen to them discussing different ways to use them in sentences. One of my boys said today, "I don't think moms could ever be extinct (vocab word)" and another wrote, "I collapsed on the stairs. My forehead was exposed."

Amber Bowden
Kindergarten Teacher
Kamloops, B.C.

Notice that student-friendly synonyms are provided for the vocabulary words (e.g., collapse — fall; exposed — uncovered). Don't you love the illustrations that bring the words to life?

Words in Context: An Alternative to Text Talk

Andrew Biemiller and Catherine Boote (2006) have developed an alternative to Text Talk that has been studied and proven to be effective in accelerating vocabulary learning, especially for students with low levels of vocabulary development. The method targets K–2 students, is used as a whole class procedure with read-alouds, and requires 30 minutes a day throughout the school year to get the best results. About 30 books are used during the year, one per week. The method, described below, can also be used as a framework for intervention lessons with a small group.

The vocabulary words chosen from the read-alouds should not be rare, but rather words that children are likely to hear and eventually encounter in elementary school. When the method is used as a whole class activity, some of the words will challenge most students, while other words will challenge only some. When the method is used for intervention with a small group, more differentiation can occur in the choice of vocabulary words. The teaching procedure follows.

Words in Context

- **Day 1:** Read the entire book without interruption and then discuss.

- **Day 2:** Reread the book, teaching about eight vocabulary words. After reading a sentence with a target word, stop and reread the sentence. Then provide a simple definition that fits the context in which the word is used. At the end of the lesson, reread the sentences that contain target words and provide the definitions again.

- **Days 3 and 4:** Reread the story twice, teaching eight new words each time. As on Day 1, reread the sentences and provide the definitions again at the end of the lesson.

- **Day 5:** Review with students all 24 words taught during the week. Provide a new context sentence for each word, but continue to provide the same definition for each word.

Research indicates that using this procedure should result in students learning about 400 out of 720 words taught, or 55 percent (Graves 2009, 44–45).

Other Ways to Encourage Children to Interact with Words Taught

Students become interested and enthusiastic about words when teachers are also interested in them and support students in both understanding the words and using them. The following activities and approaches encourage students to interact with vocabulary words.

Making Choices

In this game-like activity, (Beck 2002, 56–57), the teacher provides some examples and non-examples related to a vocabulary word. For instance, when working with the vocabulary word "intrigue," the teacher might say, "If I say an example of something that might *intrigue* you, say 'intrigue. If the example is something that does not intrigue you, don't say anything." For "intrigue," the teacher might offer the following examples:

- Snow in summer
- A flying saucer
- A peanut butter sandwich
- A new book
- A little dog

Accept any response as long as the child is able to justify the response.

Word Wizard

Word Wizard, (Beck 2013, 16) which is generally used after Text Talk or other vocabulary development activities, encourages children to show off their vocabulary knowledge. Once a child can define three words on the Text Talk wall (See **Teaching Vocabulary from Read-Alouds: Text Talk Is Proven to Work**, p. 156), the child may choose to wear a Word Wizard hat and carry cards on which the three words are printed throughout the school. Adults or other students know to ask the child for definitions of the words.

Freerice.com

Freerice is a non-profit website that supports the **United Nations World Food Programme**. Students develop vocabulary online in a game-like setting while providing rice to hungry people.

http://freerice.com/#/english-vocabulary/1634.

Monitoring Word Learning

How do teachers know if vocabulary instruction is increasing student vocabularies? Teachers use visible learning by talking and listening to students; for example, encouraging students to illustrate a word in context ("Draw me an insect that is *camouflaged*"); encouraging them to act out a situation in which they use the word; listening to students at centres; and sharing retellings. However, a group-administered procedure that can be used to assess words taught has been validated with K–2 students. The procedure, the Two-Questions Vocabulary Assessment shared by Kearns and Beimiller can be used by any teacher, using the words he/she chooses. It is much less time consuming than a one-on-one assessment. For complete details on how this procedure can be replicated, see *http://school.gogpg.com/Portals/1/Assess%20 Well/2010%20Kearns-Biemiller%20Two%20Questions%20 Article.pdf*

> Visible learning also involves listening for learning happening.

Check It Out!

www.dictionary.com: Includes a daily crossword

www.m-w.com: Includes quizzes and games

www.wordsmith.org: Learn a new word every day: A.Word.A.Day

Choosing Vocabulary Words to Teach

Generally, words should be chosen that

- Are necessary for comprehension
- Are useable and interesting to the students; some come from the children
- Can be used across the curriculum; content words like "predict"
- Are related to other vocabulary being taught (e.g., in an inquiry, science, social studies)

Beck (2002) describes three tiers of words from which teachers can choose:

- **Tier 1:** Basic words that are well known and used often (e.g., "house," "milk")
- **Tier 2:** Words used by mature language users in a wide range of contexts (e.g., "jealous," "huge")
- **Tier 3:** Low-frequency words, which are often limited to specific content areas but ultimately give students "word power," (a term coined by Neuman and Roskos 2012) as they move up the grades (e.g., "amphibian," "reptile"). The inquiry approach naturally promotes tier 3 or content area words.

In most classrooms, it is best if teachers focus mainly on tiers 2 and 3. It is also appropriate for students to suggest words.

Words Worth Teaching: Closing the Vocabulary Gap **by Andrew Biemiller (2009)**, differentiates words that most children know by Second Grade; those that 40 percent to 80 percent of children know by the end of Second Grade; those that 40 percent to 80 percent of children know by the end of Sixth Grade; and "difficult" words known by fewer than 40 percent of Sixth Graders.

How many words should a high-school graduate know?

According to Michael Graves (2009), Snow has argued that high school graduates need to know 75,000 words in English (Snow and Kim 2007). The good news, according to Graves, is that English consists of a very small number of frequent words, and an extremely large number of infrequent words. The most frequent word, *the*, accounts for almost 10 percent of the words in a typical text.

The first 100 most frequent words account for almost 50 percent; the first 1,000 account for almost 70 percent; the first 5,000 account for almost 80 percent; the remaining 100,000 plus words account for the remaining 20 percent.

Multiple Paths to Literacy

How Many Words Should Be Taught?

The number of words to teach depends on the needs of the students. Some children need a great deal more instruction in vocabulary. Students living in high-needs communities generally benefit from accelerating their vocabulary knowledge.

Research indicates that teachers can directly teach at least 800 word meanings during each year of K–2 (20 words per week), or 2,400 word meanings in three years (Biemiller 2009). Beck (2002) recommends about 400 words per year from K–2. This amounts to two to three words a day. According to Biemiller (2009), the reality is that teaching many word meanings briefly may prove more helpful than choosing a few word meanings for more detailed instruction. Even with more intensive instruction of fewer words, most students only maintain 25 to 30 percent of words taught (Brabham and Lynch 2002).Thus, generally, the best way to increase students' vocabulary is to *teach more words* (Brabham and Lynch-Brown 2002).

How Much Time is Really Spent Teaching Vocabulary?

Canada: Andy Biemiller's research

"At present, we spend a lot of time teaching (and assessing!) reading mechanics — the skills needed to read words on pages. But we spend almost no time on systematically building vocabulary. Until we do so, we cannot see significant gains in reading *comprehension* for the majority of disadvantaged children — children whose vocabularies are well below average." In fact, Canadian research reported by Biemiller (2000) indicates that vocabulary acquisition in Kindergarten and Grade 1 is little influenced by school experience, based on finding that young First Graders have about the same vocabulary (Peabody Picture Vocabulary Test) as older Kindergarten children. Cantalini reported the same result for Second Grade.

United States: research shared by Susan B. Neuman and Tanya S. Wright

The research findings are very similar to the Canadian research. Limited vocabulary instruction was found across the board. "It's been one of the most resistant-to-change skills in early literacy," Ms. Neuman said. "Generally, children come into school with vocabulary at one point and leave with vocabulary at the same point." Students in poverty — the ones prior research shows enter school knowing 10,000 fewer words than their peers from

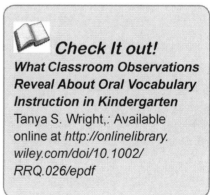

Check It out!
What Classroom Observations Reveal About Oral Vocabulary Instruction in Kindergarten Tanya S. Wright,: Available online at *http://onlinelibrary. wiley.com/doi/10.1002/ RRQ.026/epdf*

higher-income families — were the least likely to get instruction in academically challenging words.[1]

Effective Techniques for Developing Oral Language and Comprehension: Before, During, and After Read-Alouds

Before Reading

Try a picture walk of the book cover(s). A picture walk is one form of "guided looking" (visual literacy) that can be used before a read-aloud or a shared reading to help children access their background knowledge and vocabulary related to a new text, so they can make predictions. A very few new words may also be introduced if they are directly related to the photos/graphics.

Prompts might include the following:

- Tell me about the cover of this book.

- Let's play the game I Already Know. Tell me what you already know about _____. Say, "I already know or think I know _____." Based on student responses the teacher may begin to complete a KWLM organizer especially when dealing with non-fiction text (See KWLM, p. 166). Reviewing a Table of Contents with non-fiction text also supports anticipation and prediction.

- "I think I will learn_____."

- We have read another book about this topic. The title of the book was _____. How do you think the two books are similar? How might they be different?

- The author of this book is _____. Another book we read by this author was _____.

- Tell your partner what you predict will happen in this book. Say, "I predict that _____" or "I think I will learn____."

Consider the following cautions about conducting picture walks:

- Do not drag out a picture walk before reading the text. Doing so may destroy the joy of the read-aloud/shared reading experience as the children wait to get into the book.

- Picture walks can certainly destroy the excitement of the read-aloud if the ending and story line are shared

> Visual literacy generally involves helping readers to read actions, photos, charts, maps, and graphs.

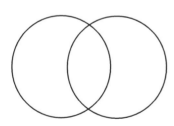

---

1 *Education Week*, May 16 2013, http://www.edweek.org/ew/articles/2013/02/06/20vocabulary_ep.h32.html?intc=es

before the reading. Instead of doing a picture walk for the complete text, why not limit it to the cover(s) and perhaps the first few pages, just to help children get into the text.

Teachers often interrogate their children with too many questions during a picture walk. Instead use just a few prompts that are open-ended, such as "Tell me about the cover of the book," rather than "What do you see on the cover?" or "What is this on the cover?"

During Reading

When reading a story, stopping frequently to discuss the photos or the text will likely cause students to lose track of the story line. It is more effective to stop during a rereading of the story. Discuss photos, graphics, and concepts, teach vocabulary words, and provide opportunities for student use during the rereading. Frequent stopping during the first reading of non-fiction texts is not a problem since there is no story line to disrupt.

After Reading

Play I Remember: I Remember is an open-ended effective strategy developed by Jerome Harste to encourage children to listen carefully to read-alouds and/or conversations and then share something they remember that they heard.

Play "Say Something": "Say Something" is an open-ended effective strategy to get the conversation going. Children may say something to a partner (turn and talk) or to a small or large group.

Play "On the Page-Off the Page": This activity supports listening and reading comprehension. A question is asked by a teacher or a student and the students come to understand that the answer may be in the book (on the page) or off the page (inference), in their heads. This is an important understanding for students to come to terms with.

Use the "I Remember" Strategy (See p. 236)

Use "Dialogic Reading Prompts" to support oral language and comprehension: See **Dialogic Reading**, p. 169.

Create a "Story Innovation" to scaffold oral language, writing, and comprehension: See **Story Innovation**, p. 214.

Use a "Cloze" to scaffold oral language and comprehension (See p. 213).

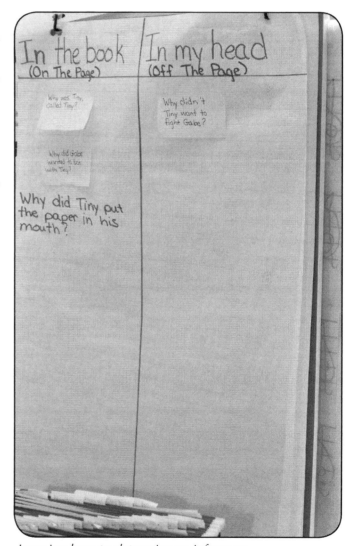

Learning how to determine an inference.

Do "Guided Looking." Beck (2002) suggests using a guided looking approach with Text Talk (See **Teaching Vocabulary from Read-Alouds: Text Talk Is Proven to Work p. 156**). Go back to certain pages, photos, and graphics to discuss. This is a great time to teach vocabulary words in context.

Guided Looking Leads to Guided Responding

It is important that children can take what they learn from guided looking and use this knowledge to support "guided responding" — the teacher guides the children to respond to a text through writing, art, or drama (acting it out).

KWLM

The teacher may choose to complete a KWLM organizer based on student responses (See **KWLM and KWHLAQ, p. 326**).

> **KWLM** chart
>
> **K**: What do we know or think we know about…?
> **W**: What do we want to know about…?
> **L**: What did we learn about…?
> **M**: What more do we want to learn about…?

Teacher Questions and Prompts: Increase Talk and Comprehension

Research reported by John Hattie (2009) indicates that teachers ask 300 to 400 questions per day, and the majority are low-level cognitive questions — 60 percent involve recall (e.g., What was the name of the dog in the story?); 20 percent are procedural (e.g., Where is your pencil?); and only 20 percent require children to think. Closed-ended questions (questions that have only one correct answer, already known and expected by the teacher) make up 82 percent of the questions asked.

Richard Allington (2006) talks about how teachers often interrogate their students, often using low-level questions such as "What is the color of her dress?" rather than encouraging a literate conversation. Unless the teacher is testing student knowledge of color names, there is likely no real benefit to asking this closed-ended question. However, higher order questions such as "Why do you think…?" or a prompt such as "Tell me about this photo" (perhaps followed by a second prompt: "Tell me more") would result in much more student talk. Conversation elicited by open-ended prompts could result in much more useful assessment data for the teacher to consider when planning for the next step in instruction.

Types of questions and prompts

- Open-ended questions elicit extended responses. There is no single right answer, and the question cannot be answered by one word.

- "How" and "why" questions often encourage students to make inferences.

- Factual questions require recall of details directly from the text.

- Inferential questions do not have answers that are directly stated in the text.

- Opinion questions ask for an opinion; there is no single right answer.

- Text–self questions connect the text to the reader's/listener's own experiences — beyond the here and now, extending to the past and into the future.

- Text–text questions connect the text to another book or movie students have read, watched, or listened to.

- Prediction questions require making a prediction; there is no single right answer.

- Authorship questions encourage the reader/listener to think like the author.

- Vocabulary questions encourage the reader/listener to define one or more words.

(Adapted from Shedd and Duke 2008, 25)

Examples of higher order questions to use

- Why do you think…?

- Have you ever…? Explain….

- What does this remind you of?

- What does the author mean by…?

- If you were the author, what would you make happen next?

- What if…?

- How would you end this story?

- What other ending could the story have?

Open-ended questions are invitations to the children to produce ideas. Children will produce more oral language and express their own ideas when adults use open-ended questions or prompts. However, like most things in education, the type of questioning should not be an "either/or" issue. Use lower-level questions to elicit surface-level information, and higher-level questions to elicit deeper information and understanding (Hattie 2009).

Prompts: Tell me about…/Tell me more…
Simple prompts often result in more extended conversations with students, more often than when the teacher is leading using questions. (For a proven, research-based prompting strategy, see **Dialogic Reading**, p. 169).

> **More questions/prompts that encourage talk**
> - Talk to me about what you are thinking.
> - Share with me what you are feeling.
> - How does this make you feel?
> - What does this make you think about?

> "The test of a good teacher is not how many questions he can ask his pupils that they will answer readily, but how many questions he inspires them to ask him which he finds hard to answer." —Alice Wellington Rollins

What About Student-Initiated Questions?

According to John Hattie (2009), analyzing the questions students ask is more important than teacher questioning. Structuring class time that provokes student questions and conversations is powerful. Why do students ask fewer questions as they move up the grades?

> "The best way to find things out … is not to ask questions at all. If you fire off a question, it is like firing off a gun — bang it goes, and everything takes flight and runs for shelter. But if you sit quite still and pretend not to be looking, all the little facts will come and peck round your feet, situations will venture forth from thickets, and intentions will creep out and sun themselves on a stone; and if you are very patient you will see and understand a great deal more than a man with a gun does."
>
> —Elspeth Huxley, from *The Flame Trees of Thika: Memories of an African Childhood*

Repeated Interactive Read-Alouds

Use repeated interactive read-alouds to support comprehension, vocabulary, and analytic discussions. Effective techniques and strategies to use include the following:

- Teaching and using vocabulary words from a read-aloud (See **Teaching Vocabulary from Read-Alouds: Text Talk Is Proven to Work**, p. 156)

- Dialogic reading (See **Dialogic Reading**, p. 169)

- Retelling or dramatizing stories (See **A Retelling, Storytelling, and Dramatizing Centre: Encourage Book-Related Play** p. 222)

- Reading and discussing several books on the same topic

- Reading and discussing several books written by the same author

- Playing with objects related to the concepts or characters (e.g., puppets)
- Visual literacy (reading pictures, graphs, and illustrations)
- Asking open-ended questions
- Analytic talk (e.g., making predictions and/or inferences related to the read-aloud)

Interactive Dialogic Reading: A Research-Based Proven Repeated Read-Aloud Technique

Dialogic reading is an interactive read-aloud technique that has been proven very effective in enhancing early literacy skills, especially in oral language and comprehension. Dialogic reading occurs during the second and subsequent readings of the text. The adult (parent or teacher) prompts the children to talk or dialogue about that book.

CROWD is an acronym formed from the kinds of prompts adults (teachers or parents) pose to the children during dialogic reading to encourage them to talk about the book and, in the process, improve their comprehension and vocabulary:

Canadian and Snow geese with goslings in agricultural field during fall migration.

C ■ **COMPLETION prompt:** Children orally fill in blank at the end of a sentence (oral cloze). *Example:* The geese ate all of the plants in the _____.

R ■ **RECALL prompt:** Adult asks questions or provides prompts that encourage children to remember what happened in the book. *Example:* Tell me what happened on this page. What happened?

O ■ **OPEN-ENDED prompt:** Adult encourages children to tell what is happening in a picture. *Example:* Tell me anything about this photo.

W ■ **"WH" prompt:** Adult uses "wh" questions (questions beginning with "what," "where," "when," "who" and "why") to draw attention to details in the illustrations and to teach new vocabulary. *Example:* In what season do you think the photo was taken? Why do you think so?

D ■ **DISTANCING prompt:** Adult relates pictures and/or words in the book to children's own experiences outside of the book. *Example:* Tell me about any wild birds that you have seen.

A second acronym, **PEER**, covers the four steps in the dialogic read-aloud technique. Here is an example that goes with the accompanying photo:

■ **PROMPT:** Adult uses one of the types of prompts from CROWD. *Examples:* "Let's look at this picture. What is Lexus doing?" (question using a "wh" prompt); "Tell me about this picture" (open-ended prompt).

■ **EVALUATE:** Adult evaluates the child's response. *Example:* Adult evaluates the response "Climbing" to the question, "What is Lexus doing?" and determines how the response could be expanded.

■ **EXPANDS:** Adult expands the child's response. *Example:* "Yes, Lexus is climbing a tree and hanging upside down."

■ **REPEATS:** Adult repeats the prompt and asks the child for an expanded response. *Example:* "So what is Lexus doing?" Child responds with "Lexus is climbing a tree and hanging upside down."

See above for an example of dialogic reading in action, using documentation in the form of this photo brought to school and used as part of a wall story.

Using Classroom Read-Alouds to Promote Conversations at Home

It is not uncommon for parents to ask their children, "What did you do at school today?" Frequently, the response is "nothing." Using "story bits" provides the impetus to get the conversation going. Cheryl M. Sigmon[2] describes a story bit as a little object or small memento, a reminder of a story that has been read to or by the child. The story bit is usually attached to a note that is sent home. Alternatively, it might simply be an illustration created by the child on the note. For example, for the wonderful book *Hey, Little Ant* by Philip and Hannah Hoose (1998), a story bit might be a very small plastic ant or an ant sketched by the child. A red piece of paper or a sketch of a boy or girl with red hair makes a great story bit for Robert Munsch's *Seeing Red* (2013). Why not let children decide on their own story bit?

To make the most of Story Bits:

- Send home a note to parents explaining what a story bit is, its value, and how to make the story bit experience most beneficial for their children (See sample letter below). Better yet, model and debrief the experience with parents at a literacy evening for parents.

- Send a story bit home at least once a week, preferably always on the same day so that parents anticipate its arrival.

- Model the experience by role-playing in front of the class a story bit conversation between a student and an adult.

- Encourage children to role-play with a partner a conversation based on their story bit before they take it home. Listen carefully and document a few of the conversations (visible learning). Are the children extending the conversations?

The many advantages of Story Bits include promoting

- Conversations week after week
- Student retellings
- Opportunities for teachers to share with parents the "how-to" of effective conversations
- A warm and special time for children and parents to talk about books

 Check It Out!

For hundreds of Story Bit ideas by Cheryl M. Sigmon, see:

http://www.teachers.net/4blocks/article34.html

http://www.teachers.net/4blocks/article33.html

🏠⇄🏫 Dear Parents,

Today your child is bringing home a "Story Bit" — a little object or small memento that serves as a reminder of a story that has been read to or by your child in class. Please consider using the story bit to begin a conversation with your child about the book. Conversations are key to your child's oral language and vocabulary development. For your child to benefit the most from this conversation, it is recommended that you begin the discussion by saying, "Tell me about the book." To encourage your child to continue the conversation, say, "Tell me more." Make sure that your child is doing most of the talking.

Enjoy this special time for you and your child to discuss the book.

Look for more Story Bits coming soon.

---

2   http://www.teachers.net/4blocks/article34.html

🏠⇄🏫 Strive for Five: Have Effective Conversations with Your Children

Dear Parents,

Parents can make a huge difference to their children's literacy development in just a few minutes a day. Parents frequently hear about the importance of reading to their children. Children learn a great deal from being read to and reading themselves. However, conversation between the children and the parents really improves children's oral language, including vocabulary and comprehension. Most importantly, let the children lead the conversation. Extend the conversation with a simple prompt such as, "Tell me about this, tell me more!" Research indicates that prompts work much better than questions, especially those questions that have a single right answer, such as "What is the name of the girl in the story?" or questions that can be answered "yes" or "no," which often end the conversation. Open-ended questions with many possible responses work much better.

Conversations also help to create a warm and caring home environment. Such conversations can be brief and can take just a minute or two at a time. Extend conversations started by the child. Dr. David Dickinson's research indicates that mini-conversations will do the trick. He calls the encounters "Strive for Five." This involves just five brief back and forth exchanges between the child and the parent, teacher or another adult. What is important is to truly listen to the child and acknowledge what he or she has said with a comment or question. Children know when the adult is not really listening. Eye contact is important. The children have to feel that what they have to say is valued by the parent. Waiting for the child to gather his/her thoughts and respond is crucial.

Nothing is more important to children than having a special family member to share their thoughts with, to celebrate what is going well and to help them problem solve. Parents should take the time to really listen to and talk with their children. Adult–child conversations are key to oral language development, the foundation of literacy learning.

Sincerely,

⌂⇄🏫 Parents Who Make a Big Difference

Dear Parents,

Oral language, what children understand when listening and how effectively they can express themselves in the primary grades strongly predicts how well they will do in reading, listening, and writing, right into high school.

Parents can make a huge difference to their children's language development. Research indicates that certain ways parents interact with their children are key. Overall, the most effective parent interactions revealed parents who use the following strategies:

- "Just talked" a great deal to their children. They generally used a wide range of vocabulary.

- "Tried to be nice." They used high rates of approval and encouragement (e.g., *I like the way you...*) and few prohibitions (e.g., *Stop! Don't!*).

- "Told children about things." They provided a great deal of information about the world. They also talked to the children about word meanings.

- "Gave children choices" rather than simply ordering them or making demands.

- "Listened" and responded to what the children said.

In the end, spending as much time as you can really listening to your children, talking with your children, and encouraging your children will make a huge difference that will pay off throughout their school careers and for the rest of their lives. The time you spend with your children and how you spend that time is crucial.

Sincerely,

Having a conversation with dad!

More High-Yield Strategies and Instructional Techniques to Scaffold Oral Language and Comprehension

For additional crucial strategies and techniques to scaffold oral language and literacy learning in general, see the chapters listed below

- Chapter 1: **Effective Teachers, Effective Schools: When it Comes to Teaching, One Size Does Not Fit All.**
- Chapter 4: **Oral Language**
- Chapter 5: **Making Conversations Powerful**
- Chapter 7: **Play, Self-Regulation and Literacy Learning K–2: How Teachers Make It Work**
- Chapter 10: **Key Centres that Support Literacy, Inquiry and Play**
- Chapter 11: **Learning to Write, Writing to Learn**
- Chapter 12: **Assessment, Documentation and Scaffolding of Writing**
- Chapter 13: **Inquiry-Based Learning: What We Really Know…**

Closing Thoughts

The development of oral language is a most critical component of any Kindergarten–Grade 2 program. Teachers also need to consider the important role that parents play in supporting students' language development. Parents have already helped their children learn to communicate in the home environment, before coming to school. Teachers can further enhance students' language by providing parents with easy activities that they can use daily to extend this knowledge at home. The activities are typically done "on the run". Many suggestions for effectively developing oral language at home and at school are provided in this book. Chapters 7 – 10 bring oral language and comprehension to life through play, self-regulation, and literacy learning in the K–2 classroom.

Play, Self-Regulation, and Literacy Learning K–2

How Teachers Make It Work

This chapter defines key terms and explores how play, literacy, and self-regulation can effectively support one another. However, this work can be challenging. For example, how does one define play? Is play-based learning the same as learning through play? What does play-based learning really mean anyway? Classroom examples will reveal how learning through play, self-regulation, and literacy learning can effectively support one another.

It is true that young children play and discover many things on their own. It is also true that children need adult scaffolding, assistance, and guidance. "We will not have done our best for young children if we deny them the path to learning they seek through play, but we also will not have done our best if we fail to provide instruction" (Schickedanz 1994,46; Leong and Bodrova 2012).

> There is a consensus that play is difficult to define. And, it is not the only context for children's learning (Whitebread 2012). That is, playing generally involves learning but not all learning is play-based. Moreover, it is important to acknowledge that not all play is equally effective in terms of learning.

What is Play?

There is no common definition of play (Saracho and Spodek 2006). The best one can do is to describe the functions and effects of play.

This definition from the York Region District School Board (with thanks to Beatte Planche and Denese Belchetz) provides the gist of play using these keywords: playful, engaging, planned, purposeful. Planned and purposeful indicate a clear role for the teacher/early literacy team.

Play-Based Learning

*Playful and engaging while being very well **planned** and **purposeful**. Planning begins with knowing each young learner to allow us to respond with purposeful assessment and instruction which is differentiated as needed."*

- YRDSB, February 2010

Check It Out!

Exploring Play, Spotlight on Young Children, NAEYC 2015

> **Not *all* play is equal and not *all* learning is play-based.**

> Quality play experiences are likely to support well-developed memory skills, language development and self-regulation. This often leads to enhanced school adjustment and improved academic learning (Bodrova and Leong 2005).

> Play helps children practice self-regulation because good players play according to the roles and rules of pretend; they must behave in a way that conforms to the play (Neuman and Roskos 2007).

The Functions and Effects of Play

Play is serious business for children. It performs many functions and has many effects on child development. Some of these include the following:

- Creating
- Sharing
- Planning
- Having fun
- Taking perspectives and understanding other points of view
- Developing empathy
- Developing concentration, impulse control, self-regulation, and problem solving
- Developing social imagination and self-confidence
- Exploring, self-discovery, using one's imagination (imagining)
- Pretending
- Socializing, developing social skills and co-operation
- Building relationships
- Scaffolding early literacy/mathematics/cross-curricular skills
- Enhancing brain and motor development, higher order thinking, language development
- Expressing personal thoughts and feelings
- Making choices
- Inquiring and developing curiosity
- Problem-solving
- Risk-taking
- Making sense of the world
- Developing music, art, physical, fine and gross motor development
- Learning

(Adapted from *What is Play? Playing is Learning,* Elementary Teachers' Federation of Ontario 2012.)

What Research Tells Us about Play, Play-Based Learning and Early Learning

It is evident from watching and listening to children at play that childhood play often results in some degree of learning. Most researchers seem to agree that including play in the early childhood curriculum is a necessary condition for ensuring optimal growth and development in young children (Bodrova and Leong 2010). But it is important to note that not all learning happens through play. Too many teachers across North America feel pressured to make all learning play-based. The research does not support this. Rather than stressing play-based learning to the extreme, educators are better off to acknowledge that much learning occurs through play but not all learning is play-based.

"Play is real work; the thinking and language that occur during play represent authentic learning as children confront problems, construct realities, and communicate concerns and ideas through talking, writing and taking part in the arts" (David Booth in Burke 2010, 7). John Hattie's meta-analyses indicate that the effect size on learning for play is 0.50. To make sense of this number, is it important to know that "The effect size (ES) of 0.40 sets a level where the effects of the innovation enhance achievement in such a way that we can notice real-world differences, and this should be a benchmark of such real-world change" (Hattie 2009, 19). Therefore incorporating play into the curriculum results in some positive difference(s) to learning. But play alone is clearly only one piece of the puzzle, one route to positive outcomes. For example, the ES for teaching strategies is 0.60; for vocabulary programs, 0.67; for reciprocal teaching, 0.74; for phonics instruction, 0.60; for repeated reading, 0.67. The how of play-based learning or learning through play is also key.

Research has not indicated any one best approach to scaffolding play. "Effective teachers use a variety of approaches that combine elements of educator-guided and child-directed activity" (Full Day Kindergarten Program Guide British Columbia 2010, 13). There is also room and a need for both child-initiated play and teacher-initiated play. "It is NOT that 'anything goes' or is so structured by adults that the children get no opportunity for creative input" (Diamond 2009, 77). The role of adults in supporting children's play is complex. This area would benefit from further research (Whitbread, 2012).

Learning through Play

"You can discover more about a person in an hour of play than in a year of conversation." —Plato

Play is a window into visible learning. "In play, children represent and transform the world around them, providing other children and adults with a window into their thoughts and perceptions, and often helping adults to see the world in new ways" (BC Early Learning Framework 2008).

John Hattie ranked influences related to learning outcomes from very positive effects to very negative effects on student achievement. Hattie found that the average effect size of all the interventions he studied was 0.40. That means about half the students in any class get the effect of 0.40 or greater while half get less than 0.40. Therefore he decided to judge the success of influences relative to this "hinge point" (0.40), in order to find an answer to the question **"What works best in education?" An effect size (ES) of 0.40 indicates factors that resulted in simply average student success.**

Child-Guided Experience + Adult-Guided Experience = Optimal Learning (Epstein 2014).

> The role of the educator during play is twofold: Observer and Active Participant.

> "When we join children in their world of play, we unlock the door to their inner lives and meet them heart to heart" (Cohen 2008, 40).

According to researchers Hirsh-Pasek and Michnick Golinkoff (2003), the level of children's play rises when adults play with them. The variety of play children engage in also increases when adults join in. The joining in is different than controlling. Controlling makes children follow the adult's agenda and does not lead to as much cognitive development as when adults follow the children's lead.

Adult scaffolding is so important. "Nowadays young children spend less time playing with their peers and more time playing alone, graduating from educational toys to video and computer games" (Bodrova and Leong 2004, 4). For many young children, school is the only place where they will have the opportunity to learn how to play. However, parents and caregivers must be guided to understand the importance of play, what it looks like, and how to scaffold play at home. It is becoming increasingly clear that without adult support, scaffolding purposeful play, the play of many children will remain immature, never destined to become fully developed (Leong and Bodrova 2012).

Important Understandings for Parents and Caregivers

Parents often underestimate the importance of play and playing with children of all ages. Some feel that play is a waste of time. It is crucial that teachers attempt to change this mindset and advocate more playfulness at home and at school. Learning through play and intentional teaching are not mutually exclusive. "Research on early learning and development shows that when children are properly supported in their play, the play does not take away from learning but contributes to it" (Bodrova and Leong 2003).

 **Linking Literacy and Play**

Dear Parents,

It is important that we encourage young children to play. When children are playing with others, they are often developing vocabulary (as they talk and listen), curiosity, imagination, self-regulation, and often specific literacy and numeracy skills and understandings. However, parent support for play is crucial.

- Encourage your children to play with others. Although computers are fun and beneficial, nothing replaces playing with someone.

- Talk to your children about their play. Have them describe and even plan their play before they begin (What are you going to play? What are you going to play with? e.g., props). Also, talk about their play after they are done. What happened? Was it fun? Why or why not?

- Encourage your children to extend their play scenario over several days.

- Provide your children with multi-purpose props to stir their imaginations. A paper plate for example might be used as a Frisbee, a space ship or a hat. Play dough is also great. Of course, dress-up clothes help to improve "acting."

- Pencils, paper, magazines, and books are useful realistic props that encourage "writing" and drawing of grocery lists, a menu for a restaurant, and making appointments when pretending to run a dentist's, doctor's, or veterinarian's office.

- Encourage your child to play out a scene from a book you have just shared. Alternatively, young children often prefer to make up their own story about the character(s) and act it out.

Young children develop literacy by using their imaginations as they role-play with others. Help your child by providing props and talking with him or her about the play experience. You might even enjoy occasionally being part of the role-play yourself!

Sincerely,

Current Ongoing Research

Higher quality early childhood programs have been shown to enhance children's development and have long-lasting effects on adult productivity and social participation. In contrast, the absence of such programs predicts poor developmental progress over time.

E4Kids is a 5-year study that is following a large group of three and four year olds who participated in childcare, Kindergarten, and preschool programs. The children are now being tracked and the programs they attend through to the early years of school are being analyzed to determine what makes effective, quality programs.

http://education.unimelb.edu.au/news_and_activities/projects/E4Kids

Moving from Immature Play to Mature Play

It is important for teachers, caregivers, and parents to understand how to spot the differences between mature and immature play and how to help children move from immature play to mature play.

Check It Out!

Great play articles, stressing mature play, available on the web:

Assessing and Scaffolding Make-Believe Play, Bodrova and Leong (2012)
http://www.naeyc.org/files/yc/file/201201/Leong_Make_Believe_Play_Jan2012.pdf

Curriculum and Play in Early Childhood Development, Bodrova and Leong (2010)
http://www.enfant-encyclopedie.com/pages/PDF/Bodrova-LeongANGxp.pdf

Chopsticks and Counting Chips, Bodrova and Leong (2003)
http://www.naeyc.org/files/yc/file/200305/Chopsticks_Bodrova.pdf

The Importance of Being Playful, Bodrova and Leong (2003)
http://www.ascd.org/publications/educational-leadership/apr03/vol60/num07/The-Importance-of-Being-Playful.aspx and

Playing is Learning (ETFO)
http://www.etfo.ca/Resources/ForTeachers/Documents/Playing%20is%20Learning.pdf

PROPS

Immature Play

Immature play is most evident in toddlers, preschool, and Kindergarten children. Characteristics of immature play in children include:

- Repeating the same play actions over and over, day after day, such as washing the dishes or feeding the baby
- Using realistic props but being unable to use their imaginations to use props symbolically during play (e.g., paper plate as a steering wheel)
- Taking on the same stereotypical play roles day after day (e.g., firefighter)
- Engaging in parallel play (they play next to each other, not with each other)
- Arguing and fighting over props and roles
- Rarely sustaining play for longer than 10–15 minutes before moving on to another activity
- Rarely able to describe their play in any detail before beginning

Mature Play: Teacher (and Parent or Caregiver) Scaffolding is the Key

More creative, imaginative, and sophisticated or mature play should be happening in preschool, Kindergarten and the primary grades. Research with preschool and Kindergarten teachers (Bodrova and Leong, 2001) found that they achieved the best results when they focused on supporting mature play. The children in these classrooms not only mastered literacy skills and concepts at a higher rate, they also developed better language and social skills (Bodrova and Leong 2004).

Research indicates that mature play supports oral language (conversation), imagination, creativity, and improved self-regulation. It demonstrates the following characteristics:

- Children are able to imagine and use open-ended props symbolically (e.g., paper plate as a steering wheel). Teachers scaffold by providing many multipurpose open-ended props (often made of natural materials) that can stand for different objects and provide the students with opportunities to discuss which props will be needed and how they will be created and used. Open-ended props are often more beneficial than educational toys! Not all materials have to be open-ended, however. Some realistic props may also be useful. Literacy materials such as pencils, crayons, computers, tablets, and books can support both play and literacy.

■ Play is not limited to stereotypical roles. For example, roles in a hospital are not limited to doctor and patient but may also include dietitian, ambulance driver, and laboratory technician. Teachers scaffold by having discussions after going on field trips (e.g., hospital), watching a video, or reading a book and joining in the play.

ROLES

■ Flexible themes as determined by the children are included. For example, the doctor goes to the dry cleaners to pick up her lab coat. Teachers scaffold by encouraging the children to make up stories related to the play and to create play plans.

FLEXIBLE PLAY THEMES OR SCENARIOS

■ Children plan their play ahead of time and debrief after the play. They have fewer arguments and disputes. Self-regulation is improved. Teachers scaffold by providing provocations in the form of read-alouds, videos, and field trips. They also encourage written play plans and discussions of roles and props. When using videos and field trips, teachers encourage students to focus on the roles of the characters.

PLAY PLANS

■ Children extend their play over long blocks of time (at least an hour daily including play planning and debriefing) and even over several days. Teachers scaffold by reviewing the previous day's play plan and encouraging the children to extend the play rather than starting new play each day. Teachers may also join in the play.

EXTENDING THE PLAY

Scaffolding Mature Play, Oral Language, and Self-Regulation

Defining Self-Regulation: Differing Viewpoints

"**Self-regulation** is a deep, internal mechanism dependent on cognitive skills or executive functions (EF) that underlie mindful, intentional, and thoughtful behaviours of children. It is the capacity to control one's impulses both to stop doing something (even if one wants to continue doing it) and to start doing something (even if one doesn't want to do it). Self-regulated children can delay gratification and suppress their impulses long enough to think ahead to the possible consequences of their action, or to consider alternative actions that would be more appropriate" (Bodrova and Leong 2005, 32). "Self-regulated learning is a process that assists students in managing their thoughts, behaviours, and emotions in order to successfully navigate their learning experiences" (Zumbrunn 2011, 4). "This ability to both inhibit and enact specific responses is a skill used not just in social interactions but also in thinking. In fact, research indicates that these two facets of self-regulation are related. Children who cannot control their emotions at age four are likely not to be able to follow the teacher's directions at age six and will not become reflective learners in middle and high school (Bodrova and Leong 2005, 32)". "Across a range of studies, the emotional, social, and behavioural competence of young children — such as higher levels of self-control and lower levels of acting out — predict their academic performance in first grade, over and above their cognitive skills and family backgrounds" (Raver and Knitzer 2002, 3).

According to Stuart Shanker, self-regulation is how a child deals with stress and recovers.

The five stress areas defined by Shanker (2013) are: 1) the biological domain, the level of energy 2) the emotional domain, feelings and moods 3) the cognitive domain, memory, attention, problem solving 4) the social domain, the capacity to understand social situations and function optimally in them 5) the prosocial domain, the development of empathy and values involving the stress of putting someone else's interests ahead of your own. These stressors, according to Shanker affect the five senses: sound, sight, touch, smell, and taste.

Research shows that 5 year olds today are behind in EFs (executive functions) compared with 5 year olds of a couple of generations ago (Diamond 2009). See http://www.excellence-earlychildhood.ca/documents/diamond_2009-11ang.pdf

Scaffolding Self-Regulation

Many books and articles have been written about self-regulation. In the end, a number of key factors support student self-regulation. These include teachers:

- Creating a warm and caring low-stress classroom culture where children want to come to school. Examine how a change in teaching philosophy can help awaken the passion for learning in students (Scott and Marzano 2014). This requires creating an environment in which it is okay "not to know," where errors are welcome. Reduce stress! The Person-Centred Approach facilitates this by helping students to feel free from threat, both physically and psychologically. This environment can be achieved in a relationship with a teacher who is deeply understanding (empathic), accepting (having unconditional positive regard), and genuine (congruent). The teacher demonstrates that he/she really cares for the student, empathizes, "sees their perspective and communicates it back to the student so that he/she has valuable feedback to self-assess." This results in fewer resistant behaviours and higher achievement (Hattie 2009, 119). For a strong example of this low-stress environment, see **Window on the Classroom: Jane's Story,** p. 109.

- Talking to students and extending conversations. This approach relies on the personal qualities of the teacher to build a non-judgemental and empathic relationship.

- Helping students to develop social imagination (Johnston 2012) and empathy. Empathy is the ability to understand and share the feelings and/or perspective of another. Developing social imagination is key to developing positive social skills and empathy, problem solving, self-regulation and comprehension. According to Johnston, it is what makes relationships work or not, which is the foundation of our society! Carefully chosen stories and fairy tales with strong characters will help support social imagination. Learn how to promote kindness in the classroom and understand the power of stories in engaging students (Scott and Marzano 2014).

> Self-regulation skills and early literacy learning help to develop the whole child. "By focusing on self-regulation as one aspect of high-quality early childhood and early elementary education, it is likely that socioeconomic disparities in achievement can be substantially reduced" (Blair, Protzko, and Ursache 2011, 31).

- Promoting discussion around critical literacy issues (e.g., perspective as found in *Jack and the Beanstalk*; see **Critical Literacy**, Chapter 14).

Developing Comprehension of Story, Social Imagination, and Self-Regulation Using Character-Rich Read-Alouds

It is through characters, real and imagined, that readers, listeners, and viewers become engaged, comprehend the story, and develop social imagination and self-regulation. Characters bring the plot (fiction, biography, autobiography) to life. As children truly learn to *read characters*, they come to understand themselves, their classmates, and others from different perspectives. Encourage students to talk about

- Character Traits
- Character Feelings
- Character Motives (what they want)
- Character Relationships
- Character Change

These discussions are a great way to get the children to connect with the character(s) and revisit and use important vocabulary! Finally, encourage the children to share and celebrate characters.

Celebrate characters by creating and sharing character mobiles

- Model how to make a character mobile. In the middle draw and label the character. Then draw and label four things that you know about the character. Next, cut and string each part and hang it up.
- Then have the children create their own character mobiles. Children may need help stringing the parts together. This is a great activity to do with older buddies. Children should have an opportunity to share their mobiles.

Through teacher scaffolding and the emotional connection to characters, young children develop empathy and compassion. "Feelings are an important facet of character. When students recognize a character's feelings and the changes that occur in those feelings over time, they gain insight into the very nature of the character's struggles" (Keehn et al. in Roser and Martinez 2005, 98). As they make connections, they begin to understand that they are not alone in feeling the way they do. *Franklin's Bad Day* by Paulette Bourgeois and Brenda Clark is a great read-aloud

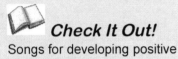

Check It Out!
Songs for developing positive character traits: http://www. songsforteaching.com/ charactereducationsongs.htm

that helps children sort through their feelings and learn about self-regulation.

Through classroom discussions, writing, art, and drama, students may also learn how to cope with problems and how to generate constructive solutions. They gain more control or power over their own lives, more self-regulation. Children's literature can be an effective non-threatening way to deal with social issues and self-regulation, and to improve the classroom, school, or community environment. Of course, emotion vocabulary and character trait vocabulary need to be intentionally taught.

"Without an emotional attachment to learning, lasting learning simply doesn't happen" (Graves 1999, 116).

"There is no link between curricula with a systematic and explicit focus (i.e., teacher-directed) and negative social-emotional outcomes for children. I should add, on the contrary focused teaching supports self-regulation" (Shanahan and Lonigan 2013).

Additional Ways to Scaffold Self-Regulation

- Scaffolding student engagement by using books and activities that are just-right and motivating: Provide "managed choice" (Allington). Use activities students can do and want to do. Motivation is key!

- Using focused teaching when teaching strategies and introducing activities; use the gradual release of responsibility model: explain, model, guided practice, and independent practice.

- Helping students both to know the strategies (metacognition) and independently use the strategies.

- Providing effective specific feedback: choice words.

- Praising the efforts and not the person.

- Knowing where students are going and having a clear plan as to how they will get there.

- Helping students to know what they are striving for too!

- Helping students to see activities as purposeful.

- Helping students to "self"-assess.

- Encouraging independent and partner problem-solving.

- Holding class meetings daily to build community and problem solve; encourage student voice and choice for all.

Classroom Rules
Take care of ourselves
Take care of each other
Take care of this place

Beginning with big ideas or life rules works well. As the rules are introduced, brainstorm with the children and create shared writing, providing examples: We take care of ourselves by… We take care of each other by… We take care of the world or this place by… Children may choose to initial their suggestion(s). Add to the chart when appropriate.

- Helping students to understand how to have a conversation.
- Adopting few rules but ensuring that the students are involved in setting them and enforcing them.
- Ensuring structure and routines are in place daily.
- Displaying student work proudly and using it meaningfully (See **Documentation**, Chapter 9).
- Minimizing activities or feedback that results in competition and comparison.
- Encouraging some games that require students to follow directions and take turns such as a barrier game (See p. 203), Simon says, and any games with rules.

- Teaching students how to give feedback and respond after a game, both as a winner and a loser. In Jane's class, she teaches the children how to respond through role-play. "We role play what we could say to the game 'winner,' and I do like them to acknowledge them as such. A friendly 'congratulations, you won the game,' 'I guess you're the winner!' while shaking the winner's hand is an important initiative they learn. The winner's response should include a positive affirmation also. A cheerful enough 'It was fun to play with you,' 'maybe next time you will win,' 'it was a good game,' 'thanks for playing' are all appropriate. It helps to bring some element of humour into these role-plays. They just love it when I play the poor sport, pretending to cry or stomp on the ground because my friend won. They, of course, do not like to see themselves in my enactments!"

- Scaffolding a growth mind-set by helping the students to develop an understanding of what the brain is and what it does for you; how to take care of the brain and help it to grow; the importance of conversations and reading to brain development. The more you have to work to succeed, the more the brain develops.

Sharing *Pete the Cat* books is a good way to help students develop a growth mind-set and grit. A growth mindset means believing in oneself (for example, believing that one can develop the literacy skills essential for life-long learning). Grit can be defined as persistence, resilience, and stamina. No matter what challenges Pete encounters, he understands that maintaining grit and self-regulation is key. Pete encourages others not to give up in the face of adversity. He continually repeats the refrain, "It's all good!" Pete really learns to take charge of his self-regulation in the book *Pete the Cat and His Magic Sunglasses*.

Pete the Cat in Kindergarten

Pete the Cat is a loveable story character created by the musician, James Dean and Eric Litwin. I discovered Pete the Cat and I fell hard for him. He is a fun dude who goes a' strolling down the street wearing his brand new white or school shoes that he loves. The stories mix music raps with the words, and we love to sing a good story. Listen here to some of "Rocking In My School Shoes": http:teachertube.com/viewVideo.php?video_id=259640

The question becomes why do I love him so? The colour book simply identifies different colours as Pete steps in different things with his white shoes. But this doesn't seem to affect Pete's festive mood—no matter what colour his shoes acquire, Pete keeps on movin' and grooving; and singing along his funky song...and it's all good. In his fourth picture book, Pete the Cat loves (and sings about) the buttons on his yellow shirt, but when they op off one by one, he doesn't panic. The story subject matter is pre-kindergarten at best, identifying colours, moving through different locations in a school, or introducing math concepts. The authors missed the opportunity to do colour blending for Pete's sake!!! However it is Pete's demeanor that caused me, and my students, to fall in love

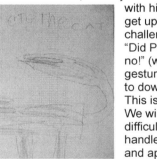

with him. Pete does not get upset at things that challenge him in his day: "Did Pete cry? Goodness, no!" (we even use a hand gesture waving it from up to down when saying this). This is the most attractive part of the book! We will encounter challenges and difficulties in our daily lives and we need to handle them with maturity, responsibility and aplomb. This is the lesson Pete offers children of every age. In kindergarten we are trying to accept responsibility for our actions. Should we make a bad choice, we learn that far more good comes from taking responsibility for our actions than trying to hide our mistake. When showing off what we know to Mrs. Patsula (that is what we call our testing), we overhear or see that other children may know more, less or different things than us. The message in school, as in the Pete books, is "It's all good."

As our inquiry takes us deeper, we will be focusing on our different gifts and talents that we bring to the classroom environment and celebrating our differences as well as our similarities. And at the end of the day, the message continues to be, "It's all good" as indeed, it is! Readers who need a reminder not to sweat the small stuff will find a model of unflappability in Pete to guide their daily interactions. Come join in the Pete love affair.

With thanks to Kas Patsula

Help the children to notice the different roles in a field trip, not just the items or objects. This will enrich their play.

The more elaborate the play scenarios, the more time is needed for planning. This time is invaluable (See **Window on the Classroom: Play Plans: Why I am Hooked!**).

A play plan is a way for children to incubate ideas.

The book begins with Pete being grumpy but his mood quickly becomes more positive when he puts on a pair of magic sunglasses. However, after the sunglasses break and his good mood is still maintained, Pete learns that *he* controls his mood, his self-regulation and not the pair of magic sunglasses.

- Identifying and removing stimuli (stressors) that may cause distractions and confusion (classroom organization).

- Helping students to understand what it feels like to be calm and what it feels like to be stressed.

- Helping students to understand what they might do to help themselves calm down.

- Providing lots of time for extended reading and writing (Allington 2002, 2006) talk and play.

- Using play plans.

Scaffolding Self-Regulation Using Play Plans

When children work together to plan their play, they incubate their ideas. They have to decide on roles, props, and scenarios. To make these decisions together, they have to discuss their impending play, come to some agreement, and get the props ready by gathering or making them. They then work together to sketch the plan, which includes the roles, props, and scenarios. A great play plan prompt is "What will you need for the play?" The plan results in clearly defined rules and roles. In a restaurant centre, for example, the customer is not the chef and is expected to pay for the meal before leaving. The staff cannot sit down and rest if customers are waiting to be served. This demonstrates self-regulation by staying in the role. However, in one Toronto Kindergarten class, one restaurant worker who had taken on two roles deviated when he announced to his teacher after five minutes that he quit because "it is too hard to work two jobs!"

The result is improved oral language (including vocabulary), stronger writing and social skills, more imaginative (mature) play and improved self-regulation. The play plans may simply be drawings with or without letters or words.

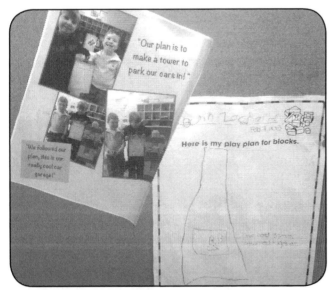

The play plan and the finished product!

Window on the Classroom:
Play Plans: Why I am Hooked!

I have spent time in classes where play plans have been used successfully. However, I was given the wonderful opportunity to introduce play plans for the first time to a Kindergarten class. This was a real revelation.

Before Play Plans: The previous day I had worked with the children at their centres. Much of the play could be described as immature play and rarely did the children stick with anything for any length of time. There was much solitary parallel play. There was little oral language, few conversations, and self-regulation appeared weak.

Day 1 of Play Plans:

Play plans were introduced. The concept of the play plan was modelled for the whole class as the teacher provided a think-aloud and sketched a plan. The children were then intentionally divided into small groups. It was felt that it would be best for the classroom teacher to form small groups for the introduction of play plans. In subsequent days, once the children began to understand how to create play plans, they were often given "managed choice" (i.e., choice, but not anything goes) among the classroom centres and the choice of partners. On day one, working with the support of a teacher or an assistant, each group drew and discussed their plan with the adult and the others at the table. The play plans then were enacted at centres. Debriefing with the whole class followed.

> Recommendation: Provide a play plan journal at each centre. Children learn much from each other by sharing their play plans simply by having the journal available. This is a great way to incubate ideas!

It was clear from day one of play plans that I did not do enough modelling or spend enough time with the children sketching and discussing their plans before the play began. Some of the children created individual plans resulting in much solitary parallel play rather than planning together to support more interactive, mature play (terms coined by Vygotsky, Bodrova, and Leong). However, the first experience with play plans exhibited real benefits. The children were more focused on their play. There was more student stick-to-itiveness and grit evident. The play was more peaceful... fewer arguments and disputes erupted. They were not simply running from centre to centre, from prop to prop. There was managed choice and there was much more calm and discussion than was evident prior to play plans. The children were learning to play collaboratively with others at centres, rather than playing with the same individuals day after day. Their imaginations were being stimulated. The play was not repetitive. The class discussion, the sharing at the end of centres, the end of the day, was also powerful. Many of the children shared how much they learned and how much they enjoyed the experience.

Next Steps: Continue with play plans at least several times a week. Extend play plans from day to day rather than starting over each day. Children build on their play and the play of others. Where possible, teachers should immerse themselves in the play when appropriate. Take time to really listen to the children at play. Spend lots of time with the students as they sketch and discuss the plan, stressing roles, available props, and props they will create. Consider removing some of the realistic props and add more open-ended props. From time to time, use read-alouds to provoke play and inquiry. Create and use wall stories (See The Power of a Wall Story Centre, p. 208) based on centre activities.

What Research Tells Us about Play and Early Literacy Development

- Play develops children's oral language, comprehension, and storytelling abilities

- Pretend play provides practice in early literacy processes

This singing word play develops phonological awareness in a fun way.

- Word play develops phonological awareness

- Play in a literacy-enriched setting increases literacy behaviours

- Play helps build background knowledge

- Play makes reading and writing fun

(Adapted from Neuman and Roskos 2007.)

Types of Play

Forms of play are varied and include pretend play, socio-dramatic play, constructive play, physical play, and playing games.

Pretend play is generally a social or small group activity where a group of children share an alternative reality, perhaps acting as if they are different people in another place and time. Other times pretending is a solo activity. Pretend play can also involve projecting imaginary objects and properties, or using one object as if it were another. Over forty years of research shows that pretend play is one of many routes to positive developmental outcomes (Lillard, Lerner, Hopkins, Dore, Smith, and Palmquist, 2012).

Socio-dramatic play is a sequence of make-believe in which two or more players collaborate to construct roles and actions around a common theme. The many possible benefits of socio-dramatic play include improved "self-regulation" among young children who are prone to be highly impulsive (Whitebread 2012).

An episode of socio-dramatic play involves four basic elements:

- Theme: what the episode is about
- Action plan: a series of actions or rituals appropriate to the theme
- Roles: theme-appropriate characters
- Language: both language about the episode and in-role language (Primarily Play 2011)

Check It Out!

For an excellent review of the effectiveness of pretend play on children's development see *The Impact of Pretend Play on Children's Development: A Review of the Evidence* by Angeline S. Lillard, Matthew D. Lerner, Emily J. Hopkins, Rebecca A. Dore, Eric D. Smith, and Carolyn M. Palmquist, *Psychological Bulletin* (August 20, 2012) http://www.faculty.virginia.edu/ASLillard/PDFs/Lillard%20et%20al%20(2012).pdf

"The primary context in which preschool and Kindergarten children learn self-regulation is make-believe play that is intentional, imaginative, and extended. In such play, children take on different roles, where they first discuss and then act out a pretend scenario, using props in a pretend way" (Bodrova and Leong 2005, 34).

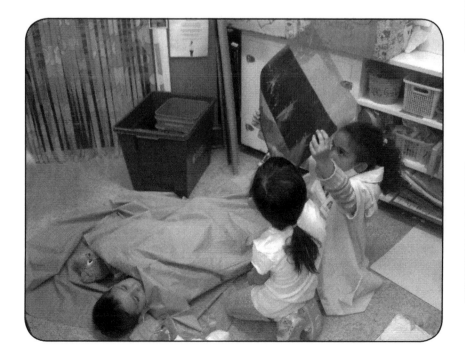

Without a play plan, socio-dramatic play often remains immature. In this hospital centre, the play plan called for x-rays as one of the props, adding another element and character to the play, the x-ray technician.

Constructive play is an organized form of play that is, in many ways, goal oriented and thoughtful. Children who are engaged in constructive play use materials to create something, which increases in complexity as they get older. With its rich capacity to teach children to problem-solve, connect, understand, and be inquisitive in their play, constructive play is an important part of an early-learning environment. It uses open-ended materials and allows children to think about the functions of the materials they are using. It can involve playing or constructing with three-dimensional materials like blocks, but it may also include Playdough and recycled materials where children get to decide what to make and how to use the materials.

Physical play and playing games with rules, such as hopscotch and rough-and-tumble play, assist sustained attention in conventional school situations (Pellegrini and Bohn 2005; see also Pellis and Pellis 2009); such games also assist emotion/self-regulation. While playing rule-based games with their friends, siblings, and parents, young children are learning a range of social skills related to sharing, taking turns, and understanding others' perspectives (DeVries 2006).

Apps that Support Early Learning

 Play apps

When using play-based apps in the classroom, it is best when students can share a device and interact with a partner. Talk will occur and collaboration can happen with some of listed apps. The device can provide access to some manipulatives that you might not have in your classroom.

My PlayHome by Playhome Software Ltd.

Toca Boca AB has a play series of apps:
Toca Tea Party
Toca Hair Salon
Toca Doctor
Toca Robot Lab
Dirt Movers: Construction Counting by RatCat Software LLC
Cars in the sandbox: Construction by Thematica — Educational and fun apps for kids
Geared 2 by Bryan Mitchell

Puzzle Apps

Butterfly Colorful Puzzles — Jigsaw puzzles for toddlers and young children by Mafooly:

Puzzle Evolution HD by wei hong

Mousefish by Jake MacMullin

Chatterpix by Duck Duck Goose

Doodle Buddy for iPad-Paint, Draw, Scribble by Pinger Inc.

Board Games

Snakes and Ladders by eQuadriga Software Pvt. Ltd.

4 in a Row — Deluxe HD by Fat Bird Games

 LEGO® Apps

LEGO® Duplo Circus

LEGO® Duplo Food

LEGO® Duplo Ice Cream

LEGO® Duplo Zoo

LEGO® Duplo Train

LEGO® Duplo

LEGO® Juniors Create & Cruise

LEGO® City Fire Hose Frenzy

LEGO® City My City

LEGO® Movie Maker

Closing Thoughts

This chapter clarified the functions and effects of play, mature play and immature play, the importance of play plans and how to support self-regulation and social imagination by linking play to read-alouds.

The next chapter will focus on effective strategies to link play and literacy learning at centres or stations.

Play at Centres or Stations

Learning centres are specific locations inside and outside the classroom. For example, provide children with magnifying glasses to examine rocks, sticks, leaves, and insects. Then encourage them to go on a hunt for nature items and make a collage. Provide materials that help children list and classify, that facilitate children's active learning in a variety of curriculum areas.

Clearly defined learning centres offer multiple opportunities for young children to engage in listening, speaking, reading, writing, viewing, and representing frequently through play and inquiry. According to the International Reading Association and the National Association for the Education of Young Children (1998), the activities must be developmentally appropriate; that is, challenging but achievable with sufficient adult support. Providing students with some choice generally supports engagement and self-regulation. Some centres may be permanent, while others may be established temporarily and changed throughout the year following the interests and needs of the students.

Bring the outdoors in and look carefully!

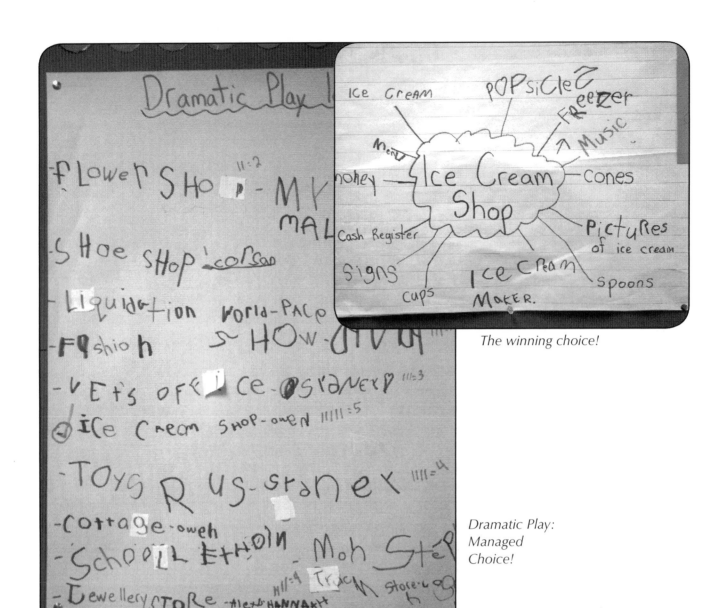

Dramatic Play

- flower shop - MK MALL
- shoe shop corsan
- Liquidation world - pace
- Fashion show-aven
- vets office - granexp II:3
- ⊘ ice cream shop - owen IIIII=5
- toys r us - granex IIII=4
- cottage - owen
- school ethiopia - moh sto
- jewellery store - alex & hannaht

Ice cream · POPSICLES · Freezer · Music
Menu · money · Ice Cream Shop · cones
Cash Register · signs · cups · ice cream Maker · pictures of ice cream · spoons

The winning choice!

Dramatic Play: Managed Choice!

Ice Cream Menu

Cup Sizes | Cones
- Small - Plain
- Medium - Sugar
- Large - Waffle

Choose from the menu.

Setting the Stage for Kindergarten Success... Spotlight on Jane's Classroom: Intentionality

My happy discovery has been that the more intentional I become in prioritizing my students' needs for character growth above all else, the greater their initiative, confidence and success seems to become with all areas of cognitive learning as well. This results in greater opportunities for undisrupted small group and especially one-to-one teaching that I find so pertinent to my work, especially with early literacy learning.

My practice each September is to act very intentionally on my awareness that the first four to five weeks of school holds tremendously high investment potential for the entire remainder of a school year. The healthier and more effective a learning community I can establish in the beginning of the school year, the smoother ongoing transitions and hurdles seem, whether planned or unexpected.

What I want my classroom to be is not a place where children behave in certain ways mainly because they feel controlled by the teacher but rather where they feel respected, empowered, and motivated by my confident expectation that they will exercise tools of self-control and self-reflection as they face and attempt to negotiate the many challenges they'll encounter. From the beginning of the year, I also try to establish the concept that our classroom is a safe mistake-making environment.

During the first weeks of school, my objective is almost solely to learn as much as I can about the children's needs and respond to them as the appropriate opportunity arises. If I do this well, I have assurance that I will more than make up any "lost" time in "teaching" the academics. Time is very precious especially since Jane's school offers just a half-day Kindergarten program.

My many visits to Jane's classroom have revealed students who develop a growth-mindset along with high levels of literacy learning. They believe in themselves as readers and they love to read! Jane's intentionality from day one is key to their success.

"The hallmark of developmentally appropriate teaching is intentionality. Good teachers are intentional in everything they do — setting up the classroom, planning curriculum, making use of various teaching strategies, assessing children, interacting with them, and working with their families. Intentional teachers are purposeful and thoughtful about the actions they take, and they direct their teaching toward the goals the program is trying to help children reach" (NAEYC Position Paper 2009, 10).

- Conversation Station
- Sorting Station
- Barrier Game Centre
- Storytelling, Retelling Drama Centre
- Wall Story Centre
- Listening Centre
- Construction/Building Centre
- Treasure/Wonder/ Discovery/Inquiry Centre

Adult–child conversations are key to the child's oral language development.

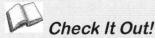 **Check It Out!**

Let's Talk about Listening from the Ontario Literacy and Numeracy Secretariat: http:// www.edu.gov.on.ca/eng/ literacynumeracy/inspire/ research/talk_about_listening.pdf

Suggested Permanent Centres

There are an infinite number of engaging and developmentally appropriate centres and activities. However, when considering the size of most classrooms, only a limited number of centres may be included at any one time. The Centres or Stations listed in the sidebar (some described in Chapters 8, 9 and 10), some appropriate for both indoor and outdoor, have been very carefully selected and recommended. The activities chosen generally promote social interaction, language, and inquiry. These research-based centres provide great potential in scaffolding engagement, language enrichment, and learning. Long blocks of time (at least an hour) are needed to plan the play (See **Play Plans**, this chapter), undertake the play, and debrief the learnings.

Conversation Stations

Research base

- Young children's language development is critically dependent on their opportunities to converse with an adult (Clay, 2002).

- Adult–child relationships in early childhood programs are important to children's security, self-confidence, and learning (Soundy and Stout 2003, 13). Adult–child conversations can scaffold positive adult–child relationships as the teacher and the child(ren) get to know one another in an intimate setting of 1–1 or up to 1–2. Unlike conversing with a child as they come in first thing in the morning or after recess (when routines might more likely be disrupted and management might become a bigger problem), the conversation station is a planned activity, part of the schedule.

- **Conversation Stations** allow effective and engaging language development to be systematically included in everyday experiences in the classroom.

- One essential component of effective communication is thoughtful listening, which is modelled at the conversation station.

- Also see Chapter 5 for the importance of conversations and the "how-to" of effectively scaffolding and extending conversations, the focus of this station.

In school and at home, children are expected to listen to adults nearly half the time they are interacting (Wolvin and Coakley 1988). Thoughtful listening has to be modelled.

The how-to of conversation stations

Typically, the conversation (5–10 minutes) is between the teacher or another adult and a student. The conversation may begin with the question, "What would you like to talk about today?" This affords a child the opportunity to express inner thoughts, to share something that he or she normally would not share in front of the whole class. Sometimes the child uses this time to describe a problem or to complain about others. During these instances, the teacher can use the time for active problem solving. The teacher may actively need to provoke the conversation to get it started using any of the following methods:

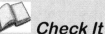

Check It Out!

Find out all about conversation stations: http://www.oise. utoronto.ca/balancedliteracydiet/ Recipe/00160/

- Using open-ended questions or prompts.

- Displaying and using props, paper and writing utensils, photos, wall stories (See **The Power of a Wall Story Centre p. 208**), inquiry posters, anchor charts, KWLM charts (See **Inquiry Posters, KWLM, and Anchor Charts**, Chapter 13), books and magazines; pretending to talk to a friend on the phone or talking to a doll or a stuffed puppy to model a conversation.

- Using a talking-stick passed between the teacher or other adult and the student. Only the person with the stick is allowed to extend the conversation. This activity supports self-regulation.

Orally summarize the conversation at the end of the session, stressing key vocabulary. Document the learning. Keep track of how often each child visits the centre and their level of involvement. Encourage the children with the weakest oral language skills to visit the centre at least once a week.

 ## *Sorting Stations*

Research base

Sorting activities support vocabulary building, oral language, and the development of critical thinking skills such as classifying and categorizing (Bauman 2004). As children undertake hands-on sorting activities using photos, books, and other manipulatives, they learn to group them according to like attributes such as color, shape, texture, and genre. Students develop and demonstrate verbal reasoning by talking about the reasons for their sorts. Teacher modelling is very important.

- Predetermined categories or closed sorts (e.g., sort the pictures into two groups representing living and non-living things) requires less decision making.

- Open categories or open sorts (children are given the items and asked to figure out how they can be sorted) require more decision-making. They allow children to demonstrate more problem-solving as they look for the common features among the items.

Check It Out!

Sort it Out! by Barbara Mariconda is a great picture book to read to children that promotes the concept of classifying, categorizing, and sorting. For additional picture books and ideas for parents and teachers to support literacy learning, go to http://www.sylvandellpublishing.com/Parents.htm

Flood! Interactive Book Sorting Tool: Students can use this resource, from PBS Kids' *Between the Lions,* to sort books online.

Also, enjoy singing and sorting coins with Michael Mitchell as he sings his song "Canada in my Pocket" at https://www.youtube.com/watch?v=82P4Ta40E14

Sort and match provinces and states as you sing along:

Canada: https://www.youtube.com/watch?v=gi-UTq0i5so

United States: https://www.youtube.com/watch?v=I1vFDZvwpfU

The how-to of sorting stations

- Begin by modelling one or two examples of sortings dualistically; that is, items that belong to a category and those that do not. For example, try photos of foods they have eaten vs. foods they have never eaten. This is called a closed sort.

- Move to higher-order thinking by having the children sort the same food photos into food categories such as fruits, vegetables, breads, meats. This is also called a closed sort.

- Challenge the students to determine the sorting categories themselves. This is called an open sort. This sort is more challenging still. The students then explain their reasoning.

A superb lesson that demonstrates book sorting using observation and comprehension to categorize books can be found at http://www.readwritethink.org/classroom-resources/lesson-plans/book-sorting-using-observation-145.html.

Students explore whether books can be included in multiple categories and whether some groups can be broken down further. Next, students work with a partner to sort twelve books. They orally explain their sorting criteria and then record in writing what categories they used and why. Students may also compare and contrast two books using an online Venn diagram. What a great way to be introduced to many new books!

Promoting books and learning how to categorize different genres!

Multiple Paths to Literacy

Window on the Classroom: Jane's Class Learns All About Attributes and Sorting

Primary teachers plan a great variety of sorting, patterning, and comparison tasks for children to engage in as part of the general math curriculum. I find these tasks an especially superb opportunity to build vocabulary in a nicely systematic way for easier retrieval. In my class, after learning to sort and compare, or create patterns using common attributes such as color, shape, size etc., I expand and build on these experiences over time to include many other categories that are revisited frequently throughout the year. We compare and contrast items or picture representations (also of people) by attributes such as texture; thickness; length; height; function (clothing, tools, furniture); temperature; flexibility (bendable, squishy, stiff etc); material (wood, rubber, plastic, glass etc); speed; volume (louder or softer/quieter); movement; mood/emotion/character traits, etc. I create a visual/tactile gesture to help the children remember the attribute label and regularly find moments of opportunity for reinforcing these labels or the contents within the categories during any of the many transitions in the day. For example, as we wait for everyone to return from putting away snack containers, the children might chant the attribute names with me as they imitate associated gestures for the various categories introduced to that point. The gestures are always simple and mimic as clearly as possible the particular attribute. I point to my eyes for "color" reminding us that our eyes are different "colors"; draw a long horizontal line to indicate "length"; reach an arm up high for "height," bend slightly with an imaginary heavy item in my arms to represent "weight," create a circle and show it changing to a triangle shape with forefingers and thumbs of both hands together to represent "shape"; rub my fingers and thumb together to indicate "texture" and so on.

Returning to these categories again and again throughout the year makes it easy to add new ones and far more likely that, when encountering interesting new words as I read to them, children will actually have somewhere specific to "file" some of them with easier later retrieval for the purpose of telling or writing their own stories, or for vocabulary predication as they read their own books. They also become much more precise in their ability describe and compare when engaged in math tasks! By about

 **Check It Out!**

Margaretha Ebbers, "Science Text Sets: Using Various Genres to Promote Literacy and Inquiry," *Language Arts* 80.1 (September 2002): 40–50.

January, the children will have learned a dozen categories or more, which, while we'll still gradually add onto, will be used for the remainder of the year to reinforce and build the vocabulary that belongs to each.

What I love best about helping them build their vocabulary in this way is that it draws in all children. This includes those requiring more movement in their learning day to those who may only be at a beginning English language level and who benefit from the frequent repetition of a few words in each category, to the strongly attuned language user who loves to know the meaning of new words like "lumbered." I explain to children, who generally have little experience with physical "files," that it is helpful to imagine our brains as containing many, many little boxes all waiting to be filled with things we learn. The fuller they get, and the more often we "open" them to use what's already in them, the more useful they become to us. As we retrieve information (maybe vocabulary words), we start to remember what is in them without having to think hard about it anymore. I also talk to them about the concept of neural pathways, describing them as little "roads" in our brains that gradually connect to other "boxes," making all learning stronger. Each time we travel to a "box" to use something from it, those "roads" get thicker and stronger and longer, and our travels become easier and faster. This is why, I explain, when we learn something new, it can feel a little tricky at first. The more we practice a new skill, the stronger and wider the "roads" become, the more other boxes they connect with, and the easier and more automatic our learning. Children love the idea of growing "new roads" in their brains, and yes, I have been asked on occasion by parents about this strange phenomenon!

Creating a picture of a brain with boxes and roads also really seems to help some children take more ownership and acceptance of the necessary obstacles along the way to learning anything well, and they will often proudly relay their "persistence" (another word we use often!) in their efforts. Sometimes children will also announce that they "got a new box" (sometimes for something like soccer or piano they've begun learning outside of school) or when I confirm a particular success, they respond with something like "Yeah, my counting road is getting longer!"

Barrier Game Centre

Research base

Current research (NELP 2008) indicates that to get the most reliable prediction of how well young students will do in reading comprehension as they advance through the grades, one should look at all of their oral language skills including both receptive and expressive language (vocabulary, grammar, and listening comprehension). Barrier games are an excellent tool for developing and monitoring students' oral language skills, both listening and speaking skills. Being able to understand and follow directions and give clear directions are important skills throughout life.

The how-to of effective barrier games

This is a paired activity in which students sit on either side of a barrier. Students should not be able to see what the other person is doing. The students take turns giving instructions to the other person to complete a task. Because they cannot see the other person's work, listeners must listen intently and speakers must be precise in the directions they give. When the task is completed, the barrier is removed and the students compare their work. This can lead to interesting discussions about which directions were incomplete or unclear and the importance of listening closely (active listening). Students learn to ask for clarification as they self-monitor and recognize possible points of confusion.

Types of barrier games

There are different types of barrier games. The level of difficulty within each game should be adjusted based on student needs. All barrier games potentially support self-regulation.

- **Making Something**: The speaker makes something (perhaps builds something, using blocks). The speaker provides clear directions so that the listener can replicate exactly what was built.

- **Recreating a picture:** The speaker describes a picture he/she has to encourage the listener to try to replicate it. For example, the speaker draws shapes or simple figures on a piece of paper and asks their partner to reproduce the picture, following their instructions. The speaker might draw the picture beforehand or design the picture on the spot.

- **Adding details/color to a picture:** Both the speaker and the listener initially begin with the same picture.

> The purposes of barrier games are to scaffold speaking, listening, and comprehension skills by providing students with the opportunities to give and follow directions effectively. In the process, students are taught the importance of including key details when giving directions, asking questions for clarification (active listening), and self-monitoring (metacognition).

For students who experience some difficulty following directions:

- Children should not wait until the end before monitoring how effectively the directions are being given and followed. For example, when introducing barrier games have the listener stop and compare his work with that of the speaker after each direction is given and followed. Encourage the listener and speaker to self-assess and discuss the game to that point. Do the products of the listener and the speaker match? Why or why not? Effective and immediate self-assessment is crucial.

- Encourage the listeners to use the Jerome Harste *I Remember Strategy* (p. 236) after being given a direction. The listener repeats what he/she remembers of the directions to the speaker before trying to follow the directions. Then the speaker provides feedback regarding the accuracy of what was remembered.

The speaker tells the listener what details/colors/ objects to add to the picture to match the changes already made by the speaker. For example, each student has a copy of the same book, turned to the same page. They also need colored shapes or letters to complete the task. One student gives directions such as, "Put a big blue square on the apples; put a small red circle under the house." Both students place the markers on the book. The students compare their pictures and discuss what is similar and what is different. They should be encouraged to talk about what caused confusion and how the directions could have been given more clearly or alternatively how the listener could have listened more closely.

Specific barrier games

Simple Sequence or Pattern Making: Describe successive items in an array or sequence such as bead threading.

Matching Pairs: Take turns describing objects or pictures. One player describes an item until the other locates and displays its matching pair. Repeat the process until all items are paired.

Assembly: Assemble pictures or objects from a choice of component parts; for example, making a clown's face.

Construction: Describe the steps in building a particular construction; for example, a block construction.

(Adapted from ABC Literacy Primary Literacy Resource *Talking and Listening Key Stage* 2, 18–19, Northern Ireland Education and Library Boards.)

Battleship, a fun challenge using coordinates, is a commonly played barrier game.

Students can use a variety of materials to create a barrier game including blocks, pictures, LEGO®, objects, letters, shapes, colored tokens, or colored pencils, markers, or crayons. Both students, the speaker and listener, have identical materials available. Linking barrier games to cross-curricular learning helps to reinforce new concepts and vocabulary.

A barrier game.

Multiple Paths to Literacy

Using the gradual release of responsibility model with barrier games

Use the gradual release of responsibility model to develop good listeners and speakers with barrier games. This three-step model — I do it, we do it, you do it — is useful in so many teaching situations.

Step 1: I do it

Modelling is the key to a successful gradual release of responsibility. You and a student demonstrate a barrier game in action, perhaps using an interactive white board. Think aloud, stressing position words such as (on top, middle, bottom), prepositions (under, beside, next to, over) and right/left, and language related to size, shape, and color. Help the children to understand the importance of providing specific instructions. For instance, when using a picture of a dog, demonstrate the changes that might occur if the directions stated, "Draw a tree near the dog" versus "Draw a large green tree behind the dog."

Step 2: We do it

Enact a barrier game with the teacher being the speaker and each student in the class being the listener and doer at the same time.

Step 3: You do it

Partners, one being the listener and one the speaker, play the barrier game. The listener has to indicate to the speaker when he/she has completed the task following the speaker's directions.

Closing Thoughts

The next chapter suggests other potential permanent centres including Storytelling and Retelling. A Wall Story Centre, also described, can be used to scaffold storytelling and retelling (oral language) and promote reading and writing. Teachers can get a great deal of mileage from a Wall Story Centre.

Task feedback describes how well the student has performed a given task. See examples of effective task feedback: http://vimeo.com/38247060.

Definitions/Explanations
The barrier game activity gives students the opportunity to use and learn language related to size, shape, color, prepositions (under, beside, next to, over), position (top, middle, bottom), and right/left.

 Check It Out!
http://www.pinterest.com/jamiemet/barrier-games/

http://www.playingwithwords365.com/2011/11/barrier-games-great-for-language-enrichment/

http://www.talkingmatters.com.au/resources/downloads/cat_view/2-barrier-games

http://mrsmclennan.blogspot.ca/2012/03/barrier-games.html

Storytelling and Retelling

Wall Stories, Story Documentation, Mystery Boxes and Story Innovations

Storytelling and Retelling

Storytelling and retelling are important activities (Benson and Cummins, 2000). Retelling helps the teacher to monitor student comprehension and ability for oral expression. Retellings indicate

- What the student remembers
- What the student deems important
- How the student organizes and sequences information
- How the student makes sense of the text
- What personal connections the student makes
- How well the student can infer (read between the lines)

Retelling fiction helps the student to remember the story, make sense of the story, sequence the story, and use some of the story vocabulary. The act of retelling also helps the student to understand what makes a story. Retelling should be more than simple regurgitation of what the text was about, more than beginning, middle, and end. Students can also learn to infer character motivations, missing pieces of the plot, and what might happen after the end of the story. Most importantly, retelling allows the student to put the text (fiction/non-fiction) into his/her own words.

Retelling: Focus on Character, Higher-Order Thinking and Inference Generation

"Inference generation, monitoring and knowledge of story-structure persisted as consistent predictors of more general reading comprehension" (Cain and Oakhill 2012 in Stahl 2014, 385).

 Storytelling Apps

Three Little Pigs Puppet
   Theatre for Kids by Duncan
   Cuthbertson
Puppet Pals HD by Polished
   Play, LLC
Sock Puppets
LEGO® Friends Story Maker
My Story-Book Maker for Kids
   by HiDef Web Solutions
Mother Goose on the Loose Felt
   Board by Software Smoothie

"Diagnosing and remediating comprehension difficulties in third grade and beyond can often feel like aiming at a moving target" (Stahl 2014, 388). Don't wait. Start with listening comprehension using read-alouds, videos, wordless picture books and discussion.

Questions or prompts to scaffold higher-order thinking, inference

- What is/are/were the problems of the character(s)? What makes you think so?

- What is/was the character thinking? What makes you think so?

- What did the character do to solve the problem?

- Did the character solve his/her problem? What makes you think so?

- Did the character do the right thing? Please explain.

Retelling non-fiction

When retelling non-fiction, students are encouraged to use charts, maps, tables, captions, headings, pictures, and academic vocabulary such as words from science and social studies.

The Power of a Wall Story Centre
Promote Reading, Writing and Oral Language

I am hooked on wall stories. They are versatile and limitless in their potential to scaffold young learners. Wall stories are typically 8 to 12-page stories created as a shared or interactive writing. Wall story text is supported with real photos (often of the children), pictures cut out of magazines, and/or illustrations drawn by both the teacher and/or the children. It is important to note that although wall stories have the word *story* in the title, they may also be a retelling of a non-fiction text or experience. The real strength of the wall story is that the text is meaningful to the children since it is often based on a shared experience. This makes the text inviting and engaging. The children want to revisit it often. Frequent retellings effectively scaffold the development of oral language and background knowledge.

Wall stories are displayed on the wall, a form of environmental print, for children to revisit as they read around the room. Additionally, wall stories can be used as a centre activity and when taken down can be made into class Big Books. Children also love having their own copy of a wall story to take home and share with their families.

"Children's retellings shift from remembering just a few ideas in random order to recalling many ideas in a well-connected sequence" (McGee and Richgels 2003, 40).

Practice in retellings improves comprehension, grasp of story concept, critical thinking, and oral language development (Benson and Cummins 2000). Assessing retellings is one piece: Retellings must be taught, not just assessed.

There are two main types of wall stories: those that support writing by having the children sketch the illustrations that go with the stories, and those that have the children write or retell the stories using letters, words, and punctuation to support photos.

Multiple Paths to Literacy

Research base

Wall stories serve many purposes. Research indicates that rich language environments include print with which the children have a personal connection and are posted at eye-level in the classroom (Prior and Gerard 2004, 3). Wall stories serve this purpose. Frequent retellings using wall stories as provocations effectively scaffold the development of oral language and background knowledge. As the children experience shared, independent, and small-group reading as well as modelled, shared, and interactive writing, they develop their knowledge of the concepts of print (including punctuation), high-frequency words, letters, letter–sound correspondence, and word-family knowledge; phonological awareness, and increased fluency. Wall stories can also be used to develop fine motor skills as the children develop their ability to sketch and write. The ability of the wall story to encourage the use of environmental print (including the word wall) is an additional strength. Just having environmental print around the room does not guarantee its use. The weakest literacy learners typically regard environmental print as wallpaper and rarely use it. But having the children make use of it through engaging activities that promote reading and writing is a real strength of the wall story.

> Do you have little wall space? Try this… Trifold Presentation Boards at centres. (Thank you Toronto for this great suggestion!) They can be taken down, stored, and revisited at another time. It works beautifully for the wall story. Digital wall stories may also be created on an interactive whiteboard.

The How-to of Effective Wall Stories

Wall stories are often based on the class's shared experiences. They are not necessarily stories but often personal recounts. First, the children must have an experience about which they can write and draw, such as a field trip, their observations of the life-cycle of a classroom butterfly that emerges from the chrysalis, or the story of a sick classroom pet that visits a veterinarian's office. The experience may also be the retelling of a read-aloud or a movie

Teachers can ensure that Wall stories promote retelling and conversation.

they have watched together. Or, it may be an innovation on a story where the character(s), the setting, some of the events, or even the ending is changed. Four great books to use to create wall story innovations are *Brown Bear, Brown Bear* (Bill Martin Jr. and Eric Carle) and the following books by Eric Carle, *The Very Grouchy Ladybug, The Very Busy Spider*, and *The Very Hungry Caterpillar*. Folk and Fairy Tales also make great wall stories as retellings or innovations. Children also love it when through their names or pictures, they become part of the story.

Check It Out!

Why not use a song along with a wall story? *"Today is Monday"* has been a traditional song about what children eat that was adapted into a book by Eric Carle. It could easily be made into an innovated wall story. Food is always an engaging topic. Jim Rule has done a nice job of creating a CD titled *Too Much Fun All in One* that includes "Today is Monday." There is a clip at http://www.songsforteaching.com/jimrule/clip/todayism.mp3

See some Kindergarten children having fun at http://www.youtube.com/watch?v=JtN7ixHO4c8
http://www.youtube.com/watch?v=2oqOGGpmsQY&feature=related.

Consider teaching the following skills with wall stories.

- Concepts of print (including punctuation)
- High frequency words
- Recognizing their own names and the names of classmates. This is especially important in the first few months of Kindergarten.
- Letters, letter/sound knowledge
- Word family knowledge
- Phonological awareness (see **Play at a Syllable Centre**, p. 105)
- Increased fluency
- One-to-one matching
- Vocabulary development

Wall stories develop many skills that support both reading and writing. It is important that the teacher intentionally teach the skills that support the needs of the students using many strategies, including thinking-aloud. Teachers have to decide what supports and challenges are best included in the wall story. If the wall story is going to be used by the children for reading around the room and/or centre activities, then the text needs to be written clearly and at a just-right difficulty level. It cannot be too hard or the children will not experience success. It must not be too easy or the children will learn very little. There must be both challenges and supports to scaffold the learning. Too hard or too easy means that the children will not remain engaged with the activity. Wall stories when taken down make great class Big Books.

When planning a wall story, consider if using a repetitive pattern is required. Which sight words should be included? Would including word families to support rhyme be helpful? How much print should there be on a page? Should the wall story be written by the teacher as a modelled or shared writing experience with the students involved solely in the creating of the illustrations? Or, should the text also involve interactive writing where the children share the pen by writing some letters, words, and/or punctuation?

Concepts of print, high frequency words, and names: Think aloud as you create and reread the wall story with the children. Have the children come up and take turns identifying high frequency words, names, and punctuation. Use Wicki Stix or a fly swatter with a small window cut out to frame or "hug" the high frequency words or names and/or the punctuation.

Letters, letter/sound knowledge: Wall stories are great for focusing on letters and their sounds. Since the skill of fluent letter recognition is a very important goal to achieve by the end of Kindergarten, teaching letters and their sounds through the wall story should be stressed. In addition to letter names and sounds, reinforce the concept of first letter, last letter and eventually the middle letter. Wall stories frequently use innovations of a read-aloud or shared reading. The innovation often includes some of the children's names as part of the story. Using student names to teach letters and sounds is a primary teacher strategy that really works.

Word family knowledge and phonological awareness: Be sure where possible to include word families in the wall story. Word families help children to rhyme, an important skill in phonological awareness. Word families and rhyming both help children to read and to write. Use a wall story to teach the rimes or word families and to rhyme with the children orally. The key word families are found on the Wylie and Durrell list (See Wylie and Durrell, p. 298,). Begin with a few of the most high-frequency word families such as /at/ and the word family /ame/ since they will likely see and hear the word "name" often.

This is a section of a class wall story on animal vision. All of the presentations can become a class Big Book.

Increased fluency: The more the teacher reads the text aloud while tracking and has the children join in using a choral or echo read, the more fluency they will develop. All the other experiences with the wall story, including the centre activities listed below, will also support improved reading and writing.

One-to-one matching: Cut up sentences and words. A motivating way to get the children involved with the wall story is having them do one-to-one matching. This requires the teacher to write the wall story on sentence strips. The children are called up one at a time and are required to match each sentence strip with the corresponding sentence in the wall story. The use of patterned text and rhymes can make the exercise more or less challenging depending on the student's understanding of phonological awareness.. For example, the retelling of an innovation of *The Very Hungry Caterpillar* by Eric Carle might look like this: *Jason was hungry. Jason ate one apple. But he was still hungry. Jason ate one cookie. But he was still hungry. Jason ate one cake. But he was still hungry. Jason ate one carrot. But he was still hungry. Jason ate one cabbage. Then he was full.* The first sentence would be easy to match since it is different and sounds like the beginning of a story. The second sentence will give the children confidence since it is easy to match since apple begins with a short or soft "a" sound. The pattern is expected and therefore should not cause problems. But all of the other non-pattern sentences except for the last one may be more challenging for some even with the pictures of the foods since they all begin with a hard c sound. All of the rest of the words in each sentence complete a common pattern, *Jason ate one*. The last sentence, Then he was full, should always bring closure. This is an important clue for the children to know.

One-to-one matching helps the children develop many literacy skills including an understanding of directionality, the concept of story sequencing, the concept of a word, the concept of beginning and ending letters, and knowledge about letters, sounds (phonological awareness) and phonics. The children find it fun to each have a copy of one of the pictures or illustrations that they then have to match to the appropriate script. Oral language practice occurs, as the children have to defend their matches.

Vocabulary development: One of the most exciting uses of a wall story is to improve vocabulary through activities that develop better word choice. Generally, a wall story is originally written using familiar vocabulary. However, in time with repeated readings it is advisable to brainstorm million dollar words or yummy words to use to energize the wall story. At different times, the teacher may choose to focus on adding descriptive words or improving action words. In one class, the teacher focused on descriptive words when using an innovation for Bill Martin and Eric Carle's *Brown Bear, Brown Bear*. A line from the script originally read "Brown Cow, Brown Cow, What do you see?" The teacher asked the children to make the animals more interesting so the line became "Spotted brown cow". Black snake became "Slithery black snake." If using text with dialogue, show the children how to change *said* to yelled, screamed, asked, whispered…

Simply add the new word on a sticky and place the sticky over the word being changed or place the additional word being added on a sticky above the text with a caret.

Creating Individual Student Wall Stories

A number of formats can be used to create individual wall stories. These include a copy of the original wall story, a wall story cloze, a modified wall story cloze, "illustrate me," "tell the story," "order me," and many activities to use with wall story word cards.

Original wall story: Each child gets a little book (mini) version of the wall story. Each page is illustrated. This booklet goes home accompanied by a letter to the parents explaining that their children may be able to read a lot, a little or perhaps just a few words. All children can discuss the experience around the wall story and tell the "story". Reading the text over and over will develop fluency.

A wall story cloze: In a traditional cloze, every fifth word is deleted and the child has to fill in the blanks with a word that sounds right, looks right, and makes sense. But in a wall story cloze, in Kindergarten– early Grade 1, one or two carefully chosen words are enough to be deleted. High frequency words, student names, and word families are the best to delete. The children have the real wall story in front of them to use for support.

A modified wall story cloze: In a modified wall story cloze the first letter of the deleted word may appear at the beginning of the blank. Additionally the deleted words may appear on the page for the children to select from to fill in the blanks.

Illustrate me: A wall story with only text but no illustrations is provided to each child. They then have to create all of the pictures.

Tell the story: Only the wall story illustrations are provided. The children have to create the text alone or with a partner. They are free to create their own innovation of the text as long as it goes with the illustrations.

Order me: Each child or pair is given a set of wall story sentence strips. The sentence strips are mixed up and then the children place them in story order and check against the original wall story. They also may be given a small booklet (8–12 pages) in order to glue the sentence strips in story order, illustrate them, and take the booklet home. (See **Letter to Parents and Caregivers: Wall Stories p. 214**)

Word cards: Many activities can be done with the wall story word cards: For this activity the wall story word cards and a mini-copy of the wall story are provided. The word cards can be placed on the corresponding words on the mini-wall story. They also may be glued on to the mini-wall story.

1. *The word cards may be sorted in alphabetical order.*

2. *The word cards may be sorted into words that begin with the same sound or end with the same sound.*

3. *The word cards may be sorted into piles with identical word cards. Then the words are counted and the results recorded. e.g., The 7; you 4.*

4. *The word cards may be sorted according to how many letters in each word.*

Wall story Big Books: Wall stories that have been created into Big Book format are used by the children. If the books have been laminated, the children can do activities that require them to write on the wall story. They may be asked to circle high frequency words, names, or rhyming words. They might be asked to circle the first letter in each word or the first word in each sentence. They may be asked to circle or underline all uppercase letters and all punctuation.

🏠⇄🏫 *Home-School Connections*

Wall Stories

Dear Parents:

Your child is bringing home a piece of writing called a wall story that we wrote together. Wall stories are based on the class's shared experiences such as a field trip, baby chicks hatching in the class or a book we read together. They are typically 8 to 12-page stories although they can be nonfiction text as well. Wall stories are displayed on the wall for children to revisit as they read around the room. Sometimes the children add the illustrations.

Please prompt your child to tell you all about the experience that prompted the writing of the wall story. Then ask your child to retell the piece based on the pictures. Finally help your child to read the piece. Your child may be able to read a lot, a little or perhaps just a few words. Point to each word as you read it with your child. The most important thing is to talk about the wall story and enjoy it with your child.

Over the next few weeks, help your child to read it over and over. Reading helps develop writers and writing helps develop readers.

Additional wall stories will be coming home monthly.

Sincerely,

Story Innovations Make Great Wall Stories

A story innovation is a story written as a shared writing experience based on a familiar story. The new text is very similar to the original story pattern but innovations such as changing the characters, the setting, the verbs, or the dialogue may occur. These changes occur when new vocabulary is used to create the innovation.

Use a familiar pattern or refrain from books such as *Rosie's Walk* by Pat Hutchins or *Brown Bear Brown Bear* by Bill Martin Jr. and Eric Carle. Innovate by changing the animal ("Black stallion, Black stallion, Who do you see?") or adding the children's names.

While learning about *community* in social studies why not innovate *Brown Bear* using community helpers?

The shared writing may look like this:

Police Officer, Police Officer, Who do you see?
Doctor, doctor, Who do you see?
Carpenter, carpenter, Who do you see?

Other Eric Carle books that lend themselves to innovations are *The Very Grouchy Ladybug, The Very Hungry Caterpillar*, and *The Very Busy Spider*. Stories like these that have patterns or repeated phrases often work well.

Use *Deep in the Forest* by Brinton Turkle (a fractured fairy tale, a take-off on *Goldilocks and the Three Bears*) to create a text innovation as a shared writing with the children. What a great opportunity for children to experience how they too can write a book using an innovation by simply including their names in the text. The story innovations can then become wall stories.

Check It Out!
Story innovation is a way for children to develop vocabulary and reading fluency while enjoying talking, writing, and reading. The new text is easy to read because of the familiar patterns from the original story. See "Story Innovation: An Instructional Strategy for Developing Vocabulary and Fluency" by Priscilla L. Griffith and Jiening Ruan, *The Reading Teacher* (December 2007): 334–338.

Window on the Classroom: Clarice's Story Innovations

One very creative teacher did a story innovation on Brian Wildsmith's *Cat on the Mat*. Her shared writing innovations and her letter home encouraging the children's families to participate follow:

"This is a rewriting we did of Cat on the Mat. I also made it into a magnetic wall story, which the children love to move around (words and pictures). You should see the rewriting (innovations) sent from home, done with me at school, and done independently! This story often helps the emerging readers/writers really take off!!" —Clarice Bloomenthal.

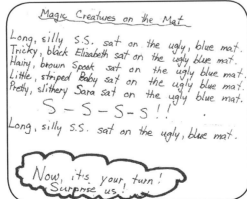

Magic Creatures on the Mat

Long, silly S.S. sat on the ugly, blue mat.
Tricky, black Elizabeth sat on the ugly blue mat.
Hairy, brown Spook sat on the ugly blue mat.
Little, striped Baby sat on the ugly blue mat.
Pretty, slithery Sara sat on the ugly blue mat.
S - S - S - S ! !
Long, silly S.S. sat on the ugly, blue mat.
Now, it's your turn!
Surprise us!

Kids on the Table

Shandy jumped on the table.
Ben jumped on the table.
Rachel jumped on the table.
Brandyn jumped on the table.
Kristen jumped on the table.
STOP!!!
Shandy sat on a chair!

Story Innovations

Dear Parents,

We enjoyed reading *Cat on the Mat* by Brian Wildsmith. It is a simple story that begins "The cat sat on the mat" and then follows using the same pattern with the dog, the goat, the cow, the elephant, and then Ssspsstt! Finally, the story ends with the first line being repeated. Have your child read it to you. On the back of this letter are three different versions or innovations we had fun writing. We changed the characters, the action word (verb), and/or the location (noun). In one version, we added some interesting words (adjectives) to tell about the characters. Have fun rewriting your own version at home using pets, family members' names, or familiar objects. Do several and send them to school for us to enjoy. Add illustrations and color too! Do the printing for your child if needed. Try this with Home Reading books too. It's good practice for spelling, reading, and writing.

Clarice Bloomenthal

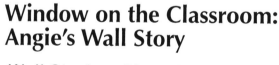

Window on the Classroom: Angie's Wall Story

Wall Stories, Class Books and Inquiry: Bird Nest Discovery

Family engagement is important for furthering the inquiry way of thinking with students. Sharing inquiries or wonderings with families through open houses, personal emails, newsletters, and/or blog entries keeps families informed of the discussions and learning occurring at school. Parents can ask similar questions or support the in-class inquiries with their own field trips, walks, or investigations. An example of parent engagement in inquiry learning is one in which a family sent regular digital photos of the process of eggs hatching. The family discovered a bird nesting in their barbecue. The family took photos over a two-week period and emailed the photos to our class. The student shared the photos and discussed the changes he saw at home in his barbecue.

Moments occur in classrooms all the time. It's important to be open and seize the opportunities when they arise. The use of wonderings can be integrated into the literacy block. Digital photos provide excellent stimuli for wall stories. The class engaged in daily discussions about the photos of the nest and the egg development. Each day the students participated in an interactive writing activity that provided a sentence that matched the photo. During the daily discussions on the changes in the photos, some wonderings naturally occurred. These wonderings were posted and then read-aloud. Shared reading texts were selected to help support the learning. A small group facilitated by the teacher investigated their wonderings. The wall story pages were put together in a book format to be read and reread. Smaller copies of the book were created for individual book bins. One of the students told a story of the life cycle of a bird and the class captured and wrote a book about this authentic experience. This became a powerful text for rereading and sharing with families.

Children retell this story repeatedly, at home and at school

Inquiries can be written in the form of a wall story. The story can recount the events of a field trip. The lifecycle of a butterfly as seen in class can be written up as a wall story to be revisited by students. A wall story might also show a photo of a provocation and then students' faces and a thinking bubble above the face indicating their initial wonderings. A wall story may also be a final product of new learning that occurred about a specific class inquiry such as worms, bird nests, or changes over time.

Digital photos can be printed and glued on 11 x 17 paper. Interactive writing can be done as a class to document the thinking about each photo.

Digital photos can also be embedded in a Word document or in SMART Notebook or other interactive software and displayed for the class. The wall story may become a centre. Students can work with the teacher to create a shared text that can be revisited throughout the day.

A School District Documents its Success

The Story of Success at the Thames Valley District School Board: Oral Language Development and Educator Professional Learning

With special thanks to Valerie Nielsen, Diana Goodwin, Rose Walton, Kim Gain and educators from the Thames Valley District School Board.

The action research undertaken by the Thames Valley District School Board really belongs to the educators. It resulted in essential findings around

1. *The influence of photo documentation on student engagement and oral language achievement*

2. *Implications for educators and students*

Action research is a practical approach to professional inquiry in any social situation. Stenhouse advocated that "curriculum research and development ought to belong to the teacher" (Stenhouse 1975, 142). He insisted that "it is not enough that teachers' work should be studied: they need to study it themselves" (Stenhouse 1975, 143).

As you can see from **Educators' Voices** below, the strength of the pedagogical documentation was not the documentation itself but the feedback it gave to educators as to how to improve their teaching and more effectively scaffold student learning. Visible learning is evident from studying the documentation.

Beginning in 2012, multidisciplinary teams of educators, administrators, speech and language staff, and research and assessment personnel from the Thames Valley District School Board became engaged in this professional inquiry through action research. The results of using effective provocations to enhance oral language in Junior Kindergarten to Grade 2 classrooms were studied. The inquiry began because of quantitative and qualitative data that demonstrated one key finding: educators need support in developing effective "talk spaces" where oral language is valued as an essential component of program planning supporting student learning and achievement. Students benefit from "reading the walls."

During the first phase of the inquiry, teams explored documentation (such as wall stories) as a provocation to oral language expression and development.

"Documentation must serve to advance learning, not merely capture it" (Ritchhart et al. 2011, 38).

Task procedures

The purpose of this analysis was to determine the impact of photo documentation on student oral responses. Educators were asked to engage in photo documentation of a whole group activity by taking a minimum of ten photos of students involved in a classroom activity. Four days later, each educator selected five students exhibiting varying levels of oral language development and met with each student individually. Each student was prompted with, "Remember when we did [group activity]? Tell me about that." The educator scribed each student's response verbatim. The educator then placed one of the photos that was taken during the activity on the table in front of the student and said "Look what I have — a picture about [group activity]. Tell me about that." The educator again scribed the student's response verbatim. Finally, the educator placed ten photos of the activity on the table in front of the student and said, "Look, I have more pictures of [group activity]. Tell me about that." The educator again scribed the student's response verbatim.

Analysis

Oral responses from twenty-nine students were collected from the educators and analyzed in order to determine the impact of using photo documentation on students' oral responses. Responses from the three conditions (no photos, one photo, and multiple photos) were analyzed and compared.

Results

Throughout this inquiry, educators noticed that students were much more engaged and responsive when they had photos to offer reminders of past experiences. When offered the opportunity to review photo documentation, students extended their descriptions and elaborated in more detail. Educators recognized the value of pedagogical documentation for purposes of student assessment and teacher practice reflection. More specifically, with the support of speech language pathologists, they were able to answer the following questions:

1. *How does authentic photo documentation impact the oral language of early years students?*

2. *Specifically, how does it support the students' abilities to recount a past classroom experience?*

Without photo documentation for support
Prompt: "I heard that you celebrated 100 Days at school last week! Tell me about some of the things that you did."

- Oral language content was limited.

- About forty percent of the students could not recall/relay one relevant event.

- Many comments were off-topic.

- Most students required numerous prompts even to respond at all.

> Collaboration between educators and speech language pathologists (SLP) is crucial. Each provide their level of expertise and together is better!

> "I don't know. We got to hand out cards and that's all I know. That's ALL I know." —Carmen, Kindergarten

"I made a mask and Mrs. Turner put it together and she put and I picked a pink long thing. I had a 100 Day band. We watched a 100 Day movie but it was a Valentine's Day movie but it was the 100 Day movie. That was it." —Sophia, Kindergarten

"We poured candy in a bowl and we turned off the lights because we wanted to. And we — did I tell you about when we ate the snacks? And we did calendar and we counted all the way to 100! And you know the fishes on calendar? We are never taking off the big fish because it's our groups of 10s. And we made it to 100. And we made the glasses. Mrs. Turner made like the glasses parts. She cut out the holes so we could see. Our part was putting on 100 dots. And Mrs. Turner put the little strip on the back. And we got to wear them. And we brought different candies. **These pictures are reminding me of what we did on 100 Day!**" —Kennedy, Kindergarten

- Many of the students were not engaged in the conversation and were anxious to terminate the exchange.

With minimal photo documentation (one photograph)....

Prompt: "Look what I have! It's a picture of your 100 Day celebration!"

- The recount improved slightly, as did the level of engagement, but the interaction was once again brief and short-lived, and the students were anxious to terminate the exchange.

With strong photo documentation (many photos)....

Prompt: "Look what I have! Lots of pictures of your 100 Day celebration!"

- The **content** of the oral language in the recount increased significantly!

- The students were **excited and much more engaged** in the communication exchange.

- Prompts were seldom required.

- **Joint attention and focus** were supported.

- **Topic maintenance** improved.

- The interaction lasted much longer!

- The language moved from the relaying of one event or a short list of activities (without documentation), to **more complete, detailed comments and explanations using specialized vocabulary.**

- Depending on their oral language level, some students **labelled**, some **commented**, some **asked questions.**

- One student **sequentially explained the procedure** for making the glasses (the oral foundation for procedural writing).

- The use of **procedural language** improved (first, next, then, finally).

- Best of all, some students **commented on their learning!**

- **The authentic documentation assisted with the recall and students were then able to use their language to recount the events of the day, thereby gaining significantly more experience and practice in oral expression — a key for our students!**

In addition:

- **The language samples obtained were authentic and excellent for assessment/analysis** (i.e., setting oral language goals … past tense, question formulation, pragmatic skills, etc.)

- The photos also **ensured a high level of student engagement** and provided **authentic content** for ongoing one-on-one, small group oral language sessions … **linked with the classroom and the learning that was taking place.**

Educators' Voices

- "Students and parents are drawn to the documentation displays. This leads to increased discussion, deeper reflection, and celebrations of learning."

- "I have learned much from pedagogical documentation. Without a doubt, the most important skill I have learned is how to interact more effectively with my students. I am learning to ask more open-ended and thought-provoking questions in our conversations. I am learning to stop giving answers and waiting to discover the answers together. Most importantly, I am beginning to truly 'listen' deeply and carefully to the amazing ideas my students have to share."

- "My experience with documentation has led me into a deeper relationship with each of my students as I spend more time focusing on the process of their learning and dialoguing with them."

- "This opportunity has taught me how to look more closely and capture those unplanned teachable moments."

- "Documenting student work shows children that what they say and do is valued enough to be caught and then displayed for others or for them to see."

- "I look forward to continuing on this journey using the power of documentation as a tool to support oral language, which is so essential especially in early and primary years."

Summary of the Findings: Documentation Alone is NOT Enough

Results indicated that the use of photo documentation had a positive impact on both the quantity and quality of students' oral responses. Specifically, student responses were more elaborate and detailed and included more frequent use of complex sentences, procedural language, descriptors, content-specific vocabulary, and inquiry when one or more photos from the activity were presented to the student. Large differences in student abilities to stay on topic and in the number of "empty" responses (no response or "I don't know") were observed when photo documentation was not provided.

The second phase encouraged a deeper inquiry into the use of effective questioning along with documentation as a means to inspiring higher-order responses representing student thinking. Educators pored over articles and evidence-based research all highlighting the impact of higher order questioning on student oral response. The team discovered a strong connection between the use of pedagogical documentation and intentional and well placed questioning. The practice of documenting authentic and meaningful learning increased student engagement while the questioning assisted with deeper elaboration and quality detail. Educators came to understand that students are more committed to their learning when they have the opportunity to see the experience recorded through documentation in the form of photos, videos, and audio. One further observation noted by a team of educators was the notion that students seemed to enjoy the opportunity to explain, comment, and share their thinking through extended oral language when they are involved in activities where their creativity is allowed to flourish through independent design evidenced through student choice and voice.

Pedagogical documentation is strengthened by multiple perspectives. "—it is a means to learning about how children think and learn" (*How Does Learning Happen? Ontario's Pedagogy for the Early Years*, 2014, p.21). It promotes dialogue among parents, children, and educators. It adds transparency to classroom experiences and creates visible traces for parents, providing parents with opportunities to know both what and how their children learn at school (Buldu 2010). Accountability was evident "on the walls and in the halls."

> I have witnessed beautiful documentation panels in classrooms around the world. However, frequently they are educator created and little is done with them to involve students in either making them or using them. They appear only as wallpaper. Documentation often takes a great deal of educator time to create and educators need to utilize the documentation as valuable student "talk spaces." The important research from the Thames Valley District School Board in London, Ontario, validates this.
> Why not incorporate a wall story centre and act on the valuable data provided?

A Retelling, Storytelling, and Dramatizing Centre: Encourage Book-Related Play

Research base

Retellings and dramatizations can effectively scaffold the development of oral language, background knowledge, comprehension, and self-regulation (Benson and Cummins, 2000).

The How-to of Making a Retelling and Storytelling Centre Work

Within the story/text

Helping young learners to understand how to retell a story is an important activity. Retelling helps the student to remember the story, make sense of the story, sequence the story, and use some of the story vocabulary. The act of retelling helps the student to understand what makes a story. Most importantly, it allows the students to put the text into their own words.

Many children need to be taught how to retell effectively. Teachers can help in the following ways:

- Modelling and encouraging the students to think about the setting (time, place, characters), theme (problem or goal), main events, and the ending.

- Supporting the retelling in the correct sequence (beginning, middle, ending).

- Using a story map or another structure to support story retelling (See **Story Map**, and **Implementing the "Who Wanted But So Then" technique** this chapter).

- Providing or supporting the students as they make puppets of the characters to use as props.

- Providing a picture story map (using pictures instead of words) or a **story board** (See p. 236) to be able to tell the story.

- Encouraging the students to take turns retelling the story in sequence using **retelling cards** as props: The name of the story is_____. The characters are _____. First _____. Next_____ Then _____. It ended when_____.

- **Using Talking Sticks:** The students at the centre sit in a circle. Talking Sticks are a tool to aide discussions and retellings. The person in the circle holding the stick is able to retell the section without interruption. It is best not simply to pass the stick to the person next in the circle as this is too predictable and others may lose interest knowing that their turn is not next. Keep the circle small (4–6) so that everyone gets a turn holding the talking stick and a turn to retell a portion of the story.

The students may work together as partners or small groups to plan, create, and share mystery boxes. Each box will be different. What a great centre activity.

Sock puppets is a useful K-6 app that allows students to choose a puppet and scenery to create and share a quick play. They can record their own voices for the puppets.

- **Passing the book around the circle:** Each child gets a turn retelling a page until the whole story has been retold.

- **Using a series of pictures representing key parts of the story:** Students put the pictures in the correct order and retell the story.

Using Mystery Boxes:

A mystery box includes items that support the comprehension, prediction, and retelling of a read-aloud (Pearman, Camp, and Hurst 2004, 768). The boxes can be made by the teacher, a class, individual students, or groups. The items in the boxes can be used before reading to introduce a story (to support prediction) and build anticipation or after reading as a response activity such as a retelling. The items need to convey the main points of the story. They can be used to follow the unfolding of the story's plot. Literacy mystery boxes have the power to motivate and encourage students to engage actively in reading and listening.

 Acting Out Stories, Nursery Rhymes, and Fairy Tales: A Centre

Acting out a story, nursery rhyme or fairy tale is a great way for a child to retell the text and also to indicate to the teacher how much of the text was understood. Teachers may choose to begin with retelling the story and modelling for the children how to act it out. The second time around the teacher retells the story and pauses for the children to do the actions. Finally, the children may simply follow the pictures in the text and act out the story. Acting out nursery rhymes and fairy tales works especially well because of frequent repetitive patterns. Book acting is especially beneficial for ELL children whose receptive language is often stronger than their expressive. They may be able to understand the story but not be able to retell it verbally. But acting it out allows them to retell without words successfully.

Be a character

An effective way to retell or act out a story, nursery rhyme, or fairy tale is to have the children take turns being a character. To *be a character*, children must imagine that character's feelings and emotions, which often results in developing empathy, imagining different perspectives, developing social imagination, often resulting in improved self-regulation.

Beyond the story/text: Using story innovations

Students may be encouraged to use their imaginations to play beyond the text. This occurs as students attempt to expand and extend the existing story elements by using an innovation on a story where the character(s), the setting, some of the events, or even the ending is changed. Prop changes may be required as the players step outside the framework provided by the text.

Retelling/Rewriting Text Improves Reading Fluency and Comprehension (See Karen's example below).

Window on the Classroom: Karen's Grade 1–2 Class

This year I had a couple of students who struggled with text. One boy in particular, Jonathan, used meaning and structure so much that it overrode his ability to use visual information. Once prompted, he could see his error and with support, could correct it. I had used wall stories, interactive writing, and easier level texts with him as strategies to make the process of reading and using information strategically easier. I had worked with him and two others in my class on a level 10 text called *Birthday Balloons*. Because I know that a student's own oral thoughts are easier to recall and read for a struggling reader, I tried another strategy. As a group of three students, I had them retell the story in their words from beginning to end, managing to clarify their thoughts into a reasonably lengthy text that they could then reread. I recorded the retell, revising parts that they suggested while keeping the story intact. We reread it together, making sure it was how they wanted it to be. I was careful not to change it but to encourage some of the vocabulary from the story that they could easily access. They each had a part to draw, beginning, middle, or end. I typed the text, added their drawings, and made copies. I did another guided reading with this text, with less support, as it was a known story and it was their composition. I was surprised in one way, but not in another, that Jonathan was able to read the text with more skill. He read fluently, and was able to pause, check initial letters, and monitor his reading with more accuracy. I noticed this and praised him for his use of strategies, and let him know that this was what he could do with new books as well.

> "When children are clearly getting left behind by their faster-learning classmates, it is very important to work with reading and writing together" (Clay 2001, 11).

We did a second book retell of another level 10 with pictures that I recorded and typed up. Again, he was able to pay attention to the text in a more focused way and monitor his reading more closely. Both of these texts simply printed out on paper went into their book boxes as familiar text that they could control.

My feedback to him was that he should use his excellent understanding of what makes sense in a story and slow down enough to notice the letters at the beginning in order to make the good word prediction. He should also use checking. He was able to use this teaching point in subsequent new books in higher levels, especially when I was able to "jump in" and prompt for it. Although he didn't quite make the minimum expected level in reading by June, this strategy was one that proved to be successful for him, and one that I will add to my repertoire of strategies with hard-to-teach readers in future. It confirms for me that we have to instruct the learner where he is at, and that familiar text used in different ways supports and scaffolds learners across those gaps that other kids navigate more easily.

 ## A Storytelling Centre: Not Simply Retelling

One of the best ways to develop oral language is to develop storytellers. As with any other skill, there is considerable variation within a class in storytelling ability. One child may tell one-word stories while others are able to tell complete stories involving a beginning, middle, and end that is sequenced and makes sense. Often the first stories that Kindergartners tell are retellings of stories that they have heard.

It is important to remember that many Kindergarten–Grade 2 students don't tell stories as we think of stories, with a problem, climax, solution…. They do, however, begin by sharing a series of events known as a personal recount about their family or friends. They consider this to be a story.

It is often hard to take the time to listen to the "stories" that students often want to share at less than opportune times. However, it is important that teachers make the time where possible to listen and even extend the conversation. Some children love to tell you stories but others may need more group storytelling to give them the confidence they need. Most importantly, they all must believe that the teacher feels that they have something worthwhile to say and is interested in what they have to say.

> Sharla Peltier notes that storytelling is "a natural area that we as Aboriginal people can draw upon as a form for oral history, language retention, extending memory capacity, and learning and practicing formal English language. It is also a great way to bring adults and Elders in to connect with children and to make program content and activities culturally relevant" (Ball 2006, 96).

How Students Become Storytellers

Students learn to tell stories by:

- Listening to lots of stories read to them and talking about stories (See **Read-Alouds**, Chapter 6)

- Retelling stories

- Being involved in story innovations (See **Story Innovations**, Chapter 9)

- Using and contributing to wall stories (See **Wall Stories**, this chapter)

- Listening to many stories being told and being involved in interactive storytelling (See **Teachers Tell Stories, this page** and **Interactive Storytelling,** p. 228)

- Using Wordless Picture Books and other props to incubate ideas (See **Storytelling Using Wordless Picture Books p. 231–234,** and **Effective Group Techniques to Encourage Reluctant Storytellers,**(See p. 229-231)

- Acting out stories, nursery rhymes and fairy tales (See p. 231)

- Singing songs from song picture books (See p. 242–244)

- Dramatic play and story playing (See p. 237–240)

- An adult scaffolding their talk beyond the present to the past and/or the future (See **Extending Conversations,** See p. 127).

They also become storytellers when teachers know how to support student storytelling effectively.

Teachers Tell Stories

Most K–2 teachers read aloud to their students at least several times a week (although at least once daily is preferable) but research indicates that teachers as storytellers occurs less frequently. Telling stories is very important because just as reading aloud, it can develop oral language skills, including vocabulary. However, telling stories has other real advantages. Telling stories engages the children because:

- Storytellers are even freer than story readers to use gestures, body language, and a variety of tones and inflections to make the story come to life.

- Storytellers often use props (as simple as a hat) to bring the story to life.

Young children's first attempts at storytelling are often the retelling of stories they have heard. Teachers will agree that many of the words, characters, actions, and story sequence are often identical or very similar to a story they have heard (Isbell 2003, 20).

- Unlike a storybook read-aloud that has text that may be too challenging for some, in storytelling the teacher can ensure that the text is at an appropriate level by simply showing the pictures and telling the story using student-friendly language.

- Nothing excites young children more than a story that the teacher tells that is personal. Young students want to know all about their teacher. Personal teacher stories often help the children to understand that their teacher has a life beyond the classroom.

Window on Miriam's Classroom

During my first year of teaching, an interesting incident happened. The principal's voice came over the intercom in my classroom. "Miss Gordon" he said, "Your mother is on the line." I remember the shock and amazement of one little girl who then said to me "Wow, you have a mother??"

- K–2 students typically want to be able to do what their teacher does. A storytelling teacher leads to storytelling students.

- Children love it when the teacher creates a story innovation by including their names in the story (See **Story Innovations,** (See p. 214-216).

- Wall stories help children to understand the concept of story and enjoy innovated stories.

- Telling stories can easily lead to acting them out.

Children learn that if you can think it, then you can tell a story.

What I can think, I can say.

Interactive Storytelling

Interactive storytelling occurs on the second or subsequent retellings by the teacher. Teachers tell the story, but in subsequent retellings, the students are prompted to join in. Children often spontaneously join in at the end of a line to complete a rhyme. Children may also be prompted to join in when there is a pattern or a repetition of a refrain such as in the Gingerbread Man: *Run, Run as fast you can! You can't catch me I'm the gingerbread man* or when the lines end with rhyming words. Nothing engages the children more than having storytelling props that they can use. Character props can be drawn on tongue depressors while masks can be made using paper plates.

The Story Playing Technique

The story playing technique (Paley 1990) allows children to act out stories that they have dictated and the teacher has written. Students love this since it is their personal stories that are written by the teacher and that they then discuss and act out. This technique follows these steps:

- Child dictates a story and teacher writes it.
- Teacher rereads aloud what the child dictated.
- Other children ask questions or make suggestions regarding changing the story.
- A group of children act out the story.

Assess Student Storytelling Skill Using the Primary Storytelling/Personal Recount Rubric.

Storytelling/Personal Recount Rubric

Student's Name: _____ **Date:** _____

Ask the student to create a story. A wordless picture book, pictures, a grab bag, or other prop may be used as an idea incubator if necessary. Indicate the quality of the student's story/personal recount relative to the story structure identified below.

Story Structure	Unprompted	Prompted	Not Provided
A beginning is stated			
Characters are identified			
Setting is shared			
A major event is described			
Events are shared in a logical sequence			
An outcome is shared			
An ending is stated			
Other			

Effective Group Techniques to Encourage Reluctant and/or Struggling Storytellers

Some children may be reluctant to begin a story or even a conversation. Others many simply struggle. Small group storytelling may be less threatening for such children and ultimately will get them to become more confident storytellers in the future. It is often challenging for primary teachers to be able to find the time for as much small group work as they would like and that some children desperately need. Volunteers, buddies, and paraprofessionals can be used effectively to provide this kind of support using the following techniques.

Round-Robin or sentence stories: In this instance, start the story off. The children each take turns adding a sentence to the story. Starting with a fairy tale that they are familiar with works well. Retell the fairy tale. Let the children know that they can change the fairy tale in any way they want. With Jack and the Beanstalk, for example, model by saying, "Jack's mother asked Jack to go and sell her bicycle since they needed the money to buy food."

Theme stories: Pick any theme or let the children pick a theme; for example, *living things* from science or *my family* from social studies. Again, get the children started. They each add to the story.

Descriptive stories: Begin the story by using boring words.... No adjectives or adverbs. For example model a think-aloud: "I was thinking of a story about a lady and a dog. The lady and dog came in to the classroom." Ask the children what they think of the story. What picture are they making in their heads? How could you make the story more interesting? Create a shared or modelled writing; for example, "A huge Golden Retriever pulled the woman in the pink polka dot dress into the classroom." Now ask the children to tell you what they think happened next... Complete the story. Try another one.

Picture stories: Use a motivating picture to get the talk going. Now help the class to create a story around the picture. Use these transition words — first, then, next, then, finally — as you move from child to child. Using pictures taken during classroom activities is always popular. The children can more easily make connections and stay engaged.

String stories: Use a length of string about one metre long to model this activity. Lay it on the floor. What shapes does it make? You may create letters or a line indicating a road or make a circle representing a balloon. As a shared writing experience, create a story about the string. Repeat the activity with a different shape. Now give each child a string and let each determine what it is and what the story will be about.

Grab-bag stories: Fill a bag with small objects such as toy animals, toy vehicles, or toys given out by fast food chains. Ask children to shut their eyes and each pick two items. Have them talk to a buddy about the two items (incubating ideas). Children then choose one of the items that reminds them of something they

Story Wheel is a digital storytelling app for the ipad and iphone. The first student or the whole class chooses an image by spinning the story wheel, and then respond with a a 30 second narration. This technique supports storytelling.

http://storywheelapp.com/about_story_wheel.xhtml

have at home or something that has happened to them. They then tell their partner the "story" or personal recount related to the item.

Finish-the-Story: Tell a story just about to the end. Have the children take turns coming up with different endings.

Begin-the-Story: Share the ending to a story. Have the children take turns coming up with different beginnings.

Acting out nursery rhymes: Begin by discussing nursery rhymes in general. All of them provide at least a recount, if not a story. Begin by naming just one nursery rhyme with which the children are familiar. Write its name. Share the nursery rhyme and have the children join in. Then model for the children how to play the game. Explain that you are going to stand in the middle of the circle and act out a part of the nursery rhyme. Have them suggest what part of the nursery rhyme you were acting out. Have them explain why they think you acted out that part. Then brainstorm two nursery rhymes and begin a list. Review the rhymes and have the children join in. Now, have children take turns doing the pantomiming and playing the game.

Storytelling Using Wordless Picture Books

Wordless picture books (books without words or just an occasional word or phrase) are interpreted entirely through a sequence of illustrations. It is important to note than there are two categories of wordless picture books: those that tell stories and those written around a concept. Concept books focus on a specific topic, such as the alphabet, numbers, or colors. In all picture books, the children are supported in developing visual literacy — their ability to read the pictures and illustrations. As children follow the pictures, they verbalize the action in their own words, a process that also builds vocabulary, comprehension, and story structure. In wordless picture books, the children really become the storytellers and are much freer to interpret the stories in their own way. Wordless picture books are excellent to use with all children, especially those just learning English and those struggling with decoding and/or comprehension. They support the development of both vocabulary and grammar through conversation. Using wordless picture books allows all children, no matter what their vocabulary or decoding skills, to read, discuss, and act out the same book. There is no one right retelling so creativity and imagination is supported. Typically wordless picture books are more economical to purchase.

 Check It Out!
"The Story" in *Frog and Toad are Friends* by Arnold Lobel.... Children will be able to connect to the concept of how hard it is at times to come up with a story to tell.

 Check It Out!
The National Centre for Family Literacy (www.famlit.org) is a great online resource to help teachers support parents/ caregivers in the development of their child's literacy. See "Talking About Wordless Picture Books: A Tutor Strategy Supporting English Language Learners."

Great Traditional and Wordless Storybooks

 Check It Out!

Check out these four wonderful wordless picture books by Canadian authors:

Baker, Liza. *Under the Sea*. Toronto: HarperCollins Canada, 2003.

Dornbusch, Erica. *Finding Kate's Shoes*. Toronto: Annick Press, 2001.

Gutierrez, Elisa. *Picturescape*. Vancouver: Simply Read Books, 2005.

Reid, Barbara. *Zoe's Sunny Day*. Toronto: Scholastic Canada, 2002.

Friendship

Briggs, Raymond. *The Snowman*. New York: Penguin Group, 2002.

Carle, Eric. *Do You Want to Be My Friend?* New York: Penguin Group, 2002.

Mayer, Mercer. *A Boy, a Dog, a Frog and a Friend*. New York: Penguin Group, 2003.

———. *Frog on His Own*. New York: Penguin Group, 2003.

———. *One Frog Too Many*. New York: Penguin Group, 2003.

McDonnell, Patrick. *South*. London: Little Brown & Company, 2008.

Rogers, Gregory. *The Boy, the Bear, the Baron, the Bard*. New York: Roaring Brook Press, 2007.

Rohmann, Eric. *My Friend Rabbit*. New York: Square Fish, 2007.

Wiesner, David. *Sector 7*. Boston: Houghton Mifflin Harcourt, 1999.

Family

Alborough, Jez. *Hug*. Somerville, MA: Candlewick Press, 2005.

Baker, Jeannie. *Home*. Toronto: HarperCollins Canada, 2004.

McCully, Emily Arnold. *First Snow*. Toronto: HarperCollins Canada, 2003.

Ormerod, Jan. *Sunshine*. London: Frances Lincoln, 2005.

Turkle, Brinton. *Deep in the Forest*. New York: Penguin Group, 1992.

Social Skills (Sharing, Bullying, Behaviour)

dePaola, Tomie. *The Knight and the Dragon*. New York: Penguin Group, 2002.

Dewey, Ariane. *The Last Laugh*. New York: Penguin Group, 2006.

McGrath, Meggan. *My Grapes*. Toronto: Scholastic Canada, 2001.

Popov, Nikolai. *Why?* New York: North-South Books, 1998.

Routines (Bedtime, Getting Dressed)

Geisert, Arthur. *Hogwash*. Boston: Houghton Mifflin Harcourt, 2008.

Ormerod, Jan. *Moonlight*. London: Frances Lincoln, 2005

Rathmann, Peggy. *Good Night, Gorilla*. New York: Penguin Group, 2004.

Schories, Pat. *Breakfast for Jack*. Honesdale, PA: Boyds Mills Press, 2004.

Wiesner, David. *Free Fall*. Toronto: HarperCollins Canada, 2008.

———. *Tuesday*. Boston: Houghton Mifflin Harcourt, 1997.

Humorous

Hutchins, Pat. *Rosie's Walk*. New York: Simon & Schuster Children's Publishing, 1998.

Yoo, Tae-Eun. *The Little Red Fish*. New York: Penguin Group, 2007.

Stories (General)

Alborough, Jez. *Tall*. Somerville, MA: Candlewick Press, 2007.

Aliki. *Tabby: A Story in Pictures*. Toronto: HarperCollins Canada, 1995.

Anno, Mitsumasa. *Anno's Journey*. New York: Penguin Group, 2002.

Baker, Jeannie. *Window*. New York: HarperCollins Publishers, 1991.

Bang, Molly. *The Grey Lady and the Strawberry Snatcher*. New York: Simon & Schuster Children's Publishing, 1996.

Banyai, Istvan. *Re-Zoom*. New York: Penguin Group, 1998.

———. *Zoom*. New York: Penguin Group, 1998.

Blake, Quentin. *Clown*. New York: Henry Holt & Company, 1998.

Crews, Donald. *Truck Board Book*. New York: HarperCollins Publishers, 1997.

Day, Alexandra. *Carl's Masquerade*. New York: Farrar, Straus & Giroux, 1992.

———. *You're a Good Dog, Carl*. New York: Square Fish, 2007.

Dematons, Charlotte. *Yellow Balloon*. Honesdale, PA: Boyds Mills Press, 2004.

dePaola, Tomie. *Pancakes for Breakfast*. New York: Houghton Mifflin Harcourt, 1978.

Edens, Cooper. *The Christmas We Moved to the Barn*. Toronto: HarperCollins Canada, 1997.

Enderle, Judith Ross. *Six Creepy Sheep*. Honesdale, PA: Boyds Mills Press, 2003.

Faller, Regis. *Polo: The Runaway Book*. New York: Henry Holt & Company, 2007.

———. *The Adventures of Polo*. New York: Henry Holt & Company, 2006.

Fleischman, Paul. *Sidewalk Circus*. Somerville, MA: Candlewick Press, 2004.

Geisert, Arthur. *Oops*. Boston: Houghton Mifflin Harcourt, 2006.

Guilloppé, Antoine. *One Scary Night*. Jericho, NY: iBooks, 2005.

Hutchins, Pat. *Changes, Changes*. New York: Simon & Schuster Children's Publishing, 1987.

Jenkins, Steve. *Looking Down*. Boston: Houghton Mifflin Harcourt Publishing, 2003.

Keats, Ezra Jack. *Clementina's Cactus*. New York: Penguin Group, 1999.

Krahn, Fernando. *Amanda and the Mysterious Carpet*. Boston: Houghton Mifflin Harcourt, 1985.

Lee, Suzy. *Wave*. San Francisco: Chronicle Books LLC, 2008.

Lehman, Barbara. *Museum Trip*. Boston: Houghton Mifflin Harcourt, 2006.

———. *Rainstorm*. Boston: Houghton Mifflin Harcourt, 2007.

———. *The Red Book*. Boston: Houghton Mifflin Harcourt, 2004.

———. *Trainstop*. Boston: Houghton Mifflin Harcourt, 2008.

Liu, Jae Soo. *Yellow Umbrella*. La Jolla, CA: Kane/Miller Book Publishers, Incorporated, 2006.

Mayer, Mercer. *A Boy, a Dog and a Frog*. New York: Penguin Group, 2003.

———. *Frog Goes to Dinner*. New York: Penguin Group, 2003.

———. *Frog, Where Are You?* New York: Penguin Group, 2003.

McCully, Emily Arnold. *Picnic*. Toronto: HarperCollins Canada, 2003.

———. *School*. Toronto: HarperCollins Canada, 2005.

Polhemus, Coleman. *The Crocodile Blues*. Somerville, MA: Candlewick Press, 2007.

Rohmann, Eric. *Time Flies*. New York: Random House Children's Books, 1997.

Schories, Pat. *Jack and the Missing Piece*. Honesdale, PA: Boyds Mills Press, 2004.

———. *Jack and the Night Visitors*. Honesdale, PA: Boyds Mills Press, 2006.

———. *Jack Wants a Snack*. Honesdale, PA: Boyds Mills Press, 2008.

Schubert, Dieter. *Where's My Monkey?* Honesdale, PA: Boyds Mills Press, 2004.

Sis, Peter. *Dinosaur!* Toronto: HarperCollins Canada, 2000.

———. *Ship Ahoy!* Toronto: HarperCollins Canada, 1999.

———. *Trucks, Trucks, Trucks*. Toronto: HarperCollins Canada, 2004.

Van Ommen, Sylvia. *The Surprise*. Honesdale, PA: Boyds Mills Press, 2007.

Weitzman, Jacqueline Preiss. *You Can't Take a Balloon into the Metropolitan Museum*. New York: Penguin Group, 2001.

Wiesner, David. *Flotsam*. New York: Houghton Mifflin Harcourt, 2006.

Wildsmith, Brian. *The Apple Bird*. Don Mills, ON: Oxford University Press, 1983.

Yum, Hyewon. *Last Night*. New York: Farrar, Straus & Giroux, 2008.

Storytelling Using Story Maps

A story map is a way to organize information from a story. It teaches students the features of story structure, which can be used for prediction and comprehension in reading and for story retelling either orally or in writing. After a read-aloud or shared-reading experience, the teacher fills in a story-map chart by having students identify the following information from the story:

- Title and author (teachers may also want to identify the illustrator)
- Characters and the setting
- What happened at the beginning, middle, and end of the story

Alternatively, students outline three or four main events (e.g., using first, next, and then) and then tell how the story ended. See http://www.readwritethink.org/files/resources/interactives/storymap/

Storytelling Using Who Wanted But So Then

This is an alternative way to retell the main points in a story. This is also a great way to retell fairy tales.

Implementing the "who wanted but so then" technique

1. The teacher models the technique for students by completing a Who Wanted But So Then chart for a familiar story.

2. Students may then use this technique on their own when retelling the main points in a story by identifying

- The character(s) (*Who*)
- What the character(s) wanted (*Wanted*)
- What was preventing the character(s) from achieving the goal; i.e., the problem (*But*)
- What happened next (*So*)
- What finally happened (*Then*)

Implementing the "who wanted but so then" technique: A real life example

The teacher models the technique for students by completing a "**Who Wanted But So Then**" chart.

Try this amazing wordless picture book and share a fractured fairy tale: *Deep in the Forest* by Brinton Turkle. This retelling of the Goldilocks story is a charming twist on a classic children's story. The illustrations really bring the story to life. The expressions on the faces of the little bear, the little girl, and the parents clearly reveal emotions and lead into feeling words as well as character trait vocabulary. Vocabulary (not exclusive):character(s), character trait(s), feeling(s), face, expression, illustrations, curious, fearful, shy, frightened, afraid, surprised, startled, shocked, amazed, happy, disappointed, mischievous, stunned, angry, loving, and creep(ing). Sharing this fractured fairy tale helps children understand perspective, an important element of critical literacy.

Who Wanted But So Then is a great technique for students to use when they come in from recess and have a problem to relate!

Who Wanted But So Then	
Story Title	Aladdin
Who	Aladdin, a street urchin
Wanted	to marry Princess Jasmine, they love each other
But	she can only marry a prince.
So	the genie saves Aladdin's life and together they save the kingdom from Jafar, the king's evil advisor.
Then	Jasmine is permitted to marry Aladdin and they live happily ever after.

Storytelling Using Story Boards

A story board is another activity that can be used to summarize a story. It can also be used to facilitate an oral retelling or as a **starting** point in a writing activity.

- Students draw pictures to represent what happened at the beginning, in the middle, and at the end of the story.

- The pictures can be used to help organize the oral retelling of the story.

- The pictures can also help students plan what they want to write when they are ready to write independently.

A large story board can be drawn on chart paper to summarize a class story, or smaller versions can be provided for a centre or individual activity (See http://harrybrake.files.wordpress.com/ 2012/07/framing-the-text-using-storyboards-to-engage-students-with-reading.pdf)

Storytelling Using Sketch to Stretch

Copies of the book(s) should be at the centre for the students to refer back to.

Use the **I Remember Strategy:** After listening to a read-aloud or reading a book, students think of something they remember and choose an "event" or fact to sketch. Students who need a stimulus may consider:

- What I learned
- What I liked
- What I felt
- The most important part

Each student shares his or her sketch with a partner or with a small group and describes the sketch's contents and the reason the sketch was created.

Storytelling Using Playing Beyond the Story

It is not uncommon for a story to provoke play and inquiry beyond the story itself. Reading the walls in Alissa's Kindergarten class told such a story.

Window on the Classroom: Alissa's Class Where the Walls Tell the Story

As I walked around Alissa's class and read the walls, it was clear that they told a story: a story of an exciting Kindergarten classroom where the teacher grabbed those teachable moments. This resulted in the effective linking of literacy, numeracy, inquiry, and play. This is Alissa's story

Alissa very effectively used a teachable moment after reading *The Door Bell Rang* (1989) by Pat Hutchins to her class. In the process, she also developed math skills and understandings, and the reading–writing connection. In the book, Victoria and Sam are just sitting down to a plateful of Ma's cookies when the doorbell rings and two of their friends arrive to share the feast. The doorbell rings again and again and each time the number of cookies per person dwindles until at last there is only one cookie per person and ... the doorbell rings again! (Luckily, it's Grandma arriving with a huge plate of cookies. And "No one makes cookies as good as grandma!!" — a refrain repeated throughout the book.)

A number of activities originated after we read *The Doorbell Rang*. We worked through a series of math problems using pretend cookies where we focused on sharing them with a certain number of friends. Initially, I chose this text for a math focus to introduce the students to the idea of fractions and dividing wholes into equal pieces. I had no idea how many things would come out of this text! One reason I love Full-Day Kindergarten!

This book led to discussions involving critical literacy, about sharing and dividing items fairly, and this was emphasized at classroom centres, such as playdough, where kids had a habit of taking huge chunks for themselves, and only giving a small amount to the other students in the group.

The children also had the idea of writing a letter to Grandma to ask her for her recipe and I thought this was a perfect opportunity to focus on interactive writing with a small group. Most of these students were Junior Kindergartners who had a pretty good grasp of basic sight words, and they were using resources, such as the word wall, to help them with spelling. It was amazing to see how these students helped each other, and took turns "sharing the pen" with me and their peers. We were also focusing on letter writing at this time as we had a post office at our dramatic play centre, so this was another way to demonstrate how to write a letter, and provide guidance and support for students to practice this independently.

Once "Grandma" wrote back to us, we extended this activity by developing and following recipes (procedural writing and math focus again), and we did some baking! The experiences led to lots of conversations about types of ingredients, measurement units, etc. We ended this activity by working with the same group of students to use interactive writing to write back to Grandma to share our experience. The students were very engaged throughout these activities, and it was so neat how it touched so many curriculum expectations! More importantly, it did so in a meaningful and authentic way by constantly building upon and extending student learning — something I feel is the backbone of full-day Kindergarten!

The Doorbell Rang is a great book to act out and is perfect for Reader's Theatre too. It also supports student understanding of self-regulation.

Enjoy *The Doorbell Rang* read-aloud at http://www.youtube.com/watch?v=BXtu90JnDkM

Sharing pretend cookies

Writing a cookie recipe using vanilla

Some math problems were developed using real cookies, and students got to use them as a tool to solve the problems accurately.

Multiple Paths to Literacy

Taking the recipes home to try!

In the process of grabbing that teachable moment, Alissa ensured that the curriculum expectations were not forgotten.

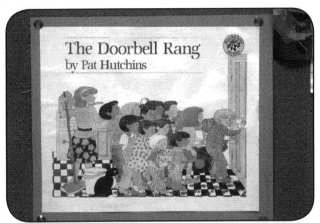

The Doorbell Rang
by Pat Hutchins

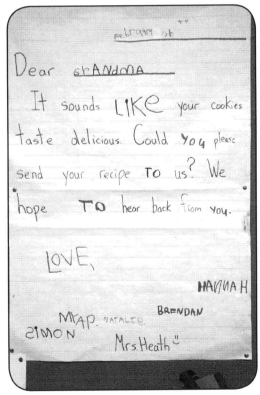

February 26

Dear GRANDMA

It sounds LIKE your cookies taste delicious. Could you please send your recipe TO us? We hope TO hear back from you.

LOVE,

HANNAH H

MYA. NATALIE BRENDAN
SIMON Mrs. Heath

A letter to Grandma… a real reason to write. Grandma writes back! The excitement in the room when the letter arrives!

March 5th, 2013

Dear Simon, Mya, Natalie, Brendan, Hannah, Mrs. Heath and the rest of your class:

Thank you for your lovely letter! I love hearing from children. You sure are super writers! Your teachers must be proud of you.

I really do love baking – especially when it's for all of my grandchildren and their friends! Chocolate chip cookies are one of my most favourite things to bake! I am happy to share my recipe with you. Do you think you can bake them as good as mine? The recipe is on the next page. It's kind of a secret recipe though, so be sure not to share it with anyone else! Shhhh!! ☺

Good luck with your baking, and I hope the cookies turn out. Make sure Mrs. Heath doesn't keep them in the oven too long, or else they will burn! I hope you write back to me to let me know how the cookies turn out. Send me pictures too, if you can!

Looking forward to hearing from you soon,
Grandma

P.S. If I have 10 cookies and 5 friends to share them with, how many cookies do each of my friends get?

Documentation: Full-Day Kindergarten Curriculum Expectations	
Personal and Social Development	
1.2	Demonstrate the ability to take turns in activities and discussions.
2.5	Interact co-operatively with others in classroom events and activities.
Language	
OL 1.4	Follow and provide one- and two-step directions in different contexts.
W 4.3	Write simple messages.
W 4.4	Begin to use classroom resources to support their writing.
W 4.5	Experiment with a variety of simple writing forms for different purposes and in a variety of contexts.
Mathematics	
NS1.3	Begin to make use of one-to-one correspondence in counting objects and matching groups of objects.
NS1.11	Investigate and develop strategies for composing and decomposing quantities to 10.
M2.2	Demonstrate, through investigation, an awareness of non-standard and standard measuring devices, and strategies for using them.
Science and Technology:	
2.2	Make predictions and observations before and during investigations.

Closing Thoughts

The storytelling and retelling centre is an important one. Wall Stories can effectively scaffold the storytelling. Chapter 10 shares the research-base and the how-to of implementing nine additional hands-on key centres including those that support listening, art, building, phonics, word work, and inquiry.

Key Centres that Support Literacy, Inquiry and Play

  Chapter 10 highlights nine key hands-on centres that support literacy, inquiry, and play. The centres include: listening, construction/ block and building, art, discovery/wonder, treasure/wonder/ inquiry, an additional wonder centre, alphabet, phonics, and word work, and a reading centre.

A Listening Centre

The listening centre provides students with the opportunity to listen to and join in to music, stories, and non-fiction, with or without accompanying text. The students may also create and record music using different instruments and materials at this centre. The traditional view of a listening centre involved a tape recorder and a few cassettes; however, technology has now expanded this concept to include a computer, tablet, iPod, and other wireless devices. Texts such as narrative, poetry, rhymes, jokes, cheers, reader's theatre scripts, and songs are especially effective for fluency development.

Research base

The listening centre is incredibly important from preschool–Grade 2. It provides all students with the opportunity to listen, read and sing. Through the listening centre, students develop reading fluency and enjoyment, concepts of print and phonological awareness skills (Rasinski and Padak, 2001). Singing becomes a vehicle for teaching reading and fluency. Students hear fluent reading being modelled. Material meant to be performed works well. If the passage is meant to be performed, it has to be rehearsed or practiced repeatedly, which is key to fluency. The performance of a passage makes the practice meaningful to students. They will want to perfect their reading, phrasing, and pausing so that the performance is as effective as possible.

Students learn that fluent reading involves reading smoothly, without hesitation and with expression. It is important for students to understand that speed does not equal reading fluency and that the whole purpose of reading is comprehension. Reading comprehension in K–2 is very dependent on fluency.

"Effective fluency instruction moves beyond automatic word recognition to include rhythm and expression in reading" (CIERA Report #2 2008).

Use music to develop reading fluency:
http://www.scholastic.com/teachers/top-teaching/2012/12/using-music-improve-reading-fluency

I like to read, sing, and have fun at the listening centre.

Songs from Song Picture Books at the Listening Centre

A great deal of singing is important in the primary grades. Singing and language development are definitely related. Songs support phonological awareness, which is an important skill used when developing reading and writing fluency. Memorized songs when supported by music and the written word can be a valuable resource for learning to read and write (Jalongo 1997). Songs also support vocabulary building and the development of oral language structures. This is especially important for English language learners. Furthermore, singing is fun and promotes the active participation of all. Children typically love songs and they love to create and sing their own versions. A song picture book is an ideal way to motivate the children to read, write, sing, talk, and draw. Song picture books are typically illustrated versions of well-known songs, chants, and musical finger plays. Most use rhyme, repetition such as a chorus or refrain, and predictable structures such as the days of the week or numbers (for example, *There were 10 in the bed and the little one said roll over, roll over... There were 9 in the bed and the little one said...*).

Multiple Paths to Literacy

Song picture books support literacy by:

- Building on familiarity and enjoyment
- Providing repetition and predictability
- Developing fluency
- Expanding vocabulary and knowledge of story structures
- Promoting critical thinking and problem solving
- Fostering creative expression and language play including phonological awareness

(Adapted from *Using song picture books to support emergent literacy* by Mary Renck Jalongo, Deborah Ribblett and Deborah McDonald : http://www.freepatentsonline.com/article/ChildhoodEducation/20851402.html).

"One particular type of book, the song picture book, is uniquely well suited for supporting children's growth in art, music, literature and language" (Jalongo 1997, 1).

Children's Song Picture Books

Adams, P. *There was an Old Lady Who Swallowed a Fly*. Auburn ME: Child's Play-International, 2003.

Aliki. *Go Tell Aunt Rhody*. New York: Simon & Schuster Children's Publishing, 1996.

Aylesworth, J. *Old Black Fly*. New York: Henry Holt & Company for Young Readers, 1995.

Beck, I. *Five Little Ducks*. London, England: Orchard Books, 1992.

Binch, Caroline, et al. *Down by the River: Afro-Caribbean Rhymes, Games, and Songs for Children*. Toronto: Scholastic Canada (Illustrated song collection), 1996.

Brett, J. *The Twelve Days of Christmas*. New York: Penguin Group, 2004.

Carle, E. *Today Is Monday*. New York: Penguin Group, 2007.

Christelow, E. *Five Little Monkeys Jumping on the Bed*. Boston: Houghton Mifflin Harcourt, 2006.

Dale, P. *Ten in the Bed*. Somerville, MA: Candlewick Press, 2007.

Glazer, T. *On Top of Spaghetti*. New York: Scholastic, 2006.

Hammerstein, O., and R. Rodgers. *My Favorite Things*. Toronto: HarperCollins Canada, 2001.

Hale, S. J. *Mary Had a Little Lamb*. New York: Penguin Group, 2004.

Ho, M. *Hush! A Thai Lullaby*. New York: Scholastic, 2000.

Hoberman, M. A. *A House Is a House for Me*. New York: Penguin Group, 2007.

Hudson, W., and C. Hudson. *How Sweet the Sound: African-American Songs for Children*. (Illustrated song collection). Toronto: Scholastic Canada, 1997.

Hurd, T. *Mama Don't Allow*. Pine Plains, NY: Live Oak Media, 2004.

Ivimey, J. *Three Blind Mice*. New York: Little Brown & Company, 1990.

Jones, C. *This Old Man*. Boston: Houghton Mifflin Harcourt, 1998.

Jorgensen, G. *Crocodile Beat*. New York: Simon & Schuster Children's Publishing, 1989.

Keats, E. J. *Over in the Meadow*. New York: Penguin Group, 1999.

Kellogg, S. *There Was an Old Woman*. New York: Simon & Schuster Children's Publishing, 1984.

Kennedy, J. *The Teddy Bears' Picnic*. New York: Simon & Schuster Children's Publishing, 2000.

Kovalski, M. *Jingle Bells*. Markham, ON: Fitzhenry & Whiteside, 1998.

La Prise, L. *The Hokey Pokey*. New York: Simon & Schuster Children's Publishing, 1997.

Langstaff, J. *Frog Went A-Courtin'*. New York: Harcourt Children's Books, 1955.

———. *Oh, A-Hunting We Will Go*. New York: Simon & Schuster Children's Publishing, 1991.

Mallet, D. *Inch by Inch: The Garden Song*. Toronto: HarperCollins Canada, 1997.

Paparone, P. *Five Little Ducks: An Old Rhyme*. New York: North-South Books, 1995.

Parton, D. *Coat of Many Colors*. Toronto: HarperCollins Canada Ltd., 1996.

Peek, M. *Mary Wore Her Red Dress and Henry Wore His Green Sneakers*. Boston: Houghton Mifflin Harcourt, 2006.

Raffi. *Baby Beluga*. New York: Random House Children's Books, 1992.

———. *Down by the Bay*. New York: Random House Children's Books, 1988.

———. *Shake My Sillies Out*. New York: Random House Children's Books, 1988.

———. *Everything Grows*. Burlington, MA: Rounder Books, 2004.

Reid, B. *Two by Two*. Toronto: Scholastic Canada, 2002.

Seeger, P. *Abiyoyo*. New York: Simon & Schuster Children's Publishing, 2001.

Soto, G. *The Old Man and His Door*. New York: Penguin Group, 2002.

Spier, P. *The Fox Went Out on a Chilly Night*. New York: Random House Children's Books, 1994.

Thiele, B., and G. D. Weiss. *What a Wonderful World*. New York: Simon & Schuster Children's Publishing, 1995.

Wadsworth, O. A. *Over in the Meadow*. New York: North-South Books, 2003.

Weiss, N. *If You're Happy and You Know It*. New York: HarperCollins Publishers, 1987.

Westcott, N. B. *Peanut Butter and Jelly: A Play Rhyme*. Toronto: Penguin Group Canada, 1992.

———. *Skip to My Lou*. New York: Little, Brown Books for Young Readers, 2000.

Winter, J. *Follow the Drinking Gourd*. New York: Random House Children's Books, 1992.

Zelinsky, P. O. *The Wheels on the Bus*. New York: Penguin Group, 2001.

Check It Out!

One of the most amazing song picture books ever written is *Hey, Little Ant* by Phillip and Hannah Hoose (Berkeley, CA: Tricycle Press, 1998). The book includes the musical score and is written in rhyme, which is great for phonological awareness. The story tells of an ant that is about to be squished by a little boy. The ant and the boy argue back and forth. The story is left open-ended with the question, "What do you think that kid should do?" This question leads to great and sometimes heated discussions and ultimately to predictions. The illustrations support visual and critical literacy, interpreting perspective. (You can access a free teacher's guide and listen to the song at the *Hey, Little Ant* website: www.heylittleant.com)

A Construction/Block/Building Centre

Research base

The block centre is very important (Colker 2008). It promotes learning across developmental domains such as:

- Social and emotional
- Physical
- Language and literacy
- Science and math

Skill development during block play

Social and emotional: Perseverance when building; co-operation, problem solving and self-regulation when planning and building with a partner or group; following classroom safety rules

Physical: Large(gross) and small(fine) motor skills; hand-eye coordination; visual discrimination to select blocks by visually comparing the sizes and shapes of the blocks available.

Language and literacy: Learn academic vocabulary such as shapes (arch, cylinder, triangle, rectangle); building terms such as enclosure, bridge; comparison terms such as shorter, longer, smaller, lighter; spatial words such as under, over, through, on top of, inside. Create labels for structures; create wall stories and class books by taking photos and writing about the event; participate in oral language practice, including many conversations.

Science and math: Counting, comparing, measuring, building ramps and pathways; **architecture and engineering:** "To build tall and complex structures that don't topple over, young builders apply principles of architecture and engineering, such as

- Bases of structures must be stable
- Structures must be balanced
- Ramps are strong when they are supported
- Columns can support arches and bridge spans
- Tunnels will collapse if they are not built into well-supported structures
- Long unit blocks and strong hollow blocks are best for framing foundations" (Colker 2008, 17).

Stages of Block Play
1. *Carrying blocks*
2. *Piling blocks and making roads*
3. *Connecting blocks to create structures by making:*
   - Bridges
   - Enclosures
   - Designs
4. *Elaborate designs*

Window on the Classroom: Ramp and Bridge Inquiry and Play in Angie's Class: Curriculum as Lived

One afternoon in the block centre, two boys had an argument about what they had built. I sat and listened to them. One child said they had built a ramp because the car could go down it. The other child stated they built a bridge because you could go under it. I posed a question, "What are the differences between a ramp and a bridge?" I located some non-fiction books about ramps and bridges and found some clips on Discovery Education. We investigated different types of bridges and ramps and some students learned that sometimes you need a ramp in order to get onto a bridge. Children worked in teams to build ramps and bridges. As an observer, I watched as children built and debated whether there were two separate things or if the ramp and bridge went together as one. No wonder there was debate, this was not a clear cut situation. Students used foam blocks, sticks, wooden blocks, and our big Gorilla Block set to create different types of ramps and bridges. This inquiry led to some discussion about which ramp was the fastest. Does the height of the ramp influence the speed? Does the material of the ramp make the car go faster or slower?

We read about the purposes of ramps and bridges and together we made some observations. Some students were so interested in this inquiry that they continued to keep it as a focus when they went to blocks throughout the entire year. Through reading non-fiction books, looking at digital photos of bridges and watching short video clips of bridges and ramps, students developed a building vocabulary and used the words consistently throughout the year.

Angie was able to integrate aspects of

- The planned Ontario provincial science curriculum: conduct simple investigations through free exploration, focused exploration, and guided activity, using inquiry skills (observing, questioning, planning an investigation, carrying out the investigation, and communicating findings by exploring the effects of changing the slope and the construction material of a ramp), "curriculum as planned".

- The "curriculum as lived," by grabbing the teachable moments and following two of the students.

Check It Out!

Great read-alouds to support a bridge and ramp inquiry:

Bridges! by Carol A Johmann and Elizabeth J Rieth

Bridges, by Susan Canizares and Daniel Moreton, 2012

Iggy Peck, Architect by Andrea Beaty and David Roberts, 2007

Also, see the story of *Iggy Peck Architect, following your dreams*: https://www.youtube.com/watch?v=hRj4FBX6pHw

Let's Try It Out with Towers and Bridges: Hands-On Early Learning Activities by Seymour Simon, Nicole Fauteux, and Doug Cushman, 2003

Pete the Cat: Construction Destruction by James Dean, 2015

Roberto: The Insect Architect by Nina Laden, 2000

Roll, Slope, and Slide: A Book about Ramps by Michael Dahl, illustrated by Denise Shea, 2006

Cars and ramps... what great inquiry and play! Which ramp was the fastest? Does the material of the ramp make the car go faster or slower?

Ontario, The Kindergarten Program 2006, OVERALL EXPECTATIONS

By the end of Kindergarten, children will:

1. Demonstrate an awareness of the natural and human-made environment through hands-on investigations, observation, questioning, and sharing of their findings;
2. Conduct simple investigations through free exploration, focused exploration, and guided activity, using inquiry skills (observing, questioning, planning an investigation, carrying out the investigation, and communicating findings);
3. Demonstrate an understanding of and care for the natural world;
4. Investigate and talk about the characteristics and functions of some common materials, and use these materials safely;
5. Recognize and use safely some common forms of technology.

SPECIFIC EXPECTATIONS: investigate, in various ways, how different forces make things move (*e.g., observe the effect that wind has on different objects, explore ways in which different toys move*)

Props to extend play and elaborate block building include:

- People figures (families and community helpers)
- Farm, zoo, and other animals
- Trees and other landscaping items
- Traffic signs
- Cars, trucks, and other vehicles
- Phones and phone books
- Blueprints for buildings
- Child-size hard hats
- Paper, notebooks, clipboards, and writing tools
- Individual student created drivers' licenses for the block centre
- Fiction and non-fiction books, home magazines, architectural digests

(Adapted from Colker 2008, 17)

Great Books to Support Literacy Learning, Play, and Inquiry at the Block Centre

Construction and Demolition

1. *How A House Is Built* by Gail Gibbons
2. *Hammers Nails Planks* by Thomas Jackson
3. *Bam Bam Bam* (A Demolition Story) by Eve Merriam
4. *Up Goes The Skyscraper* by Gail Gibbons
5. *Harry's House* by Angela Medearis
6. *Building a House* by Byron Barton
7. *The House That Max Built* by Maxwell Newhouse
8. *Tools* by Ann Rosen
9. *Arches to Zigzags: An Architecture ABC* by Michael Crosbi
10. *Raise the Roof* by Anastasia Suen and Elwood Smith

Houses and Buildings

(For People and Animals)

1. *House Is A House For Me* by Mary Ann Hoberman
2. *Castle* by David Macaulay
3. *This House Is Made Of Mud* by Ken Buchanan
4. *Pyramid* by David Macaulay
5. *A House for a Hermit Crab* by Eric Carle
6. *13 Buildings Children Should Know* by Annette Roeder
7. *Look at That Building* by Scot Ritchie
8. *This is Our House* by Michael Rosen

Block Play and Buildings

1. *If You Take a Mouse to School* by Laura Numeroff
2. *Changes, Changes* by Pat Hutchins
3. *The Three Little Pigs*
4. *Block City* by Robert Louis Stevenson
5. *The Three Little Wolves and the Big Bad Pig* by Eugene Trivizas

Window on the Classroom: Bonnie's Class Learns All About Construction, Play, and Literacy

Inspired and motivated by Miriam's visit (*Learning to Write and Loving It*) I set out to transform our Imagination Station (dramatic play centre) into a space where children were free to construct and create but the key was that they had to plan and write before they ever touched a single block. I covered the walls in the cozy space with giant sheets of old building plans (blueprints) from an architect, which we discussed, set out a giant tub of wooden blocks, a small carpet on the floor (wooden blocks are really quite loud when they crash!), added a book stand that held clipboards with pages that said "My Building Plan" (play plans) and lots and lots of pencils. As a class, we did some research on design and construction by looking at different buildings as well as reading some books about architects, building, and creating. The children really love the book *Look at that Building*. I also bought *Building a Home*. It talks about all of the tradespeople involved in building a home. Today the children were plumbers, carpenters, electricians... so many rich words are being used, and they are reading and writing away!

> Use mainly open-ended questions when discussing the creations at the block centre... Extend the talk with "Tell me more..." Post photos of completed structures to share with others to enable a degree of permanence to their structures (See **Play Plans**, p. 188).

We had a shared writing experience and generated a list of words to post in their new design centre about construction. Every single child was able and eager to write. Every single child was successful. Every single child knew that he or she was a writer.

A budding architect... his face says it all!

Also, note encouragement for play plans on clip boards.

Window on Kathy's Classroom: Linking Literacy and Play at Home and at School

I received a great idea from Kathy Steele, Surrey School District in British Columbia, that demonstrates how teachers can effectively link literacy and play, both at home and at school. It is a take-off on the idea of sending home a stuffed animal and a journal, one child at a time. The child then brings the stuffed animal and the journal back to school and shares the adventures with the group. I had wanted to change it up and so I brought in a copy of *Architectural Digest* magazine. We talked about designing and building structures. I then put some pattern blocks into a bag along with a large scrapbook/class journal called *Architectural Digest*. On the inside cover I included a letter to parents to let them know their child could keep the materials for a couple of days, build a structure with the blocks, and represent it in some way in the "digest" — diagram, writing, photo... Everyone enjoyed their time in adding to the book and some students found it particularly engaging. Of course, there were the added benefits of more writing at the block centre, and the parents understanding a little more about the learning and application of children working with blocks.

 ### *An Art Centre*
Research base

Visual arts (painting, drawing, collage, and modelling) and literacy go together like coffee and donuts or jelly and peanut butter. Pictures and print work together, to help children to think, to share their thinking, feelings, stories, and imaginations. "Children's art has the capacity to say what words often cannot" *Young Learners Experiences in Art*, Art Gallery of Nova Scotia and the Nova Scotia Department of Education 2009, 9).

Students benefit where they are guided to understand the six elements of visual arts: line, shape, form, space, texture, and color. Art and art conversations make thinking visible. Art is also a mediator of oral language. Although art is supported across the curricula and in many places in the classroom, the Art Centre is designed to allow students freedom to use materials of various

See an enlightening talk by Elliot Eisner: "What do the Arts Teach" https://www.youtube.com/watch?v=h12MGuhQH9E.

shapes, textures, and sizes in order to create. The activities result in student engagement and generally are self-directed, but some teacher direction is also important. For example, many teachers encourage students to draw but do not provide the support. I was one of those teachers. I knew there was something missing but I did not know how to draw myself. For many practical ideas on how to teach drawing, see *Talking, Drawing and Writing Lessons for Our Youngest Writers* by Martha Horn and Mary Ellen Giacobbe. Also enjoy a superb book by Ann Pelo listed below and Ed Emberley's Drawing *Book of Animals , Drawing Book of Trucks and Trains, Drawing Book of Faces, the Fingerprint Drawing Book* and the mini-lesson below. Visit www.janBrett.com to learn about drawing, from video demonstrations.

The how-to of making it work

In her book *The Story in the Picture Inquiry and Art Making with Young Children* (2009), Mulcahey stresses the importance of teaching children to think like an artist. This is the foundation of scaffolding art and a great place to start.

> Thinking like an Artist[3]
>
> - Look at things very closely (look for the details)
> - Look at things in different ways (different perspectives)
> - Take risks (There is no one right way to be an artist)
> - Dream and imagine

"Too often we rush through our lives, seeing but not truly taking the time to really see. What is beneath our feet? How big a world of mystery awaits us if we only pick up a magnifying glass or microscope? We must take time, look carefully to truly see". Kas

Kas encourages her students to use all of their senses.

---

3   Adapted from Mulcahey, p. 13.

Check It Out!

The Art Gallery of Nova Scotia and the Nova Scotia Department of Education, *Young Learners Experiences in Art*, 2009. This beautiful book honours young children's curiosity and imagination through the visual arts and celebrates collaboration between the NS Art Gallery and the NS Department of Education.

Althouse, Margaret Johnson and Sharon Mitchell; "*The Colors of Learning: Integrating the Visual Arts into the Early Childhood Curriculum,*" 2002.

Bell, David, 2012; *Talking about art with young people: Conversational strategies for aesthetic learning in early childhood settings*; International Art in Early Childhood Research Journal., Volume 4, Number 1.

Gandini, Lella, Lynn Hill, Louise Cadwell and Charles Schwall; 2005; *In the Spirit of the Studio Learning from the Atelier of Reggio Emilia*; Teacher College Press; USA.

Hetland, Lois, Ellen Winner, Shirley Veenema and Kimberly M. Sheridan; 2013; *Studio Thinking 2*; Teachers College Press; USA.

Kolbe, Ursula; 2005; *It's Not a Bird Yet*; Peppinot Press; Australia.

Mulcahey, Rosemary Christine; 2009; *The Story in the Picture: Inquiring and Art making with Young Children*; Teacher College Press, NY, USA.

Pelo, Ann; 2007; *The Language of Art Inquiry-Based Studio Practices in Early Childhood Settings*; Redleaf Press, St. Paul Minnesota, USA.

Vea Vecchi; 2010; *Art and Creativity in Reggio Emilia Exploring the Role and Potential of Ateliers in Early Childhood Education*; Routledge; USA.

Window on the Classroom: Mini-lessons Looking Closely:

Observational Paintings in Angie's Class Tell an Important Story

Throughout the year, I involved our class in many observational painting tasks. I brought in pumpkins, lilacs, pussy willows, plants and peonies and provided different art opportunities. Sometimes we did direct lessons on mixing colors; sometimes our lessons were on brush strokes or use of space. All year long, the students had opportunities to revisit and build on their observational skills and create paintings from what they saw.

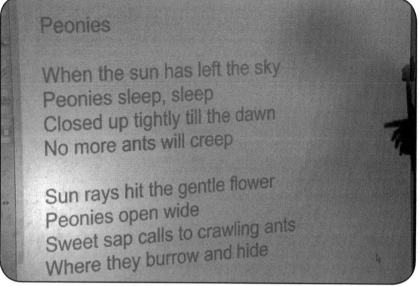

Integration of art and phonological awareness with thanks to Lea Ann Lear, York District School Board.

As an educator, I was amazed when I laid out the finished products and examined the results. It was always easy to identify the paintings of the students who were having the most academic struggles in the class. As I looked more carefully at the paintings, I discovered that these students were having issues with spatial awareness. Their vases were on one side of the page and the flowers on the other side. At the end of the year another spatial issue occurred. We discussed the shape of the peony petals.

One of the students noticed the heart shaped petals that went together to create a sphere. As the students went off to paint, I noticed one student who painted shapes, including a heart, but they were not connected into a flower. He had seen the shapes but had not noticed how they fit together. This became a next step for instruction not only in painting but also in building tasks. I realized more barrier type games would also be important (See **Barrier Games**, p. 203). Using LEGO®, I created modified instructions and asked the students to recreate the objects. Examining the positioning of photos in read-alouds also helps. Another student had very limited exposure to painting tasks and he had spatial awareness issues in other areas. I worked side by side with him and painted next to him. While I painted and I spoke aloud about the positions of the brush strokes, he was able to follow along. His painting was put together in a cohesive manner. This child needed coaching and guidance in art just as he did in other subject areas.

Artwork is another lens through which to look at how a child views objects in their surroundings. I learned that the observational paintings also provided valuable information on a child's spatial awareness.

Observational painting of lilacs. We are learning how to make purple.

Creating colors

Observational painting before intentional mini-lesson

Observational painting after intentional mini-lessons.

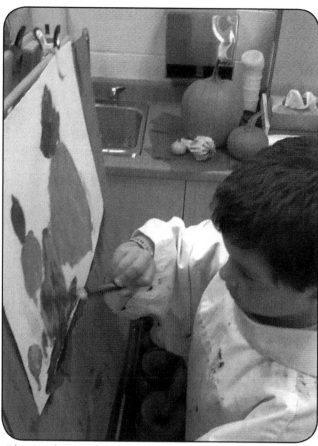

The students' observational skills improved greatly by having continued opportunities to conduct observational paintings throughout the year.

Talking with Students: Art Conversations

Art conversations are important. They extend thinking and reflection and indicate to the student that you value their ideas. The conversations may occur before, during and after the activity. Where possible encourage the students to look closely at the subject, touch it, and perhaps smell it before they begin to create. Point out or better yet elicit details of color, texture, line, and form.

An art conversation!

Key art vocabulary to stress, concepts, and descriptors

Size: big, huge, gigantic, tiny, small

Attribute: clean, dirty, soft, hard

Location: near, beside, above, below, on top, under, between

Quantity: many, a few, none, most

Shapes: circular, sphere, triangular, cylinder, rectangle, oval, triangle

Textures: smooth, rough, soft, bumpy, silky

Colors and metaphors: as black as the sky

Mixing colors to create colors

The teacher prompts the students to notice the shades of color, the petal sizes, and the shapes in the bouquet. "Notice as an artist" is the invitation prior to the painting task.

Really looking closely!

Students Talking with Students: Art Conversations

"In critiquing, complimenting or stating what they notice in another child's art, students are demonstrating restraint to listen to another child, taking turns and accepting a thoughtful critique to apply either to this or future works. It moves children from their egocentric nature to a more self-evaluative and critical thinking mode as they begin to symbolize what they know and feel. It is a direct connection to literacy learning through the act of 'reading' the artwork", writing/talking/critiquing the piece". —Kas

(See Mini-lesson: http://vimeo.com/38247060) to show children the strength of effective, specific student–student feedback).

Providing Art Feedback: Don't Make Assumptions

Making comments on students' art can be tricky. If you are not sure what the child has created, it is better to make general comments on the elements of the art: colors, lines, shapes, texture rather than make a statement such as *the dog is huge…* when in fact there may not be a dog in the picture. Better yet encourage child talk, by prompting with *tell me about this….*

Two ways to respond to a student's question: "Do you like my picture?"

- Tell me about your picture: Do you like it? Why or why not?
- Find and share one specific praise point with the artist.

Besides talking about their art, encourage the students to write the "story" behind the piece. Art promotes storytelling. One young artist labelled her art: "I think and then I draw a line around my think." (*Young Learners Experiences in Art*, Art Gallery of Nova Scotia and the Nova Scotia Department of Education, 2009, 6).

Young children should become acquainted with works of art through field trips to museums and the sharing of books and videos that often leads to students replicating the style of famous artists as demonstrated on the next page.

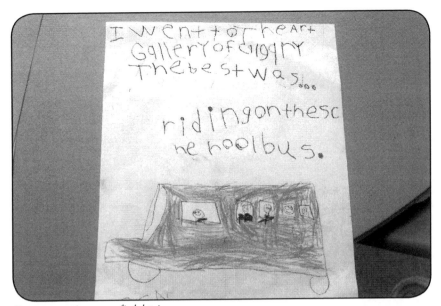

Documenting our field trip.

A self-portrait, just like Picasso!

 Check It Out!

Art related Canadian read-alouds
Canada in Colors, Per-Harrik Gurh, 2011
Chester's Masterpiece, Melanie Watt, 2010
The Imaginary Garden Andrew Larsen, 2009
Painted Circus, Wallace Edwards, 2007
Picturescape, Elisa Gutierrez, 2007
Augustine, Melanie Watt, 2006

More art-related read-alouds
Louise Loves Art, Kelly Light, 2014
Key quotes: "To be a great artist you have to notice everything." "I love Art! It's my imagination on the outside."

Mix It Up! Herve Tullet, 2014
Color Dance, Ann Jonas, 1989
Colors Everywhere, Tana Hoban, 1995
Color Zoo, Lois Ehlert, 1997
The Art Lesson, Tomie, de Paola, 1989
Looking Closely through the Forest Frank, Serafini, 2008

Social imagination and art are keys to developing self-regulation and a growth mindset. Here are some suggestions for books that support these learnings:

the dot, Peter H. Reynolds, 2003 and The Dot Song: http://mrsharrisonk.wordpress.com/2014/09/20/the-dot-song/
Beautiful Oops!, Barney Saltzberg, 2010
little blue and little yellow, Leo Lionni, 1959

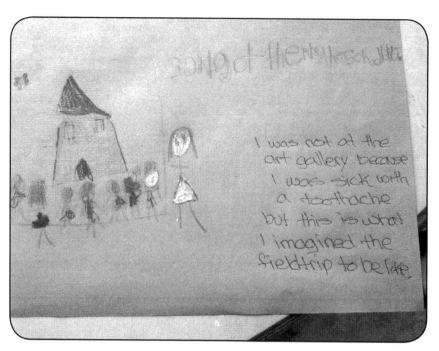

Documenting our imagined field trip.

I was not at the art gallery because I was sick with a toothache but this is what I imagined the fieldtrip to be like.

 ### *A Discovery/Wonder Centre*

Research base

The Discovery/Wonder Centre often contains a variety of materials related to nature, science, and technology. It affords specific opportunities for students to explore, observe, classify, and sort materials in order to infer and predict. This gives them a greater understanding of their environment and technological concepts. The centre fosters curiosity and wonder, while encouraging inquiry and discovery. Working at this centre scaffolds oral language, reading, and writing development. The main purpose of the centre is to encourage asking and answering questions, wonderings, talk and problem solving and in the process to get to know the students.

Window on the Classroom: Colette's Classroom Makes Discovery Work

The explore and discover centre came about as the children's curiosity piqued each time they learned something new, or when they found things they were wondering about. Soon, the centre became alive as the children began to take it over and brought in different things to explore. The centre was filled with things such as leaves, rocks, plants, a crystal, a spider, water in a glass, etc. If something crawled into our class, it was placed in the centre. I provided tools for them to explore, discover and wonder. They had paper to record their wonders and discoveries that we discussed at the end of the week. After carefully examining a dead roach with a magnifying glass, a child wrote, "Oh, that's an example of once living!" Some children were crouched over a spider counting the legs, while checking the book on spiders to verify

their findings. The children were making all sorts of wonderful connections. They also had magnifying glasses, a scale, literature, and writing implements to help them become more effective mini-scientists. One child even brought in paper and a homemade folder from home to place in the centre. It was a very simple, but popular centre, mainly due to the ownership the children felt for the centre. The centre kept on evolving throughout the year, integrating all curriculum areas. Such phenomenal Kindergartners!

It was a very simple, but popular centre, mainly due to the ownership the children felt for the centre.

Encouraging the Use of a Thinking Routine at Centres: I See-Think-Wonder

Ritchhart, Church, and Morrison (2011, 55) recommend using the I See-Think-Wonder Thinking Routine. "The routine emerged out of our interest in harnessing the power of looking closely, not only at art but also with a wide variety of objects and stimuli, as a foundational element of much of our learning." Also try this:

THINK / PUZZLE / EXPLORE from
http://www.pzartfulthinking.org/think_puzzle_explore.php

A routine that sets the stage for deeper inquiry

1. What do you <u>think</u> you know about this artwork or topic?

2. What questions or *puzzles* do you have?

3. What does the artwork or topic *make* you want to *explore*?

We *See-Think-Wonder* about butterflies.

Treasure Wonder Inquiry Centres

Children love to bring treasures from home to place at the centre for others to enjoy.

Window on the Classroom: Celebrating Looking Closely and Making Thinking Visible in Heather's Classroom

Making Thinking Visible: We have been taking time each day to look closely, as part of our Treasure Inquiry. Each day a different student brings a hand-picked treasure from home as the muse for our critical thinking conversations and writing. We take photos using our iPads and use PicCollage to create our images. I preset the page layout in our class book and we insert the PicCollages after the student has presented. Students record their voices sharing what they see, what their treasure makes them think of (analogies), and what they wonder. We plan to finish our Inquiry in December and will be publishing our book for families to enjoy and share at home, as well as including hard and digital copies in our classroom library. I enjoy starting this centre at the beginning of the year. This enables the children to learn about each other based on what they choose to bring in and the ensuing conversation that results.

Family Treasures: Celebrating Diversity while Supporting English Language Learners

The article *Family Treasures: A Dual-Language Book Project for Negotiating Language, Literacy, Culture, and Identity* (Roessingh 2011) describes how English language learners, using objects of cultural and personal relevance, brought from home, generated stories of "Family Treasures." Parents were requested to choose something of family value. They were asked to spend some time having a conversation with their child around the family treasure: how did it come to be in the family, who did it belong to and why was it important. Were there any special memories linked to the treasure? The children then brought their treasure to school. Their stories were shared and questions were encouraged. In small-group contexts, the stories were transcribed into English, often illustrated by the children, and uploaded to a website for perma-nent sharing, rereading, and exchange in both English and their original language. These stories also provided an opportunity for students to develop identity, pride of family and culture and the acquisition of rudimentary technology and early literacy skills. "Most of all, we want to create a learning environment for curios-ity, wonder, imagination, respect for, and interest in diversity and fun!" (http://www.duallanguageproject.com).

> Enjoy Family Treasures:
> http://www.duallanguageproject.com/booklets.html
> http://www.duallanguageproject.com/booklets1011.html

Use Google Translate (https://translate.google.com) to write an e-mail in a parent's native language.

The dual language book project is supported by the following ideas:
1. We want to involve the family and especially the parents in telling their children family stories that are interesting and that will expand or "stretch" their mother tongue vocabulary.
2. We want to link this vocabulary to an object that has family and cultural relevance — a family "treasure."
3. We want the child to bring the object to class, where we can support the storytelling in English in small group work. We will write the stories in English and the first language of each child.
4. We want to target "next words to know" — and purposefully challenge the children to learn many new words related to the Family Treasures project.
5. We want to encourage word play, through recycling activities and games that will lead to deep understanding of word meanings.
6. We want to link the children's stories to good children's literature on the same theme that can be explored for meaning and personal connection.
7. Most of all, we want to create a learning environment for curiosity, wonder, imagination, respect for, and interest in diversity, and fun!

Source: http://www.duallanguageproject.com

Another Discovery/Wonder Centre

There are many ways to make a wonder centre work. Georgia Heard and Jennifer McDonough share examples in their book *A Place for Wonder,* 2009. They suggest using chart paper to make a wonder wall with the title: What do you wonder? They also suggest including sticky notes and markers and a wonder bag. Children write down their wonder questions directly on the chart paper during centre time or on sticky notes any time a wondering comes to them during the day. The wonder bag is used to store all of their wonderings on sticky notes. A wonder of the week is selected to "research" as a class, from all of the children's wonderings.

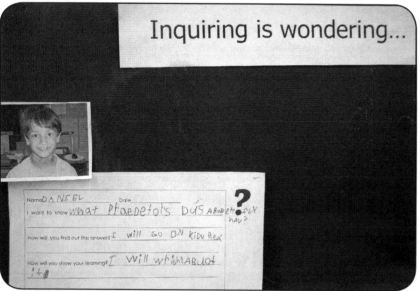

Inquiring is Wondering.

Ensure that the children put their names on the questions to support "translation" and transcribing. Watch for non-fiction topics to emerge from the wonderings, which are great for researching. A conversation ensues during wondering time where children discuss, research, and share their findings in order to answer the wonder of the week question. It is important that the students understand that there are two types of wonderings: Research Wonders and Heart Wonders:

Research Wonders: The answers come from thinking and researching.

Heart Wonders: The answers come from using brains and hearts, e.g., "What makes a best friend?" There is no specific research to support the wondering.

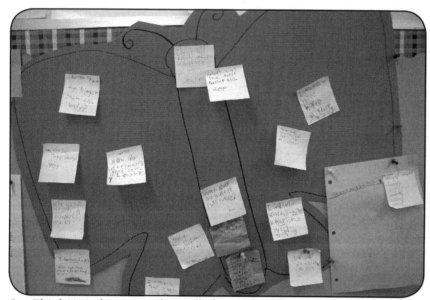

See-Think-Wonder A wonder wall about butterflies.

Writing Centres

Writing occurs at many centres. For examples of engaging writing opportunities and the research base, see Chapters 11 and 12.

Alphabet, Phonics, and Word Work Centre

Research base

Research in recent years has informed teachers that word work is an important aspect of a comprehensive early childhood literacy program. Teachers often use the terms *word work, word learning, word study,* and *word solving* interchangeably. *Word study* is the body of knowledge that includes phonics and spelling. It involves a range of instructional activities that focus attention on words and word elements. This focused attention is called *word solving* in reading and writing (Fountas and Pinnell 1998). Research indicates that the most critical factor supporting fluent word reading is the ability to recognize letters, spelling patterns, and whole words effortlessly, automatically, and visually (Adams 1990).

Word work goes beyond learning individual words, although this too is important. It helps students to develop the strategies and skills necessary to become successful readers and writers. For more on **Phonics**, see Chapter 1, p. 46–51. The Wylie and Durrell 37, key word families and the key high frequency or pop up words can be found on p. 297.

Word learning, in fact, is not so much about learning individual words as about learning how the written language works (Fountas and Pinnell 1998)

Although phonics must be taught formally, it is through lots of successful reading and writing opportunities that students develop and use their phonics knowledge. Moustafa discusses the importance of shared and partner reading to teach concepts of one-to-one matching, word identification, letter–sound correspondence, phonemes, and onsets and rimes (Moustafa, as cited in Strickland and Morrow 2000).

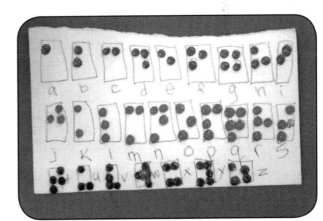

Learning the letters using Braille supports letter knowledge and critical literacy. It also reinforces learning through the senses.

Use an eye chart to enable play and alphabet learning at the same time.

Making words

"Making words" is an interactive activity where children arrange letters to make words. Children begin by making little words such as *at*. Children learn to see patterns in words. They also see how changing one letter or its place in the word often creates a new word. Eventually children can be provided with a greater number of letter cards to make a longer mystery word. Picking mystery words generated from the Wylie and Durrell 37 word families or rimes is a good idea (See table below). These help the students sort for and recognize patterns.

Building a sentence using word cards at a centre. Notice the last word card includes the closing punctuation.

Suggested Mystery Word Lists for Making Words

Word Family or Phonogram	Mystery Words(s)
all	smallest
ame	farmers
an	addition, planets
at	Saturday, scratch
It	stopping, biggest
in	friends, spring
ump	trumpets
est	present
ick	tricks
op	stopping, computer
ight	lights
eat	stranger
ain	animals
ide	spider
ell	smallest, baseball
ing	walking, stopping

A Cozy Reading Centre

Research base

Encouraging reading at a reading centre allows the teacher to:

- immerse students in a situation in which books are being enjoyed

- familiarize students with a variety of books; encourage students to revisit a book that has been previously read by the teacher

- offer students an opportunity to engage in an activity that might not be self-selected during activity time

- develop student concepts of print and book knowledge

- develop student reading fluency and comprehension

Join the book club!

Most importantly a reading centre with many books available motivates reading as a social experience (Allington, 2002). This is extremely important because recent research indicates fewer elementary aged students are motivated to read. This is a serious problem.

- The percentage of Grade 3 students in Ontario who report they "like to read" declined from 76 percent in 1998/99, to 50 percent in 2010/11.

This is a well-loved routine.

- In Grade 6, the percentage of students who say they "like to read" declined from 65 percent in 1998/99 to 50 percent in 2010/11

- In addition, only 21 percent of Ontario children in Grade 3 report that they read together with a parent or guardian "every day or almost every day."

(Source: http://www.peopleforeducation.ca/wp-content/uploads/2011/12/People-for-Education-report-on-students-reading-enjoyment-Reading-for-Joy.pdf).

For the *how-to* of making a reading centre work well, see **Books, Magazines, Newspapers, Centre Materials**, Chapter 3. However, reading is encouraged everywhere.

According to Allington, 2002, with managed choice, students do not have an unlimited range of task or topic choices, but it is less common to find every student doing the same task and more common to observe students working on similar but different tasks. Managed choice often results in greater student ownership and engagement.

Closing Thoughts

Teachers and parents can successfully scaffold play and self-regulation by most importantly creating a warm and caring low stress culture where children want to be. Relationships are key! How adults talk to children and what they say (choice words) is crucial. Adults also need to provide engaging materials and activities, encourage mature play and play plans and become involved at times in the play setting. Providing children with managed choice (Allington, 2002) and voice and effective feedback is also important. Really listening to the feedback from the children is even more important than the adult–child feedback provided.

Chapters 11 and 12 provide the research-base and the how-to of effective writing programs across the curricula, across the day.

Being a word detective. Play and literacy learning are not mutually exclusive!

Learning to Write, Writing to Learn

"Learning to write assists children in their reading; in learning to read, children also gain insights that help them as writers. But writing is more than an aid to learning to read; it is an important curricular goal. Through writing children express themselves, clarify their thinking, communicate ideas and integrate new information into their knowledge base."

—*Every Child a Reader*, CIERA 1

Writing (including drawing) helps children to make sense of their world. It also develops skills in letter recognition, phonics, print awareness, phonological awareness, oral language, and comprehension. This chapter provides teachers with key understandings for supporting early literacy learning effectively with a focus on writing and the reading–writing connection (See also Chapters 7-14 for examples of writing that supports play, inquiry, and self-regulations). For a more thorough review of early literacy teaching and learning using a writing focus see *Learning to Write and Loving It!* (Trehearne 2011). Excerpts from the book are included in this text.

Research on Writing in K–2: What It Really Tells Us

The research is clear. It is not only developmentally appropriate but also crucial to support writing beginning in preschool. Children typically arrive at preschool believing that they are already writers, or at least that they will become writers. It is important that their expectation becomes a reality beginning on the first day. The quality of writing support for 4-year-olds is highly related to their language and literacy growth at the end of Kindergarten and Grade 1 (Dickinson and Sprague 2001). Unfortunately, the sad but honest truth is that writing, like oral language, is often a curriculum casualty, neglected in many K–2 classrooms, while reading gets most of the focus.

Writing is an activity that promotes both alphabet letter knowledge and phonological awareness. Writing also helps children to understand concepts of print, including the fact that the end of a line is not always the end of a thought (Snow, Burns, and Griffin 1998).

Teacher enthusiasm for writing goes a long way!

Primary students need to write, write, write. Believe in the students and help them to believe in themselves as writers.

The Reading–Writing Connection

In her landmark research, Dolores Durkin (1966) discovered that the parents and caregivers of children who had learned to read before coming to Kindergarten had read with their children. However, they did more than this; they did "literacy on the run" on a regular basis. They sang with their children, rhymed, pointed out letters on signs, and wrote to and with their children. They also gave their children many writing opportunities. It became clear that early readers generally are very interested in writing and many write long before they read.

Canadian researchers reviewed K–3 studies conducted in Canada, the United Kingdom, and the United States on early writing. The findings, published in a paper entitled "The Influence of Early Writing Instruction on Developing Literacy" (Harrison, Ogle, McIntyre, and Hellsten 2008), indicated that writing instruction should begin at the outset of formal schooling, which is usually Kindergarten (either Pre-Kindergarten/Kindergarten or Junior-Kindergarten/Senior-Kindergarten). They also discovered that early writing

- Enhances early reading (word identification, decoding, passage comprehension, and word reading)
- Supports the development of phonological awareness, the alphabetic principle, and phonics

The High-Yield Strategies of Effective Writing Programs

Learning to write can seem daunting to young children, but a number of high-yield (or non-negotiable) strategies can help children develop both the skill and will to write. Perhaps the most important factor is the classroom environment, especially the relationship between the teacher and the child (John Hattie 2012).

Be enthusiastic about writing

When teachers show excitement about writing and write with the children, the children will respond to that energy (Polochanin 2004).

Establish developmentally appropriate goals and believe in the students. Don't underestimate what they can do. See the descriptions of emergent, early, and transitional writers, writing stages and targets, trait-based scoring scales, emerging beginning writers (often preschool to early Grade 1) and early–transitional writers (Grade 1–2), in Chapter 12.

Window on the Classroom: In Memory of Jo Simpson, an Exceptional Educator

I had the honour and pleasure of spending time in Jo Simpson's Kindergarten class, in Oswego, Illinois. Jo had the children write a great deal from the first day. By spring, she had many very skilled and engaged writers in her classroom. These children developed writing skills and saw themselves as writers. This was no accident! They were frequently encouraged to self-select their own writing topics. They were taught that their art was also very important. They were taught to look carefully in order to include many details when they drew. They listened carefully for details during read-alouds. They learned how important details are to developing the trait of ideas. Additionally, they wrote across the curriculum — in science, social studies, and math. Using mentor texts and mini-lessons, the children learned the craft of writing. In Jo's class, the students did many inquiries and delved deeply into topics so that they remained excited about their writing. They wrote many individual student books, especially informational texts. They worked on a page a day while being involved in an inquiry or project. But most importantly Jo had high expectations for her students and they had high expectations for themselves. These high expectations are exemplified by this writing sample from an end of Kindergartner in Jo's class.

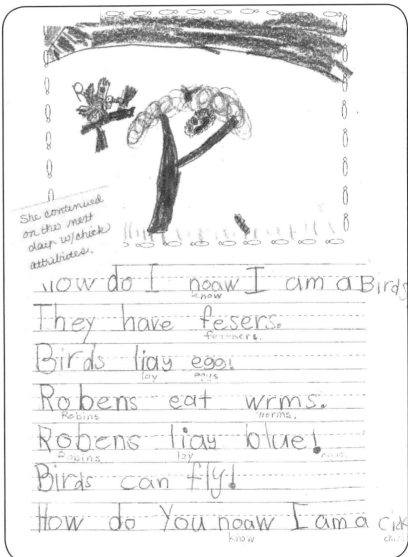

Can't you hear the great voice in this piece? Due to Jo's selection of read-alouds and modelled writing mini-lessons, this child has learned how to ask and answer questions when writing.

Goals for beginning and early writers

It is important to have clear goals for students and to plan with the "end" in mind. Specifically, beginning and early writers must be helped to

- Understand what writing is (i.e., speech written down)
- Understand why people write (i.e., for real purposes)
- Understand how to write, and how to assess writing in different genres using the traits or qualities of good writing
- Use appropriate language to talk about their writing and the writing of others
- Understand how to revise and edit (and that the two are different)
- Want to write often
- Feel a sense of joy in writing
- Use different genres (kinds of writing) for different audiences
- Think of themselves as writers
- Take risks
- Make the reading–writing connection
- Develop a love of reading and listening to good literature

According to Mem Fox, "If you don't have clear expectations, how can children know what to aim for? If you don't have the highest expectations, how do you know if you're not underestimating what your students can do?" (Spandel 2001, 318).

Assessment
Feedback
Instruction
Documentation
Feedback

Feedback: student-teacher, student-student, teacher-student.

Often these techniques that support teaching and learning occur concurrently, during the process of teaching and learning.

Use assessment and effective feedback to drive instruction

Having developmentally appropriate goals and informally assessing the children's writing on a daily basis are crucial to documentation, providing effective feedback, and effective instruction. It is important to look not only at what children write, but also at how they write. Catch them in the act! (See Writing Stages and Targets p. 301).

Write daily and often

"We believe that if children (or adults for that matter) are to learn to write well, they need lots of experience with writing. There is no such thing as too much writing if you are trying to develop yourself as a writer. The more you do it, the easier it becomes for you to continue to do it and the more you learn about how it gets done" (Ray and Cleaveland 2004, 24). Children will write a great deal when the activities are engaging and when they see a purpose. Children need to write daily during writing workshop but also across the day.

> "Every child is entitled to excellent instruction that includes daily opportunities and teacher support to write many kinds of texts for different purposes, including stories, lists, messages to others, poems, reports and responses to literature." (IRA and NAEYC 1998, 42)

Establish a purpose and audience for writing and scaffold topic choice

Children are more successful and motivated when they see a purpose for writing and are given a choice of what to write and are supported in coming up with a topic. This also supports self-regulation. The teacher's task is to recognize opportunities for authentic writing and to help the children take advantage of these opportunities. Functional experiences provide a real purpose for writing (making a list, writing a note, writing a letter that requires a reply, taking a survey and so on). Encourage the children to ask themselves, "What is my purpose?" and "Who is my audience?" (i.e., "Who am I writing this to?"). (See **Writing Messages, Reports, and All About Books**, this chapter, and an **All About Bees** book p. 358).

> **Purpose + Audience = Form**
> (Ontario Education 2005, 29).

Incubating ideas (used with permission from Mila Tamaoka, Webling School, Hawaii).

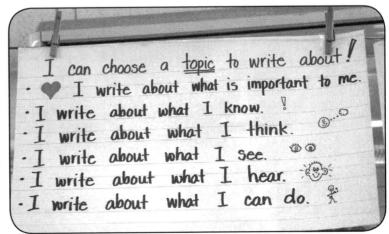

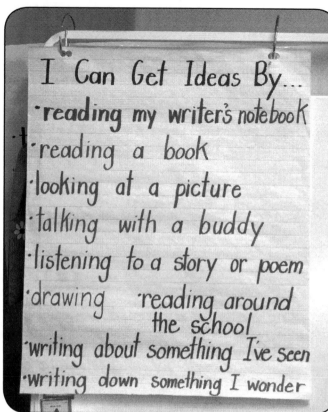

Shared writing scaffolds topic choice.

Develop Motivated Readers and Writers through Purposeful Writing. The Secret: Writing Letters and Notes

Nothing develops a young writer's voice like writing a letter to a real audience, especially when there is the expectation that the recipient will write back. Writing friendly letters enables the children to develop personal relationships with the people to whom they are writing and allows them to share information. Children love to write to their friends, their families, and their teachers. However, the ultimate letter-writing experience for young children is often writing to a classroom stuffed toy, since to the children, the toy is truly "real."

Window on the Classroom: Introducing Zink the Pink

I witnessed first-hand engagement in writing and significant development as readers and writers when my daughter and, three years later, my son were in First Grade. Their teacher introduced a stuffed cat named Zink the Pink to the class. Both children wrote letter after letter to Zink and both were thrilled every time they received a response. My daughter was saddened in January when she came home and informed me that Zink was moving to Australia. Any experienced teacher would understand why Zink needed a holiday!

Multiple Paths to Literacy

Window on the Classroom: Wags in Diana's Class

At a Kindergarten workshop in Toronto, I described to the group how my children's teacher, largely using Zink, made them into motivated and skilled writers. Diana Bruni, a Kindergarten teacher in Toronto, took the idea back to her class. Soon after, she emailed me with the subject line *Zink the Pink Idea Big Success in My Class*. It is through her voice and photographs that Zink the Pink and other Magic Creatures come to life for primary teachers.

Dear Miriam,

I attended a Kindergarten workshop you gave on October 1 in Toronto. I enjoyed your seminar immensely and walked out of there with a book full of ideas I was eager to try implementing in my JK/SK class. One idea struck me in particular. You mentioned that your daughter's Grade 1 teacher used Zink the Pink to motivate her class to write. Well, that night I happened to be shopping when I saw this huge huggable dog that I immediately fell in love with. As soon as I saw it, I knew that this was my Zink the Pink. I spoke to the manager of the store and he was very kind and agreed to donate the dog to my class. I have no shame about begging when it comes to my kids!

I had read a story (*The Puppy Who Went to School* by Gail Herman) early on in the year about a dog that followed his owner to school and got into all kinds of trouble. The dog's name in the story was Wags so I decided to name our dog after him. I had already taken my own dog, Candy, to school for the day a couple of times and my kids loved her, so I knew they were going to love Wags too. You should have seen their faces when they saw this beautiful 6-foot-long dog. Their smiles could not have gotten any bigger!

Dear Kindergarten Parents,

Please allow me to introduce myself. My name is Wags. I am a big, floppy dog that lives in your child's Kindergarten class. I am very happy to be their special friend. The children sing their Hello Song and come up and give me a big hug every day at the beginning of class.

One of my favourite things to do is write letters to my new friends in Mrs. Bruni's class. I hope you will encourage them to write letters back to me too, because I love getting letters even more than I like writing them! Sometimes my friends will write letters to me at school but please help them to write me letters from home too. Then they can bring them to school and mail them in my special "doggy" mailbox in the classroom. I will read their letters and write back to them.

Today I gave each of my new friends a sheet of my special doggy paper that I hope they will use to write me a letter. Please encourage your child to ask me questions and to write their own words if they can. I love when they draw me pictures too.

It was very nice talking to you. Please come in and visit me at school anytime.

Love,

Wags in his reading tent. Also, notice his mailbox.

Wags wrote the class letters telling them how much he loved to read and write and asked them to write letters to him. I had made a special mailbox for Wags in the shape of a doghouse and I made up his own set of "doggy" stationery on the computer as well. The response from my kids was beyond my wildest dreams. They are writing Wags letters at school and writing him letters from home without any prompting from me whatsoever. I try to make sure that every child gets at least one letter from Wags each week but now I can understand why Zink had to go to Australia! The kids are loving it, I'm loving it, the parents are loving it too. Thank you so much for the great idea. In 20 years of teaching, I have never seen Kindergarten kids so eager to write.

I bought a special play tent (Wags' Reading Tent) for Wags to live in and the kids love taking turns visiting him there where they read him their letters or stories. Even the older kids in the school will stop by for a hug from Wags now and then. My Grade 6 Kindergarten helpers even asked me why I hadn't done this when they were in my class!

I have lots of future plans for Wags. The possibilities are endless really. I would also like to host an early literacy night for parents called *Reading and Writing with Wags*. We sing songs about Wags, we are going to write stories about Wags, and we'll even attempt to make up our own book about Wags and his adventures. Perhaps Wags will be the next Clifford! I just had to write and let you know how one of your stories has sparked such a writing frenzy in my classroom. Many thanks again.

Sincerely, Diana Bruni, JK/SK Teacher, Transfiguration School, Toronto, Ontario

P.S. Your idea was so successful that I decided to make up my own special teacher mailbox as well. Now the kids mail me letters and drawings too and I write back on my own stationery.

Wags invites students to read to him. A real reason to write and read!!

Diana also sent a letter home so that family members might support their children's writing (See previous page).

A year later, I received the following email from Diana. Just feel the excitement in her class!

Hi Miriam,

I'm not sure if you remember me or not but I think you'll probably remember my classroom mascot dog Wags. I just wanted to let you know that I've gone to the next level (or 2!) with your idea. Wags got a girlfriend as a present from Santa this year named Wiggles. Wags proposed to Wiggles on Valentine's Day, they got married with a full Italian doggy wedding and they just had six gorgeous puppies a couple of weeks ago! It has been the most amazing experience ... interesting and fun for me and my parent volunteers and the kids just love it.

Wags, Wiggles, and a puppy.

My reading and writing scores are much, much higher and I'm pretty sure I can attribute that to Wags and Wiggles. Thanks yet again for sparking the whole idea!

Diana Bruni
Transfiguration School, Toronto, Ontario

Dear _____,

Thank you so much for helping to make our wedding day so special. We had the best day ever! Thank you for making us such a beautiful wedding card too.

We took the train to Quebec City for our honeymoon. We stayed at a fancy hotel. We went tubing down a big, big mountain. That was scary! We went skating too. It was very cold in Quebec City but we had lots of fun. Look at the back of this letter to see our honeymoon pictures.

Love,
Wiggles and Wags

Sierra creates a wedding book. She wrote and wrote and wrote!

Any letter from Wags and Wiggles is loved… even generic ones!

Wags and Wiggles: An Update from Diana, 2015

Any experienced Kindergarten teacher will tell you that there is no one right method to encourage the development of emerging literacy skills in their young students. Wise teachers will use a flexible and balanced literacy approach that encompasses a wide variety of different strategies, including daily read-alouds, self-selected reading, shared reading and writing, word study and phonics, guided play, mini reading/writing lessons, the use of writing centres, as well as guided reading and writing for those students ready for that degree of scaffolding. Children need to see firsthand that reading and writing are important ways that people use to communicate and they need to be given daily opportunities to engage in these types of activities. Most of all, children need to have a real, valid reason to read and write and they need to do it often, from the very beginning, at whatever stage they happen to be at. They also need to be given the opportunity to share their reading and writing skills with others and receive positive reinforcement for their efforts. Getting parental support in further nurturing literacy skills at home is also key.

One of the most exciting, successful, and comprehensive approaches I have used to motivate and encourage my Kindergarten students to read and write is by using our class mascot, a large loveable stuffed dog named Wags, as a major part of my literacy program. At the beginning of the year, I introduce Wags to the children (and to their parents during curriculum night) as my special school reading and writing dog. Of course, Wags is incredibly smart because he lives at school all the time and his absolute favourite things to do are reading and writing. I explain to my students that Wags is very excited about teaching them to read and write too so they can become just as smart as he is. Each class begins with our "Hello" song, with each child taking turns to come up to greet, hug, and kiss Wags.

A morning greeting with Wags.

It's a great way to start the day and the children never tire of the silly big hugs and licks he gives them. Wags plays a central role in our classroom. We bring him to the school library each week in his wagon and the student leader of the day gets the honour of choosing a good doggy book for him (the Biscuit and Clifford series are his favourites!). The children love snuggling up with Wags on the floor and reading him books. They enjoy working together to design and build him new doghouses with the big wooden blocks. The children also love to draw and cut out paper bones and make paper strip spaghetti for him, as these are his favourite foods (this is an excellent way to develop fine motor skills as well). Wags asks to be the stable dog when we perform our annual Christmas Nativity play and he always joins us for our senior Kindergarten graduation celebrations, resplendent in his own graduation gown and cap.

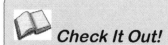

The Wags mailbox.

In my Kindergarten literacy program, Wags writes a short, two or three sentence letter to the class each week. We read and reread his letter each day that week, focusing on different instructional elements, depending upon the needs of my students. Wags usually asks the class a question in his letters and this gives us added motivation to write a class letter back to Wags. The children are also encouraged to write their own letters to Wags during class time at the writing centre, stocked with special doggy stationery and envelopes, as well as at home, with the help of their parents or older brothers and sisters. I always provide the children with the opportunity to share their letters with the rest of the class as this provides good modelling and motivation for each other and we never fail to applaud each child's efforts, no matter which writing stage they happen to be at. The children mail their individual letters in Wag's special doggy mailbox at the writing centre and Wags gives them one of his special stickers to thank them for their letter. Most importantly, Wags always writes each student a letter back using his own personal stationery (again, usually only a short two sentence reply, often including a new question to invite another letter back). The children are always so excited when they get their own personal letter from Wags!

I always knew getting a reply letter back from Wags was important to the children (who doesn't love getting their own handwritten

Check It Out!

Make letter writing to parents a weekly part of your classroom program: FRIDAY LETTERS connect students, teachers, and families through writing (Newman and Bizzarri, 2011).

Multiple Paths to Literacy

mail?) but I never realized just how important these individual letters from Wags were until one of my former parents happened to mention to me that her son, who was by then in Grade 3, still had all of his letters from Wags posted on his bedroom wall, even 4 years later. I was taken aback because I had no idea just how much those letters meant to him. Wow! Now that really is powerful!

I have used Wags in various ways over the years and the children love reading and writing about all of his many exciting adventures. Sometimes I will ask the children to write a letter on a specific topic and we assemble these letters to him and make a variety of class books for him (e.g., "Our Christmas Letters to Wags"), which we then take turns bringing home and sharing with our families. We've organized birthday parties for Wags complete with doggy biscuits we've baked for him and "doggy" dance music like "Who Let the Dogs Out?" and games like "Doggy, Doggy, Who's Got the Bone?" Santa Claus has given Wags a special girl friend named Wiggles for Christmas in response to his letter stating that he was lonely when we all left school to go home. Some years Wags and Wiggles have gotten engaged around Valentine's Day and we have planned and organized full-blown Italian weddings, food and all! You should see the girls all dressed in their finest flower girl dresses and the boys in their ties and top hats and the entire school attending. The children all create their own hand-written invitations to invite family and friends to the wedding. Most exciting of all, later in the year, Wags and Wiggles have then had puppies, which the children get to take home and babysit for the evening. All of these activities of course have a reading and writing component attached to them. For example, when the children take one of the puppies home they are asked to read them a doggy book at bedtime and then draw pictures and write us a letter telling how they spent the evening together. For the wedding, the children read the wedding vows and create special wedding cards for them, which they share with the guests. So, as you can see, not only is Wags a central part of my literacy program, he is also a wonderful vehicle for teaching family life as well. Best of all, I have never seen my students so engaged in reading and writing before and their literacy scores have improved dramatically in response.

Thank you Wags and Wiggles for helping my students become the best readers and writers they can be!

Check It Out!

Try these great read-alouds to support letter writing *with voice:*

Augustine by Melanie Watt, 2006).

Dear Mr. Blueberry by James Simon, 1991

Dear Peter Rabbit by Beatrix Potter, 1995

Frog and Toad Are Friends (The Letter) by Arnold Lobel , 1970

I Wanna Iguana by Karen Kaufman Orloff and David Catcrow , 2004

The Jolly Postman or Other People's Letters by Janet and Allan Ahlberg , 1986

The Secret Life of Squirrels by Nancy Rose , 2014

Lilly's Purple Plastic Purse by Kevin Henkes , 1996

Mouse Letters by Michelle Cartlidge, 1993

Mouse's Scrapbook by Michelle Cartlidge, 1995

Window on the Classroom: Teachers Learning from Teachers: Zink the Pink, Wags and Wiggles all began with Clarice Bloomenthal

This story and others like it did not start with Zink but with Clarice Bloomenthal, a former student teacher of mine, and her "Magic Creatures" puppets. Clarice always established a growth mindset when she taught. All of the children believed in themselves and became writers and readers in a joyful classroom environment, which involved writing to and receiving letters from the Magic Creatures. Better yet, here's one of the Magic Creatures, Super Snake, to tell the story (see p. 281).

A letter from the Magic Creatures to the Students

January 18, 2015

Dear Boys and Girls,

We are the *Magic Creatures*. We have come to live in your class, to be your friends. We love getting letters from you. Tell us all about you. What is your favourite color? What do you like to eat? What is your favourite thing to do? Do you like summer more than winter? What centre at school do you think is the most fun?

Your teacher tells us that you are very good illustrators too so please draw us some pictures to go with your writing.

We promise to write back to you. So, please write to us soon!

Love,

The Magic Creatures

Writing to Magic Creatures

Date:

 Dear Parents:

Children love to write letters to their friends, family members, and teachers. However, we also now have *Magic Creatures* for the children to write to. Today your children are bringing home this letter about the *Magic Creatures*: Super Snake, Sara Snake, Baby Snake, and Elizabeth the Skunk. Have your children tell you all about the *Magic Creatures* experience. Share their excitement! Help them write and draw to one, some, or all of the Magic Creatures. Then wait for a response!

Sincerely,

A Letter from Super Snake

Dear Miriam,

When you invited Clarice to write an article about how Magic Creatures helped to teach reading and writing in her primary classroom, I, Super Snake, decided I would do it for her. After all, who am I but a combination of her inspiration, love of teaching, creativity, and wacky sense of humour all rolled up into a very handsome, semi-retired stuffed animal with personality plus. Along with my fellow Magic Creatures, Sara Snake, Baby Snake, and Elizabeth the skunk (a charming little stinker who mixed up the pocket charts each night), we wrote daily letters to the children and received wonderful replies. At first, they were mainly drawings plus signatures but they evolved over the months into delightful missives using correct and invented spelling. We were so proud and had such fun creating exciting adventures in the classroom! We dressed up for every special occasion, had birthday parties, invited guest Magic Creatures in when we went on trips, and sent emails from all over the world. In case you are wondering, there were also journals and many other forms of writing in the classroom but always, we were the favourites.

Clarice was mystified when a student's relative visiting from Japan already knew about me before she came to Canada, as she had read about the classroom in a Japanese book that was never located. Thirty years later, a patient of Clarice's daughter, Dena, an obstetrician, gave Dena a book written many years ago by her mom. It was about the difficult adjustment of moving from Japan to Canada and the unexpected joys of Grade 1. Miriam, there are even pictures of yours truly in the book! When Clarice visited the young woman the day after she gave birth, the first thing she said, even before showing off her new baby was, "How is Super Snake?"

Oh, Miriam, I could go on and on! It's truly inspiring to know that even though Clarice and all us Magic Creatures are semi-retired, our legacy lives on in classrooms all over the world. You have told Clarice about so many wonderful teachers who use Magic Creatures in an amazing variety of ways with incredible success and we are thrilled!

Scaffolding letter writing.

The Magic Creatures

Dear Elizabeth

Dear S.S.

Dear Sara

Dear Baby

Dear Spook

Magic Creatures!

More Purposeful Writing with an Audience in Mind

Message boards, note passing at a post centre, writing question-and-answer reports, perhaps as a culmination to an inquiry, and writing books are all forms of writing with an audience in mind.

Message boards

A message board is a written show and tell. There are three stages in implementing a successful message board. First, explain to the children the purpose of a message board and various message models. Second, give the children opportunities to write messages and support them in their message writing. Finally, encourage the children to share their messages.

> Learning to read and write messages gives children information about common words from slightly different perspectives, which seems to help them to understand more about the ways in which written words work (Clay 1991).

From the beginning of Kindergarten, it is important to write messages to the children. The messages will often include a combination of conventional print and pictures. You might begin the day with a morning message, which communicates something special that is happening that day, such as a field trip, birthday, or visitor. You might also write a message before recess or home time reminding the children to wear their mittens, to take home their reading, or to avoid the mud on the playground (the latter message might be adhered to by some!). The goal is for the children to learn that people use a message board to communicate for authentic reasons. Of course, you can also make good use of the message board for finding and noting high-frequency words, beginning and ending consonants, and making a rhyming word. However, the main reason for the written communication is to share a message with the whole class. Additionally, the

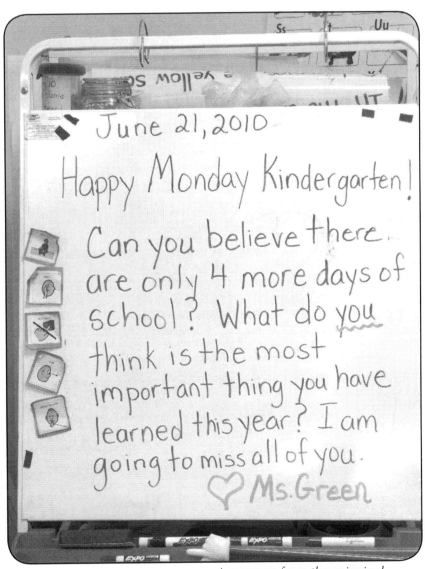

A message from the principal.

principal, parents/caregivers, and students from other grades are also encouraged to come into the classroom and share their messages on the Message Board. How motivating it is for the children to get messages from other adults and peers!

Window on the Classroom: Amber's Kindergarten Class in Kamloops B.C.

"I implemented the class messages and news board. I explained it before recess and by lunch it was full, so we read all the contributions together, erased it and started again.

Children may choose to explain their messages to ensure that others can understand them. It is important that young children can "drite" = draw and write, even if they are the only ones to understand the writing.

Window on the Classroom: Message Boards at the End of the Day or After Recess

Another good time to encourage message board writing is after recess and at the end of the day. Children often come in from recess wanting to share what happened on the playground but the reality is that 1–1 sharing, adult–child is sometimes not feasible. At the end of the day, prompt the children to write about

Multiple Paths to Literacy

something that they did that day at school that they might then share with their parents/caregivers when they get home. This may help to reduce the number of times that children respond with the word *nothing* when asked by a family member, "What did you do in school today?"

I learned about the after-recess news board approach after one of my workshops. A teacher left me this anonymous note:

After recess, children are always anxious to tell you what happened on the playground — there are too many to listen to. I have them write what happened and put it on the "news board." I use real newspaper as a border and put a blank sheet in the middle for them to tell their story.

The message board can also be used to solve personal problems. In one Kindergarten class, a little boy used the message board to enlist the help of others in finding his cat.

A real reason to write!

Note passing at a post centre

Creating a post centre in the classroom is a method of legitimate note passing. It is one way to encourage the children to write notes to one another. Create a chart with each child's name in a box at least the size of a small sticky note. Leave a pad of small sticky notes and a few pencils beside the wall chart. Encourage the children to write to each other. How do you try to ensure that each child gets at least one note? Give the children a list of the names of all the students in the class at the beginning of the year. Ask them to check off the name of each class member as they write, before writing to the same person twice.

Writing news

Children always have lots of news they want to share, such as experiences that have happened to them outside of school. Why not create a news centre where they can write and illustrate their news?

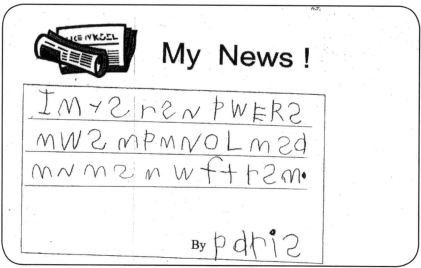

My News !

IMYSreN PWERS
MWSmPMNOLMSd
MNMSMWFttSM.

By pdris

The author, Paris, explained to the teacher: "I put a period because my idea stopped!"

Check It Out!

Here are some wonderful question-and-answer books to read aloud:

Do Bees Sneeze? And Other Questions Kids Ask about Insects by J. K. Wangberg , 1998.

How Do Flies Walk Upside Down? Questions and Answers about Insects by Melvin and Gilda Berger, 1999.

I Wonder Why Snakes Shed Their Skin and Other Questions about Reptiles by Amanda O'Neill , 1996.

I Wonder Why Triceratops Had Horns and Other Questions about Dinosaurs by Rod Theodorou , 1994.

Why Do Dogs Have Wet Noses? by Stanley Coren , 2006.

Why Do Volcanoes Blow Their Tops? Questions & Answers About Volcanoes & Earthquakes, 2000.

Why Don't Haircuts Hurt? Questions and Answers about Your Body by Melvin and Gilda Berger , 1999.

You Asked for It! Strange but True Answers to 99 Wacky Questions by Marg Meikle and Tina Holdcroft , 2000

For even more question-and-answer book titles, see the Early Literacy Telecollaborative Project (www.earlyliterature.ecsd.net) and click on Predictable Books.

Writing Question-and-Answer Reports: Inquiries

Emerging and early writers can write simple reports. A question-and-answer report (or book) can be a great culminating activity to an inquiry as can an All About Book.

Reports are often a response to a question a child or adult has. What more authentic reason to write can there be than for a child to pick a topic of interest to investigate? Introduce the activity by sharing a question-and-answer book with the children as a read-aloud.

All About...Books are typically very simple. By the end of Kindergarten, the books generally consist of at least one illustration or photo and at least one line of text per page (See Chapter 14 for an example of text from an All About Bees book created in Kindergarten).

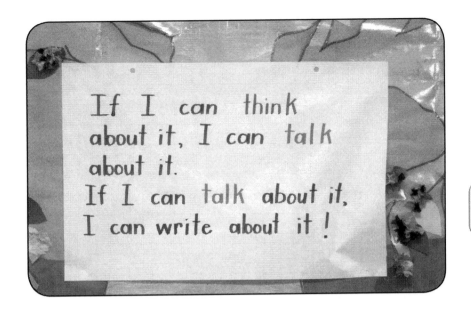

Students believing in themselves as writers is crucial.

Conduct Mini-Lessons

Daily short, focused, mini-lessons must occur based on children's needs. The gradual release of responsibility model provides the best support. Modelled writing (I do it), shared writing (we do it) while you think aloud, guided writing (we do it in a small group), and then independent writing (you do it) are the most important approaches to scaffolding the writing craft. Mini-lessons help the students to understand the traits of writing, and how to improve their writing by using those traits.

Use read-alouds and mini-lessons to help students to understand the difference between ideas and voice.

IDEAS	VOICE
Things I see (details)	How I feel (emotions)

Keep a Writer's Notebook

Published authors frequently keep a writer's notebook. A writer's notebook is simply a notebook used to store ideas, memories, special words, drawings, mementos, souvenirs, photos, ticket stubs, stickers, and stamps. Some children have even included a special leaf from the playground; some of their pet's fur; a piece of their baby blanket; a list of special (yummy) words; a list of numbers, alphabet letters, or their friends' names; a picture of a toy taken from a newspaper ad; and lots of drawings. The whole purpose of a writer's notebook is to remember special ideas, times, people, or things to motivate writers to write!

Introducing the idea of a writer's notebook

- If you have any writer's notebooks kept by children from past years, display and discuss some of the pages. Nothing motivates young writers to write more quickly than celebrating the writing of other children. "If he can do it, I can do it too!"

Items for a writer's notebook.

- Read aloud the wonderful picture book *Lilly's Purple Plastic Purse* by Kevin Henkes. The story describes Lilly bringing her plastic purse to school for show and tell. She cannot wait to show her purse and interrupts the teacher's read-aloud in her excitement. Ask the children to speculate as to why the author used a purse and specifically a purple plastic purse in the story. The real story is that the author was sitting in an airport waiting for a plane when he looked over and saw a little girl holding a purple plastic purse that played music. He got out his writer's notebook and wrote purple plastic purse. If he had not written it down, he would likely have forgotten about the purple plastic purse. That is where he got the idea to write his book.

- As a shared writing, make a list of possible items that might be recorded in a writer's notebook.

Scaffold Parental Support: A Letter to Parents

🏠➡️🏫 *Home-School Connections*

Keeping a Writer's Notebook

Dear Parents,

Published authors frequently keep a writer's notebook. A writer's notebook is neither a journal nor a diary. It is simply a notebook used to store ideas, memories, special words, drawings, mementos, souvenirs, photos, ticket stubs, stickers, stamps, and so on. Some children have even included a special leaf from the playground; some of their pet's fur; a piece of their baby blanket; a list of special (yummy) words; a list of numbers, alphabet letters, or their friends' names; a picture of a toy taken from a newspaper; and lots of drawings. The whole purpose of a writer's notebook is to remember special ideas, times, people, or things to motivate writers to write!

One Grade 1 student described a writer's notebook as a spark that could light a fire. Our goal is to use a writers' notebook to spark your child's writing.

On _____, every child will receive his or her very own writer's notebook. Please talk to your child about the purpose of the writer's notebook. Then discuss and plan an item or two that your child will bring to school by _____ to be glued into their very own notebook. The class will add to their notebooks as the year goes on.

Thanks very much for your support.

Sincerely,

Use modelled and shared writing and reading often

There are numerous opportunities in every classroom for you to write as the children watch—and sometimes help—with suggestions of what to write. As children watch, you write (modelled writing) and as you read the text together, they learn a great deal about writing and reading. Think-alouds while you write help children to understand what is going on in the writing process.

"I put an exclamation mark at the end of the sentence because I want the reader to understand that I love Benji a lot."

Dictation: The Pros and Cons of Dictation/Scribing

Dictation (scribing what the child says) helps children to understand the purposes of writing and the speech–text connection (What I think about, I can say, and what I can say, I can write).

Through dictation, children are also supported in learning phonics, the conventions of print, capitalization, and punctuation. On the other hand, dictation provides limited value for teaching children to read and write. Few children are able to read back what they dictate because their oral language is generally at a much higher level than their reading and writing ability. A highly verbal child who is able to dictate very complex sentences may become frustrated when she or he is unable to read back the scribed sentences. This is problematic as many children learn to read, at least in part, by reading and rereading what they have written.

Scribing, therefore, must not be used to the exclusion of the children's writing or minimize their writing in any way. Independent writing is crucial. Children need to write a great deal.

Scaffolding Writing by Using Writing Innovations

"Sometimes, teachers are reluctant to trust that children will discover their own topics ... Letting children arrive at their own topics requires patience on the part of the teachers" (Feldgus and Cardonick 1999, 97). While allowing children to arrive at their own topics does require patience, it also requires a great deal of teacher support. Children often get their writing topics from mini-lessons during a writing workshop. Often they experience read-alouds or shared readings followed by modelled, shared, or guided writing. Finally, each child "gives it a go." Using patterns from great children's literature can motivate young children to write. For example, after reading *Rosie's Walk* by Pat Hutchins, you could begin with a shared writing (See **Elizabeth's Crawl**, next page) and then have the children use the pattern to create their own text. The poem "Bugs" by Margaret Wise Brown begins and ends with the line "I like bugs," and children love it (See the shared writing innovations that follow).

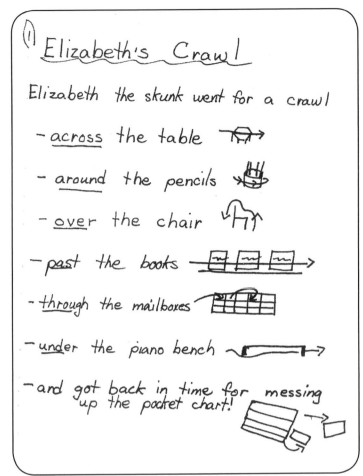

Elizabeth's Crawl

Elizabeth the skunk went for a crawl
- across the table
- around the pencils
- over the chair
- past the books
- through the mailboxes
- under the piano bench
- and got back in time for messing up the pocket chart!

Innovation on Rosie's Walk.

Dads

I love Dads.
Tall Dads, short Dads,
Fat Dads, skinny Dads,
Any kind of Dads.
I love Dads.
A Dad in a hockey game,
A Dad going jogging,
A Dad in a truck,
A Dad at school.
I love Dads.
Sportsmen Dads, smart Dads,
Nice Dads, joyful Dads,
I LOVE DADS!

Innovation on Margaret Wise Brown's "Bugs."

Using Popular Music to Improve Reading and Writing

Genia Connell, a Third Grade teacher, explains effective methods using popular music to improve reading and inspire writing. She has adapted the ***See, Think, and Wonder*** thinking routine (Ritchhart, Church, and Morrison 2011, 55) that stresses looking carefully to ***Hear, Think, and Wonder*** when listening closely to a song. The students listen carefully at least two times and each time they complete a different section of the thinking routine. A copy of the song lyrics is then handed out to each student and reread with a partner for fluency development. The song lyrics and/or the melody then inspire writing, such as personal narratives and poetry. See http://www.scholastic.com/teachers/top-teaching/2014/10/use-popular-music-improve-reading-and-inspire-writing

Mr. Vasicek's Classroom Music Playlist provides a great variety of songs to use in classrooms. See http://www.scholastic.com/teachers/classroom_solutions/2011/01/mr-vasiceks-classroom-music-playlist.

> Try the Hear-Think-Wonder thinking routine along side See-Think-Wonder.

 Check It Out!
See the lesson "Creating a Class Pattern Book with Popular Culture Characters" at www.readwritethink.org

Taylor Swift has written two songs about bullying, "Mean" and "Shake it Off." Swift talks with students about the importance of reading and writing, how one supports the other, and how she writes about her personal experiences. Swift also finds that keeping a writer's notebook is important. See http://www.scholastic.com/taylorswift.

Music in the Inclusive Classroom by Melody McGrath Taylor (2014) is designed to support both the music specialist and the classroom teacher.

 ### Support daily play to develop writers

Literacy learning and play support each other. Writing often emerges naturally as children play. Dramatic play at various classroom centres, often referred to as Imagination Stations, may lead children to write grocery lists, menus, receipts, and even a chart listing a patient's medications at the hospital centre. However, children do not automatically choose to write; they often need to be nudged. One of the ways that you can nudge a young writer is to make sure appropriate resources are readily available and discussed, such as a notepad and pencil next to the telephone at the restaurant/pizza parlour centre and a prescription pad and a pencil or marker at the hospital centre (See **Play** in Chapters 7–10).

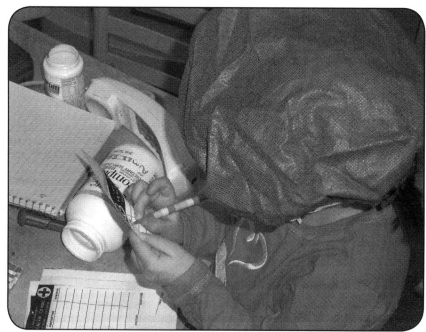

Doctors write prescriptions!

Other ways to link writing and play include having conversations with the children about their play before they begin and having them create play plans (See Chapter 7). Writing after centres encourages children to reflect on their play and to record or report their thoughts.

Create a rich oral language program

An oral language program that includes mini-lessons to teach vocabulary and builds on the children's own background knowledge is the foundation of effective writing instruction. Time must be spent encouraging children to incubate their ideas through drawing, role-playing, and talking before writing. (For many practical ideas on creating a vocabulary-rich environment, see Chapters 4–5.)

Incubating ideas through drawing and talking. **Thinking routine: Think-Talk-Write**.

Use read-alouds and shared reading daily

Read-alouds and shared reading can and should support writing. The effectiveness of their use, however, depends on what texts you choose and how you connect the reading to the writing. Ralph Fletcher and JoAnn Portalupi (1998), among others, have stated that literature may be the most important influence of all for writing development. However, they also explain that simply enjoying good literature will not enable most children to become effective writers. It is through mini-lessons (craft lessons), reading and rereading, talk, and writing that children learn what effective authors do when they compose.

"Pretend play is a valuable part of early literacy development … In fact the amount of time children engage in pretend play is correlated to their performance on language and literacy assessments" (Van Scoter and Boss 2002, 6).

Teachers can facilitate language and literacy development through play-based literacy instruction (Snow, Burns, and Griffin 1998).

"In a classroom the writing and reading floats on a sea of talk" (James Britton in Fletcher and Portalupi 2001, 36).

"How much does shared reading relate to writing? Much as steel beams support an office building, so does reading support writing" (Bean and Bouffler in Strickland and Morrow 2000, 113).
There is a close relationship between the kinds of texts children experience in read-alouds/shared reading and what they choose to write and are able to write (Duke and Bennett-Armistead 2003). For example, lists are one of the easiest and most authentic forms of writing and there are great read-alouds to support list making.

Check It Out!

Try these Mentor Text read-alouds to support list making

Bunny Cakes by Rosemary Wells, 2000

Don't Forget the Bacon by Pat Hutchins, 1989

Frog and Toad Together by Arnold Lobel, 1979

Scaredy Squirrel by Mélanie Watt, 2008

Squirrel's New Year's Resolutions by Pat Miller and Kathi Ember , 2010

The Right Word: Roget and His Thesaurus by Jen Bryant and Melissa Sweet, 2014

The Very Hungry Caterpillar by Eric Carle, 2002

Wallace's Lists by Barbara Bottner and Gerald Kruglik , 2004

Using mentor texts and mini-lessons helps students to understand

- That there are different genres of writing
- What the characteristics of these genres are
- When and how to use these genres

It is advisable to read aloud a number of texts by the same author so that the children become familiar with the author's style. Frequently, young writers will try to replicate the style in their own writing. Try to pick mentor texts where the author is also the illustrator, such as books by Patricia Polacco and Kevin Henkes. The children connect well to these types of texts because when they write, they are also both author and illustrator.

Chrysanthemum: *a great read-aloud to support critical literacy.*

K–2 students may also write mentor texts. Do not underestimate the importance of peers sharing their writing, especially books they have written. By celebrating the writing of their classmates on a daily basis, children are encouraged to believe that they too can achieve success in their writing.

Use everyday activities to motivate

Everyday activities in the child's life are another source of inspiration and dramatized stories sometimes make children eager to write (Clay 1991). The power of an experience, a concrete object, a discussion, a picture, or a drawing used as a lead-in to writing should not be underestimated (Strickland and Morrow 2000). Encourage children to label their drawings. Once children are comfortable constructing spelling for individual words, they typically will begin to apply their newfound knowledge to (longer) written texts (Neuman and Roskos 1998).

Very often the urge to write comes from a story shared with a group of children, chosen by the teacher or read by a child who has authored a text (Clay 1991).

Include many non-fiction writing opportunities

Contrary to the popular assumption that young children's first writing is narrative, educators have found that Kindergarteners and First Graders write many non-narrative compositions in which they provide information about familiar topics (Tompkins 2000). There is ample evidence that children are quite comfortable with expository or informational writing even before they enter Kindergarten (Neuman and Roskos 1998). Non-fiction writing is the most functional and commonly used form of writing. Projects and inquiries engage children in using reading and writing for multiple purposes while they are learning about topics meaningful to them (IRA and NAEYC 1998). (See Chapter 14, **Reports: An Example of an All About Book,** p. 358)

Children who realize the functional relevance of written language are more likely to be motivated to explore its use for their own purposes. Such purposes include writing notes and letters, and making and using lists.

Encourage both Invented and Conventional Spelling

Encourage invented spelling
Invented spelling, a form of kid writing, is an important step for emerging and early writers.

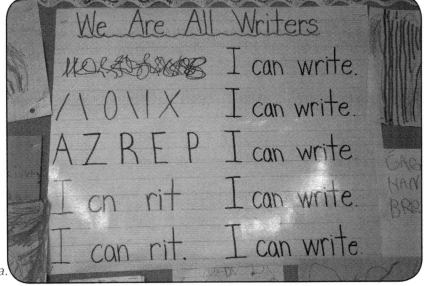

Use environmental print to help the children understand how writing progresses in K–2 , with thanks to Alissa.

Studies suggest that temporary invented spelling may contribute to beginning reading. Every child is entitled to writing experiences that allow the flexibility to use non-conventional forms of writing at first (invented or phonic spelling) and then, over time, to move to conventional forms (IRA and NAEYC 1998).

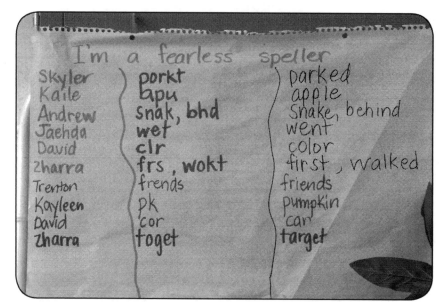

Celebrate their spelling! Used with permission from Sue Ann Goshima, Gustav H. Webling Elementary School.

Scaffolding Conventional Spelling

Spelling rules that work

According to Richard Gentry (author of *My Kid Can't Spell!*) there are only three spelling rules appropriate for children in Grades 1–2:

Rule 1: Always put a u after q.

Rule 2: Every syllable has either a vowel or a y.

Rule 3: When a word ends in silent e, drop the e when adding an ending that begins with a vowel (like = liking).

(Source: J. Richard Gentry, *My Kid Can't Spell!*, Heinemann, 1997, 83–84.)

Encourage the correct spelling of for-sure or pop-up words

Even by the Spring of Kindergarten, children should be encouraged to copy correctly in their everyday writing a core group of high-frequency words. These words include the children's own names, the names of some of their classmates, and the following *for-sure* or *pop-up* words (since they pop up all the time):

For-Sure or Pop-Up Words			
a	and	he (she)	I
in	is	it	of
that	the	to	was

Multiple Paths to Literacy

Surprisingly, twelve simple words make up approximately 25 percent of the words children will encounter in their reading up to the end of Third Grade! (Note the word *she* has been added to make it 13.) All of these words should appear on the classroom word wall, as they are important for children's writing.

A few simple pop-up words that are key to reading and writing in the early years.

By the end of First Grade, at least 70 percent of what children read and write is composed of approximately 100 words.

High-frequency or pop-up words, end of First Grade, spelling words end of Second Grade:

1	**a	16	before	31	go	46	into	61	**of	76	than	91	**was
2	about	17	big	32	going	47	**is	62	*on	77	**that	92	we
3	after	18	but	33	*had	48	**it	63	one	78	**the	93	went
4	all	19	by	34	has	49	just	64	*or	79	their	94	were
5	am	20	came	35	have	50	like	65	our	80	them	95	what
6	an	21	can	36	**he	51	little	66	out	81	then	96	when
7	**and	22	come	37	her	52	look	67	over	82	there	97	where
8	*are	23	could	38	here	53	make	68	play	83	*they	98	who
9	*as	24	day	39	him	54	man	69	put	84	this	99	will
10	asked	25	did	40	*his	55	me	70	said	85	**to	100	*with
11	*at	26	do	41	how	56	mother	71	saw	86	too	101	would
12	away	27	don't	42	**I	57	my	72	see	87	two	102	*you
13	back	28	*for	43	if	58	no	73	she	88	up	103	your
14	*be	29	*from	44	I'm	59	not	74	so	89	us		
15	because	30	get	45	**in	60	now	75	some	90	very		

* indicates the top 25 words ** indicates the 12 most frequently read words K-3 (included in the top 25).

Learning word families (also called rimes or phonograms) is also important to early reading and writing. Children who can recognize and use word families will be able to read and write hundreds of words. There are 37 key word families for the primary grades. These 37 word families allow children to read and write nearly 500 primary-level words. Begin with a few in Kindergarten. Also see **How Important is Phonics and How is it Best Taught?** p. 50 and **A Helpful Phonics Guide** on p. 50.

Common Phonograms

ack	ain	ake	ale	all	ame	an	ank	ap	ash	at	ate	aw
ay	eat	ell	est	ice	ick	ide	ight	ill	in	ine	ing	ink
ip	it	ock	oke	op	ore	ot	uck	ug	ump	unk		

(Source: R. E. Wylie and D. D. Durrell, "Teaching Vowels Through Phonograms," *Elementary English 47* (1970): 787–791.)

Create a literacy-rich classroom

A literacy-rich physical environment is also important. For example, highly visible print labels on objects, signs, and bulletin boards in classrooms demonstrate the practical uses of written language (IRA and NAEYC 1998). Message Boards provide important opportunities for shared reading and writing. Songs, poems, and word walls are also important. Environmental print must be used or it will go unnoticed.

Being a word detective.

Children are encouraged to read it, copy it, and to use the words and labels in their writing (Neuman and Roskos 1998). The ideal is to have many, many Little Books, Big Books, eBooks, Chapter Books, newspapers, and magazines for the children to examine alone and with a partner. Give them time just to "read." Also, include and highlight the children's published books in your classroom collection. Ensure that each child is given a classroom book bag or book box in which to store familiar texts that he or she can "read" and enjoy over and over again.

Book boxes encourage student choice and independent reading. This results in more time reading and less time looking for books.

Closing Thoughts

This chapter has focussed on motivating and meaningful writing activities for K-2 students. The next chapter shares the trait-based scoring scales. It also demonstrates assessment, documentation and the scaffolding of student writing through effective writing conferences.

Assessment, Documentation and Scaffolding of Writing

Before assessing writing, teachers, students, and parents must have a good idea of what is developmentally appropriate to expect of young writers. Start with an understanding of the traits and writing stages and with clear targets. Writing conferences provide the opportunity for intentional teaching using mini-lessons. Conferences also allow for the celebration of the students' writing.

Writing Stages and Targets

Typically, in Kindergarten–Grade 2, three writing stages are evident: emergent, early, and transitional or developing. A child may move back and forth between the stages, depending on the day and what he or she chooses to write. Literacy skills and understandings are evident in each stage although they tend to be somewhat fluid between stages. Skills and understandings provide a guide for assessment, documentation, and instruction. It is important to understand that the skills, understandings, and dispositions listed below provide good examples or illustrations but are not exhaustive.

Emergent Writers (typically preschool–Kindergarten)

Writing Behaviours	Literacy Skills, Understandings, and Dispositions
The term emergent literacy comes from the work of Marie Clay. It is a landmark term that says to parents/caregivers and teachers that literacy begins at birth and is constantly emerging. There is no magic age or developmental level when children are deemed ready to write. They begin to write as soon as they can think and have the ability to scribble.	■ Knows that writing is speech written down and that it communicates an idea ■ May initially rely primarily on pictures (without print) to convey meaning ■ May use squiggles, sticks, wavy lines, and scribbles ■ Can draw pictures with recognizable shapes ■ Can create letter-like units or forms ■ May use an individual letter only (may be repeated) ■ May use random, non-phonetic strings of letters ■ Can copy print (not necessarily correctly) ■ Usually prints own name so that it is recognizable ■ May use one letter to represent a word ■ Can create words using invented spelling ■ Can contribute ideas to shared and interactive writing ■ Can describe their own writing and drawing ■ Begins to understand the concepts of author, illustrator ■ May see themselves as writers although some do not consider themselves writers until they know how to write the alphabet

Early Writers (typically Kindergarten–Grade 1)

Writing Behaviours	Literacy Skills, Understandings, and Dispositions
Early writers are developing more consistency in their appropriate use of concepts of print and sound–symbol correspondence. They use invented spelling and their approximations become more accurate as the years go on. Early writers are more successful with many initial consonants and a few final consonants, and occasionally even find success with the middle of a word. Completely random strings of letters rarely appear, as even early writers know that not just anything goes. Their repertoire of high-frequency words is growing, in both reading and writing. These words are often called glue words, islands of certainty in a sea of print, or for-sure words, and they generally appear on word walls. Use of upper and lowercase letters becomes more appropriate. Typically, by the end of Kindergarten early writers can write at least one complete sentence or thought using invented spelling and appropriate closing punctuation.	Understands that print is functional — it can be used to get things done in everyday life ■ Uses pictures with print ■ Understands the concepts of author, illustrator ■ Creates words regardless of spelling ■ Knows the directional pattern on the page (left to right, top to bottom) ■ Leaves spaces between words ■ Uses some initial consonants correctly while using invented spelling ■ Uses some final consonants correctly while using invented spelling ■ Can correctly print their own name ■ Can spell a few other words conventionally ■ Can create phrases (two or more words) ■ Uses a pattern to scaffold occasionally ■ Begins labelling and using titles ■ Creates a sentence (a complete thought), leaving spaces between words, regardless of spelling ■ Begins to use uppercase letters at the beginning of proper names and sentences ■ Begins to use upper and lowercase letters appropriately more consistently ■ Writes some high-frequency words or no-excuses words (may be copied) ■ Begins to experiment with closing punctuation (period, question mark, exclamation mark) ■ Can create several sentences about a subject ■ Chooses a writing topic independently ■ May create their own "book" ■ Able to read some of their own writing, even after a few days ■ See themselves as readers and writers

Transitional or Developing Writers (typically Grade 1–2)

Writing Behaviours	Literacy Skills, Understandings, and Dispositions
Transitional writers are developing even more consistency in their appropriate use of sound–symbol correspondence. They still use some invented spelling mainly for unfamiliar and un-phonetic spellings but their approximations become more accurate as the years go on. Transitional writers are more successful with many initial consonants and final consonants, and more frequently find success with the middle of a word. They know that not just anything goes. Their repertoire of high-frequency words is growing, in both reading and writing. These words are often called glue words, for-sure words or no-excuses words — islands of certainty in a sea of print — and they generally appear on word walls. Use of upper and lowercase letters becomes more appropriate. Typically, by the end of Grade 2, transitional writers can write at least two indented paragraphs on a related topic or theme. They use varied and simple-complex sentence structures.	■ Uses writing to get things done in everyday life (e.g., writes lists, notes; uses a range of text forms to suit the purpose and audience) ■ Sees a purpose for writing and wants to write often ■ Uses pictures with print that support one another ■ Understands the concepts of author, illustrator ■ Spells unfamiliar words using a variety of strategies ■ Develops a personal voice in writing ■ Uses patterns to support writing ■ Incubates ideas before writing, including using a writer's notebook ■ Identifies the topic, purpose, audience, and form for writing, initially with support and direction ■ Gathers information to support ideas for writing in a variety of ways and/or from a variety of sources ■ Uses labels and titles ■ Begins to understand the difference between editing and revising and uses both ■ More consistently uses uppercase letters at the beginning of proper names and sentences ■ More consistently uses upper- and lowercase letters appropriately ■ Writes high-frequency words or no-excuses words correctly (some may be copied) ■ Uses closing punctuation (period, question mark, exclamation mark) ■ Can create several sentences about a subject ■ Writes a paragraph on a related topic; by the end of Grade 2 at least two indented paragraphs on a related topic or inquiry (e.g., reports) ■ Develops skill and enjoyment in sharing their writing ■ Develops an understanding of the writing process ■ Writing demonstrates the reading–writing connection ■ Uses varied sentence structures grouped into paragraphs ■ Uses greater variety and more maturity in word choice ■ Begins to understand and write from a perspective; writing supports critical literacy ■ Creates own "books" ■ Able to read most of their own writing, even after a few days ■ Chooses a writing topic independently ■ Publishes some of their texts using different formats, such as PowerPoint ■ Shares their writing with others ■ Develops skill in self-assessing own writing ■ See themselves as reader and writers

Trait-Based Scoring Scales: A Strong Framework for Clear Assessment and Feedback

Trait-based scoring scales or looking at children's writing through the traits provides a common language for teachers, children, and parents/caregivers, and a consistent approach to assess and teach writing from classroom to classroom and grade to grade. The traits provide a great framework for providing important and clear feedback to children and for them to self-assess their own writing and that of others. "When we present students with clear criteria, we turn on the lights" (Spandel 2001, 5). The scoring scales provide diagnostic information for writing just as a running record does for reading. For example, a writer might be strong in ideas but weak in organization or vice-versa. Students using self-assessment become self-reflective. Their feelings about their writing do count. They, along with their teacher, have to determine where to go next. Students often find being assessors of their own or other's work motivating.

> The traits also help to link the reading–writing connection. Through listening to read-alouds, reading a variety of genres themselves, conversations, and teacher scaffolding the children come to understand what makes writing strong. Sharing mentor texts is crucial.

> Assessment and feedback don't work best after writing. They are best done during writing.

The Traits Defined: The six traits are the six qualities, elements, or characteristics that define good writing.

Ideas: A clear message; the content of the piece; the main theme or idea, together with the details that develop that theme. One can see (picture), hear, smell, touch, or taste what is being described. Through rich details, both written and/or drawn, the reader can easily deduce the general idea.

Organization: The structure of the piece; the logical ordering of the piece. Text and pictures support one another. Sentences relate to each other and to a common theme.

Voice: The heart and soul of the individual writer. Voice is what captures the reader. It makes the reader "feel." Voice is supported by both words and drawings. Voice comes through loud and clear when the writer writes from the perspective of a person, place, or thing or speaks to the audience (e.g., as in writing a letter).

Word Choice: Million-dollar or yummy words move the reader. The words and drawings paint the picture.

Sentence Fluency: Letters and words form readable phrases and sentences. The piece is easy to read aloud; sentences begin in a variety of ways; sentence lengths vary.

Conventions/Presentation: Concepts of print, spelling (invented spelling and for-sure words), capitals, and punctuation; readable text; pleasing presentation

---

Trait-Based Scoring Scales: Emerging Beginning Writers (often Preschool to Early Grade 1)

Use trait-based scoring scales with writers who write, whether scribbles, picture writing, labelled pictures, letter and number shapes, letter strings, or a single "sentence."

	Exploring	Developing	Accomplished
Ideas	■ Marks on paper ■ Meaning "lives" with writer as he or she writes	■ Letter/number shapes ■ Pictures ■ "Take a guess" ■ Reader creates meaning through inference/guessing ■ Minimal detail	■ Recognizable letters/numbers ■ Recognizable pictures ■ Reader can easily infer general idea ■ Pictures often carry more meaning than text ■ Detail in picture: face, fingers, toes, movement, etc. ■ Writer can "read" text back and elaborate
Organization	■ Random use of space	■ Pattern-centred, left-to-right, etc. ■ Beginning of ordering of text and pictures	■ Balanced look ■ Definite left-to-right "writing"; pictures thoughtfully centred or placed ■ Events in order ■ Co-ordination of text and pictures ■ May write "the end"
Voice	■ Bold lines ■ Use of color ■ Voice expressed through dictation	■ Pictures show mood/feeling ■ Exclamation points or periods ■ BIG LETTERS ■ Multicolor pictures	■ Recognizable as "this child's piece" ■ Unique flavour, style ■ Expressive pictures ■ Expression of feeling in text ■ Writes from the perspective of a person, place or thing ■ Speaks to the audience e.g., letter
Word Choice	■ Scribbles ■ No real letter/ number shapes yet	■ Recognizable letter/number shapes ■ Borrowing from environmental print ■ Labels ■ Letter strings — may be difficult to read even with writer's help	■ Easy-to-read letter/number shapes ■ Some recognizable letter-string words ■ Variety of words

	Exploring	Developing	Accomplished
Fluency	▪ No letter/ word strings yet ▪ Dictates sentences to go with writing	▪ Letter strings suggest beginning sentences: ilpdg (I like to play with my dog). ▪ Not translatable without help ▪ Dictates multiple sentences	▪ Letter strings form readable sentences: I lk to pl w m dg (I like to play with my dog) ▪ Dictates a whole story, personal recount, or informational piece
Conventions	▪ No recognizable conventions yet ▪ Can point to conventions in environment	▪ Places punctuation randomly in text ▪ Scribbles imitate look and shape of text ▪ Writes readable name on paper, which may or may not be spelled correctly ▪ Writes one or two readable words (often using invented spelling)	▪ Improving use of conventions of print ▪ Includes a title ▪ Writes name on work and spells it correctly ▪ Writes (may copy) several or many readable words including no-excuses words ▪ Use of I (capitalized) ▪ Periods placed correctly ▪ Other closing punctuation attempted

(Adapted from Vicki Spandel, *Creating Writers Through 6-Trait Writing Assessment and Instruction*, 3rd ed. New York: Addison-Wesley Longman Inc., 2001: 353–354.)

The best part of me is my face.Mentor text:
The Best Part of Me *by Wendy Ewald*

Trait-Based Scoring Scales: Early–transitional Writers (Grade 1–2)

Use trait-based scoring scales with writers who are writing words, sentences, and paragraphs.

	Exploring	Developing	Accomplished
Ideas	■ Uses pictures and/ or minimal text to share ideas ■ Writes for several purposes ■ Reader can infer main idea ■ Writer can read text back	■ Pictures becoming more detailed ■ Text has expanded to at least several sentences ■ Attends to details in written text ■ Writes for several purposes ■ Fairly easy for reader to read text	■ Pictures and/or text detailed; convey clear meaning ■ Writing makes a point ■ Typically the text carries more meaning than the pictures ■ Writes for many purposes ■ Easy for reader and writer to read and understand. ■ Shows knowledge of the topic
Organization	■ Text has a definite beginning and end ■ May use a title and The End ■ Pictures and text go together	■ Uses multiple pictures or multiple sentences that go together ■ Uses a title, lead, and The end or conclusion ■ Indicates a beginning (e.g., "One day…") ■ Sticks with one topic	■ Strong lead ■ Ending evident ■ Engaging and thoughtful title ■ Pictures and text go together ■ All text and pictures in logical order ■ Uses word organizers or transition words to make connections; to provide a structure (e.g., first, then, next, after…)
Voice	■ Text/pictures show definite mood/ feelings ■ Shows awareness of audience ■ Uses exclamation points, underling and BIG letters to indicate strong feelings	■ Creates pictures and text that produce an emotional response in the reader; feelings ■ Uses exclamation points, underlining and BIG letters to indicate strong feelings ■ Indicates wanting to connect with the audience by using words such as You and by asking direct questions	■ Engaging text ■ Projects personal point of view ■ Writes from the perspective of a person, place or thing ■ Speaks to the audience (e.g., letter) ■ Listener enjoys hearing text read aloud ■ Text moves the listener ■ The voice in the text often gives away the author's identity to those who know the author ■ The text, including photos/ illustrations has personality

Multiple Paths to Literacy

	Exploring	Developing	Accomplished
Word Choice	▪ Uses recognizable words ▪ Uses nouns, adjectives, and verbs, generally correctly ▪ Often uses words to label pictures, signs	▪ Tries new words ▪ Uses words to help the reader visualize ▪ Uses words to prompt feelings	▪ Uses "million dollar" or "yummy" words — new words that cause the typical child to stretch ▪ Uses striking unexpected phrasing ▪ Uses words that spark imagery and/or mood
Fluency	▪ Writes at least one complete thought, one complete sentence	▪ Writes more than one sentence ▪ May use sentence patterns such as I love my mom, I love my school ▪ Text is easy to read aloud	▪ Writes one or two paragraphs ▪ Varies sentence beginnings ▪ Varies sentence endings ▪ Varies sentence lengths ▪ Uses connecting words: first, then, after, so ▪ Uses dialogue where appropriate ▪ Flows nicely when read aloud
Conventions	▪ Improving use of conventions of print ▪ Includes a title ▪ Writes name on work and spells it correctly ▪ Writes many readable words ▪ Use of I (capitalized) ▪ Periods placed correctly ▪ Other closing punctuation attempted	▪ Uses periods, question marks, and exclamation marks correctly ▪ Experiments with semicolons, colons, quotation marks ▪ Uses capitals on I, names, and beginnings of sentences ▪ Spelling correct on most simple words such as those with four or fewer letters ▪ Generally includes name, date, and title	▪ Uses periods, commas, question marks, quotation marks, and exclamation marks correctly ▪ Uses capitals correctly and consistently ▪ Spelling correct on most one and two syllable words, including no-excuses words ▪ Writers can self-identify the presence of spelling errors in most cases ("It doesn't look right") ▪ Grammar is correct in most cases ▪ All words are readable; text is easy to read

(Adapted from Vicki Spandel, *Creating Writers Through 6-Trait Writing Assessment and Instruction*, 3rd ed. New York: Addison-Wesley Longman Inc., 2001: 353–354.)

Teach Children to write with VOICE by:

▪ Writing messages and notes

▪ Writing from the perspective of a person, place or thing

When responding to "I'm done!" teach the children that writers often say, "When you're done, you have just begun."

Using Assessment Results

Assessment results help to determine student interests, how much time should be spent on each instructional approach, and which mini-lessons should be highlighted. Assessments also help to clarify potential writing topics based on their interests and writing forms and genres.

A great deal can be learned by using assessments "on the run" during shared, interactive, guided, and independent writing. An important factor to note is the degree of student engagement in writing. How often have you heard: "I'm done" or "I don't know what to write"? Help the students to understand that they are never done. When one piece of writing is finished, one of two things may happen: another one is started or a previous piece is revised.

A helpful wall chart (used with the permission of Mila Tamaoka)

Assessing, Teaching, and Celebrating Writing through Writing Conferences

Daily writing, celebrations, and sharing of individual children's writing and feedback are crucial. A writing conference is any discussion that focuses on a child's writing. It can occur at any time: "on the run" as you move from child to child or in a public forum with a small or large group of children listening in. A writing conference can be initiated by the teacher or by the individual writer.

The two main reasons for writing conferences are to scaffold learning (through assessing and teaching) and to celebrate each individual's writing. Nothing encourages writing more than celebrating children's work. Scaffolding and celebration will result in developing in children both the skill and will to write.

Writing "conferences" (conversations) often occur while the children are engaged in the act of writing. Examining a piece of writing is an authentic form of assessment. The students should also be self-assessing their writing. Student–teacher and

According to Regie Routman (2005), conferences may celebrate, validate, encourage, nudge, teach, assess, and/or set goals. A writing conference (generally less than five minutes) usually occurs one-to-one, with teacher and student. Either the teacher or the student may ask for a conference. Small group conferences where peers listen in (and sometimes provide feedback) also work.

teacher–student feedback are both important. This is the heart of a writing conference.

Feedback:
The Heart of a Writing Conference

There are several keys to strong feedback:

- Helping the students to understand the traits or characteristics of strong writing: what they are working towards (See trait-based scoring scales p. 306-309)

- Developing a collaborative learning environment so that students feel comfortable talking about and sharing their writing

- Having the student read a part of their writing aloud helps the writer and the listener to listen for fluency and voice

- Timing the feedback, where possible using a teachable moment

- Knowing the most effective way to have a conversation around student writing: what to say and how to say it. Providing feedback is tricky. One never wants to discourage a writer. On the other hand providing honest feedback in an encouraging way is important. Empty comments like "Nice work" don't tell writers anything specific about their work. The type of feedback provided by a teacher will be mimicked by students when giving each other feedback. Respond mainly to the content of the piece

- *Always* encourage the child to do most of the talking

- Encourage the child to self-assess. Useful prompts include the following: "Tell me about your writing." "What's one smart thing you did today (or yesterday) as a writer?" "What is one thing you could do better as a writer?"

> The keys to *sentence fluency*: beginning sentences in different ways; using a variety of sentence lengths.

  Talking Tom Cat is a fun app for K-3 students. Students can read their sentences to the app and Tom the Cat will read it back to them. It is a good way to motivate students who are are reluctant to read aloud.

> Be specific with your feedback. For example, "All of the details you include such as the rain pelting down and all of the water rushing in the streets help me to make a picture in my head." Or, "I can tell by this sentence that you really care about the topic. Your voice is coming through."

Student Self-Assessment:
Thinking Like a Writer

Self-assessment is very important. In the process of self-assessment, students develop metacognition and determine for themselves what they think the next steps should be to improve their writing. In the early grades, this self-assessment is likely to occur through teacher scaffolding. This may involve reading the self-assessment tool to/with the student and then helping to document the student responses as needed. The student–teacher conversation provides more feedback and possible next-steps.

The following revision self-assessment tool focuses only on developing meaning and focuses on five traits. Editing deals with conventions, the sixth trait, such as spelling and punctuation. An editing checklist is also included below.

My Revision Checklist

Ideas   Organization   Voice   Word Choice   Fluency

	Yes	No
This is what I think of my writing		
Ideas		
My writing		
Has a main idea	☐	☐
Has enough detail (and not too much).	☐	☐
Readers will be able to picture what I am writing about	☐	☐
Organization		
My writing		
Has a good title	☐	☐
Has a beginning, middle, and end	☐	☐
Tells the ideas in order	☐	☐
Has a lead or beginning that "grabs" you	☐	☐
Has a strong ending	☐	☐
Voice		
My writing:		
Sounds like me	☐	☐
Shows that I care about the subject	☐	☐

Will make the readers feel _____

Word Choice

My writing uses some million-dollar or yummy words such as _____

A very good word that I used or could use _____

Fluency		
I begin my sentences in different ways	☐	☐
Some of my sentences are long; some are short	☐	☐

Self-Assessment: Editing (Including Conventions)
Early–Transitional or Developing Writers (Typically Grade K–1)

How did I write today?

A one-on-one conference

Name:_____

Date:_____

This self-assessment is read to each student and discussed before any choices are made.

	Yes	Sometimes	No
I wrote my **name** on my work.	☺	☺	☹
I started writing in the right place.	☺	☺	☹
I left meatball spaces between the words.	☺	☺	☹
I copied a word from the Word Wall, the wall, or a book.	☺	☺	☹
I wrote some for-sure or pop-up words correctly.	☺	☺	☹
I wrote some little words correctly from my head.	☺	☺	☹
I used kid writing to write words that were really hard for me.	☺	☺	☹
I used an uppercase letter at the beginning of my sentence.	☺	☺	☹
I used an uppercase letter at the beginning of my name.	☺	☺	☹
I used a period, exclamation mark, or a question mark (.!?) at the end of my idea.	☺	☺	☹
I read it over after I finished writing to make sure that it made sense and all of the words were there.	☺	☺	☹

(Adapted from *Learning to Write and Loving It!* © Miriam P. Trehearne 2011).

Self-Assessment: Editing (Including Conventions) Transitional or Developing Writers (Typically Grade 1–2)

Name: _____

Date: _____

Title: _____

		Yes	No
1.	I spelled all "no-excuses" or "pop-up" words correctly.	☐	☐
2.	I used kid writing to write some words that were really hard for me.	☐	☐
3.	I used periods, question marks, and exclamation points correctly.	☐	☐
4.	I used a capital letter for "I."	☐	☐
5.	I rubber-banded or stretched words to help me spell them correctly.	☐	☐
6.	I used a capital letter to begin my sentences	☐	☐
7.	I used a capital letter to begin all names and in the right places in my title.	☐	☐
8.	I spelled all the words the best that I could.	☐	☐
9.	I used quotation marks around the words that characters said.	☐	☐
10.	I read it over after I finished writing to make sure that all of the words were there.	☐	☐

I used _____ to help me spell.

_____

Parents/caregivers and administrators also become part of the process through classroom visits, conferences, portfolios, and other forms of documentation.

Closing Thoughts

"[There is a] synergy between reading and writing. Reading inspires and excites children about the possibilities awaiting them as writers, and acquaints them with the structure of text and books and the conventions of written language. Writing allows them to use what they've gleaned from reading as they craft their own stories, poems and factual texts. And because of their writing efforts, children approach written text with a heightened awareness and understanding of print, text and genre" (Taberski 2000, 176).

Reading and writing are connected. Children learn to write from understanding the traits, qualities, or characteristics used by authors in good literature shared by teachers. As teachers model, demonstrate, and explain, children are able to assess the qualities of good writing. This enables them to understand how to assess and revise their own writing, to make it even better. There is no question that, compared to reading, writing remains a curriculum casualty. There is no doubt that a greater emphasis needs to be placed on writing, oral language and comprehension, not only during the literacy block but also across the day.

The next chapter emphasizes the important roles of writing, oral language, and comprehension, across the curricula, during inquiry learning. In the process, children solve problems, make sense of their world, and communicate with others.

Inquiry-Based Learning: What We Really Know...

> "A child is not a vessel to be filled, but a lamp to be lit." —Hebrew Proverb

Inquiry-Based learning and self-regulation (Chapter 7) along with play-based learning (Chapter 7) have become hot terms in the culture of primary teachers. It is crucial that all educators start with common definitions and shared understandings for these terms. For instance, what does the research indicate? Which pedagogical approaches are most effective in supporting inquiry-based learning? Agreement on educational definitions, or the lack thereof, for the term inquiry-based learning makes it very confusing. This chapter provides some clarity. It also provides practical examples of how K–2 teachers using inquiry-based learning also support strong literacy programs. Educators should always start with planning that implements the **Essential Elements and High-Yield Strategies of Effective Grades K–2 Literacy Programs**, see Chapters 1-3.

Defining Inquiry-Based Learning: Little Agreement!

There is little agreement from class to class, school to school, as to what constitutes inquiry-based learning as well as its degree of effectiveness when used in preschool/primary classrooms.

The definition used in this book is that inquiry-based learning is a pedagogical approach that attempts to support students in becoming thoughtful, motivated, collaborative, and innovative learners capable of engaging in their own inquiries and thriving in a world of constant change (adapted from the Ontario Literacy and Numeracy Secretariat 2013). Inquiries often engage children in using reading, writing, listening, and speaking for multiple purposes while they are learning about topics meaningful to them. The inquiries typically support the curriculum as planned (e.g., by

> The **essence of inquiry:**
> "Inquiry ... requires more than simply answering questions or getting a right answer. It espouses investigation, exploration, search, quest, research, pursuit, and study. It is enhanced by involvement with a community of learners each learning from the other in social interaction" (Kuklthau, Maniotes, and Caspari 2007, 2).
>
> "The meaning of 'knowing' has shifted from being able to remember and repeat information to being able to find and use it." —Nobel laureate Herbert Simon, 1996
>
> Introductions to inquiry-based learning can be found at https://www.edu.gov.on.ca/eng/literacynumeracy/inspire/research/CBS_StudentInquiry.pdf and http://teachinquiry.com/index/Introduction.html and https://www.edu.gov.on.ca/eng/literacynumeracy/inspire/research/CBS_InquiryBased.pdf

the province or state) and/or the negotiated curriculum as lived (grabbing those teachable moments). The inquiries may be over in a day or may go on for weeks or even months.

Negotiating the curriculum provides kids with things worth thinking, talking, reading, and writing about! We do know that children learn best when the concepts, vocabulary, and skills they encounter are related to things they know and care about and when the new learnings are interconnected (Copple and Bredekamp 2009). Student choice and voice, where possible, is very important. Young children naturally construct knowledge as they participate with others as they inquire, experiment, solve problems, play, and learn together. They also need direct teaching involving scaffolding through modelling, demonstrating, explaining, and guided practice (Routman 2005; Neuman and Roskos 2007). Effect Size (ES) for direct instruction = 0.59 (Hattie 2009, 297).

Teachers can use the key ideas underlying inquiry-based learning in any classroom. Using real-life issues to motivate students, challenging them to think deeply about meaningful content, and enabling them to work collaboratively are worthwhile practices.

Research on Inquiry-Based Learning: How Effective is it Really?

There is very little research (in refereed journals) on the effects of inquiry-based learning at the primary level. What is available is typically high-school based. Additionally because the definitions and the learning look so different from one type of inquiry to another, from one classroom or school to another, it is hard to try to compare and make sense of the results. What we do know is that "The effectiveness of inquiry-based learning depends on the guidance provided by teachers. For example, teachers should guide students to develop a good question for investigation, monitor their inquiry process, and provide guidance when they encounter difficulties. Teachers should give students ongoing feedback and encourage them to constantly assess their own learning" (Canadian Education Association 2014, online). As outlined by the Galileo Educational Network (2008) rubric to guide inquiry, which is supported by a large body of research, a constellation of processes needs to be in place to maximize the impact of inquiry-based education. These elements include scaffolding activities, formative feedback loops, and the adoption of powerful questioning strategies to guide the learning process.

Research (again, mostly at the high-school level) also suggests that inquiry-based approaches to learning positively impact students' abilities to understand core concepts and procedures. Research also suggests that students are likely to develop as engaged, self-directed learners in inquiry-based classrooms and that inquiry does promote thoughtful literacy.

"Once children are helped to perceive themselves as authors and inventors, once they are helped to discover the pleasure of inquiry, their motivation and interest explode" (Malaguzzi 1998, 67).

"It is important to recognize that not all learning opportunities call for an inquiry approach ... It is a misconception that inquiry-based pedagogy means letting go of the class and following students to self-direct all aspects of their learning. Students' thinking can be limited when confined to their own experiences" (The Student Achievement Division, Ministry of Ontario, 2013, 5). Additionally, most K–2 students have limited researching abilities using both reading and writing; however, there are other ways to inquire.

Inquiry-Based Learning Promotes Thoughtful Literacy

"Thoughtful literacy" is a term coined by Richard Allington, amongst others. Thoughtful literacy is not a separate kind of literacy but rather the umbrella for all literacy learning across the curriculum. It involves having students actively engaged in "deep thinking" in complex and critical ways while reading, listening, speaking, writing, and representing. Thoughtful literacy teaching and learning focuses on educating the whole child in all aspects: academic, moral, social, and emotional. "One of the best ways to increase student thinking is to make sure you have a curriculum that provides kids with things worth thinking about and that offers kids enough depth that they can actually think" (Allington quoted in Preller, 2001. 2). Inquiry learning typically provides such an engaging curriculum. When students are getting their information from multiple sources, they are required to compare, synthesize, evaluate, and summarize. These higher-order thinking skills typically occur during an inquiry. Studies indicate that teachers who promote thoughtful literacy have students who routinely produce superior work in various forms of assessment. In addition, their students read and write more and differently than students in more typical classrooms. They talk more and make more connections across texts and across conversations. The quality and quantity of classroom talk is different (Allington 2006, 119). Fostering thoughtful literacy really matters for all learners but especially for struggling literacy learners. **Teaching students how to think rather than what to think is the key to all learning.**

In Support of Inquiry-Based Learning

Of course, "the effectiveness of inquiry-based learning depends on the guidance provided by teachers" (Canadian Education Association 2014, online) but it has the potential to foster the following:

- Engagement of children's curiosity about a topic of interest to them and sharing as the curriculum emerges

- Encouragement of questioning, problem solving, and higher-level thinking

- Oral language (academic vocabulary) and background knowledge development

- Growth in early literacy and cross-curricular knowledge and skills by connecting student wonderings to the big ideas of the curriculum, including critical literacy

- Establishment of a culture of classroom inquiry that can teach students to question and wonder while posing questions important to them

- Understanding that it is okay not to know everything

- Facilitation of student ownership and pride in their work

Cautions around Inquiry-Based Learning

Despite the vast potential of inquiry-based learning, there is also the danger of becoming so wrapped up in an inquiry that strong, focused literacy teaching, carefully aligned to student needs, falls by the wayside. There is also the danger that not enough time and energy will be available in order to "cover" the mandated curriculum effectively. How does one get it all in? Effective cross-curricular integration is the only answer. "If teachers merely elicit and run with student questions without framing overarching curricular goals and essential questions to support them, there can be no guaranteed and viable curriculum" (McTighe and Wiggins 2013, 58).

Not all inquiry questions are essential questions. Small group instruction will be necessary to help some students form questions, share ideas, and build upon each other's thoughts. For some students, an inquiry way of thinking and expressing their learning is not going to come naturally. It will be essential for explicit instruction in this area. Setting up provocations around the room will not instantly result in inquiry thinking and learning. The educator needs to be the guide on the side.

Strong inquiry questions are key. Often they spark discussion and debate. Questions may be teacher crafted, teacher provoked, or student created. "One good question can keep a whole class going for a long time; a bad one produces little more than a simple answer" (McTighe and Wiggins 2013, 43). At times, inquiries go on for far too long. Teachers have to know when it is time to "Let it go"; not all inquiries need to be extended. Mini-inquiries are also important (See examples p. 333).

Getting Started: Guided Discovery

Whether student generated or teacher generated, it is crucial that the teacher scaffold the inquiry to support strong literacy teaching and learning (See **Chapter 14 for many examples**).

Student-generated inquiries

Student wonderings often lead to inquiries. They may become individual, small group, or whole class inquiries. However, inquiries don't have to be completely student generated without teacher scaffolding. Teachers can and often should provide provocations to generate student inquiries (See Angie's Mitten Inquiry p. 333).

Teacher-provoked inquiries

A major challenge for teachers is not having enough time in the day. Cross-curricular integration is crucial. This often occurs as the result of a teacher-initiated question or shared experience (e.g., a read-aloud, video, or field trip, based on a key concept in the mandated curriculum (See **What's the Buzz about Bees?** A Critical Literacy Learning Story, p. 346). As long as the students are engaged and the learning is connected, a teacher-provoked inquiry can be just as effective, or even more effective, than a student-generated one.

> "Inquiry offers common background knowledge and discourse in a meaningful, relevant topic of current importance—something being studied in the real world, not just made up for the students to learn. I think of the inquiry learning as a river. I have the plans in my head first, but I am actively listening to my students and searching for those 'teachable moments' when I need to stray from my planned path onto a tributary stream. I still know the grand scheme and can get back to my main flow with ease. I want their input, which comes through their engagement so I prepare for those streams of student-generated flows of learning under the general umbrella of the inquiry topic." Kas Patsula

Scaffolding an Inquiry

There is no script to inquiry-based learning; however, five phases are typically evident: engage, question, plan, explore, and report/reflect/celebrate at the end.

ENGAGE

Phase 1: Engage

Engage or provoke children's curiosity about a topic of interest to them, often by reading aloud, using artifacts or pictures, or sharing a common experience. Grab those teachable moments!

Get to know the students before moving forward with an inquiry. Marie Clay describes "roaming around the known" as a procedure where the teacher takes the time to really listen to and watch the students working in their comfort zone to get to know their strengths, weaknesses, and interests before determining the best learning path.

Online Resources to Engage Inquiry

Provocations

http://passionatelycuriousinKindergarten.blogspot.ca/2012/10/provocations-for-learning.html defines and provides classroom examples of provocations for learning.

https://www.pinterest.com/dpearlylearning/provocations-for-learning/ provides a visual list of provocations used in Kindergarten classrooms.

Photo provocations

Always check each time to ensure that photos are appropriate for your learners!

http://www.earth-pics.com/photo-of-the-day provides an engaging photo of the day.

http://www.insectimages.org/ provides images of insects.

http://sciencekids.co.nz/images.html provides images of animals.

www.worldbookonline.com/kids/browsepictures provides images of animals.

Wonders of the Day

http://wonderopolis.org/ is a free site that posts a wonder of the day. You can explore wonders and vote for your favourites. The site has a section to filter by grade level and by topic. Questions such as "Why is Ice Slippery?" and "How is Glass Recycled?" are explored and defined for students. There is a "listen to" option as well as a text option. Always check each time to ensure that wonders are appropriate for your learners!

 *Check It Out!*

Great Read-Aloud Picture Books to Support Inquiry

I Wonder (2013) by Annaka Harris and John Rowe stands out as one of the most amazing books available. It successfully provokes inquiry and curiosity while helping children understand what inquiry is all about. (See more from I Wonder on p. 362)

Questions, Questions (2011) by Marcus Pfister shares wonderings written in rhyming couplets such as "How do birds learn how to sing? What brings summer after spring?" (Caution: not a single answer is provided, which can be annoying for some young learners.)

Fascinating Canada: A Book of Questions and Answers (2011) by John Robert Colombo will stimulate inquiry and spark the sense of surprise in the minds of readers who know something about Canada (but not as much as the author!).

The Wonder Book by Amy Krouse Rosenthal (2010) lists wonderings such as "I wonder who left something under the tooth fairy's pillow?"

What Do You Do With an Idea? (2013) by Yamada Kobi and Mae Besom is a superb book that helps children understand what an idea is and what we can achieve with an idea: "And then I realized what you do with an idea…. You change the world." "Some people make fun of others' ideas. But believe in your ideas; don't give up." "It's okay if it's different and weird and maybe a little crazy." This book strongly supports self-regulation (Chapter 7), stick-to-it-iveness, and critical literacy.

Anything is Possible by Giulia Belloni and Marco Trevisan (2011) strongly supports self-regulation (Chapter 7), stick-to-it-iveness, and using one's imagination, stressing that "anything is possible." *If Kids Ran the World* by Leo and Diane Dillon (2014) states,

"If Kids ran the world, we would make it a kinder, better place." This book strongly supports critical literacy. Help the children make a text–text connection with Judith Viorst's book *If I Were in Charge of the World*

Phase 2: Question

QUESTION

Children formulate **questions** or **wonderings**… Often children start with a wonder statement, which sparks an inquiry. The students' questions may be spontaneous or teacher-generated, essential questions based on key curriculum concepts. McTighe and Wiggins define these questions as "essential for students to continuously examine so as to come to an understanding of key

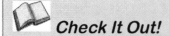

Check It Out!

A Wonder Poem: "I WONDER" by Jeannie Kirby: http://www. englishforums.com/English/ TeachingPoemWonderJeannie-Kirby/pcmzr/post.htm

One teacher's view: "The most important factor in inquiry learning is to ensure an authentic question propels the students' learning forward. It is a question of interest outside of the classroom in real-world application and it is generous enough to cover much of the cross-curricular curriculum". —Kas Patsula

An inquiry poster is an important instructional tool. To learn more about the research-base of inquiry poster use, see "Vocabulary Visits: Virtual field trips for content vocabulary development" in Blachowicz and Obrochta (2005).

ideas and processes" (2013, 14). They are provocative, open-ended (lack one "right" answer), generative, and require *uncovering* the depth of the topic rather than simply *covering* it. Often the answers are not stated in a text (on the page). Answers are often inferred (off the page) and depend on different perspectives. The wonders may be research wonders or heart wonders. According to Heard and McDonough (2009), a research wonder is just that… a wonder that you must research in order to find the answer, such as "Why do dogs have wet noses?" A heart wonder is only answerable from your mind and your heart… such as "What makes a good friend?" (See **Treasure Wonder Inquiry Centres p. 260** and **Another Discovery/Wonder Centre p. 262**).

Asking questions and making sense of the information lies at the core of all inquiry (See Ontario Ministry of Education, *Getting Started with Student Inquiry*, 2011). Essential questions must engage the students and provide needed curricular understanding. Posting essential questions in the classroom and referring to them often is helpful. Prompts for furthering inquiry discussions include, "What are you thinking now?" "What wonderings do you have?" "What does this make you think of?" Wonders can also be grouped into categories. Inquiry posters, anticipation guides, and KWHLAQ charts (See this chapter) are also great ways to "roam around the known": What do the students really know or think they know about the inquiry topic?

Roaming around the known using an inquiry poster and an anticipation guide

Inquiry poster

The purpose of an inquiry poster is to help open the inquiry and then to play a central role in the ongoing discussion of the key concepts and vocabulary. The poster mainly consists of photos or drawings related to the inquiry and helps stimulate language use by activating prior knowledge about the topic. The visuals often help the children to make sensory connections with the main inquiry content.

The poster can be introduced by prompting with, "Tell me what you see." As students contribute words or ideas, the teacher writes them on the poster or on sticky notes placed on the poster. The children simply share their ideas and their excitement as they make connections. Extend the conversation by prompting them to describe what they might hear, see, and feel if they were in the pictures. This is a good opportunity to teach important vocabulary for the inquiry (See p. 156, **Text Talk**).

Honeybees

This is an inquiry poster used to introduce an inquiry on bees. The poster is a great vehicle for developing and assessing vocabulary and background knowledge. Thank you Kas for sharing this very thoughtfully created bee inquiry poster.

Teachers need to keep coming back to the poster throughout the inquiry. They make changes based on discussions of "what we know" versus "what we thought we knew." As the teacher shares read-alouds or video clips related to the inquiry, new vocabulary and concepts are added and existing vocabulary is noted. The students become more knowledgeable and confident as they encounter repeated, related vocabulary.

Anticipation guide

An anticipation guide, like an inquiry poster, helps to stimulate language use by helping the students activate prior knowledge about the topic through discussion. It helps to introduce some of the key concepts while providing clues about the unit content. It can also be used at the end of the inquiry to see if students' beliefs and understandings have changed. The easiest way to explain an anticipation guide is by providing the example below. This guide was used to stimulate discussion at the beginning of an inquiry on bees.

All About Bees	YES (I agree)	NO (I don't agree)
1. We need bees.		
2. Bees are insects.		
3. Bees make honey from pollen.		
4. Honeybees and bumblebees live in caves.		
5. All bees can sting people.		
6. Bees and flowers help one another.		

Before the inquiry: The teacher shares the anticipation guide statements one at a time. Students are asked to select a response to each statement and to share their reasoning during a discussion with a partner. Group sharing follows.

After the inquiry: Students are asked to reconsider their initial responses in light of what they have read, heard, and experienced during the unit. Group sharing follows.

From a KWLM chart to an KWHLAQ chart

Similar to a KWLM anchor chart (See p. 166), a KWHLAQ chart, developed by Silvia Rosenthal Tolisano, is a great system for documenting student understandings and for monitoring and documenting ongoing student learning, especially when undertaking an inquiry with a **critical literacy focus**.

http://langwitches.org/blog/2011/07/21/upgrade-your-kwl-chart-to-the-21st-century/ expands on the KWHLAQ chart

KWHLAQ chart:

K: What do we know or think we *know* about...? What makes us think that?

W: What do we *want* to know about...?

H: *How* will we find out about...?

L: What did we *learn* about...?

A: What *action* will we take...?

Q: What other *questions* do we have...?

Learn more about questions, conversations, and prompts

- Understanding what a conversation is starts with understanding what a question is (p. 118)

- Some wonderful question-and-answer books to read-aloud (p. 121)

- Create question-and-answer books or reports (p. 286)

- Make Conversations Powerful: Chapter 5

- Effective prompts and questions to extend conversations (p. 166–169)

- Get everyone talking using strategic conversations (p. 132)

- Teacher questions and prompts to use with read-alouds: increase talk and comprehension (p. 166–167)

- Types of questions and prompts (p. 167)

- What about student-initiated questions? (p. 168)

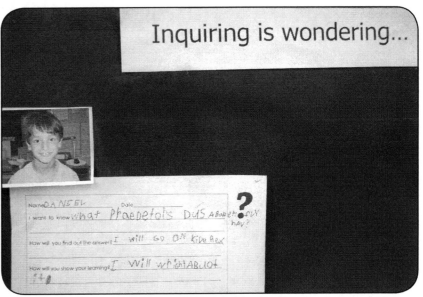

Daniel is making a statement about his inquiry. Inquiry is wondering: "What I want to know; how I will find it out; how I will share my learning."

Sharing our wonderings.

Phase 3: Plan

Children plan ways to inquire and how to show others what questions they asked and what they found out. Providing each child with his or her own **inquiry notebook** is a great way for them to document the process. The notebook may contain questions sketches, diagrams, findings, and thoughts, similar to a writer's notebook, (See **Keep a Writer's Notebook** p. 287.)

PLAN

How will we find
out the answers to
our wonders?
— we can go on googul
— we can ge, te the
  butterflay conservatort
— we can woch a video
— we can look on kid rex zoe
— we can look in a book
— we can gsc sumple

The plan: How will we find out the answers to our wonders?

Phase 4: *EXPLORE/COLLABORATE/DISCOVER/ CREATE*

EXPLORE/COLLABORATE/ DISCOVER/CREATE

When children put their inquiry plans into action, they sometimes make mistakes. It is important to stress that this trial and error is all part of the research and experimentation process, which will help their brains to grow (See **Window on the Classroom: Jane's Story**, p. 109; see also **Building the Brain Smarter and Stronger**, p. 118.)

Children need access, of course, to appropriate sources to explore their inquiries. There are so many wonderful print and online sources that it would be impossible to list them all, but see a sampling of specific suggestions throughout this chapter and the list of online resources at the end of the Chapter 14.

Phase 5: *COMMUNICATE/SHARE FINDINGS/ REFLECT/CELEBRATE*

Children report and reflect, sharing different perspectives. **It is important that they learn *how* to share effectively with an audience. Teacher modelling is crucial (See Rubric for "Animal VISION inquiry below).** They also learn from each other. Students could engage in a wide range of writing tasks about their inquiry topics or class inquiries. Dictation apps or voice recordings is one way to differentiate for learners. See the list of online resources at the end of Chapter 14 for more ideas. Check with your principal or board to inquire about access to software for your students.

Window on the Classroom: Accesses Information and Presents Effectively

Student's name _____ Rubric for "Animal VISION" challenge /20

	1 point	2 points	3 points	4 points	Inspiration
Presentation	Student requires **multiple reminders** to "speak like a teacher".	Student requires **occasional reminders** to "speak like a teacher".	Student requires **NO reminders** to "speak like a teacher"— just does it.	Student **exceeds presentation expectations** and "speaks like a teacher".	
Response to teacher and student questions and comments.	Student **cannot field questions** or comments and teacher must do so on their behalf.	Student fields questions and comments with **extensive teacher support**.	Student fields questions and comments with **some teacher support**.	Student fields questions and comments with **NO teacher support** and exceeds expectations.	
Ability to quote one resource (website, book, spoke to expert, other…)	Did not use a resource.	Can vaguely site resource but it is ambiguous.	Can **quote one resource** with specifics (mom and I looked this up on website…)	**Can quote more than one source (I used a website and this book that dad and I read…)**	
Demonstrating understanding through speaking (i.e. able to explain/ talk about the "animal vision".)	Does not know any facts about their animal's vision.	Able to describe their animal's vision with **one distinct fact**.	Able to describe their animal's vision **with two to four distinct facts**.	Able to describe their animal's vision with **five or more distinct facts**.	
The project will be marked out of 20 and 5 points are awarded simply for completing task.					

> "From day one, I establish a culture of sharing, listening, questioning on topic, which puts the sharer in a position of authority and expertise on that which they are sharing. It allows 4 and 5 year olds to 'be the teacher' and hold the class' attention on a topic of their choosing. This cultivation of confidence, respect, sharing of interests and ideas allows the teacher to better understand each student, and thus to better meet their needs throughout the year, while preparing the class for strong risk-taking in literacy and learning". Kas Patsula

Thank you to Kas Patsula for sharing this rubric. It helps provide important student feedback and understanding on the how-to of effective communicating, sharing and celebrating. It also supports student reflection and self-assessment. See Chapter 9 p. 211, student sharing a zebra vision inquiry report.

Wall stories

Wall stories (**See The Power of a Wall Story Centre** p. 208) can be used for all sorts of classroom purposes, including inquiries. A wall story might begin by showing a photo of the provocation with students' faces and a thinking bubble above to indicate their initial wonderings. Or a wall story might be the final product of new learning that occurred about a specific class inquiry such as bees, worms, butterflies, mittens, bird nests, or changes over time. Digital photos from the different stages of the inquiry can be printed and glued on 11 x 17 paper, or used in Word, SMART Notebook, or other interactive software to display for the class. Interactive writing can be done as a class to document the thinking about each photo. Students then work with the teacher to create a shared text, usually over several days that can be revisited until it is finished. Students can also create their own wonder books to share.

Window on the Classroom: Explaining Inquiry in Angie's Class

An inquiry may occur spontaneously or be planned; it might last a morning, a day, a week, a month, or even be revisited throughout the year. For example, students were wondering about the worms in the Kindergarten play area during a rainy week in the Fall. The class created a list of wonderings and worked through them together. They looked at and read informational texts about worms, stories about worms, and diagrams of worms. As the weather got colder, the conversation about worms stopped. In the spring, during a class walk to the pond, students noticed dried up worms on the pathway. This sparked a conversation about worms and generated more wonderings. Why are the worms dried up? Where were they during the winter? What is happening to worms now? Why do worms come out on rainy days? Where are they on other days? The class went back and pulled out the information they had gathered earlier in the year and added to it. The teacher took more photos and videos of worms. Dew worms were brought into the classroom to explore with magnifying glasses. The class Skyped with another Kindergarten class who had conducted a worm inquiry.

An inquiry does not have to be "finished"; a skilled teacher continues to weave student knowledge into other areas and revisits and builds upon inquiries throughout the year. A key learning, scaffolded by the teacher, was that the students attached their new learning to seasons and the effects that seasons have on plants, animals, insects, and people. While the worm inquiry appeared to be completed in November, it emerged again, renewed, in April.

Closing Thoughts

The best way to learn about inquiries is through successful examples shared by classroom teachers. Examples of both mini-inquiries and extended inquiries come to life in the next chapter.

Check It Out!
Great Professional Materials to Scaffold Inquiry and Cross-Curricular Learning

Spotlight on Young Children: Exploring Science (2013), Amy Shillady, editor

Spotlight on Young Children and Nature (2011), Amy Shillady, editor

Spotlight on Young Children and Social Studies (2006), Amy Shillady, editor

Spotlight on Young Children and Science (2004), Derry G. Koralek and Laura J. Colker, editors

Active Experiences for Active Children: Social Studies (2nd ed., 2005), by Carol Seefeldt and Alice Galper

Integrating Instruction Literacy and Science (2005), Judy McKee and Donna Ogle, editors

Powerful Learning (2008), by Linda Darling-Hammond

CHAPTER 14

Inquiry-Based Learning Comes to Life

This chapter demonstrates how teachers in K-2 classrooms successfully scaffold inquiry, play, art, technology, and strong literacy teaching and learning. Examples of both mini- inquiries that may last just a day and extended inquiries that may go on for most of the year are shared.

Mini-Inquiries

Mini-inquiries arise from students daily. These inquiries are typically brief, lasting only a day or two. Many excellent examples come from Angie's Kindergarten class. Angie really listens, watches, and follows her students!

Window on the Classroom: Angie's Mitten Inquiry, Perfect for Winter!

Canadian winters can be very cold. Dressing and undressing from recess takes a long time on a cold day. In our class, as in many Kindergarten rooms across the country, many of the little boys are fascinated by Spiderman. They have Spiderman shoes, backpacks, T-shirts, and magic finger gloves. Their attachment for their super hero outweighs their cold tingling fingers. Several of the boys said that their hands were cold but they would not take any of the mittens we offered from our extra mitten bin. They did not see why they should switch from their beloved Spiderman finger gloves into fleece-lined mittens. I spoke with our classroom Early Childhood Educator and together we set up a mitten inquiry at our water table centre. I picked up extra mittens, gloves, and finger gloves from the lost and found and spread them out around the water table. In the evenings, I filled containers with water and put them in the school freezer.

During centre time, we placed snow and frozen blocks in the water table. We placed a clipboard and pencil next to the water table and asked, "Which mittens or gloves are the warmest?" Over the week, students were drawn to the centre. They all wanted a chance to play with snow and ice inside. They took the challenge seriously and tried on different mittens and gloves. When we noticed that one of our students who normally wore the Spiderman finger gloves was over at the centre, we made our way over to observe, prompt, and discuss his findings. Too often adults give commands, such as "Wear these gloves; they are warmer." The water centre tasks allowed students the time to wear different mittens and gloves and discover for themselves which ones were the warmest.

As a side inquiry, some students who arrived later in the open centre time also learned more about absorption. Some partners discussed which mittens were the wettest and explored reasons why. This led to a class discussion on absorption and we looked at our mittens and gloves over the next few weeks after each recess. We asked who had wet mittens or gloves. Why? An extension of this mini-inquiry would be to have different materials and have students explore and make a mitten that was both warm and water resistant. In our class, the inquiry ended with students choosing to bring warmer mittens from home or borrowing warmer mittens from our bin. A few mothers thanked us because they had been telling their children to wear warmer mittens, but they could not convince them that Spiderman gloves were not best suited for our coldest Canadian days.

We know which mittens will keep our hands warmest.

Window on the Classroom: Angie's Duct Tape Challenge

It all started with a series of Tweets. I am involved in an online professional learning network on Twitter. I often seek out advice, share ideas, or put out a thought and have others expand and push my thinking. I was initially seeking suggestions on an inexpensive iPad cover and was led as a laugh to a video on how to make iPod and iPad covers out of duct tape. After several tweets and others jumping in and talking about my little learners using duct tape to make their own covers, I began thinking about my Kindergarten class.

I had a group of students who spent a great deal of time at the art centre. They plowed through tape and created the most interesting objects. We put out different types of tape and watched them explore which tape was best for each project. I had not yet thought of using duct tape with my learners. I decided that this might be a good extension for them. It would also address a part of our science curriculum in which students are expected to select different tools for specific purposes as well as state problems and pose questions as part of the design process. In addition, our art curriculum had a section on two-dimensional and three-dimensional art designs. I decided to present some duct tape to my learners to see if it would lead into an inquiry.

The challenge was an inquiry for students to explore and discover the properties of duct tape. It was also a way to bring some excitement into the classroom during a long, wintery month in Canada. Yes, as an educator in Ontario, I needed a little pick-me-up, and that's why I jumped into this challenge.

Tinkering or exploring using different materials often leads to inquiry. It is serious play!

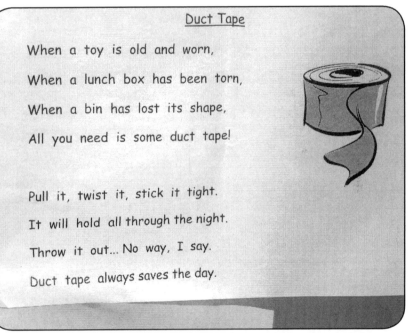

Duct Tape

When a toy is old and worn,

When a lunch box has been torn,

When a bin has lost its shape,

All you need is some duct tape!

Pull it, twist it, stick it tight.

It will hold all through the night.

Throw it out... No way, I say.

Duct tape always saves the day.

Use rhyme often as part of the inquiry to support phonological awareness. (With thanks to Lea Ann Lear, York Region District School Board.)

Steps undertaken for the duct tape investigation:

1. Explore, investigate, compare, and discuss different types of tapes: Students were put into groups and together explored four pieces of tape and recorded their observations. Together we created an anchor chart of our learning as a class. It was fascinating what they discovered and the language they used.

2. Explore, investigate, and discuss what duct tape can do: Students worked in pairs and used one long strip of duct tape. They cut, folded, rolled, crunched, and explored ways to manipulate the tape. They recorded their findings and shared them with the class.

3. View and discuss as a whole class activity how duct tape could be used: I displayed some images of things made from duct tape and we brainstormed as a class a list of what we could make with duct tape.

4. Offer the opportunity to work in groups, partners, or individually to plan: Students created a plan by drawing what they would like to attempt to make from duct tape (See **Play Plans**, p. 188).

5. Creation: Students were given generous blocks of time to create, problem-solve, and try again.

6. Recording findings: Students recorded what they discovered, what worked and didn't work.

7. Display and self-reflect: We displayed and reflected on the creations and found ways to share them with others.

As a follow up, we created art tasks later in the week. The children made items in art in 3-D sculpture format, or in a jewelry-making format.

I also placed duct tape at the building centre and the art centre during the month and observed what happened.

One discovery I made was how the students struggled to go from their plans to their actual 3-D creations. Many students created 2-D objects that reflected their plans. I re-did the activity and added some instruction on how to create 3-D objects.

It was a learning opportunity for both the students and for me. I was able to learn much about my students as problem solvers and planners. I understood my next steps were to work more with 3-D materials and to demonstrate and provide more opportunities for planning and creating in the classroom. This project also reconfirmed my beliefs that we do not have to follow someone else's procedure to create artwork. We don't need 30 items that all look the same. Students need opportunities for trial and error. Teachers need to provide open-ended activities and materials that enable children to plan and problem solve.

Cross-curricular integration is essential, especially in extended inquiries that provide deep understanding. Learners must also be actively involved, not just exposed to information. Some of the most engaging inquiries have a critical literacy focus.

Critical Literacy: Improve the World through Inquiry

Critical literacy is a form of thoughtful literacy. It is a way of thinking that helps to uncover social inequalities, injustices, and varied points of view or perspectives, often through inquiries. These discoveries might ultimately lead to social change with the focus on making this world a better place. This way of thinking (*SEEING WITH NEW EYES*) occurs as students are taught to question and challenge attitudes, values, and beliefs that lie beneath the surface as they read, listen, view, and experience. This is crucial in this age of the Internet where many students believe that everything they see, read, or hear on the Internet or on television must be true. Students are taught to challenge and analyze. Questioning to promote **discussion** and **writing** lies at the heart of a critical literacy program. It is through talk and writing that students develop new ideas. They challenge text and life as we know it (McLaughlin and DeVoogd 2004).

Critically literate students analyze and evaluate the meaning of text, oral or written, as it relates to issues of equity, power, and social justice to inform a critical stance, response, and/or action. They are aware that all discourse, including movies, photos, illustrations, television programs, and books, are created from a certain perspective or bias and they learn to examine each to see how it positions itself as they read, listen, or view. Teasing and bullying, gender and age stereotypes, playground politics, racism, homelessness, and environmental issues are frequently explored using a critical literacy lens. The goal of this form of thoughtful literacy is to prepare students for these real-world experiences. Critically literate students often go beyond the discussion by taking a stance on an issue, considering social action, and acting.

With critical literacy inquiries, children naturally work together to pursue answers to questions that matter to them. Often they

 Check It Out!
Great Critical Literacy Resources
On Transforming Wonder into Knowledge, Capacity building series, Special Edition #32, May 2013, Literacy and Numeracy Secretariat of Ontario: http://www.edu.gov.on.ca/eng/literacynumeracy/inspire/research/critical_literacy.pdf
Critical Literacy: Enhancing Students' Comprehension of Text (McLaughlin and DeVoogd 2004).
Negotiating Critical Literacies with Young Children (Vasquez 2004).
Getting Beyond "I Like the Book": Creating Space for Critical Literacy in K–6 Classrooms (Vasquez 2010).
Many Tests, Many Voices: Teaching Literacy and Social Justice to Young Learners in the Digital Age (Silvers and Shorey 2012).
Critical Literacy and Writer's Workshop (Heffernan 2004).

"Being asked to think about the text you have just read is different from being asked to recall the text you've just read" (Allington 2001, 87). An important skill involved in critical literacy is teaching students how to read photos and illustrations through guided looking by asking questions such as "Where is the photo on the page?" "Why is it there?" "How big is it?" "Why is it that size?" "Who are the characters portrayed in the photo?" "How are they portrayed?" and "Why are they portrayed in that way?"

Promote critical literacy through the following books by Kathryn Otoshi:
One (2008), is a story that teaches children how to stand up for themselves and others when they come up against people who try to intimidate them ("bullies"). The message is that it just takes one person to make a difference, to make this world a better place.
Zero (2010) is about self-esteem, stressing the importance of being yourself and finding value in who you are.

deal with student passions connected to real-world social struggles that students experience in everyday life. Critically literate students embrace a social justice way of learning, caring, and living. **Critical literacy is generally not an add-on to the classroom curriculum. It can become a way of life that exists within the mandated curriculum, an important part of the classroom culture.** Developing critical literacy skills as a young child is important because, as Aristotle observed, "the habits we form from childhood make no small difference, but rather they make all the difference."

Creating Conditions to Foster Critical Literacy Inquiries

Teachers can create conditions for fostering this kind of inquiry by

- Building a safe, inclusive classroom environment or culture that promotes inquiry: it is good to question!

- Making available thought-provoking oral, print, electronic, and multimedia texts representing diverse perspectives for students to read/view/hear.

- Acknowledging that some issues and discussions can be sensitive and uncomfortable for some students e.g., *bullying.*

- Grabbing those *teachable moments*… Those experiences… Using the curriculum as lived, as negotiated.

(See an interview with Jerome Harste and Vivian Vasquez that brings inquiry-based learning and critical literacy to life: http://curriculum.org/secretariat/snapshots/criticalliteracy.html)

Critical literacy

Four major dimensions of critical literacy should be developed:

1. *Examining multiple viewpoints in the text, such as different characters' perspectives. Many texts demonstrate the power of one character or group of characters over others (e.g., "Jack and the Beanstalk").*

2. *Thinking about power relationships between and among characters (e.g., Click, Clack Moo: Cows That Type by Doreen Cronin).*

3. *Making the reader reconsider a commonly held belief (e.g., Tough Boris by Mem Fox).*

4. *Uncovering social inequalities and injustices, developing empathy, and frequently taking action to promote social justice (e.g., The Paper Bag Princess by Robert Munch).*

Multiple Paths to Literacy

 *Check It Out!*

Books that Promote Thinking about Perspective

Children need to become more adept at understanding and interpreting the thoughts, feelings, and perspectives of others. Books written from different perspectives can really help children to understand the concept of perspective.

Two Bad Ants, http://www.houghtonmifflinbooks.com/features/thepolarexpress/tg/twobadants.shtml

Anna Aphid, http://www.curledupkids.com/annaphid.htm

Hey, Little Ant supports an understanding of perspective with a critical literacy focus: http://www.collier.k12.fl.us/WebLessons/WebQuest/heylittleant/index.htm

Duck! Rabbit! by Amy Krouse Rosenthal asks, is the creature a duck or a rabbit? It depends on your perspective: http://www.chroniclebooks.com/duckrabbit

It Looked Like Spilt Milk by Charles Shaw follows a simple pattern. It shows that by using one's imagination and different perspectives something can appear as many different things: https://www.pinterest.com/nickirolling/it-looked-like-spilt-milk/

The Lion and the Mouse by Jerry Pinkney (2010), is an adaptation of one of Aesop's fables and a wonderful Caldecott winning, nearly wordless picture book. It teaches that to make this world a better place, one needs to remember that no act of kindness is ever wasted. The book can be used to teach character lessons involving traits such as kindness, mercy, loyalty, and courage. It is also an excellent choice for practicing inference skills and the important comprehension skill of visual literacy through reading the enchanting watercolor illustrations. The author is also the illustrator, which children can relate to when they create their own books.

Kindergarten Big Idea: Children are connected to others and contribute to their world.

Supporting critical literacy = improving the world.

Character and perspective: Variations on "The Three Little Pigs"

"The Three Little Pigs" must be one of the most adapted children's stories, especially now that we understand that wolves are not bad, just misunderstood!

The Three Pigs by David Wiesner

The Story of the Three Little Pigs by Joseph Jacobs

The True Story of the 3 Little Pigs! by Jon Scieszka

Yo, Hungry Wolf! A Nursery Rap by David Vozar

Three Little Cajun Pigs by Mike Artell

Shh! (Don't Tell Mr. Wolf!): A Preston Pig Lift-the-Flap Book by Colin McNaughton

Suddenly! by Colin McNaughton (also supports making inferences and predictions)

Yum! by Colin McNaughton

Seeing multiple perspectives: An introductory critical literacy lesson

Introduce your students to the concept of multiple perspectives by using or adapting the following lesson plan: http://www.read-writethink.org/classroom-resources/lesson-plans/seeing-multiple-perspectives-introductory-30792.html?tab=4#tabs

Alternatively, use different versions of "Jack and the Beanstalk" or books listed at the following site: http://www.readwritethink.org/files/resources/lesson-docs/30792ChildrensBooks.pdf

Classroom Examples of Extended Inquiries Using a Critical Literacy Lens

Window on the Classroom: Taking Social Action to Support Vegetarians

Vivian Vasquez's magical book *Negotiating Critical Literacies in Young Children* (2004) recounts the author's experiences working with three- to five-year-old children in Kindergarten classrooms in Ontario, Canada. Chapter 4, entitled "Our Friend Is a Vegetarian," tells the story of what happened the day after a school barbeque was held for staff, students, and parents. The children, as would be expected, arrived at school excited about what happened at the barbeque the night before. One child asked if she could do a hand-count survey to see how many people had eaten hot dogs or hamburgers. She wanted to know their preferences. As the survey was being taken, the children learned that one of their classmates could not be part of the survey because he was a vegetarian and could eat neither hot dogs nor hamburgers. The children asked whose idea it was to serve only hamburgers and hot dogs and found out that it was a committee decision, which included parents, teachers, and the assistant principal as chair. The children decided to write a letter to the assistant principal, which their teacher scribed.

The letter read, "If we don't eat food we'll die. We have to get new hot dogs and hamburgers. You can ask Anthony's daddy what you can buy because Anthony is a vegetarian" (Vasquez 2013, 105). The children thought seriously about the wording: *We* (meaning all of us) and *have to* (meaning this is not negotiable).

When the children did not receive a response after two weeks, they wrote a second letter, which was even more forceful. It ended with "What happened to the letter I gave you from before?" This time they did get a response and were invited down to the assistant principal's office to share their thoughts on what food could be served next time. They then decided that they should make all the school principals in the area aware of this issue so that no other children would be left out. This letter included a survey for the principals to complete (See below).

> "Children who learn using curriculum that is based on what matters to them are more likely to feel that what they are learning is important in their lives" (Vasquez 2013, 27).

ABOUT VEGETARIANS SURVEY

What is the name of your school? _____

Do you have a school barbeque?	☐ Yes ? ☐ No
Do you know if you have vegetarians at your school?	☐ Yes ? ☐ No
Do you think it is fair not to have food for vegetarians?	☐ Yes ? ☐ No
Are you going to have vegetarian food if you have vegetarians?	☐ Yes ? ☐ No

(Vasquez 2004, 109)

These children found a real reason to write. Their writing has voice because they found something worthwhile to write about and they have an audience in mind. By reading the survey above, using their own words, you can hear the wheels turning, their thoughts being formed. Think of all that they learned in the process, all the mini-lessons on word choice and persuasive writing that came out of a teachable moment.

> Persuasive Writing

Window on the Classroom: Taking Social Action on Gender Issues

Vivian Vasquez also provides the following example from her Kindergarten class when the students, focusing on visual literacy, discussed a Royal Canadian Mounted Police poster.

Curtis: Who are those again?

Patrick: Oh, Mounties.

Julia: When I grow up I can be one!

Curtis: No, you can't! There are no girl Mounties in the poster.

Roger: When I grow up I will be a horse.

Emily: You can't be a horse; you're a person not an animal!

Patrick: There are boys and men and there are no girls in the picture because…. Girls are not like boys, are they?

Teacher: So do you mean that you don't think they can do this job? That being a Mountie is a boy thing to do? Does anyone have anything they'd like to say about that?

Girls: Yeah!!... (Vasquez 2010, 23–25)

Then the students discussed some photos in books on Mounties, making text–text connections.

Andrea: Wait, Wait, Wait… It's the same again, It's all the same again… it's all men and no girls!

Jessica: This poster and this book does not make things equal.

Then the students took action by writing a letter to the Mounties stating, "Could you please change the poster because there are girls in the Mounties" and providing their example (Vasquez 2010, 31). Great inquiries are based on kids' lived experiences and can have a real-life impact.

Window on the Classroom: Heather's LOVE Story

This is a love story on two counts: the learner (Kindergarten student) became absorbed in a topic he loves and the teacher (me) was reminded of why I love emergent curriculum and the opportunities it provides.

This story resonates with me as an example of what can happen when time and space are created for inquiry and play. Since September, a student had been building trains in the classroom on a regular basis. His personal love of trains created a deep and meaningful context to look closely, learn about, and contribute to our larger community. This train-inspired play ebbed and flowed throughout the whole year of Kindergarten. It inspired him to look closely at trains he saw around the city and form his own theories and questions, which he then brought back into the classroom.

> "We asked our students what their take-aways were and one student shared: Building was fun but getting food to the families made me feel happy."

One day he asked, "I wonder how many different kinds of trains there are?" We discussed different ways that he could explore this question. For the next three weeks, he played with finding his answer. I carefully chose the word "play" because I want to highlight that play does not only mean toys, play does not mean a free-for-all.

He poured over different books about trains, built conceptual models using blocks, and used the act of drawing to organize what he knew and formed new questions. My role as the teacher was to actively listen, engage in conversations, observe, and introduce the skills he needed within the context of his personal passion. For example, while publishing his own book about trains, it became the right time to learn about how numbers help us keep our pages in order and how words can add meaning to illustrations.

This All About Trains student created book reflects student choice and voice.

When our class decided to participate in the Construction Jr. contest using the non-perishable donations we had been collecting as part of the mayor's annual food drive, Gabriel had developed the skills to analyze the Canadian Pacific Holiday Train and help us recreate it. While the building of the train was important, our greater connection to why we were collecting food was essential. As

a teacher, my greatest hope is that every student has the same opportunity to follow their passions and find a way to contribute to our global community in a way that is meaningful to them.

Another Critical Literacy Inquiry: Being Different is Being Unique

This inquiry helps the students to not only accept differences but also to celebrate them by understanding what makes each individual unique.

Window on the classroom: Kas and Jennifer and the Uniqueness of Names

What's in Your Name?

The power of a name and its value has long been immortalized in prose, poetry, and religious ceremony. Everyone recognizes himself or herself by name. The question is: What does my name mean and how does a name influence a person's character? The students investigated the power of their names and how their names tell an amazing story relating to family, place or origin, meaning and culture.

The students took home a questionnaire, "What's in Your Name?" which was completed by the students and their parents and returned to school. With the support of the teacher or another adult their questionnaire was typed up into a story they shared. Students had input into the color and font of the typed print.

As their stories were being typed and prepared, students received information about self-portrait work. As an introduction to the self-portrait task, they were provided a template of a face, body middle and legs to personalize using pencil crayons. The three different pieces were placed together to create a person who represented the student. The head looked like the student, the personalized story went at the central part of their body and their legs/feet were also colored and attached at the bottom.

🏠⇄🏫 What's In YOUR Name?

The inquiry this year revolves around language, stories, and the power of words. Everyone has a story - please take the time to sit down with your child and share the story of their name. _____

Full name: _____

Is there a name in another language? _____

Origin of name: _____

Who named your child? _____

Meaning of name (if known): _____

Is there a story associated with your child's name? _____

_____

_____

The children then described their feelings about their names.

"My name is Moe. It is an English name but I don't know what it means. My dad named me and I am named after my grandfather. When I hear my name I feel cool, fun, and handsome and that is it. If everyone in the world was named Moe there would be too many Moe's and you would not know which mom was calling which Moe!"

📖 *Check It Out!*
Great Name Books and Songs

Chrysanthemum, 2008, by Kevin Henkes

Like Me and You, 1985, words and music by Raffi

The Name Jar, 2003, by Yangsook Choi

My Name is Elizabeth, 2011, by Annika Dunklee and Matthew Forsythe

Cross-Curricular Learning and Critical Literacy: An Extended Inquiry about Bees

Kas Patsula, a K–2 teacher from Calgary, Alberta, Canada, masterfully demonstrates through the following example how her students try to make this planet a better place through inquiry using a critical literacy focus. Note the richness of the content, the academic vocabulary, the balanced literacy, and the meaningful art integration. This extended inquiry in K–2 classrooms went on for most of the year, although not daily. I have seen a number of extended inquiries but rarely have I seen one as strong as this one. Much of the strength comes from the intentionality of the ongoing planning. Literacy remained central in this inquiry. Student Engagement was high.

Window on the Classroom: What's the Buzz about Bees? Kas's Critical Literacy Learning Story

Our Kindergarten, Grade One, and Grade Two students took on an inquiry about interdependence and ecology in order to help them ultimately understand that all things are connected and what their role is in the global community. This critical literacy inquiry was teacher-generated or provoked. We opened by asking the students to consider the following quotation attributed (but without solid proof) to Albert Einstein:

> "If the bees disappear off the surface of the globe, then man would have only four years of life left. No more bees, no more pollination, no more plants, no more animals, no more man." —Einstein

We returned to this quote over the course of our inquiry, asking ourselves whether or not this statement was true, how to determine this and ultimately what this might mean for the planet and ourselves. What we do know for sure is that around 2006 commercial beekeepers began noticing that their honeybees were disappearing. In order to contemplate these larger issues, it was necessary to build a strong foundation; in other words, we needed to understand the bee.

Using various resources including photographs, movies, books on bees, guest speakers, a visit in the schoolyard, and a visit to a bee farm, we studied the physiology of the bee and witnessed a working hive in action. Very rich opportunities for conversations and oral language development were provided. Students also used a variety of learning strategies in our bee explorations from art, drama, film clips, computers, cameras, videos, and so on, incorporating all subject areas in a year-long inquiry. This became a real-world catalyst for learning.

Check It Out!
Saving the Bees – Real-World Catalyst for Learning

Vanishing Bees@http://www.nrdc.org/wildlife/animals/bees.asp

Science Kids: Fun, Science, and Technology for Kids@http://www.sciencekids.co.nz/

Amazing portraits of bees from *National Geographic* @: http://www.nationalgeographic.com/features/140114-bee-native-macro-photography-insects-science/#.VWeV8N7bKUk

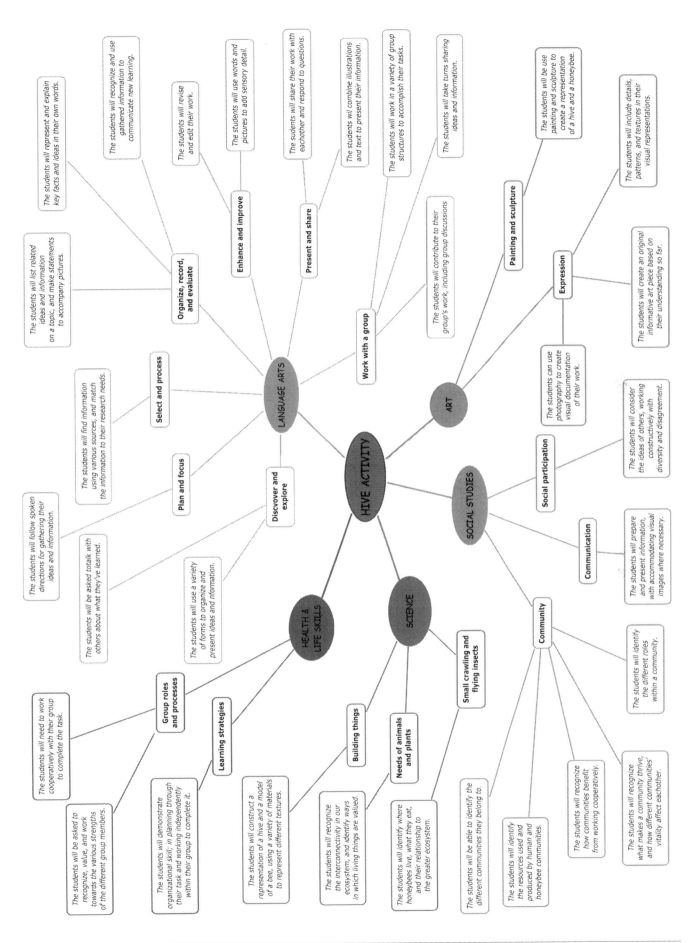

The students will represent and explain key facts and ideas in their own words.

The students will recognize and use gathered information to communicate new learning.

The students will revise and edit their work.

The students will use words and pictures to add sensory detail.

The sudents will share their work with eachother and respond to questions.

The students wil combine illustrations and text to present their information.

The students will work in a variety of group structures to accomplish their tasks.

The students will take turns sharing ideas and information.

The students will be use painting and sculpture to create a representation of a hive and a honeybee.

The students will include details, patterns, and textures in their visual representations.

The students will list related ideas and information on a topic, and make statements to accompany pictures.

Organize, record, and evaluate

Enhance and improve

Present and share

Painting and sculpture

The students will contribute to their group's work, including group discussions.

The students will create an original informative art piece based on their understanding so far.

Work with a group

LANGUAGE ARTS

ART

Expression

Select and process

The students will find information using various sources, and match the information to their research needs.

The students can use photography to create visual documentation of their work.

HIVE ACTIVITY

The students will follow spoken directions for gathering their ideas and information.

Plan and focus

The students will consider the ideas of others, working constructively with diversity and disagreement.

Social participation

SOCIAL STUDIES

The students will be asked totalk with others about what they've learned.

Discover and explore

Communication

The students will prepare and present information, with accommodating visual images where necessary.

The students will use a variety of forms to organize and present ideas and nformation.

HEALTH & LIFE SKILLS

SCIENCE

Community

The students will identify the different roles within a community.

The students will need to work cooperatively with their group to complete the task.

Group roles and processes

Learning strategies

Building things

Needs of animals and plants

Small crawling and flying insects

The students will be asked to recognize, value, and work towards the various strengths of the different group members.

The students will demonstrate organizational skill; in planning through their task and working independently within their group to complete it.

The students will construct a representation of a hive and a model of a bee, using a variety of materials to represent different textures.

The students will recognize the interconnectivity in our ecosystem, and identify ways in which living things are valued.

The students will identify where honeybees live, what they eat, and their relationship to the greater ecosystem.

The students will be able to identify the different communities they belong to.

The students will identify the resources used and produced by human and honeybee communities.

The students will recognize how communities benefit from working cooperatively.

The students will recognize what makes a community thrive, and how different communities' vitality affect eachother.

Inquiry-Based Learning Comes to Life

347

PHYSIOLOGY
- HEAD, THORAX, ABDOMEN
- 6 LEGS ON "
- 4 WINGS " "
- 2 ANTENNAS
- POLLIN BASKETS
- PROBOSIS
- COMPOUND EYES

- COMPARE BEE TO HUMAN VISION (ULTRAVIOLET & COMPOUND EYE)
- DIFFERENT TYPES OF BEES (BUMBLE, HONEY, BLUE ETC.)

BASIS IS ALBERT EINSTEIN QUOTATION...

COMMUNITY
- JOBS WITHIN THE HIVE TO FACILITATE WHAT IS BEST FOR ENTIRE HIVE COMMUNITY
- DRONES (CARED FOR BY GIRLS & NURSE BEES
- QUEEN BEE LAYS EGGS & MATES W/ DRONES
- FORAGERS
- GUARD BEES
- NURSE BEES

BEES

HOME/HIVE
- PIGGY-BACKS ONTO COMMUNITY & JOBS
- MAKE-UP OF HIVE IN HEXAGONAL CELLS TO BIRTH BEES AND/OR STORE HONEY/WAX
- HIVE DISEASES LIKE COLONY COLLAPSE SYNDROME
- PROPOLYS - CURE TO STOP INFECTION W/IN HIVE I.E. WRAP AN INVADING MOUSE THEY (BEES) KILLED TO STOP ROT & INFECTION SPREADING!

EXPERTS
HONEYBEE FARM
ZOO HORTICULTURIST (FLOWER PREFERENCE FOR BEES & HOW CAN WE MAKE BEE-FRIENDLY SPACES?)
URBAN BEEKEEPER PROPONENT

BY PRODUCTS
- DEFINE NECTAR
- " HONEY
- " POLLINATION
- COTTON CLOTHING
- WOOD HOMES / FURNITURE
- FRUITS & VEGETABLES
-

HAZARDS
COLONY COLLAPSE
MONO CROPPING
- LESS BEES?
- BEES DYING DUE TO MAIL STRIKE OR DELAYS AS FARMERS MAIL QUEENS
- LACK OF FOOD DUE TO INDUSTRIALIZATION & URBAN SPRAWL

FLOWERS & POLLINATION
- PARTS OF A FLOWER AND THEIR PURPOSE
- STUDY WHAT FLOWERS BEES PREFER & WHY, I.E. BEES LIKE TO WALK ON FLOWERS (POLLIN BASKETS) VS BUTTERFLIES LIKE TRUMPET SHAPED LIKE BLUE BELLS TO SUCK.
- ARTISTIC REVIEW OF FLOWERS I.E HOW DOES GEORGIA O'KEEFE & MONET SEE FLOWERS.
- BEE ULTRAVIOLET VISION ART
- EXPERIENCE GROUP NECTAR SUCKING TRAVEL
- UNDERSTAND POLLINATION

The beginning of the intentional planning.

As we dug deeper into the fascinating world of the honeybee, the themes of community and interconnection continued to lend themselves fluidly to our inquiry. With an amazing social structure so complex that it nearly rivals our own, the students were able to make beautiful connections to our lifestyle in the topic of community: what defines the bee, how bees change over time, how bees flourish, and how bees are unique. Exploring the roles and responsibilities of bees, both within their hive and in their ecosystem, led naturally to an understanding of the students' own roles and responsibilities within the multitude of communities to which they belong.

Students learned that bees are a current focus for scientists due to their apparent decline and the potentially disastrous effects on our food sources. By learning about the diminishing numbers of bees and the ecology, the students began to make good choices. They came up with a plan as to how to draw the bees into the community for the betterment of the community as a whole.

> The bee focus became a critical literacy issue that the students decided to act upon!

Balanced Literacy Instructional Approaches Used in this Inquiry

This inquiry is not the full curriculum. However, since time is so precious and integration has been proven to be effective, cross-curricular skills and approaches such as read-alouds, oral language development, phonological awareness, reading, and writing are intentionally made a part of the inquiry.

Read-alouds and Media Literacy

There are numerous strong bee read-alouds and movies, fiction and nonfiction, many with enriching academic vocabulary.

Check It Out!

Clan Apis by Jay Hosler is the "biography" of a honeybee named Nyuki written as a graphic novel. This scientific comic book tells the story of hive life. The story is told by Nyuki with help of her sister Dvorah (a Hebrew word for bee), a dung beetle named Sisyphus, and a sarcastic flower named Bloomington.

Check out these other bee books:

A Short History of the Honey Bee by E. Readicker-Henderson and Ilona McCarty. The everyday importance of the bee remains the main message of this book. Approximately forty percent of the world's food supply including apples, tomatoes, and strawberries is dependent on pollination by honeybees.

The Biography of a Honeybee by Naida Dickson. This is a story about all of the job opportunities for a honeybee, told by one honeybee. This book promotes student writing as a bee. Writing as a bee promotes writing with voice.

Busy Busy Bee by Karen Wallace (non-fiction)

Are You a Bee? by Judy Allen (non-fiction)

The Life and Times of the Honey Bee by Charles Miucci (non-fiction)

The Honey Makers by Gail Gibbons (non-fiction)

What if there were No Bees? by Suzanne Slade (non-fiction)

The Hive Detectives: Chronicle of a Honey Bee Catastrophe by Loree Griffin Burns (non-fiction)

The Honeybee and the Robber by Eric Carle (fiction)

Phonological Awareness

During read-alouds, we furthered our inquiry knowledge, but we also practiced literacy skills, including phonological awareness, using the language from the book. For example, children practiced clapping "colony collapse syndrome" for the number of syllables. Together we practiced rhyming inquiry vocabulary including the parts of a bee. Students turned to a friend and challenged them to rhyme a word of choice as I roamed and listened to determine if more clarification of the task was still necessary. All day long, I asked students to do different things such as, "Give me a word that rhymes with *bee*"... "How many syllables in the word *mandibles*?" (See **Phonology and Phonological Awareness** on p. 104 for more on this topic.)

Phoneme segmentation

Using a phoneme segmentation sheet called Elkonin boxes, students worked with different inquiry words to move their fingers or an object such as a counter into each box representing individual sounds in the words (See **The Sound (Phonemic Awareness) Segmenting Centre: A Three-Step Intervention Lesson Framework that Works!** p. 105). For each phoneme, students moved a counter to a box in a left-to-right progression. An alternative to using ready-made Elkonin boxes is to have students draw three boxes on sheets of paper or dry-erase boards giving them the independence to create their own boxes for centre fun learning. Their job was to put the marker in the appropriate box to indicate the position of the sound in the word (bee=b/e). Once they demonstrated a beginning understanding of this skill, they practiced the skill with the game, "Secret Language." Children and the teacher clapped and said words from the inquiry. They then challenged their peers by making "secret language" by stretching out these words such as, "bees help with pollination." The words were said very slowly, stretching the individual sounds in each word. The palms were stretched far apart: /Bbbbb/eeeee/sssss/ / hhhhh/eeeee/lllll/ppppp /wwwww/iiiii/thththth /ppppp/ooooo/

Check It Out!

Bee-dia Literacy
Some movies really stood out in this inquiry for developing vocabulary and background knowledge:

- *City of Bees*
- *Silence of the Bees*
- *Bee Movie*
- *Dances with Bees*

lllll/iiiii/nnnnn/aaaaa/shshshshsh/uuuuu/nnnnn. Students were each given a small foam ball that they tossed up in the air for each sound they heard in the inquiry word.

Oral Language
Bee academic vocabulary

The students' receptive and expressive academic vocabularies improved. Academic vocabulary included honeybee, queen bee, drone, worker bee, hive, propolis, hexagon, mono-cropping, colony collapse syndrome, interdependence, community, hazards, disasters, expert, interview, nectar, honey, flower, stamen, stylus, etc. Students also learned the bee physiology (how the bee's body parts function) and were able to name the different body parts:

1. Two compound eyes and three smaller eyes

2. Six legs

3. Honey baskets on back legs

4. Three body parts named head, thorax, and abdomen

5. Four wings

6. Mandibles, which are teeth on the outside, as bees have no inner teeth as we do

7. Any other body parts the children deemed important and worth studying during our learning...

Students were exposed to a variety of fiction and non-fiction resources. They listened to a variety of bee books and after each reading, they were taught and/or reviewed bee vocabulary. The proven method used to teach vocabulary is called Text Talk (See **Teaching Vocabulary from Read-Alouds: Text Talk Is Proven to Work** p. 156).

Using the Smart Board, students in a whole class setting viewed an image of an anatomically correct bee. Together they named the different parts of the bee and labelled the Smart Board diagram with class input from their recollection of the information. Finally, monitoring the students' understanding, students used a teacher-made honeybee scientific drawing and attached the names of the parts in the appropriate box on their paper. Cutting out the terminology at the bottom of the page allowed for fine motor practice; reading the bee vocabulary allowed for literacy practice as they worked in table groups to place each word box on their diagram. Lots of oral language was built into this activity as students discussed and negotiated why they thought a word card belonged where they said it did.

A centre activity: Using word cards to label the parts of a bee.

Going on a bee hunt.

A superb photo taken by a Grade 2 student!

From using word cards to labelling, to actually creating scientific drawings.

Taking quality photos to support vocabulary development and visual literacy

If students are going to use a camera as a tool for learning, they need to learn how to use it properly. During this inquiry, the students learned:

1. Good photographs don't come from pictures taken from the same location. Get down on the floor and look up or vice versa; take a chance and try new points of view.

2. To use the macro on the camera to photograph the bees by zooming in to grasp tiny details from the environment.

3. To focus on a subject, one must attend to the background. Is it detracting from the subject? If so, we call it "background noise" and we seek to reduce it.

4. Using the tripod can reduce the blurriness of hand-held photography. Students learned to move the tripod to alter the camera angle successfully.

5. To view everyone's photography and effectively critique the works to encourage the best photography we are capable of making. Though a communal activity (critiquing the art), it is the individual's responsibility ultimately to choose their finished piece for display in the photography show.

"I learned about the tripod and making the camera zoom in and out. The best part of using a camera is the zooming because it lets you get a really, really close up of people, bees and me too."

Oral language development in the community: Honeybee field trip

"On Wednesday October 27th, the students took a school bus to a honeybee farm. We were fuelled with lots of enthusiasm and prior knowledge about bees and bursting with excitement to see real bees in action after all the talking and reading about bees that we had done. We took a school bus, which was exciting in the first place. It took about an hour to travel to the farm. The extracting room was all new to us. We learned how the beekeepers work with the hive to obtain honey. We got to wear a beekeeper's hood, see the plates from the hive, touch the honeycombs, see a carrying crate for a queen bee who is brought from another colony and so much more. We all got a chance to view bees in their hive within a windowed area. This was amazing! Finally we got to taste honey. It was good."—Kas

I am a beekeeper.

A beehive!

Role Play: How Bees Find Their Food

The waggle dance is a term used in beekeeping to describe a particular figure-eight dance of the honeybee. By performing this dance, bees can share information with other members of the colony about the direction and distance to patches of flowers yielding nectar and pollen, to water sources, the quality of the food they have found, or new housing locations.

Bring this scientific term *the waggle dance* to life by encouraging the children to do the dance just before snack to demonstrate where the snack is and how much they like it!

Bee hive life: More role play

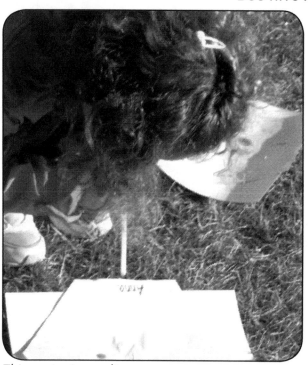

This nectar is good!

We "became" bees to experience life fully within the beehive. Students were assigned a honeycomb as a home base. Then they took their own straw to represent a proboscis, which was used to suck up the nectar. On the outside of the area, there were bowls of colored juice, each color representing different types of flowers. Since students were aware of the dangers of mono-cropping to a bee's diet and therefore healthy life, they needed to seek out a variety of flower nectars to slurp. Once students sucked up some nectar, they had to find their way back to their honeycomb. Then they set out for another batch of nectar for the hive and for their own nutrition. The difficult part was that every bee was doing the same thing, so it was very chaotic and confusing. Bees had difficulty returning to their own honeycomb. The students learned about bee communication and pheromones that help lead a bee where they need to go.

Bee Robotics

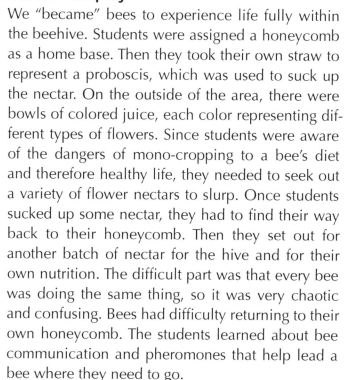

We continued our bee learning with our robotics. Students estimated how long it would take in wheel rotations from the hive to the red flower. Once they got the next robot to the red flower, they needed to turn it around and get it back to the hive. All of this work in estimation had to be programmed into the computer, downloaded to the robot, tested, and then modified if something did not go as planned. We quickly learned that it was important to place the robot carefully on the beehive. Anything less than careful placement could result in the robot occasionally stepping on the red flower but occasionally not ending up there at all. We needed to be consistent.

Bringing the Community into the School: More Opportunities for Conversation

Having experts come to the classroom is an important part of inquiry learning in that real-world problems are examined by real-world experts. These experts shared their knowledge directly with us.

The students learned much from a bee presentation by the founder of Apiaries and Bees for Communities (ABC). It is crucial to brainstorm with the students before their conversation with a guest speaker. They might even practice interviewing each other on the topic, practicing good interviewing techniques.

Ask an Expert
Good interviewing techniques include:

- Asking questions for which you do not already know the answers.

- Asking questions that require more than a "yes" or "no" answer.

- Not limiting the interview to your preplanned questions. Listening carefully to the person you are interviewing and asking any new questions that may be sparked by his or her responses.

- Always being sensitive to the feelings of the person being interviewed.

- Ending the interview by thanking the person.

One Inquiry Leads to Another: A Bee Ecosystemn.

An ecosystem includes all of the living things (plants, animals, and other organisms) in a given area, interacting with each other and with their non-living environments (weather, sun, soil, climate, atmosphere). Flowers are an essential area of study in the bee ecosystem if one wants truly to understand a honeybee. For the bees, the pollen and nectar from many flowers is an important source of fats, proteins, vitamins, and minerals. The nectar is also a source of energy. Bees gradually switched from eating other insects to flowers as their source of food. With the passage of time, bees have become completely dependent on flowers as a food source. As bees travel from one blossom to another, pollen

Check It Out!
Wonderings:
- http://wonderopolis.org/wonder/do-beekeepers-ever-get-stung/

- http://wonderopolis.org/wonder/why-do-bees-sting/

- http://wonderopolis.org/wonder/why-do-bees-buzz/

clings to their fuzzy bodies. It is then transferred to other flowers of the same species. This pollinates or fertilizes the plant. Plants then can produce their own fruits and seeds. But which flowers are the most helpful to pollination?

For more practical examples of inquiry and specifically a bee inquiry, see http://www.journeytogetherfdk.com

Ask an expert: More conversation, background knowledge, and vocabulary development

A Zoo Naturalization Specialist visited the class and shared information about which flowers bees prefer. She talked about the school garden and what we could do to attract more bees to it. She explained that bees like flowers with big centres that they can walk upon as they suck the nectar with their proboscis. Some flowers preferred by bees include Asters, Black-Eyed Susans, Goldenrod, Huckleberry, Lupine, Coneflower or Echinacea, Rhododendron, Sage, Snowberry, Sunflowers and Lilacs. The students were encouraged to think of questions before, during, and after the presentation.

Flower physiology introduction

Check It Out!
Pollination: http://www.youtube.com/watch?v=RuYrFwDuYn0

To understand the work of the bee, one needs to understand where they spend much of their time: the flower. Students were introduced to the term pollination and to the parts of a flower, both male and female: petal, stamen (which is an anther and filament), pistol, which is the stigma, style, ovary, and ovule. The children learned more academic vocabulary.

Critical Literacy and Bees: Taking Action

A talented Kindergarten photographer who knows how to look carefully.

Using real-life problems to motivate students, challenges them to think deeply about meaningful content. With their knowledge of bees and flowers, the students then decided they could make this world a better place. One thing they could do was to guide the local community association in planting for bee nutrition. Using our bee knowledge, we guided the gardening committee by sharing with them the flowers that attract bees to support plant life. Some examples include Marigolds, large single blossom blooms like Daisies or

Multiple Paths to Literacy

Chamomile, but nothing red as bees can't see red. We also investigated Autumn Joy Sedum, which is the flower we noticed bees clustering about in a neighbouring yard and we further investigated with the homeowner to discover its name. As we learned about the flowers that bees like, we planted Gladiolas in the classroom for each child that were then given as Mother's Day gifts, planted in our school garden, and given to neighbours for their gardens.

Art and Inquiry

Art played a big role in this inquiry. Three examples are included below.

Watercolors
Multimedia art project

Students photographed their faces as self-portraits. After cutting out each face to be the head of the bee, students added a thorax and abdomen as well as legs, antennae's, etc. to create a bee. This "love bug" piece of art was given away at Father's Day.

"This was a father's day art project still using our inquiry learning. Children made a multimedia art piece of a bee/bug demonstrating their understanding of bee physiology: clear delineation of the three body parts of head, thorax and abdomen".

"This is a really good piece of art demonstrating the child's understanding of bee physiology, plus it is aesthetically appealing and in fact, beautiful" said his teacher.

Note the detail in this art.

Celebrating Our Learning

At the "end" of the inquiry, students celebrated in their own way by sharing what each had learned. Student choice and voice is evident.

Writing and sharing bee reports: All About Bees
(See **All About Books,** p. 286.)

"All About Bees" by Caroline

Bees drink nectar from the flower. They make honey. Did you know that bees use pollen to make honey too? Bees make fruits and vegetables. Without bees we would be bare naked and hungry. Bees can fly around by making a buzzing noise.

"My Bee" by Evan

My bee is very colorful. This is called a rainbow bee because of all the colors. I kinda wanted to do it like Mrs. P., but I couldn't. I wanted to do it on my own, so I did a stripe, stripe, stripe, and I didn't mind if it was all mixed up. I really like my bee how it is. This bee is so old, it might be from the time of the dinosaurs.

A Grade 1 ELL student writes a bee story

My bee is happy and it loves flowers and nectar and my bee is a worker bee and it is going to the other flowers and it is nice bee and it has friends.

"I liked her bee story as it contained some facts about bee life including that it is a girl, sucking nectar, it is a worker and no, she does not work alone — she has many friends also working," commented the teacher.

Spring break presentations or busy bee projects

Students shared anything that they had learned about bees and in a multitude of ways including scientific drawings, paintings, photos, wall stories, creating a bee sculpture, talking about a bee book, creating a PowerPoint, or writing a report. Students self-assessed using criteria provided before they created their projects. The assessments were based on three areas: **presentation, information**, and **effort** (See **Busy Bee Kindergarten Spring Break Presentation Rubric** below).

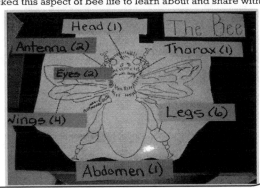

Busy Bee Spring Break Kindergarten Project

Project Criteria

❖ You may present your project in anyway that you like! You will be asked to share your project with the class sometime after Spring Break.

❖ Pick an aspect of bees that you can teach to the class: what a bee eats, how a bee creates honey, life in the beehive, what flowers does a bee prefer, what happens after a bee pollinates a flower, how a bee sees, the bee dance, how a bee helps the environment, what can we (people) do to protect the bees, talk about colony collapse syndrome, speak about the health of bees, etc. It is WIDE OPEN!

❖ Explain why you chose picked this aspect of bee life to learn about and share with us.

❖ Include a picture of your aspect of bee life – this can be a scientific drawing, an artistic drawing, a photograph or a cut out.

❖ **Have Fun!!**

❖ **BEE** happy and have a super Spring Break!

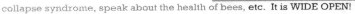

Busy Bee Kindergarten Presentation Rubric 2011

	2	3	4	5
Presentation	Hmmmm.... I don't know the information and can't answer questions	I know most of the information and can answer most questions	I really know my stuff! It's clear that I understand what I have researched and am able to answer all questions!	WHOA! I am an expert on my topic. Not only do I understand what I have researched, I can answer questions using lots of details
Information	Most of the criteria has been met	I have provided accurate information on bees including 3 facts and a picture.	I have gone above and beyond by meeting all of the criteria and adding additional information!	I have provided outstanding information and met all the criteria. I should probably have my work published!
Effort	I could have put in more effort (or, my parents did this for me)	I have worked hard and feel proud!	I am seriously awesome and worked to make a fabulous project!	My teacher has no words for how fabulous my project is!!

(With thanks to Kas Patsula)

Bee photographs/movies/books

Students used their photography learning to create a formal sharing of their bee knowledge using technology, art, and science.

Photos like this don't often happen by accident.

A play

The students shared some of their key learnings by creating and sharing a play based on the storybook, *The Wrong Book*. The children shared what they had learned about some of the dangers to honeybees, a critical literacy issue. These dangers include:

Mono-cropping: When farmers plant just one type of crop rather than a variety of species. Just like people, bees need a variety of food to eat. Farmers should plant more than one type of seed to grown in their fields.

The Tracheal Mite: A pest that enters the trachea of the honeybee and feeds off the blood of the bee. The bee becomes weak and the mites lay eggs in the back part of the trachea so the bee can't get oxygen to breathe. Each mite is smaller than a speck of dust, so you can't see them.

Colony Collapse Disorder: The name for beekeepers finding their hive empty in the spring — no dead bees inside or on the ground, just empty hives without the bees. Scientists believe it is a combination of all the pests, illnesses, pesticides, malnutrition, and pollen or nectar death hitting the bees and wiping them out.

It is easy to see why this cross-curricular inquiry was so successful. Teacher intentionality resulted in effective language learning within a warm and caring classroom environment. Note all of the opportunities for student oral language, play, and choice. Most importantly the students were engaged as they attempted to problem solve to help improve the word.

Window on the Classroom: Angie's View on Year-Long Inquiries

A year-long inquiry is also a place for whole class discussions that can lead into small group or individual inquiries. Regular walks to the neighbouring pond lead to comparisons, discussions, and many wonderings. The teacher needs to find a way to capture these discussions skillfully and guide the students through the comparisons. Observing a tree throughout the year could lead to other inquiries such as bird's nesting habits, temperature, and seasonal changes in the yard. An inquiry can be year-long or could be revisited at specific points throughout the year. Other inquiries surface and the teacher weaves back and forth among the inquiries.

Management of inquiries is always on the teacher's mind. Does everyone have to participate in each inquiry? Are there enough resources for all of the students? How do we gather resources? What will others do while some are working on inquiries? These are all valid questions that educators must ask themselves continuously throughout the day in all subject areas. The answers might be different for each room, each teacher, or each group of students. What is most important is that the educator reflects upon the questions and creates a flexible plan.

"We live in a society where people are uncomfortable with not knowing. Children aren't taught to say 'I don't know' and honesty in this form is rarely modelled for them. They too often see adults avoiding questions and fabricating answers out of embarrassment or fear and this comes at a price. When children are embarrassed by or afraid of the feeling of not knowing, they are preoccupied with escaping their discomfort, rather than [with being] motivated to learn. This robs them of the joy of curiosity. Let's celebrate the feelings of awe and wonder in our children, as the foundation for all learning. Let's teach children to say 'I don't know' and help them understand the power behind it" (Harris and Rowe 2013).

Closing Thoughts

Establish a culture of classroom inquiry. Teach students to question and wonder and to believe that it is okay not to know everything. Successful teachers are intentional. They plan ahead and effectively scaffold student learning. Inquiry can be a wonderful lens for literacy development. Focused literacy teaching, carefully aligned with students' needs and interests, need not fall by the wayside. In *Joining the Literacy Club*, Frank Smith (1988) states, "The trick is to find something involving reading and writing that interests the learner and to engage the learner authentically in that area of interest, making the reading and writing incidental" (p. 125). Use the inquiry approach as one instructional framework to help make this happen.

  ## Technology to Support Inquiry

Information-Based or Play-Based Inquiry Apps

Life Cycle of a Monarch Butterfly by Edward Gonzalez provides information on the many phases of Monarch life.

Painted Lady Butterflies by Carolina Biological Supply provides information on the lifecycle of a Painted Lady butterfly.

Bird Guide for Kids by PGS Software S.A. provides a virtual tour with bird sounds and lots of information.

Leaf Snap for iPad by Columbia University enables students to use a photo of a leaf to identify the species and provides related information.

Read-Alouds and Listening Centre Options

There are many formats of online picture books: eBooks, websites of interactive books, and videos of various readers reading aloud. iPads and iPods could be used in addition to traditional listening centres.

http://www.storylineonline.net/ features famous actors reading aloud books such as *Stellaluna* and *The Rainbow Fish*.

http://www.readtomelv.com/archived-books/ features picture books read aloud by various performers.

http://www.tumblebooks.com/library/asp/customer_login.asp online digitized trade books (requires a log in).

http://www.pebblego.com/login.php has a digital series of informational texts (also requires a log in).

Scholastic has an online series entitled BookFlix with nine categories of video storybooks featuring paired fiction and non-fiction titles. Free trial. Ontario teachers are already licensed to use the site. In Canada, go to http://education.scholastic.ca/category/BOOKFLIX; in the United States, go to http://auth.grolier.com/login/bookflix/login.php?bffs=N Check your district or school for licensing information.

Creation Apps for Demonstrating Learning

Explain Everything by Morris Cooke records student writing and voice at the same time. Students can integrate photos into the app and record their learning. The file can then be exported in many different ways and shared.

My Story by HiDef Web Solutions allows students to write and illustrate stories about their own inquiries. They can insert photos and record their voices. The stories can be shared in many ways.

Photo Story by Shutterfly integrates photos, text, and voice together to create a photo book about their inquiry. A printed book can be ordered or a free digital version can be shared.

ChatterPix by Duck Duck Goose upload photos and record the student's voice to create a video that can be exported and shared.

Pic Collage by Cardinal Blue can be used to photograph the process and create a procedure. It can also be used to document the learning of the inquiry through pictures and text.

PicPlayPost by Flambe Studios LLC combines pictures and videos together for ease of posting and sharing ideas.

Tellagami creates a cartoon. Students can create a character and record their new learning. The file can be shared in various ways.

Strip Designer by Vivid Apps is a comic strip maker that uses photos.

Comic Life by plasqu LLC enables students to create comic strips.

Doodle Buddy for iPad by Pinger is a simple drawing app that students can use to document their thinking.

Dragon Dictation (for iPad or iPod) or *Dragon Naturally Speaking* (for laptop) by Nuance Communications are licensed software programs for taking down student dictation.

WritePad by PhatWare Corp converts handwriting to text when the student writes on the screen.

My Story by HiDef Web is a digital book creator.

Book Creator by Red Jumper is a digital book creator.

Studio and Story Creator: Easy Story Book Maker for Kids by Innovative Mobile Apps is a digital book creator.

Student and Teacher Websites

www.worldbookonline.com/kids/home is a basic encyclopedia for kids.

http://kids.discovery.com/tell-me has a "Tell Me" feature that provides answers to questions such as "Why are eggs, egg shaped?" and "Is there a link between a bird and a dinosaur?"

Discovery Education has a full website of professional blogs, videos, and support materials for inspiring wonder. In Canada, the site address is http://www.discoveryeducation.ca/Canada/; in the United States, the address is http://www.discoveryeducation.com/teachers/. A free teacher resource section and a subscription are also available.

http://kids.nationalgeographic.com/kids/animals/creaturefeature/ provides videos, maps, facts, and photos on various animals such as panda bears, beavers, and chipmunks.

Once kids have learned from the pages above, have them try the *National Geographic* quiz: http://kids.nationalgeographic.com/kids/games/puzzlesquizzes/quizyournoodle-weird-but-true-animals

http://www.owlkids.com/category/chirp/animals-chirp/ has videos, information, challenges, and photos.

http://www.canadiangeographic.ca/kids/animal-facts/animals.asp provides facts about Canadian animals.

www.sciencekids.co.nz/sciencefacts.html provides animal facts and experiments.

www.biokids.umich.edu provides field guides and a "critter catalogue."

Shared Reading for Research

Use the classroom's interactive whiteboard with various online resources. SMARTNotebook, for example, can be used to create personalized shared reading texts.

Scholastic's Let's Find Out (http://letsfindout.scholastic.com/) and The Big Red World (http://clifford.scholastic.com/) magazine series offer digital subscriptions. In the United States, Scholastic has released a magazine app — Scholastic Classroom Magazines–Student Edition — that enables users to purchase the magazines and read them on an iPad.

http://ngexplorer.cengage.com/ngyoungexplorer/moreissues.html contains the digital versions of National Geographic's Young Explorer series of non-fiction magazines such as *Fur, Feathers and Scales*, *Is it Living?* and *Seasons*. The text is written in short, simple sentences for early readers, with a read-aloud feature on every page, and access is free. For a shared experience, display on an LCD.

At Home Online Reading

This list of resources for at home online reading is particularly useful when access to leveled texts is not available, such as during school vacations.

Websites

http://www.oxfordowl.co.uk/for-home/reading-owl/find-a-book/library-page provides 250 free, leveled readers in eBook format.

http://www.peekuboo.com/library#stories_tab provides simple early interactive readers.

http://www.starfall.com/n/level-c/fiction-nonfiction/play.htm?f provides early readers, both fiction and non-fiction.

Apps

Project X: The Power of Reading series from Oxford University Press is available in the App Store. Each book is priced from $5.99 to $6.99. School licensing is also available.

National Geographic Kids also has apps available. Check the app store for the following: "Look and Learn: Animals Vol. 1," "Weird But True," and "Kids Magazine." For android devices, check out the apps "National Geographic Explore for Home" and "National Geographic Explore for School." A full list of National Geographic Kid's Apps can be found at http://www.nationalgeographic.com/apps/kids

Discovery Kids Sharks interactive app has map locations, shark identification, videos, and facts.

Reviews and links to story apps for young children http://www.digital-storytime.com/

French and Multiple Language Digital Resources

http://www.tumblebooks.com/library/asp/french/ provides eBooks in French and Spanish.

http://www.childrensbooksforever.com/childrenpages/French.html provides PDF versions of picture books in French.

http://en.childrenslibrary.org/ provides PDFs of picture books in different languages.

iBooks

Look through the store in the iBooks app for picture books to read aloud or display as full class read-alouds using Apple TV and an LCD.

Over and Under the Snow by Kate Messner, illustrated by Christopher Silas Neal, provides a side view that reveals animals beneath the snow sleeping. The book provides many opportunities to dive deeper into inquiry questions.

Discovery Kids Readers series is available for download in iBooks. Topics such as sharks, favourite pets, space, and wonders of the world are available with prices from $1.99 to $2.99.

Teacher Resources for Inquiry

Teacher Blogs

http://mrsmyersKindergarten.blogspot.ca/2013/03/force-and-motion-inquiry-about-gravity.html

http://ljpsKindergartenteam.blogspot.ca/

http://www.journeytogetherfdk.com/

http://passionatelycuriousinKindergarten.blogspot.ca/2012/10/provocations-for-learning.html

http://thiskindylife.blogspot.ca/

Teacher Websites

Inquiry- and evidence-based practice: http://instep.net.nz/Inquiry-and-evidence-based-practice/An-inquiry-habit-of-mind

Provocation ideas and photos: http://pinterest.com/booknblues/provocations-and-inquiry-spaces/

Understanding by Design (Wiggins and McTighe): http://www.ascd.org/research-a-topic/understanding-by-design-resources.aspx

In her numerous publications, including *By Different Paths to Common Outcomes* (2014), Marie Clay stresses the importance and benefits of honouring individual differences and following the interests and discoveries of the individual child. Richard Allington talks about the importance of "managed choice." Teachers must make choices that work best for their students. Students must be afforded both choice and voice.

Learners take different paths to becoming literate and teachers can use different paths to get them there. There is no quick fix, no one right way. That being said, Clay, and many other experts in the area of early literacy, do not believe that anything goes. Many proven, field tested, high-yield strategies are described in this book. As we know, some teachers are much more effective than others for a variety of reasons. In fact, the within-school variance in teacher effectiveness is typically larger than the between-school variance! "A student in a high-impact teacher's classroom has almost a year's advantage over his or her peers in a lower-effect teacher's classroom" (Hattie 2012, 23).

> "There is nothing as powerful as the quality of the teacher in predicting the achievement of children. Neither parents nor socio-economic status of the family is as powerful as good instruction in shaping the academic futures of students" (Allington 2006, 142).

What teachers know, do, and care about is very powerful in this learning equation (Hattie 2003, 3). The only variable that has even more influence on student learning than teacher variance is student ability. However, "regardless of ability, we have evidence that 98 percent of all children entering Kindergarten can be at grade level by the end of first and second grade" (Allington 2010, 1).

> "The hallmark of developmentally appropriate teaching is intentionality. Good teachers are intentional in everything they do — setting up the classroom, planning curriculum, making use of various teaching strategies, assessing children, interacting with them, and working with their families. Intentional teachers are purposeful and thoughtful about the actions they take, and they direct their teaching toward the goals the program is trying to help children reach" (NAEYC Position Paper 2009, 10).

The effective teachers highlighted in this book are not clones of one another. However, all employ a variety of strong pedagogical approaches that accommodate a combination of educator-guided instruction and child-directed activity. Intentionality is key.

"Expert teachers are passionate about teaching and learning" (Hattie 2003). Being passionate about early literacy is a must. Early literacy learning can change lives, as is pointed out in a quotation often attributed to Christa McAuliffe, the high school teacher who died during the 1986 Challenger space flight: "I touch the future. I teach."

The POWER OF NOT YET!

"How we give children feedback is probably the most difficult for us to change, but it is probably the point of most leverage" (Johnston 2012, 34).

No matter the approach, literacy remains central to the cross-curricular classroom program. The teachers are passionate about this. In all cases, strong teacher–student relationships are at the heart of their success. Really listen to the teacher and student voices throughout this text. Focus on the "choice words" used by the teachers when providing timely, specific, and student-friendly feedback. Watch the teachers help the students to develop **a growth mindset**, to believe in the **power of "not yet."**

For many years, educators have focused on a balanced literacy approach. Balanced literacy involves a wide variety of activities provided consistently. These activities include the following:

- Reading and writing to/for children
- Reading and writing with children
- Reading and writing by children
- Word work
- Oral language
- Visual literacy
- Numerous forms of representing knowledge/understandings, such as through art and play

For some young children, art becomes their primary vehicle for written expression.

Balanced literacy also involves a balance of direct and indirect instruction as well as whole-class, small-group, and individual activities; and a balance of work with various genres. In Kindergarten and beyond, play and inquiry-based learning experiences are two of a number of approaches that are able to provide authentic learning and managed choice. Authentic learning scaffolds student engagement in a strong, balanced literacy program. Effective teachers keep high expectations for all students. They do not underestimate what students can do.

We now know that a warm and positive classroom culture is the key to making a strong literacy program successful. Two teachers will have very different levels of student success using a balanced

Multiple Paths to Literacy

literacy approach or learning frameworks such as the Daily 5™ or the Four Blocks™. Success depends largely on the implementation including teacher–student relationships, student–student relationships, and the classroom culture established.

Humour in schools often serves a variety of positive functions beyond simply making people laugh. Humour builds class cohesion. Research indicates that people respond more positively to each other when humour is present. It brings them together by building relationships. Humour can also facilitate cohesion by softening criticism. It also helps individuals cope with stress by relaxing them. It frequently positively affects levels of attention and interest. It is a way to keep students engaged. It supports self-regulation (Banas et al. 2011, 115–144). Angie, Jane, and Kas all establish classrooms full of humour. These are joyful classrooms that inspire curiosity and the desire to learn. They are environments where the students and teachers want to be. They are environments where I also want to be!

> "You never judge a (school) system by those who succeed in it. These people would likely succeed in any system. You judge it by those it fails" (Hamilton 1995, 94).

Research shows that the development of oral language is *the key* component of a successful literacy program. Oral language is the foundation of all literacy learning and all cross-curricular learning. It facilitates thinking, comprehending, making connections, communicating, and solving problems. It is the basis of reading, writing, inquiry, and play. It provides the foundation for developing social skills, self-regulation, and strong relationships. Oral language is instrumental in developing the whole child — heart, mind, and soul. That is why oral language is central to this book. It also needs to be more central in many classroom programs.

> "The major prevention strategy is excellent instruction" (Snow et al. 1998, 172).

Teachers can't teach what they don't know. Therefore, effective *ongoing* differentiated staff development is instrumental in scaffolding effective teaching and learning. Schools need to create time for teacher collaboration — teachers learning from teachers.

Pendulum swings have disenfranchised many children. P. David Pearson describes how it is important to "reclaim the centre" rather than taking an extreme perspective. He would rather be in the radical middle going somewhere, than in the far left or right in the ditch going nowhere (Graves et al. 1999).

I am aware of the many recent education pendulum swings. Many students will develop adequate literacy skills no matter the approach used. However, for at least twenty percent, that is not the case. Many of these students depend on public education to become literate.

I am worried. Many primary teachers are feeling the pressure to adopt certain approaches to and frameworks for teaching and learning. I offer a heartfelt caution to Kindergarten–Grade 2 teachers. Avoid the latest flavour of the month. Always ask, "Where is the research to support this practice?" Whose research is it? How credible is it? Does it appear in a refereed journal? How would or could this work in my setting? Does this seem plausible to me? If what I am already doing is working, why implement change? Teachers encourage children to question, to inquire. Teachers need to do the same. Remember the tale, *The Emperor's New Clothes* by Hans Christian Andersen? Ask questions!

My motto: "Better to be effective than politically correct." New or different is not necessarily better. The work of such notables as John Hattie, Michael Fullan, and others promotes improving teaching by building on success, on what is working, rather than looking to implement yet ANOTHER innovation.

A caution to administrators, school districts, ministries and departments of education: jumping from initiative to initiative does not work. Instead of always looking for the next innovation, schools and school districts need to build upon success — what we already know works. Innovation does not always equal improvement.

Enjoying reading and writing informational text while learning tier 3 vocabulary.

"In the end it will become clearer that there are no 'proven programs,' just schools in which we find more expert teachers — teachers who need no script to tell them what to do … Are we creating schools in which every year every teacher becomes more expert?" (Allington 2006, 185).

As Hattie (2003) says, "Expert teachers are passionate about teaching and learning." Being passionate about early literacy is a must. Early literacy learning can change lives, as is pointed out in a quotation often attributed to Christa McAuliffe, the high school teacher who died during the 1986 Challenger space flight: "I touch the future. I teach."

I am very honoured to be able to share many rich teacher, student and parent stories from across North America. Their stories, their voices, bring this book to life. These teachers are successfully "touching the future".

"We are stretching our reading muscles."

Getting off to a strong start at school and at home!

Today I had fun with my friends but what made my day was that my teacher was there. I love my teacher. April 8th

A note from Ivy to Kas.

Ivy snuck this note on my desk to discover at the end of the class. I asked her to read it to class at dismissal. I will keep this forever!

The Effect Size of teacher–student relationships according to Hattie (2009) is 0.72. Relationships can and do make a huge difference!

Intentionally learning about rectangles through play.

Multiple Paths to Literacy

Note: Additional key references and links are found under the heading **Check It Out!** throughout the book. Books for children and blogs for educators are found within the body of the text as well.

ABC Literacy. Accessed online August 2015. "Primary Literacy Resource: Talking and Listening in Key Stage 2," 18–19. Northern Ireland Education and Library Boards. http://www.belb.org.uk/downloads/lit_talking_and_listening_ks2.pdf

Adams, Marilyn Jager. 1990. *Beginning to Read: Thinking and Learning About Print: A Summary*. Champaign, IL: Center for the Study of Reading/University of Illinois.

Adams, Marilyn Jager, B. R. Foorman, I. Lundberg, and T. Beeler. 1998. *Phonemic Awareness in Young Children: A Classroom Curriculum*. Baltimore: Paul H. Brookes Publishing.

Albers, Peggy. 2007. *Finding the Artist Within: Creating and Reading Visual Texts in the English Language Classroom*. Newark, DE: International Reading Association.

Allington, Richard L. 1998. *Teaching Struggling Readers*. Newark, DE. International Reading Association.
———. 2001. *What Really Matters for Struggling Readers: Designing Research-Based Programs*. New York: Pearson.
———. 2005. *What Really Matters for Struggling Readers: Designing Research-Based Programs*. 2nd ed. New York: Pearson.
———. 2006. "What Research Has to Say About Fluency Instruction." *Fluency: Still Waiting After All These Years*. Newark, DE: International Reading Association.
———. 2008. *What Really Matters in Response to Intervention: Research-Based Designs*. New York: Pearson.
———. 2009. *What Really Matters in Fluency: From Research to Practice*. New York: Allyn & Bacon.
———. 2010. *Essential Readings on Struggling Learners*. Newark, DE: International Reading Association.
———. 2011. "What At-Risk Readers Need." *Educational Leadership* 68 (6): 40–45.

Allington, Richard L., and Patricia M. Cunningham. 1996. *Schools That Work: Where All Children Read and Write*. New York: HarperCollins College Publishers.
———. 2002. *Schools That Work: Where All Children Read and Write*. 2nd ed. Boston: Allyn & Bacon.

Allington, Richard L., and Peter H. Johnston. 2000. *What Do We Know About Effective Fourth-Grade Teachers and Their Classrooms?* Albany, NY: The National Research Center on English Learning and Achievement: http://www.albany.edu/cela/reports/allington/allington4thgrade13010.pdf. Also published in C. Roller, ed. 2001. *Learning to Teach Reading: Setting the Research Agenda*. Newark, DE: International Reading Association.

Ball, E. W., and B. A. Blachman. 1991. "Does Phoneme Awareness Training in Kindergarten Make a Difference in Early Word Recognition and Developmental Spelling?" *Reading Research Quarterly* 26 (1): 49–66.

Ball, Jessica. 2006. "Talking Points: Exploring Needs and Concepts for Aboriginal Early Childhood Language Facilitation and Supports." Concept discussion paper prepared for Public Health Agency of Canada Aboriginal Head Start in Urban and Northern Communities: http://www.ecdip.org/reports/index.htm

Banas, John A., Norah Dunbar, Dariela Rodriguez, and Shr-Jie Liu. 2011. "A Review of Humor in Education Settings: Four Decades of Research." *Communication Education* 60 (1): 115–44.

Bauman, J., and E. Kame'enui. 2004. *Vocabulary Instruction: Research to Practice.* New York: Guilford Press.

Beattie-Moss, Melissa. 2015, May 25. *Probing Question: Is Art an Essential School Subject? Phys.org, Science X network*: http://phys.org/news/2015-05-probing-art-essential-school-subject.html

Beck, Isabel L., Margaret G. McKeown, and Linda Kucan. 2002. *Bringing Words to Life: Robust Vocabulary Instructions.* New York: The Guilford Press.

———. 2002. "Taking Delight in Words: Using Oral Language to Build Young Children's Vocabularies." *Bringing Words to Life: Robust Vocabulary Instruction.* New York: Guilford Press: http://www.readingrockets.org/article/taking-delight-words-using-oral-language-build-young-childrens-vocabularies

Bell, David. 2012. "Talking About Art with Young People: Conversational Strategies for Aesthetic Learning in Early Childhood Settings." *International Art in Early Childhood Research Journal* 4 (1): http://artinearlychildhood.org

Bennet-Armistead, V. Susan, Nell K. Duke, and Annie M. Moses. 2005. *Literacy and the Youngest Learner: Best Practices for Educators of Children from Birth to 5.* New York: Scholastic.

Benson, Viki, and Carice Cummins. 2000. *The Power of Retelling: Developmental Steps for Building Comprehension.* Columbus, OH: McGraw-Hill.

Biemiller, Andrew. 2000. "Teaching Vocabulary: Early, Direct and Sequential." *Perspectives* (International Dyslexia Association Quarterly Newsletter) 26 (4): 4-7.

———. 2001. "Teaching Vocabulary: Early, Direct and Sequential." *American Educator* Spring: http://www.aft.org/periodical/american-educator/spring-2001/teaching-vocabulary

———. 2006. "Vocabulary Development and Instruction: A Prerequisite for School Learning." In *The Handbook of Early Literacy Research*, Vol. 2, edited by D. Dickinson and S. Neuman, 41-51. New York: Guilford Press.

———. 2007. *The Influence of Vocabulary on Reading Acquisition.* Canadian Language and Literacy Research Network: http://www.literacyencyclopedia.ca/index.php?fa=items.show&topicId=19.

———. 2009a. *Words Worth Teaching: Closing the Vocabulary Gap.* Columbus, OH: SRA/McGraw-Hill.

———. 2009b. "Parent/Caregiver Narrative: Vocabulary Development (0–60 Months)." In *Handbook of Language and Literacy Development: A Roadmap from 0–60 Months*, edited by L. M. Phillips, 1–42. London, ON: Canadian Language and Literacy Research Network. http://www.theroadmap.ualberta.ca/vocabularies

Biemiller, Andrew, and Catherine Boote. 2006. "An Effective Method for Building Meaning Vocabulary in Primary Grades." *Journal of Educational Psychology* 98 (1): 44–62.

Blachman, B. A., E. W. Ball, R. Black, and D. M. Tangel. 2000. *Road to the Code: A Phonological Awareness Program for Young Children*. Baltimore: Brookes.

Blachowicz, Camille L. Z., and Connie Obrochta. 2005. "Vocabulary Visits: Virtual Field Trips for Content Vocabulary Development." *The Reading Teacher* 59 (3): 262–68.

Blackwell, C. 2015. "iPads in Kindergarten: Investigating the Effect of Tablet Computers on Student Achievement." Presented at the 65th Annual International Communication Association Conference, San Juan, Puerto Rico.

Blair, Clansy, John Protzko, and Alexandra Ursache. 2011. "Self-Regulation and Early Literacy." *Handbook of Early Literacy Research*, Vol. 3, edited by Susan B. Neuman and David K. Dickinson, 20–35. New York: Guilford Press.

Blankstein, Alan M., and Paul D. Houston, eds. 2011. *Leadership for Social Justice and Democracy in Our Schools*. A joint publication with the Hope Foundation and the American Association of School Administrators. Thousand Oaks, CA: Corwin.

Bodrova, E., and D. J. Leong. 2003. "The Importance of Being Playful." *Educational Leadership* 60 (7): 50–53.

———. 2004. "Chopsticks and Counting Chips: Do Play and Foundational Skills Need to Compete for the Teacher's Attention in an Early Childhood Classroom?" *Spotlight on Young Children and Play*. Washington, DC: NAEYC.

———. 2005. Uniquely Preschool: What Research Tells Us About the Ways Young Children Learn. *Educational Leadership* 63 (1): 44–47.

———. 2007. Tools of the Mind: The Vygotskian Approach to Early Childhood Education. 2nd ed. Columbus, OH: Merrill/Prentice Hall.

———. 2008. "Developing Self-Regulation in Young Children: Can We Keep All the Crickets in the Basket?" *YC: Young Children* 63 (2): 56–58.

———. 2010. "Curriculum and Play in Early Child Development." *Encyclopedia on Early Childhood Development*: http://www.child-en-cyclopedia.com/

Boekaerts, Monique, and Lyn Corno. 2005. "Self-Regulation in the Classroom: A Perspective on Assessment and Intervention." *Applied Psychology: An International Review* 54 (2): 199–231.

Bohart, Holly, Kathy Charner, and Derry Koralek, eds. 2015. *Spotlight on Young Children Exploring Play*. Washington, DC: National Association for the Education of Young Children.

Boushey, G., and J. Moser. 2006. *The Daily 5: Fostering Literacy Independence in the Elementary Grades*. Portland, ME: Stenhouse Publishing.

———. 2009. *The Café Book*. Portland, ME: Stenhouse Publishing.

Brabham, E. G., and C. Lynch-Brown. 2002. "Effects of Teachers' Reading-Aloud Styles on Vocabulary Acquisition and Comprehension of Students in the Early Elementary Grades." *Journal of Educational Psychology* 94 (3): 465–73.

Bredekamp, S., and C. Copple. 1997. *Developmentally Appropriate Practice in Early Childhood Programs*. Washington, DC: National Association for the Education of Young Children.

British Columbia Ministry of Education. Accessed online August 2015. English Language Arts Overview: https://curriculum.gov.bc.ca/curriculum/English%20Language%20Arts/1

———. 2008. Early Learning Framework: http://www2.gov.bc.ca/assets/gov/education/early-learning/teach/earlylearning/early_learning_framework.pdf

———. 2010. Full Day Kindergarten Program Guide: http://www2.gov.bc.ca/assets/gov/education/early-learning/teach/fulldayKindergarten/fdk_program_guide.pdf

Brookhart, Susan M. 2008. *How to Give Effective Feedback to Your Students*. Alexandria, VA: ASCD.

Buldu, Mehmet. 2010. "Making Learning Visible in Kindergarten Classrooms: Pedagogical Documentation as a Formative Assessment Technique." *Teaching and Teacher Education: An International Journal of Research and Studies* 26 (7): 1439–49.

Burke, A. 2010. *Ready to Learn: Using Play to Build Literacy Skills in Young Learners*. Markham, ON: Pembroke Publishers.

Burke, Nancy. 2004. *Teachers Are Special*. New York: Random House.

Burns, M. K., J. J. Appleton, and J. D. Stehouwer. 2005. "Meta-Analytic Review of Responsiveness-to-Intervention Research: Examining Field-Based and Research Implemented Models." *Journal of Psychoeducational Assessment* 23: 381–94.

Burns, S. M., P. Griffin, and C. E. Snow. 1999. *Staring Out Right: A Guide to Promoting Children's Reading Success*. Washington, DC: National Academy Press.

Canadian Education Association. 2014. *Is Inquiry-Based Learning Effective?* Simon Fraser University: http://www.cea-ace.ca/sites/cea-ace.ca/files/cea_facts_on_ed_inquiry-based_learning.pdf

Cantalini, Maria. 1987. "The Effects of Age and Gender on School Readiness and School Success." PhD diss., Ontario Institute for Studies in Education.

Ceppi, G., and M. Zini. 1998. *Children, Spaces, Relations: Meta-Project for an Environment for Young Children*. Reggio Emilia, Italy: Reggio Children.

Center for Best Practices in Early Childhood Education at Western Illinois University. Early Childhood Technology Integrated Instructional System. Online Workshops. http://www.wiu.edu/ectiis/

Chall, Jeanne S. 2002. *The Academic Achievement Challenge: What Really Works in the Classroom?* New York: Guilford Press.

Chall, Jeanne S., Vicki A. Jacobs, and L. E. Baldwin. 1990. *The Reading Crisis: Why Poor Children Fall Behind*. Cambridge, MA: Harvard University Press.

Chand, R. K. Same Size Doesn't Fit All: Insights From Research On Listening Skills At The University Of The South Pacific (USP). *International Review of Research in Open and Distance Learning*, 8(3). Web Publication http://www.irrodl.org/index.php/irrodl/article/view/383/951

CIERA (Centre for the Improvement of Early Reading Achievement). 1998a. "Topic 1: How Can I Help Children Get Ready For Reading?" *Every Child a Reader*. Ann Arbor, MI: University of Michigan.

_____. 1998b. "Topic 2: Concepts of Print, Letter Naming and Phonemic Awareness." *Every Child a Reader*. Ann Arbor, MI: University of Michigan.

———. 1998c. "Topic 6: Reading and Writing." *Every Child a Reader.* Ann Arbor, MI: University of Michigan.

Clay, Marie M. 1991. *Becoming Literate: The Construction of Inner Control.* Portsmouth, NH. Heinemann.

———. 2001. *Change Over Time in Children's Literacy Development.* Portsmouth, NH: Heinemann.

———. 2002. *An Observation Survey of Early Literacy Achievement.* Portsmouth, NH. Heinemann.

———. 2005. *Literacy Lessons Designed for Individuals Part One: Why? When? and How?* Portsmouth, NH: Heinemann.

Cohen, Lawrence J. 2002. *Playful Parenting.* New York: Ballantine Books.

Colker, L. 2008. "Block Off Time for Learning." *Teaching Young Children* 1 (3): 14–17.

Copple, C., and S. Bredekamp. 2009. *Developmentally Appropriate Practice in Early Childhood Programs Serving Children Birth Through Age 8.* 3rd ed. Washington, DC: National Association for the Education of Young Children.

Cunningham, P., and R. Allington. 1994. *Classrooms That Work: They Can All Read and Write.* New York: Harper Collins.

D'Arcangelo, Marcia. 2003. "On the Mind of a Child: A Conversation with Sally Shaywitz." *Educational Leadership* 60 (7): 6–10.

Diamond, Adele. 2009. *Cognitive Control and Self-Regulation in Young Children: Ways to Improve Them and Why.* CEECD (*Centre of Excellence for Early Childhood Development) www.excellence-early-childhood.ca/documents/diamond_2009-11ang.pdf*

Dickinson, David K. 2001. "Teacher Rating of Oral Language and Literacy (TROLL): A Research-Based Tool": CIERA (Centre for the Improvement of Early Reading Achievement) http://www.ciera.org/library/reports/inquiry-3/3-016/3-016.pdf

Dickinson, D. K., J. B. Freiberg, and E. M. Barnes. 2011. "Why Are So Few Interventions Really Effective: A Call for Fine-Grained Research Methodology." *Handbook of Early Literacy Research*, Vol. 3, edited by Susan B. Neuman and David K. Dickinson, 337–57. New York: Guilford Press.

Dickinson, David K., and Susan B. Neuman. 2006. *Handbook of Early Literacy Research.* Vol. 2. New York: Guilford Press.

Dickinson, D. K., and K. Sprague. 2001. "The Nature and Impact of Early Childhood Care Environments on the Language and Early Literacy Development of Children from Low-Income Families." In *Handbook of Early Literacy Research.* Vol. 1, edited by Susan B. Neuman and David K. Dickinson, 263-80. New York: Guilford Press.

Dickinson, D., and P. Tabors. 2003. *Beginning Literacy with Language: Young Children Learning at Home and School.* Baltimore: Paul Brookes.

Diller, Debbie. 2008. *Spaces and Places: Designing Classrooms for Literacy.* Portland, ME: Stenhouse Publishing.

Doherty, Linda. 2004, Nov. 1. Children Drowning in the Sea of Blah. The Age Company Ltd: http://www.theage.com.au/articles/2004/10/29/1099028201302.html

Donohue, Chip. 2015. Technology and Digital Media in the Early Years: Tools for Teaching and Learning. Washington, DC: National Association for the Education of Young Children/New York: Routledge.

Dougherty Stahl, K. A. 2014. "Fostering Inference Generation with Emergent and Novice Readers." *The Reading Teacher* 67 (5): 384–388.

Dougherty Stahl, K. A., and G. Earnest Garcia. 2015. *Developing Reading Comprehension: Effective Instruction for All Students in Pre-K–2*. New York: Guilford Press.

Doyle, Mary Anne. 2014. "Marie Clay's Perspective on Preschool Literacy: Wisdom, Caution, Delight." *Journal of Reading Recovery* Spring: 35–42.

Drew, W. F., J. Christie, J. E. Johnson, A. M. Meckley, and M. L. Nell. 2008. "Constructive Play: A Value-Added Strategy for Meeting Early Learning Standards." *YC: Young Children* 63 (4): 38–44.

Duke, Nell K. 2014. *Inside Information: Developing Powerful Readers and Writers of Informational Text Through Project-Based Instruction*. New York: Scholastic.

Durkin, Delores. 1968. "Children Who Read Early." *American Educational Research Journal* 5 (2): 265–67.

Dweck, Carol S. 2008. "Brainology: Transforming Students' Motivation to Learn." *Independent School Magazine* Winter, Online Publication. Washington, DC: NAIS. http://www.nais.org/Magazines-Newsletters/ISMagazine/Pages/Brainology.aspx

Ehri, Linnea C., and Theresa Roberts. 2006. "The Roots of Learning to Read and Write: Acquisition of Letters and Phonemic Awareness." In *Handbook of Early Literacy Research*, Vol. 2, edited by D. K. Dickinson and S. B. Neuman, 113-31. New York: The Guilford Press.

Elementary Teachers' Federation of Ontario. 2012. *Playing is Learning*: http://www.etfo.ca/Resources/ForTeachers/Documents/Playing%20is%20Learning.pdf.

Epstein, Ann S. 2007. *The Intentional Teacher: Choosing the Best Strategies for Young Children's Learning*. Washington, DC: National Association for the Education of Young Children.
———. 2014. *The Intentional Teacher: Choosing the Best Strategies for Young Children's Learning*. rev. ed. Washington, DC: National Association for the Education of Young Children.

Ewald, Wendy, and Alexander Lightfoot. 2002. *I Wanna Take Me a Picture: Teaching Photography and Writing to Children*. Boston: Beacon Press.

Feldgus, Eileen G., and Isabell Cardonick. 1999. *Kid Writing: A Systematic Approach to Phonics, Journals, and Writing Workshop*. DeSoto, TX: Wright Group/McGraw-Hill.

Fletcher, Ralph, and JoAnn Portalupi. 1998. *Craft Lessons: Teaching Writing K–8*. Portland, ME: Stenhouse Publishers.
———. 2001. *Non-fiction Craft Lessons: Teaching Information Writing K–8*. Portland, ME: Stenhouse Publishers.

Fountas, Irene, and Gay Su Pinnell. 1996. *Guided Reading: Good First Teaching for All Children*. Portsmouth, NH: Heinemann.

Friesen, Sharon, and David Scott. 2013, June. *Inquiry-Based Learning: A Review of the Research Literature*. Prepared for the Alberta Ministry of Education.

Fullan, Bennett and Rolheiser-Bennett. 1990. *Linking Classroom and School Improvement*. In Educational Leadership, ASCD, May 1990, p. 13-19.

Gentry, J. Richard. 1997. *My Kid Can't Spell!* Portsmouth, NH: Heinemann.

Glaze, Avis, Ruth Mattingly, and Ben Levin. 2011. *Breaking Barriers: Excellence and Equity for All*. Toronto: Pearson Canada.

Gordon, Christine J. 2004. *Good First Teaching and Effective Early Intervention in Kindergarten: No Child Left Behind*. Featured Speaker Presentation at the 49th Annual Convention of the International Reading Association, May 2–6, in Reno-Tahoe, ND.

Gordon, Christine J., and Tyrone Donnon. 2013. "Early Literacy: A Success Story." *Education Canada* 43 (3): 16–19.

Graham, S., and M. Hebert. 2010. *Writing to Read: Evidence of How Writing Can Improve Reading*. New York: Alliance for Excellent Education.

Graves, Donald H. 1999. *Bring Life into Learning*. Portsmouth, NH: Heinemann.

Graves, Michael F. 2006. *The Vocabulary Book: Learning and Instruction*. New York: Teachers College Press.

———. 2009a. *Essential Readings on Vocabulary Instruction*. Newark, DE: International Reading Association.

———. 2009b. *Teaching Individual Words: One Size Does Not Fit All*. Newark, DE: International Reading Association.

———. 2009c, August. *Words, Words Everywhere! But Which Ones Do I Teach?* Hand-out. Minnesota Center for Reading Research: http://www.cehd.umn.edu/reading/events/summerworkshop2009/MGravesHandout.pdf

Graves, Michael F., Paul Van den Broek, and Barbara Taylor. 1996. "Reclaiming the Centre." *The First R: Every Child's Right to Read*, 259–74. New York: Teachers College Press, Columbia University.

Greene Brabham, Edna, and Carol Lynch-Brown. 2002. "Effects of Teachers' Reading Aloud Styles on Vocabulary Acquisition and Comprehension of Students in the Early Elementary Grades." *Journal of Educational Psychology* 94 (3): 465–473.

Gullo, Dominic F. K. 2006. *Today: Teaching and Learning in the Kindergarten Year*. Washington, DC: National Association for the Education of Young Children.

Hamilton, Sharon Jean. 1995. *My Name's Not Susie: A Life Transformed by Literacy*. Portsmouth, NH: Heinemann.

Hanson, Ralph A., and Donna Farrell. 1995. "The Long-Term Effects on High School Seniors of Learning to Read in Kindergarten." *Reading Research Quarterly* 30 (4): 908–33. http://www.jstor.org/stable/748204

Hargreaves, Andy, and Michael Fullan. 2012. *Professional Capital: Transforming Teaching in Every School*. New York: Teachers College Press.

Harrison, G. L., L. McIntyre, L. Hellsten, and K. Ogle. 2008. *The Influence of Early Writing Instruction on Developing Literacy*. Paper presented at the Annual Conference of the Canadian Society for Studies in Education, May, Vancouver, BC.

Harste, J. C., K. G. Short, and C. Burke. 1988. *Creating Classrooms for Authors: The Reading–Writing Connection*. Portsmouth, NH: Heinemann.

Hattie, John. 2003. *Teachers Make a Difference: What is the Research Evidence?* Australian Council for Educational Research Annual Conference on Building Teacher Quality, 19-21st October, Melbourne, Australia.

———. 2009. *Visible Learning: A Synthesis of Over 800 Meta-Analyses Relating to Achievement*. New York: Routledge.

———. 2012a. "Know Thy Impact." *Educational Leadership* 70 (1): 18–23.

———. 2012b. *Visible Learning for Teachers: Maximizing Impact on Learning*. New York: Routledge.

———. 2013. "Know Thy Impact: Teaching, Learning and Leading." *Conversation* 4 (2): http://www.eosdn.on.ca/docs/In%20 Conversation%20With%20John%20Hattie.pdf

———. 2015. "High-Impact Leadership." *Educational Leadership* 72 (5): 36–40.

Heard, Georgia, and Jennifer McDonough. 2009. *A Place for Wonder: Reading and Writing Nonfiction in the Primary Grades*. Portland, ME: Stenhouse Publishers.

Heffernan, Lee. 2004. *Critical Literacy and Writer's Workshop: Bringing Purpose and Passion to Student Writing*. Newark, DE: International Reading Association.

Helm, Judy Harris, and Lillian G. Katz. 2010. *Young Investigators: The Project Approach in the Early Years*. New York: Teachers College Press.

Hernandez, D. J. 2012. *Double Jeopardy: How Third-Grade Reading Skills and Poverty Influence High School Graduation*. Baltimore, MD: Annie E. Casey Foundation.

Higgins, Steve, Elaine Hall, Kate Wall, Pam Woolner, and Caroline McCaughey. 2005. *The Impact of School Environments: A Literature Review*. Newcastle, UK: School of Education, Communication and Language Science, University of Newcastle.

Hill, Peter W., and Carmel A. Crévola. 1999. "The Role of Standards in Educational Reform for the 21st Century." In *ASCD Yearbook 1999: Preparing Our Schools for the 21st Century*, edited by David D. Marsh, 117–42. Alexandria, VA: Association for Supervision and Curriculum Development.

Hirsh-Pasek, Kathy, Roberta Michnick Golinkoff, and Diane Eyer. 2004. *Einstein Never Used Flashcards: How Our Children Really Learn—and Why They Need to Play More and Memorize Less*. Emmaus, PL: Rodale Books.

Hoddinott J., L. Lethbridge, and S. Phipps. 2002. *Is History Destiny? Resources, Transitions and Child Education Attainments in Canada* (Catalogue RH63-1/555-12-02E). Gatineau, QC: Human Resources Development Canada.

Huxley, Elspeth. 2000. *The Flame Trees of Thika: Memories of an African Childhood*. New York: Penguin.

Isbell, R. T. 2003. "Telling and Retelling Stories: Learning Language and Literacy." *Spotlight on Young Children and Language*. Washington, DC: NAEYC.

IRA (International Reading Association). 1998. "Phonemic Awareness and the Teaching of Reading." A Position Statement from the Board of Directors of the International Reading Association: http://www.reading. org/Libraries/position-statements-and-resolutions/ps1025_phonemic. pdf

IRA (International Reading Association) and NAEYC (National Association for the Education of Young Children). "Learning to Read and Write: Developmentally Appropriate Practices for Young Children." Joint Position Statement. *YC: Young Children* 53 (4): 30–46.

Jalongo M. R., D. McDonald Ribblett. 1997 Fall. Using Song Picture Books To Support Emergent Literacy. *Childhood Education*, 74 (1): 15-22. http://www.freepatentsonline.com/article/Childhood-Education/20851402.html

Johnston, Peter H. 2004. *Choice Words: How Our Language Affects Children's Learning*. Portland, ME: Stenhouse Publishers.

———. 2012. *Opening Minds: Using Language to Change Lives*. Portland, ME: Stenhouse Publishers.

Jones, C., and D. R. Reutzel. 2012. "Enhanced Alphabet Knowledge Instruction: Exploring a Change of Frequency, Focus, and Distributed Cycles of Review." *Reading Psychology* 33: 448-64.

Jones, B., G. Valdez, J. Nowakowski, and C. Rasmussen. 1994. *Designing Learning and Technology for Educational Reform: Meaningful, Engaged Learning*. Oak Brook, IL: North Central Regional Educational Laboratory. http://www.ncrel.org/sdrs/engaged.htm

Juel, Connie. 1988. "Learning to Read and Write: A Longitudinal Study of 54 Children from First Through Fourth Grades." *Journal of Educational Psychology* 80: 437–47.

Juel, Connie, Gina Biancarosa, David Coker, and Rebecca Deffes. 2003. "Walking with Rosie: A Cautionary Tale of Early Reading Instruction." *Educational Leadership* 60 (7): 12–18. http://www.ascd.org/publications/educational_leadership/apr03/vol60/num07/Walking_with_Rosie@_A_Cautionary_Tale_of_Early_Reading_Instruction.aspx

Kame'enui, E. J. 1993. "Diverse Learners and the Tyranny of Time: Don't Fix Blame; Fix the Leaky Roof." *The Reading Teacher* 46: 376–83.

Kamil, Michael L., Peter B. Mosenthal, P. David Pearson, and Rebecca Bar, eds. 2000. *Handbook of Reading Research*. Vol. 3. Mahwah, NJ: Lawrence Erlbaum.

Kears, Gail, and Andrew Biemiller. 2010. "Two-Questions Vocabulary Assessment: Developing a New Method for Group Testing in Kindergarten Through Second Grade." *Journal of Education* 190: 31–41.

Knighton, Tamara, Pierre Brochu, and Tomasz Gluszynski. 2010. *Measuring Up: Canadian Results of the OECD PISA Study the Performance of Canada's Youth in Reading, Mathematics and Science 2009 First Results for Canadians Aged 15*. Ottawa: Minister of Industry.

Koralek, Derry. 2003. *Spotlight on Young Children and Language*. Washington, DC: NAEYC.

Krechevsky, Mara, Ben Mardell, Melissa Rivard, and Daniel Wilson. 2013. *Visible Learners: Promoting Reggio-Inspired Approaches in All Schools*. San Francisco: Jossey-Bass.

Lane, Holly B., and Tyran L. Wright. 2007. "Maximizing the Effectiveness of Reading Aloud." *The Reading Teacher* 60 (7): 668–75.

Leong, D. J., and E. Bodrova. 2012. "Assessing and Scaffolding: Make-Believe Play." *YC: Young Children* 67 (1): 28–34.

Lesaux, N. K., and Siegel, L. S. 2003. "The Development of Reading in Children Who Speak English as a Second Language." *Developmental Psychology* 25: 1005–19.

Lewin-Benham, Ann. 2011. *Twelve Best Practices for Early Childhood Education: Integrating Reggio and Other Inspired Approaches*. New York: Teachers College Press, Columbia University.

Lillard, A. S., M. D. Lerner, E. J. Hopkins, R. A. Dore, E. D. Smith, and C. M. Palmquist. 2012. "The Impact of Pretend Play on Children's Development: A Review of the Evidence." *Psychological Bulletin* August 20: http://www.faculty.virginia.edu/ASLillard/PDFs/Lillard%20et%20al%20(2012).pdf

Lipka, O., and L. S. Siegel. 2007. "The Development of Reading Skills in Children with English as a Second Language." *Scientific Studies of Reading* 11: 105–31.

Lonigan, Christopher J., and Timothy Shanahan. 2013, October. "Developing Early Literacy Skills: Things We Know We Know and Things We Know We Don't Know." *Journal of Communication and Education Language:* 340-46.

Malaguzzi, Loris. 1993. "History, Ideas, and Basic Philosophy." In *The Hundred Languages of Children: The Reggio Emilia Approach to Early Childhood Education*, edited by Carolyn P. Edwards, Lella Gandini, George E. Forman, 41-89. Westport, CT: Praeger.
———. 1998. "History, Ideas and Basic Philosophy: An Interview with Lella Gandini." *The Hundred Languages of Children: The Reggio Emilia Approach, Advanced Reflection*, edited by Carolyn P. Edwards, Lella Gandini, George E. Forman, 49-97. Santa Barbara, CA: Greenwoood Publishing.

Mandela, Nelson. 2002, 18 May. Address during the 90th Birthday Celebration of Mr. Walter Sisulu. http://www.anc.org.za/show.php?id=2879

Manning, Maryann, and Constance Kamii. 2000. "Whole Language vs. Isolated Phonics Instruction: A Longitudinal Study in Kindergarten with Reading and Writing Tasks." *Journal of Research in Childhood Education* 15 (1): 53-65.

Marzano, Robert J. 2010. "Art and Science of Teaching: High Expectations for All." *Educational Leadership* 68 (1): 82–84.

McGee, Lee M., and Donald J. Richgels. 2003. *Designing Early Literacy Programs: Strategies for At-Risk Preschool and Kindergarten Children*. New York: Guilford Press.

McGill-Franzen, Anne. 1992. "Early Literacy: What Does 'Developmentally Appropriate' Mean?" *The Reading Teacher* 46: 56–58.

McLaughlin, Maureen, and Glenn L. DeVoogd. 2004. *Critical Literacy: Enhancing Students' Comprehension of Text*. New York: Scholastic.

McTighe, Jay, and Grant Wiggins. 2013. *Essential Questions: Opening Doors to Student Understanding*. Alexandria, VA: ASCD.

MindUp Curriculum. 2011. *Grades Pre-K–2, Brain-Focused Strategies for Learning—and Living*. New York: Scholastic/The Hawn Foundation.

Morrow, R. L., and Heather Morgan. 2006. "Phonics: Explicit and Meaningful Instruction." In *Understanding and Implementing Reading First Initiatives: The Changing Role of Administrators*, edited by Carrice Cummins, Chapter 3: 31–41. Newark, DE: International Reading Association.

Mulcahey, Christine. 2009. *The Story in the Picture: Inquiry and Art Making with Young Children*. New York: Teachers College Press and Reston, VA: the National Art Education Association.

NAEYC (National Association for the Education of Young Children). 2009. *Developmentally Appropriate Practice in Early Childhood Programs Serving Children from Birth Through Age 8*. http://www.naeyc.org/positionstatements

NAEYC (National Association for the Education of Young Children) and IRA (International Reading Association). 2009. Where We STAND On Learning To Read And Write. *A Joint Position Paper. Web publication* https://www.naeyc.org/files/naeyc/file/positions/WWSSLearningToReadAndWriteEnglish.pdf

Nagy, William E., and Judith A. Scott. 2000. "Vocabulary Processes." In *Handbook of Reading Research,* Vol. 3., edited by Michael L. Kamil, Peter B. Mosenthal, P. David Pearson, and Rebecca Bar, 27-44. Mahwah, NJ: Lawrence Erlbaum.

Neuman, Susan B. 2000. "Sparks Fade, Knowledge Stays: The National Literacy Panel's Report Lacks Staying Power." *American Educator* Fall: 14–17, 39.

Neuman, Susan B., C. Copple, and S. Bredekamp. 2000. *Learning to Read and Write: Developmentally Appropriate Practices for Young Children.* Washington, DC: NAEYC.

Neuman, Susan B., and David K. Dickinson, eds. 2001. *Handbook of Early Literacy Research,* Vol. 1. New York: Guilford Press.
———. 2011. *Handbook of Early Literacy Research,* Vol. 3. New York: Guilford Press.

Neuman, Susan B., and Kathleen A. Roskos, eds. 1998. Children Achieving: Best Practices in Early Literacy. Newark, DE: International Reading Association.
———. 2012. "More Than Teachable Moments: Enhancing Oral Vocabulary Instruction in Your Classroom." *The Reading Teacher* 66 (1): 63–67.

Neuman, Susan B., and Kathleen A. Roskos, with Tanya S. Wright and Lisa Lenhart. 2007. *Nurturing Knowledge: Building a Foundation for School Success by Linking Early Literacy to Math. Science, Art, and Social Studies.* New York: Scholastic.

Neuman, Susan B., Tanya S. Wright. 2013. All About Words Increasing Vocabulary in The Common Core Classroom, Pre-K–2. New York: Teachers College Press, Columbia University.

New Teacher Centre. Accessed online August, 31 2015. "Oral Language Development: Language is a Child's Most Powerful Learning Tool." New Teacher Center, Santa Cruz, CA. http://old.newteachercenter.org/collaborative-discussions/turn-and-talk/plan#main-content

Newman, Terry H., and Sarah A. Bizzarri. 2011. "FRIDAY LETTERS Connecting Students, Teachers, and Families Through Writing." *The Reading Teacher* 65 (4): 275–80.

Northrop, Laura, and Erin Killeen. 2013. "A Framework for Using iPads to Build Early Literacy Skills." *The Reading Teacher* 66 (7): 531–37.

O'Sullivan, Julia, Patricia Canning, Linda Siegel, and Maria Elena Oliveri. 2009. "Key Factors to Support Literacy Success in School-Aged Populations: A Literature Review." Society for Excellence in Education. Canadian Education Statistics Council: http://www.cmec.ca/Publications/Lists/Publications/Attachments/201/key-factors-literacy-school-aged.pdf

Ontario Ministry of Education. 2003. *The Early Reading Strategy: The Report of the Expert Panel on Early Reading in Ontario.* Literacy and Numeracy Secretariat. Toronto: Queen's Printer for Ontario. https://www.edu.gov.on.ca/eng/document/reports/reading/reading.pdf
———. 2004. *Literacy for Learning: The Report of the Expert Panel on Literacy in Grades 4 to 6 in Ontario.* Literacy and Numeracy Secretariat. Toronto: Queen's Printer for Ontario.
———. 2005. *A Guide to Effective Instruction in Writing, Kindergarten to Grade 3.* Toronto: Queen's Printer for Ontario.
———. 2006. *The Ontario curriculum grades 1-8: Language.* Toronto, ON: Queen's Printer for Ontario.

———. 2011. *The Capacity Building Series: Getting Started with Student Inquiry*. Student Achievement Division. www.edu.gov.on.ca/eng/literacynumeracy/inspire/

———. 2013. *The Capacity Building Series: Inquiry-Based Learning.* Student Achievement Division. www.edu.gov.on.ca/eng/literacynumeracy/inspire/

———. 2013. *Paying Attention to Literacy K–12: Six Foundational Principles for Improvement in Literacy, K–12*. Toronto: Queen's Printer for Ontario.

———. 2014. *Achieving Excellence: A Renewed Vision for Education in Ontario.* Toronto: Queen's Printer for Ontario.

———. 2014 How Does Learning Happen? Ontario's Pedagogy for the Early Years, Queen's Printer for Ontario.

Opitz, M., Zbaracki, M. 2004. *Listen hear! 25 effective listening comprehension strategies.* Portsmouth, NH: Heinemann.

Pascal, Charles E. 2009, June. *With Our Best Future in Mind: Implementing Early Learning in Ontario.* Report to the Premier by the Special Advisor on Early Learning. http://www.ontario.ca/en/initiatives/early_learning/ONT06_018865. Compendium: An Updated and Annotated Summary of Evidence Implementing Early Learning in Ontario: https://www.cpco.on.ca/files/7913/8142/6914/An_Updated_and_Annotated_Summary_of_Evidence.pdf

Pearman, C. J., D. Camp, and B. Hurst. 2004. "Literacy Mystery Boxes." *The Reading Teacher* 57 (8): 766–68.

Pellegrini, A. D., and C. M. Bohn. 2005. The Role of Recess in Children's Cognitive Performance and School Adjustment. *Educational Researcher* 34 (1): 13–19.

Pellegrini, A. D., P. D. Huberty, I. Jones. 1995. "The Effects of Play Deprivation on Children's Recess and Classroom Behaviors." *American Educational Research Journal* 32: 845–64.

Pellis, S., and V. Pellis. 2009. *The Playful Brain: Venturing to the Limits of Neuroscience.* London, UK: Oneworld Publications.

Pelo, Ann. 2007. *The Language of Art: Inquiry-Based Studio Practices in Early Childhood Settings.* St. Paul, MN: Red Leaf Press.

Phillips, Linda M., Stephen P. Norri, and Dorothy J. Steffler. 2007. "Potential Risks to Reading Posed by High-Dose Phonics." *Journal of Applied Research on Learning* 1 (1): 1–18.

Pianta, Robert C. 2006. "Teacher–Child Relationships and Early Literacy." *The Handbook of Early Literacy Research*, Vol. 2, edited by D. Dickinson and S. Neuman, 149–62. New York: Guilford Press.

Pikulski, John. 1998. "IRA and Learning Disabilities: Another Update." *Reading Today* 15 (4): 39.

Preller, Paula. 2001. "Fostering Thoughtful Literacy in Elementary Classrooms." *Of Primary Interest* 8 (2): 2–3.

Pressley, Michael. 2002a. "Comprehension Strategies Instruction: A Turn-of-the-Century Status Report." In *Comprehension Instruction: Research-based Best Practices*, edited by C. C. Block and M. Pressley, 11–27. New York: Guilford Press.

———. 2002b. "Comprehension Instruction: What Makes Sense Now, What Might Make Sense Soon." *Reading Online* 5 (2): http://www.readingonline.org/articles/art_index.asp?HREF=/articles/handbook/pressley/index.html

———. 2010. "Striking the Balance: The Quest for Effective Literacy Instruction." *Education Canada* 45 (4): 6-10.

Prior, J., and M. Gerard. 2004. *Environmental Print in the Classroom: Meaningful Connections for Learning to Read*. Newark, DE: International Reading Association.

Rasinski, T. V., and N. Padak. 2001. *From Phonics to Fluency: Effective Teaching of Decoding and Reading Fluency in the Elementary School*. New York: Addison, Wesley, Longman.

Rasinsk, T. V. 2008. *Teaching Reading Fluency to Struggling Readers – Method, Materials, and Evidence. Web Publication*. http://www.coedu. usf.edu/main/departments/ce/homan/docs/Rasinski,%20Homan%20 Biggs.515.106%5B1%5D.pdf

Raver, C. Cybele, and Jane Knitzer. 2002. "What Research Tells Policymakers About Strategies to Promote Social and Emotional School Readiness among Three- and Four-Year-Old Children." Policy Paper No. 3, *Promoting the Emotional Well-Being of Children and Families*. New York: National Center for Children in Poverty. http://www.nccp.org/ publications/pdf/text_485.pdf

Ray, K. W., and L. B. Cleaveland. 2004. *About the Authors: Writing Workshop with Our Youngest Writers*. Portsmouth, NH: Heinemann.

Ritchhart, Ron, Mark Church, and Karin Morrison. 2011. *Making Thinking Visible: How to Promote Engagement, Understanding, and Independence for All Learners*. San Francisco: Jossey-Bass.

Robinson, K. 2015. "Sir Ken Robinson: Creativity is in Everything, Especially Teaching." From Creative Schools by Ken Robinson and Lou Aronica. New York: Viking. http://ww2.kqed.org/mindshift/2015/04/22/ sir-ken-robinson-creativity-is-in-everything-especially-teaching/

Roessingh, Hetty. 2011. "Family Treasures: A Dual-Language Book Project for Negotiating Language, Literacy, Culture, and Identity." *Canadian Modern Language Review* 67 (1): 123–48.

Root-Bernstein, Robert, and Michele Root-Bernstein. 2013. "The Art and Craft of Science." *Educational Leadership* 70 (5): 16–21.

Roser, Nancy L., Miriam G. Martinez, Junko Yokota, and Sharon O'Neal. 2005. *What a Character! Character Study as a Guide to Literary Meaning Making in Grades K–8*. No. 563–846. Newark, DE: International Reading Association.

Roskos, Kathleen A., Patton O. Tabors, and Lisa A. Lenhart. 2004. *Oral Language and Early Literacy in Preschool: Talking, Reading, and Writing*. Newark, DE: International Reading Association.
———. 2009. *Oral Language and Early Literacy in Preschool: Talking, Reading and Writing, 2nd Edition*. Newark, DE: International Reading Association.

Routman, Regie. 2005. *Writing Essentials: Raising Expectations and Results While Simplifying Teaching*. Don Mills, ON: Pearson Education Canada.

Rowe, Mary Budd. 1986. "Wait Times: Slowing Down May Be a Way of Speeding Up." *Journal of Teacher Education* 37 (1): 43–50.

Saracho, O. N., and B. Spodek. 2006. "Young Children's Literacy-Related Play." *Early Child Development and Care* 176 (7): 707–721.

Scarborough, H. S. 2001. "Connecting Early Language and Literacy to Later Reading (Dis)Abilities: Evidence, Theory, and Practice." In *Handbook of Early Literacy Research*, Vol. 1. edited by S. B. Neuman and D. K. Dickinson , 97–110. New York: Guilford Press.

Schickedanz, Judith A. 1994. "Early Childhood Education and School Reform: Consideration of Some Philosophical Barriers." *The Journal of Education* 176 (1): 29–47.

Schickedanz, Judith A., and Renee M. Casbergue. 2004. *Writing in Preschool: Learning to Orchestrate Meaning and Marks*. Newark, DE: International Reading Association.

Scott, Darrell, and Robert J. Marzano. 2014. *Awaken the Learner: Finding the Source of Effective Education*. Centennial, CO: Marzano Research Laboratory.

Shanahan, Timothy. 1984. "The Reading–Writing Relation: An Exploratory Multi-Variate Analysis." *Journal of Educational Psychology* 76: 466–77.
———. 2006. "Relations among Oral Language, Reading, and Writing Development." In *Handbook of Writing Research*, edited by C. A. MacArthur, S. Graham, and J. Fitzgerald, 171—86. New York: Guilford Press.

Shanahan, Timothy, Christopher J. Lonigan. 2013a. Literacy in Preschool and Kindergarten Children: The National Early Literacy Panel and Beyond. Baltimore: Paul H. Brookes Publishing.
———. 2013b. Early Childhood Literacy: The National Early Literacy Panel and Beyond. Baltimore: Paul H. Brookes Publishing.

Shanker, Stuart. 2012. *Calm, Alert and Learning: Classroom Strategies for Self-Regulation*. Don Mills, ON: Pearson Education Canada.

Shaywitz, Sally. 2003. Overcoming Dyslexia: A New and Complete Science-Based Program for Reading Problems at Any Level. New York: Alfred A. Knopf.

Shaywitz, Sally E., and B. A. Shaywitz. 2003. "The Science of Reading and Dyslexia." *Journal of AAPOS* (American Association for Pediatric Ophthalmology and Strabismus) 7 (3): 158–66.

Shedd, M. K., and N. K. Duke, 2008. *The Power of Planning Effective Read Alouds. YC: Young Children* 63 (7): 22–26.

Silver, Penny, and Mary C. Shorey. 2012. *Many Texts, Many Voices: Teaching Literacy and Social Justice to Young Learners in the Digital Age*. Portland, ME: Stenhouse Publishers.

Simon, H. A. 1996. *Observations on the Sciences of Science Learning*. Paper for the Committee on Developments in the Science of Learning for the Sciences of Science Learning: An Interdisciplinary Discussion. Department of Psychology, Carnegie Mellon University.

Siraj-Blatchford, Iram, Kathy Sylva, Stella Muttock, Rose Gilden, and Danny Bell. 2002. *Researching Effective Pedagogy in the Early Years*. Norwich, England: Queen's Printer.

Smiley, A. Patricia, and Carol S. Dweck. 1994. "Individual Differences in Achievement Goals among Young Children." *Child Development* 65 (6): 1723-43.

Smith, F. 1988. Joining The Literacy Club. Portsmouth, NH: Heinemann.

Snow, Catherine E., and Y. Kim. 2007. *Large Problem Spaces: The Challenge of Vocabulary for English Language Learners*. In *Vocabulary Acquisition: Implications for Reading Comprehension*, edited by R. K. Wagner, A. E. Muse, and K. R. Tannenbaum, 123–39. New York: Guilford Press.

Snow, Catherine, M. Susan Burns, and Peg Griffin. 1998. *Preventing Reading Difficulties in Young Children*. Washington, DC: National Academy Press.

Snow, Catherine, Michelle Porche, Patton Tabors, and Stephanie Harris. 2007. *Is Literacy Enough? Pathways to Academic Success for Adolescents*. Baltimore: Paul H. Brookes Publishing.

Soundy, Cathleen S., and Nancy L. Stout. 2003. "Pillow Talk: Fostering the Emotional and Language Needs of Young Learners." *Spotlight on Young Children and Language*. Washington, DC: NAEYC.

Spandel, Vicki. 2001. *Creating Writers Through 6-Trait Writing Assessment and Instruction*. 3rd ed. New York: Addison Wesley Longman.

Stahl, Katherine A. Dougherty. 2014. "New Insights About Letter Learning." *The Reading Teacher* 68 (4): 261–65.

Stahl, Steven A. 2001. *How Can I Help Children Crack the Code?* Presentations by CIERA-Affiliated Researchers. Web publication. Center for the Improvement of Early Reading Achievement, University of Michigan School of Education. Ann Arbor, MI. http://www.ciera.org/library/presos/2001/

Stahl, Steven A., Ann M. Duffy-Hester, and Katherine A. Dougherty Stahl. 1998. "Everything You Wanted to Know About Phonics (But Were Afraid to Ask)." *Reading Research Quarterly* 33 (3): 338–55.

Stanovich, K. E. 1986. "Matthew Effects in Reading: Some Consequences of Individual Differences in the Acquisition of Literacy." *Reading Research Quarterly* 21: 360–406.

Statistics Canada. 2006. "Sharp increase in population with a mother tongue other than English or French." *2006 Census: The Evolving Linguistic Portrait:* http://www12.statcan.ca/census-recensement/2006/as-sa/97-555/p2-eng.cfm

Steiner, Claude, and Paul Perry. 1997. *Achieving Emotional Literacy*. New York: Bloomsbury.

Stenhouse, Lawrence. 1975. *An Introduction to Curriculum Research and Development*. London, UK: Heinemann Educational Publishers.

Strickland, Dorothy S. 1998. *Teaching Phonics Today: A Primer for Educators*. Newark, DE: International Reading Association.
———. 2010. *Essential Readings on Early Literacy*. Newark, DE: International Reading Association.

Strickland, Dorothy S., and Lesley Mandel Morrow. 2000. *Beginning Reading and Writing*. Newark, DE: International Reading Association.

Taberski, Sharon. 2000. On Solid Ground: Strategies for Teaching Reading K–3. Portsmouth, NH: Heinemann.

Tarr, Patricia. 2004. "Consider the Walls." *Beyond the Journal—YC: Young Children on the Web* May. https://www.naeyc.org/files/yc/file/200405/ConsidertheWalls.pdf

Taylor, Barbara M., P. David Pearson, Debra S. Peterson, and Michael C. Rodriguez. 2003. "Reading Growth in High-Poverty Classrooms: The Influence of Teacher Practices that Encourage Cognitive Engagement in Literacy Learning." *Elementary School Journal* 104 (1): 3–28.

Taylor, Barbara M., Michael Pressley, and P. David Pearson. 2002. "Research-Supported Characteristics of Teachers and Schools That Promote Reading Achievement." In *Teaching Reading: Effective Schools, Accomplished Teachers*, edited by B. M. Taylor and P. D. Pearson, 361–74. Mahwah, NJ: Erlbaum.

Teale, William H., Kathleen A. Paciga, and Jessica L. Hoffman. 2007. "Beginning Reading Instruction in Urban Schools: The Curriculum Gap Ensures a Continuing Achievement Gap." *The Reading Teacher* 61(4): 344–48.

Technology and Young Children Interest Forum. 2008. "Meaningful Technology Integration in Early Learning Environments." *Beyond the Journal—YC: Young Children on the Web* September. http://www.naeyc.org/files/yc/file/200809/ OnOurMinds.pdf

Tindall, E., Nisbet, D. 2008. Listening: A Vital Skill. *The International Journal of Reading,* 15(6): 121-28.

Tomlinson, Carol A. 2014. *The Differentiated Classroom: Responding to the Needs of All Learners.* 2nd ed. Alexandria, VA: ASCD.

Tomlinson, Carol A., and Tonya R. Moon. 2013. *Assessment and Student Success in Differentiated Classrooms.* Alexandria, VA: ASCD.

Tompkins, G. 2000. Teaching Writing: Balancing Process and Product. 3rd ed. Upper Saddle River, NJ: Prentice-Hall.

Trehearne, Miriam P. 2003. *Comprehensive Literacy Resource for Kindergarten Teachers.* Vernon Hills, IL: ETA hand2mind. http://www.isbe.net/earlychi/pdf/trehearne_chapter_2.pdf
———. 2005. *Comprehensive Literacy Resource for Grades 1–2 Teachers.* Vernon Hills, IL: ETA hand2mind.
———. 2005. *Comprehensive Literacy Resource for Preschool Teachers.* Vernon Hills, IL: ETA hand2mind.
———. 2006. *Comprehensive Literacy Resource for·Grades 3–6 Teachers.* Vernon Hills, IL: ETA hand2mind.
———. 2011. *Learning to Write and Loving It! Preschool–Kindergarten.* Thousand Oaks, CA: Corwin Publishing.

Trelease, Jim. 2013. *The Read-Aloud Handbook.* 7th ed. New York: Penguin Books.

Van Scoter, J., and S. Boss. 2002. *Learners, Language, and Technology: Making Connections That Support Literacy.* Portland, OR: Northwest Regional Educational Laboratory.

Vasquez, Vivian Maria. 2003. *Getting Beyond "I Like the Book": Creating Space for Critical Literacy in K–6 Classrooms.* Newark, DE: International Reading Association.
———. 2004. *Negotiating Critical Literacies with Young Children.* Mahwah, NJ: Lawrence Erlbaum.
———. 2010. *Getting Beyond "I Like the Book": Creating Space for Critical Literacy in K–6 Classrooms.* 2nd ed. Newark, DE: International Reading Association.

Vasquez, Vivian Maria, and Carol Branigan Felderman. 2013. *Technology and Critical Literacy in Early Childhood.* New York: Routledge.

Whitebread, David. April 2012. *The Importance of Play.* Report On The Value Of Children's Play With A Series Of Policy Recommendations. Brussels, Belgium: Toys Industries For Europe.

Wiggins, Grant. 2012. "Seven Keys to Effective Feedback." *Educational Leadership* 70 (1): 10–16.

Wolvin, Andrew, and Carolyn Gwynn Coakley. 1988. *Listening.* Dubuque, IA: William C. Brown Publishers.

Wright, Tanya S. 2012. "What Classroom Observations Reveal About Oral Vocabulary Instruction in Kindergarten." *Reading Research Quarterly* 47 (4): 353–55, http://onlinelibrary.wiley.com/doi/10.1002/RRQ.026/epdf

Wylie, R. E., and D. D. Durrell. 1970. "Teaching Vowels Through Phonograms." *Elementary English* 47: 787–91.

Yousafzai, Malala, and Christina Lamb. 2013. *I Am Malala.* New York: Little, Brown/Hachette.

Zumbrunn, S., J. Tadlock, and E. D. Roberts. 2011. "Self-Regulation and Motivation: A Review of the Literature." Richmond, VA: Metropolitan Educational Research Consortium.

63293477R00223

Made in the USA
Charleston, SC
02 November 2016